D1603378

THINKING THROUGH ISLAMOPHOBIA

Thinking Through Islamophobia

Global Perspectives

Edited by

S. Sayyid and AbdoolKarim Vakil

Columbia University Press
New York

Columbia University Press
Publishers Since 1893
New York   Chichester, West Sussex
Copyright © S. Sayyid and AbdoolKarim Vakil, 2010
All rights reserved

Library of Congress Cataloging-in-Publication Data

Thinking through Islamophobia : global perspectives / Edited by S. Sayyid
and AbdoolKarim Vakil.
    p. cm.
"This book is the product of a workshop hosted by the Centre of Ethnicity
and Racism Studies at the University of Leeds in May 2008."
Includes bibliographical references and index.
ISBN 978-0-231-70206-5 (alk. paper)
1. Islamophobia—Congresses. 2. Islam—Public opinion—Congresses.
3. Muslims—Public opinion—Congresses. 4. Muslims—Non-Muslim
countries—Congresses. I. Sayyid, S. (Salman) II. Vakil, AbdoolKarim.
III. Title.

BP52.T45 2010
305.6'97—dc22

2010037840

∞

Columbia University Press books are printed on permanent and durable acid-free paper.
This book is printed on paper with recycled content.
Printed in India by Imprint Digital

c 10 9 8 7 6 5 4 3 2 1

CONTENTS

Acknowledgements   vii
Contributors   ix

1. Thinking Through Islamophobia   *S. Sayyid*   1
2. Out of the Devil's Dictionary   *S. Sayyid*   5
3. Islamophobia and the Crusades   *Jonathan Riley-Smith*   19
4. Is The Islam in Islamophobia the Same as the Islam
   in Anti-Islam; Or, When is it Islamophobia Time?   23
                                            AbdoolKarim Vakil
5. The Problem With Parables   *Katherine Butler Brown*   45
6. Islamophobia: From K.I.S.S. To R.I.P.   *Chris Allen*   51
7. The Voyage In: Second Life Islamophobia   *Yakoub Islam*   65
8. The Racialisation of Muslims   *Nasar Meer and Tariq Modood*   69
9. No Innocents: Muslims in the Prevent Strategy   *M. G. Khan*   85
10. 'Flooding The Embankments': Race, Bio-Politics
    and Sovereignty   *David Tyrer*   93
11. Sexualising the 'War on Terror'   111
        Adi Kuntsman, Jin Haritaworn and Jennifer Petzen
12. Governing Muslims After 9/11   *Yahya Birt*   117
13. Neoconservative Narrative as Globalising Islamophobia   129
                                            Cemalettin Haşimi
14. Asking the Law Questions: Agency and Muslim Women   135
                                              Samia Bano
15. Fear of Small Numbers? Debating Face-Veiling
    in the Netherlands   *Annelies Moors*   157
16. A Short Genealogy of Russian Islamophobia   165
                                          Madina Tlostanova

CONTENTS

17. Culturalism, Education and Islamophobia in China   *Lin Yi*   185
18. Islamophobia in Turkey   *Yasin Aktay*   195
19. Reclaiming the Turk's Head   *Mohammad Siddique Seddon*   207
20. Islamophobia and Hellenophilia: Greek Myths of Post-Colonial
     Europe   *Rodanthi Tzanelli*   213
21. Troubled by Muslims: Thailand's Declining Tolerance?   231
                             Duncan McCargo
22. 'Breaking the Taboo of Multiculturalism': The Belgian Left
     and Islam   *Nadia Fadil*   235
23. 'Don't Freak I'm a Sikh!'   *Katy Pal Sian*   251
24. 'Islamophobia': A New Racism in Football?   *Peter Millward*   255
25. Fundamental Fictions: Gender, Power and Islam
     in Brasian Diasporic Formations   *Ruvani Ranasinha*   259
26. Generating Islamophobia in India   *Dibyesh Anand*   265
27. Who's Afraid of Islamophobia?   *AbdoolKarim Vakil*   271

Bibliography   279
Index   313

ACKNOWLEDGEMENTS

This book is the product of a workshop hosted by the Centre of Ethnicity and Racism Studies at the University of Leeds in May 2008. It is the editors' pleasant duty to acknowledge the Centre's generous support and to thank those who made the day-long event possible. In particular, Marie Johnson, for the efficient handling of the logistical and administrative issues, and Ian Law, for his sustained commitment to both workshop and book, as well as for his encouragement and inspiration along the years. For the stimulating discussion which has found its way into the papers developed for this book, we and the authors record our thanks to all the participants at the workshop, and to the many friends, colleagues, and antagonists with and against whom the arguments here presented were honed. In particular we would like to thank Andrew Brockett, Gargi Bhattacharyya, Max Farrar, Liz Fekete, Barnor Hesse, Ajmal Hussain, Serena Hussain, Karima Laachir, Helen Irving, Andy Lie, Marc Lyall, Rabia Malik, Gabriele Marranci, Vera Marten, Sean McLoughlin, Shamim Miah, Ghazala Mir, Leon Moosavi, and Amir Saeed. A special mention is due to the retiring members of the Brighton Beach Reading Club. To Michael Dwyer, for unstinting and patient belief in the venture, and Leilla Talebali, without whom the book would never have seen the light of day, we extend our greatest thanks. Finally, the editors would like to acknowledge the debt they owe to their families and friends for distractions and detours, which paradoxically worked to shorten the path to the completion of this book. To Carola, Nuria and Sabira, for the sacrifices they made to allow him time to work on the book, a guilt-ridden word of thanks from AK.

S. Sayyid   *Leeds, May 2010*
AbdoolKarim Vakil   *London, May 2010*

CONTRIBUTORS

Yasin Aktay is Professor of Sociology at Selçuk University, Konya, Turkey, and Director of the Institute of Strategic Thinking at Ankara.

Chris Allen is a Research Fellow at the Institute of Applied Social Studies, University of Birmingham.

Dibyesh Anand is Associate Professor in International Relations at the Centre for the Study of Democracy, University of Westminster.

Samia Bano is Lecturer in the School of Law at the University of Reading.

Yahya Birt is a Commissioning Editor at Kube Publishing and an independent researcher.

Katherine Butler Brown is Lecturer in the Department of Music at King's College London.

Nadia Fadil is FWO Postdoctoral Research fellow at the Centre for Sociological Research of the Catholic University of Leuven.

Jin Haritaworn is a Fellow in Transnational Gender Studies at the Gender Institute of the London School of Economics.

Cemalettin Haşimi is a PhD candidate in the Department of Political Science at Johns Hopkins University.

Yakoub Islam is a UK-based internet author and cyber-activist.

Muhammad G. Khan is Tutor in Youth and Community Work at Ruskin College, Oxford and Chair of the Muslim Youthwork Foundation.

Adi Kuntsman is Leverhulme Early Career Fellow at the Research Institute for Cosmopolitan Cultures, University of Manchester.

CONTRIBUTORS

Duncan McCargo is Professor of Southeast Asian Politics at the School of Politics and International Studies, University of Leeds.

Nasser Meer is Lecturer in Sociology in the School of Social Sciences, University of Southampton.

Peter Millward is Lecturer in Sport Policy and Sport Sociology, Carnegie Faculty of Sports and Education, Leeds Metropolitan University.

Tariq Modood is Professor of Sociology, Politics and Public Policy and the Director of the Centre for the Study of Ethnicity and Citizenship, University of Bristol.

Annelies Moors is a Professor in the Department of Anthropology and Sociology at the University of Amsterdam and Programme Director of the Research Group 'Muslim Cultural Politics' at the Amsterdam School for Social Science Research.

Jennifer Petzen currently teaches Queer and Gender Studies in Berlin.

Ruvani Ranasinha is Senior Lecturer in the Department of English at King's College London.

Jonathan Riley-Smith is Dixie Professor Emeritus of Ecclesiastical History at the University of Cambridge.

S. Sayyid is Director of the Centre of Muslim and Non-Muslim Understanding at the University of South Australia and a Reader in Rhetoric at the University of Leeds.

Katy Pal Sian is a UK-based independent researcher.

Mohammad Siddique Seddon is Lecturer in Religious Studies and Islamic Studies in the Department of Theology and Religious Studies, University of Chester.

Madina Tlostanova is Professor in the History of Philosophy Department at the School of Humanities and Social Sciences, the People's Friendship University of Russia, Moscow.

David Tyrer is Lecturer in Sociology at Liverpool John Moores University.

Rodanthi Tzaneli is Lecturer in the School of Sociology and Social Policy at the University of Leeds.

AbdoolKarim Vakil is Lecturer in the Departments of History and of Spanish, Portuguese and Latin American Studies at King's College London.

Lin Yi is Associate Professor and Deputy Head of the Department of Sociology, Xiamen University.

1

THINKING THROUGH ISLAMOPHOBIA

S. Sayyid

Islamophobia, both as a term and a concept, is widely used, hotly disputed and frequently disavowed. It is seen by its supporters as having something signifi-cant to say about the times we live in, and as an important tool to highlight injustices faced by and specific to Muslims. Its detractors perceive Islamopho-bia as simply a fig leaf behind which 'backward' (sic) social practices and totali-tarian political ambitions are covered up and afforded bogus exemption from legitimate criticism and challenge. The backdrop to these debates and more generally to the mobilisations and contestations, to which they give expression, is a succession of 'moral panics' that have swept over initially Western plutocra-cies and subsequently the rest of the world, centred on the figure of the Mus-lim. To some, these moral panics are urgent wake-up calls to identifiable shifts in the politics of exclusion, hatred, and scapegoating which, with greater or lesser usefulness, Islamophobia names and defines. For others, the growing Muslim presence in major Western conurbations and the increasing restlessness of the global Islamist awakening attest to very real problems manifest in the universal values of freedom of speech, equality of the sexes and tolerance. To them, talk of Islamophobia is at best a distraction and at worst, a form of cul-tural censorship under the cover of which reactionary communitarianism and patriarchal cultural practices are allowed to go unchecked.

Those who see Islamophobia not as a polemical but as an analytical term are confronted with the paucity of its current formulation. Neither consistently defined, deployed or understood, Islamophobia comes off as a nebulous and perpetually contested category. This has allowed it to circulate widely, but ineffectively: useful, for some, to vent grievances; used, by others, to pontificate; conveniently toothless platitudes and sound bites for canvassing politicians and opinion makers unable or unwilling to see its value as a tool for justice. Questions about what Islamophobia is, often (and not unreasonably in the practical domain of public policy and everyday life) slip into questions about who exactly is and is not Islamophobic. This type of question in turn slides into others that inquire whether Islamophobia actually exists, which in turn impinges upon what, if any, relationship is there between Islamophobia and racism, or Islamophobia and Orientalism. What, in short, do we gain, and lose, by talking about Islamophobia rather than racism or Orientalism? Confronted with the whirlpool of polemics and emotions around the concept, there is a strong temptation to clear the decks, mistaking essential contestation for semantic ambiguity and thus to offer rigorous and nuanced definition by way of solution. The most common such approach, which further mistakes the etymology of the concept for conceptual definition, is to try and understand Islamophobia by breaking it down into its constituent parts: we know what Islam is, and we know what phobia means, thus we can understand Islamophobia as fear of Islam (and its cognates). While not devoid of heuristic value this approach does not help us to account for the range of phenomena marshalled by and mobilisations around references to Islamophobia.

In this book we propose a different approach. Rather than try and focus on a forlorn quest for the essence of Islamophobia we offer instead a series of reflections on the way in which the term Islamophobia (and its cognates) has been, and can be used. The aim is not to produce an idea of Islamophobia that corresponds to an analytical definition based on a single property or essence capable of unifying the multiple uses of the term in all possible situations, but rather to think it through the notion of a family resemblance based on overlapping similarities. An edited collection is ideally suited for such a task. Contributors, drawing on diverse fields of disciplinary and geographical expertise were neither mandated to subscribe to a particular understanding of the concept, nor tasked with formulating a more robust and precise definition than the ones already in circulation. Instead, they were asked to take Islamophobia seriously as a concept and reflect upon its usage. In particular, this meant considering the way in which the Muslim presence is problematised in various contexts. Problematisation is a dual operation; it asks questions but the asking also implies certain types of answers. This has the effect not only of turning the Muslim presence and all that it is said to represent into a problem, but the articulation of the problem becomes a site for various interventions directed to its resolution.

This problematisation of Muslim identity is not something that is restricted only to the Western plutocracies, and the focus on the way in which the dynamic of Islamophobia is played out in these countries should not blind us to the global range of its performance. The inflections of Islamophobia, its variations and accents are products of specific histories and trajectories. These inflections are also conditioned by the way in which the Muslim presence itself is performed. Being a Muslim can mean very different things in different places. It is possible to identify four main regions where this occurs. Firstly, there is 'Muslimistan'. This is a group of countries, which are dominated (either informally or formally) socially and culturally by the Islamicate. For all practical purposes such a grouping corresponds, a few anomalies aside (e.g. the presence of Guyana and Mozambique and the absence of Bosnia and Western Sahara), to the membership of the Organisation of the Islamic Conference (OIC). Secondly, there are the states in which Muslims either form a minority or hold a socio-economically subaltern position but where the Muslim presence, while marginal, either predates or is contemporaneous with the formation of the state. In other words, where the Muslim minority cannot be easily dismissed as recent arrivals. In this group, one can include the Muslim populations of India, Russia and China as well as countries such as Thailand. Thirdly, the lands in which Muslims are represented as newly arrived immigrants. Most of these countries are to be found in Western plutocracies, though not exclusively so. Finally, there are the regions in which the Muslim presence is either miniscule or virtual and thus problematisation of Muslim identity is vicarious based on the virtual absence of Muslims. Many of the countries of Latin America and parts of Africa and north east Asia can be included in this group. These four arenas provide the four distinct contexts for the problematisation of Muslim identity, and the ways in which Islamophobia may be deployed. Islamophobia cannot simply be over-determined by the problem of immigrants and their integration into host societies. The tendency, especially pronounced in Western plutocracies, to see immigrants and Muslims as effectively equivalent should not prevent us from seeing the other logics in which Muslims often become metaphors for invaders, traitors and woman-haters.

A global perspective on Islamophobia recognises the multiple ways of being Muslim and multiple antagonisms that it may generate. To reflect this diversity of experiences the volume is divided into two broad categories: there are chapters that construct large and sustained arguments and there are more staccato interventions, which illustrate a particular theme to which Islamophobia is attached or invoked. These can be geographically focused, in that the range of experiences described as Islamophobia are transported away from their mooring in the crucible of the post-Civil Rights universe of the Western plutocracies, but they also include little vignettes by which the banality of Islamophobia is expressed or repressed. These two types of essays are directed toward producing not a full account of Islamophobia but rather to showing the way in which the category is used analytically or polemically. The war of interpretation that ranges around this concept is not simply an academic exercise. Inevitably this book will be seen as an intervention in on-going debate rather than just a scholarly report on the polemics forged around this concept. In this sense it too is a move in the 'language game' of Islamophobia, in other words, it belongs to a genre of writing on the Muslim question.

2

OUT OF THE DEVIL'S DICTIONARY

S. Sayyid

Antisemitism is indeed a western phenomenon. It has no precedence in Islam or in the East. Jews and Muslims have lived harmoniously together for centuries. In the east, we have had despotism and dictatorship, but never had fascism or Nazism. These, too, are also western phenomena, and the west has paid dearly to combat them. What concerns me is that, first, this western antisemitism has turned into a tool for the imposition of a whole range of improper policies and practices on the people of the Middle East and Muslims in general. Secondly, I am concerned that this western dilemma may be projected elsewhere, that is [if] fascism and Nazism are suppressed in the West, they may resurface in another form in western policies elsewhere.

Mohammad Khatami

There is an epistolary short story by Woody Allen (1966) about a game of postal chess, which culminates with both players simultaneously declaring checkmate. This simultaneous declaration is the product of a protracted and increasingly acrimonious correspondence in which the two protagonists (Gossage and Vardebedian) reel off chess moves without any regard to each other's positions. The exchange of chess moves and the letters that explain them have the appearance of a dialogue but are more akin to exercises in autism. Gossage and Vardebedian conduct themselves in a manner that is consistent with postal chess: a game which, by virtue of distance, is played on two chessboards, in

THINKING THROUGH ISLAMOPHOBIA

two distinct locations. As each player moves the pieces on his board he informs the other, who in turn adjusts his chessboard accordingly so that both boards show an identical sequential array of pieces. As the story develops it becomes increasingly clear that even though the two correspondents interact as if they are playing the same game, each board in fact contains different configurations of moves. It is the illusion that one game is being played rather than two that allows both players to declare checkmate in the same move.

This short story seems to capture something of the form of the debate generated by the formation and circulation of the concept of Islamophobia. Islamophobia is widely deployed, hotly disputed and frequently disavowed. It has entered the general field of debate but it cannot establish an isomorphic relationship between itself and the phenomenon that it is supposed to marshal, and there seems to be some confusion as to what kinds of experiences Islamophobia is supposed to delimit. It is a category around which a war of interpretation is being fought, and as such it does not have one settled meaning—its meaning is precisely provided by the language game or discourse it is inscribed in. At the same time there are vigorous attempts to discredit Islamophobia as an act of shameless appeasement towards some of the most reactionary forces in the contemporary world. It seems then that most participants in the debate around and about Islamophobia assume that they are playing the same language game when in fact several distinct language games are being played. This partly accounts for the relatively rapid circulation of the category; what this proliferation of language games leaves ill-defined is the impact the concept of Islamophobia is actually having.

In the vortex of language games around Islamophobia it is possible to isolate two distinct positions. There are those for whom the concept is purely polemical and has no analytical value, and is therefore best dispensed with; and those who think that it is analytically useful and all that is needed is good, targeted research so that the concept can be operationalised in public policy. The clash between these two positions has already generated a fairly large literature.

A number of concepts have emerged since the nineteenth century to describe a set of systematic discriminatory practices: antisemitism (1879), Islamophobia (c.1918) racism (1930s).[1] In addition, there are also concepts

---

[1] Race in something akin to its contemporary usage is dated by Bernasconi and Lott to 1684. The concept of racism, however, is dated to the 1930s when it was deployed to describe the practices of the Nazi regime in Germany, practices that were similar

like Orientalism (1978), which have described the complex ways in which Islam and Muslims have been represented. These concepts do not need to have a particular essence, but it is worth considering how they relate to each other. The complex and rather convoluted genealogy of Islamophobia in both its initial form and its second coming have been well described in recent studies by AbdoolKarim Vakil and Chris Allen respectively (both featured in this volume), but the relationship between the concepts remains underexplored. One way of working out this relationship is to compare the 1997 Runnymede Trust Report (1997a) that (re-)introduced Islamophobia into public policy and discussion with the Trust's earlier, 1994 report on anti-Semitism, *A Very Light Sleeper*. The latter not only called for the enquiry which led on to the publication of the now landmark report on Islamophobia, but also already used the term Islamophobia in its conclusion, where it was rather succinctly described as 'anti-Muslim prejudice', and as another form of racism (Runnymede Trust, 1994). Thus, *A Very Light Sleeper* provides a useful way of comparing one conception of anti-Semitism with the understanding of Islamophobia which in effect came to set the terms of discussion. The comparison is helped by a degree of authorial and organisational continuity that allows the differences between the two reports to be especially illustrative.[2] Thus they provide an opportunity to reflect upon the phenomena of anti-Semitism and Islamophobia and assess the impact of how these concepts have evolved in recent years.

A Very Light Sleeper distinguishes between anti-Judaism, anti-Semitic racism, and anti-Zionism. Anti-Judaism is described as antipathy towards beliefs and values of the Jewish faith (Runnymede Trust, 1994, p. 23). This is presented as the oldest form of anti-Semitism, dating back to the 'Persian' and Seleucid Empires; however, its main focus is the period of the early Church and the Roman Empire. The report conflates the Christian denunciation of Jews as 'Christ-killers' with acts of rebellion/resistance against the imperial order by members of the Jewish population, thereby presenting the imperial authorities not as 'equal opportunity oppressors' who were more concerned to suppress any challenges to their rule regardless of its source. The antagonism that emerges out of this confrontation between empire and rebellion is directed at

---

to those being deployed by the British, French and Dutch empires. See Bernasconi and Lott (2000).

[2] Akbar Ahmed, Julia Neuberger and Nasreen Rehman were members of both commissions.

the conflation between ethnicities (Smith, A.D., 1986) and religious practices as expressions of *ethnie* rather than a polemical investment in the truth or false-hood of a religious conviction. This problem arises because of the way the report de-historicises the phenomena under study. Anti-Judaism can be found not only in the development of the Jesus movement into the Christian Church but also within 'profound secularism and agnosticism' and it may include those born and socialised as Jews. Anti-Judaism also includes theological polemics by followers of other faiths (Runnymede Trust, 1994, p. 25).

Anti-Semitic racism is based on the set of ideas that Jews are inherently dif-ferent from non-Jews and that difference is biologically determined, and cul-turally overdetermined. Anti-Semitic racism can be seen as a 're-occupation' of anti-Judaism in secular, scientific Darwinist terms. Thus, anti-Semitic racism is what made the 'Final Solution' possible. It is this form of anti-Semitism that is most familiar in contemporary times. *A Very Light Sleeper* goes on to discuss a more complex form that anti-Semitism (in general) may take which is not simply reducible to racism. This is a form of anti-Semitism, which is articu-lated with anti-Zionism.

According to *A Very Light Sleeper* anti-Zionism can be as multi–faceted as Zionism (Runnymede Trust, 1994, p. 27). The report accepts that an anti-Zionism that criticises aspects of specific Israeli government policies is legiti-mate and cannot be necessarily considered to be anti-Semitic (Runnymede Trust, 1994, p. 29). There is, however, a danger, which the report's authors are at pains to illustrate, that anti-Zionism can easily slip into anti-Semitism. To illustrate the slippery nature of this slope they outline three instances in which anti-Zionism can become anti-Semitism. First, they argue, it is anti-Semitic to 'deny the legitimacy of Israel' outside the context of scholarly debate regarding international law or the formation of Israel. The reason being that denial of the legitimacy of the state of Israel 'denies what is not denied to other people, namely nationhood and self-determination' (Runnymede Trust, 1994, p. 31).[3] Perhaps recognising the weakness of its argument here, the Report goes on to argue that: 'The overwhelming majority of Jews would certainly regard the denial of the legitimacy of the state of Israel as anti-Semitic' (Runnymede

[3] What is interesting about this argument (leaving aside the long list of peoples who are being denied a nation state e.g. Kurds, Roma, Kashmiris, nearly all the planets' indigenous aboriginal people...) is that asserting the necessity of nationhood to Juda-ism entails a rejection of positions within the Jewish community, which do not accept the necessary linkage between Judaism and nation-state.

OUT OF THE DEVIL'S DICTIONARY

Trust, 1994, p. 31). Thus, anti-Semitism becomes a subjective category by which 'an overwhelming majority of Jews' determines whether anti-Zionism is anti-Semitism.

Secondly, it is 'usually anti-Semitic' to describe Zionism as a racist ideology (Runnymede Trust, 1994, p. 31). Again *A Very Light Sleeper* makes the caveat that there are 'special contexts' in which the description of Zionism as being racist may not be racist, e.g. 'opposition from first principles to all forms of political nationalism or state religion' (*Ibid.*). The report concedes that it is not anti-Semitic to suggest that 'some Israeli Jews adopt racist attitudes towards Palestinians' (*Ibid.*), but it considers it to be anti-Semitic to generalise from this and argue that Israeli society is itself racist. (This of course, would make any structural explanation of racism or classification of Israel as being an apartheid state impossible to sustain). Third, *A Very Light Sleeper* contends that any form of anti-Zionism that equates Zionism with Nazism or specifically suggests that the Israeli persecution of Palestinians is similar to the Nazi treatment of the Jews is anti-Semitic. Any such comparison undermines the exceptional significance of the Holocaust, thus any attempt to assert that Israelis are involved in genocide of Palestinians is anti-Semitic.

Anti-Judaism, anti-Semitic racism and anti-Zionist racism are all dimensions of anti-Semitism, which according to *A Very Light Sleeper* is 'a product of the psychology of its practitioners, reinforced by the cultural and social environments' (Runnymede Trust, 1994, pp. 22; 33). The report is adamant that: '[h]ostility to the Jews is entirely one sided... it is unreciprocated... it is not the result of any particular objective factor or kind of behaviour on the part of the Jewish people' (*Ibid.*). The phenomenon of anti-Semitism that emerges from the Runnymede report is transhistorical, subjective, and unprovoked. It is not only a form of racism (Runnymede Trust, 1994, p. 57) but also seems to predate racism. Thus, anti-Semitism's relationship with racism is rather complicated; it is both a form of racism and something distinct from it. This ambiguous relationship between racism and anti-Semitism is mirrored in broader cultural practices where (at least in Anglophone contexts) within the literature on the topic there is a tendency to conjoin the two categories by the insertion of an 'and' rather than reading one (anti-Semitism) as a sub-species of the other taken as a broader category (racism). Racism's relationship with anti-Semitism is parallel rather than hierarchical. In other words, anti-Semitism shares some overlapping features with racism but cannot be subsumed into it.

Given this rather nebulous and unstable relationship between racism and anti-Semitism it is worth considering where Islamophobia fits in: is it closer to anti-Semitism or racism? *A Very Light Sleeper* concludes with a statement that would seem to point to similarities between anti-Semitism and Islamophobia:

...both Jews and Muslims are perceived by people hostile to them to be foreigners and intruders in European societies; there is a strong religious component in both kinds of hostility, dating back to medieval Christianity with Jews seen as Christ killers and Muslims as infidels; the negative stereotypes prevalent in both kinds of hostility are used to justify processes of exclusion, marginalization and discrimination; the psychological processes and the interactions between attitudes and behaviour are much the same in both instances; both require the same broad range of educational, legal and political measures to combat them; and there are links in both instances with global political relationships, specifically the international situation in the Middle East. The principal overlap lies in the fact that most racist and extremist organizations in Europe are simultaneously anti-Semitic and anti-Islamic (Runnymede Trust, 1994, p. 55).

In the last sixty years the two communities in Europe which have been subjected to some of the most intense forms of racist genocidal violence were the German Jews and the Bosnian Muslims. In both cases being Jewish or being a Muslim was not about endorsing a set of beliefs or engaging in a set of practices. When the Nazis and Serbian ultra-nationalists called, it was not just the practice but the population that they targeted.

Despite this attempt to announce a common ground between anti-Semitism and Islamophobia, subtle differences in treatment of Jews and Muslims become apparent with the publication of the report on Islamophobia. Both the reports begin by paying homage to the concept of free speech and are at pains to argue that nothing that they set out to condemn would prevent 'legitimate criticism of religion' and that they recognise the right in 'democratic' society for all kinds of practices and values to be open to criticism.[4] Yet they deal with this 'right to criticise' in a slightly different way. The report on Islamophobia suggests that when acts of 'terrorism' directed against Israeli targets occur, Muslims and their representative organisations should express regret and show solidarity

---

[4] In this light it is interesting to note that in the challenge mounted by many British 'alternative' comedians against legislation on religious hatred, the strange echoes of the similar defences mounted by comics in relation to various 'race relations' legislation during the 1970s. What is ironic is that one of the premises of alternative comedy was that it abandoned the racist and sexist staples of earlier British comedy.

(Runnymede Trust, 1997a, pp. 50-55). There is no comparative suggestion in either report that Zionist or Jewish representatives should make similar gestures of sympathy and support when Israeli governments or groups attack Palestinians.

Similarly, in contrast to the clear assertion of the unprovoked nature of anti-Semitism, some Muslims are accused of contributing to Islamophobia. The Muslim community is internally differentiated between good and bad Muslims and the activities of bad Muslims are seen as contributing to Islamophobia. No similar split is presented in the case of the Jewish communities: there are neither moderate Zionists nor extreme Zionists, let alone good Jews and bad Jews. The distinction between bad Muslims and good Muslims is played out as a distinction between Muslims and fundamentalists: the former do not become embroiled in politics, especially politics outside the nation-state. The latter use religion for 'strategic' purposes rather than for sacred contemplation (Runnymede Trust, 1997a, p. 8). Again, neither of the reports suggests that Jews should not involve themselves in the politics of the Middle East.

These differences in the two reports illustrates that despite the attempt to treat Islamophobia as equally worthy of opprobrium as anti-Semitism and/or racism, the concept that emerges is far weaker in terms of its condemnatory power. The hesitancy is, I contend, a product of a lack of understanding of Muslim identity and its significance. In *A Very Light Sleeper* there is a clear sense of what a Jewish identity is, and unequivocal support for Zionism as the political expression of Jewish autonomy. In *Islamophobia: A Challenge for us all*, there is no clear endorsement of Muslim autonomy and its political articulation (see Birt, this volume). The 1997 report lacks an understanding of Muslim identity. This failure arises from a conceptual lacuna, which has become apparent with the eruption of the Muslim political subject not only in Western plutocracies but also throughout the *ummah*. An understanding of Islamophobia in absence of an understanding of the way in which there has been a global re-assertion of Muslim identity is difficult to sustain. Thus it is important to understand how the implication of the Runnymede reports' reliance on what Barnor Hesse describes as the Eurocentric concept of racism limits understanding of both racism in general and Islamophobia in particular (Hesse, 2007).[5]

The 'Eurocentric concept of racism' extrapolates from the policies of the Nazi regime the very essence of what racism means, in doing so it presents rac-

---

[5] For an elaboration of the Eurocentric concept of racism see Hesse (2004, pp. 135–136).

ism as primarily an anti-liberal, extremist ideology (Hesse and Sayyid, 2006, pp. 13–31; Hesse, 2007). The consequence is to forestall the disarticulation of the concept of racism from Nazism/fascism and from any systematic articulation with 'normal' liberal-democratic politics. In this privileging of the Nazi experience racism emerges as an exceptional moment in the state formation of Western plutocracies, and thus is displaced from the colonial order so that racism of the British, American, French, Portuguese and Dutch polities is disavowed (Hesse and Sayyid, forthcoming). This is despite the chilling similarities between the system of segregation, subordination and humiliation established by colonial polities and the racial laws instituted by the Nazis at least prior to the 'Final Solution' (Cesaire, 2001; see also Mazower, 1998). Thus in the absence of Nazis, quasi–Nazis or self-ascribed racists it becomes virtually impossible to imagine racism, for the Eurocentric concept of racism cannot conceive of racism without identifiable racists.

Three ways out of the conundrum of methodological and ontological individualism produced by this Eurocentric concept of racism suggest themselves. First, one can rely on a notion of some sort of 'false consciousness', which allows for racists to exist even in the absence of their self-declarations. In other words, racists do not know that they are racists. Second, one could argue that racism without racists is actually the work of a cabal of crypto super-racists. In this conspiratorial mode of thinking, social outcomes can be explained by motivations of specific persons scheming in a secret, elaborate and sustained manner. Third, one could argue that racism is produced by ignorant and uninformed people rather than racists, the unintended consequences of the actions of otherwise decent people. By linking the existence of racism to racists (whether through delusion, occultation, or ignorance), the solution to racism is individual reform rather than structural transformation; because racism is what racists do, one can stop racism by educating racists or by getting others not to give cause for racists to act like racists.

The problem posed by racism without racists is compounded when we consider the case of Islamophobia. For not only is there a rejection of the argument that Islamophobia is a form of racism (since racism is what 'Nazis' do) but paradoxically, there is also an affirmation that to be an Islamophobe is justified given the 'realities' of Islam or Islamicate cultural practices. As we have seen, *Islamophobia: A challenge for us all* in its vacillation comes close to endorsing such a view, or at least to giving the impression that it may be justified. The case for Islamophobia being a form of racism, or similar to racism, continues to be contested. A manifestation of this contestation can be seen in attempts to use an etymological discussion of Islamophobia as the means of discovering its true kernel. Islamophobia, it is argued, is a misnomer since it is not 'Islam' per se which is the target of discriminatory practices but Muslims, and as such, the use of the term 'Islamophobia' prevents legitimate critique of Islamic practices. The meaning of terms, however, is a matter of their use rather than the application of an etymological rule. For the same reason that anti-Semitism has come to denote not exclusionary practices against all Semitic language speakers as such, but specifically against those of Jewish heritage, the conceptualisation of Islamophobia does not have to be bound by its etymological roots. Far too much energy is misleadingly spent in trying to use an etymological discussion of Islamophobia as a means to uncovering its essence.[6]

Etymological fundamentalism is only one of the arguments that are deployed by those who insist that Islamophobia does not exist. Another is the argument that because Muslims are not a 'race', Islamophobia cannot be a form of racism. This set of arguments rests upon making a sharp distinction between 'race' and religion—a distinction that is often inflected within discussions of racism between the idea of cultural and biological forms of racism. It can be shown without too much difficulty that the so-called 'cultural' and 'biological' forms of racism are not as distinct as is often presented (see Nasr and Modood, this volume). The difference between the biological and the cultural is translated into the difference between will and fate.[7] This distinction is difficult to sustain, for the biological cannot be so easily disarticulated from the cultural in the case of racism.

Racialised bodies were never exclusively biological; they were marked at the same time as religion, culture, history, and territories were marked and used to group socially fabricated distinctions between Europeanness and non-Europeanness. The idea that an individual can simply choose a different cultural context ignores the fact that individuals are formed by immersion into specific cultural contexts and that it is not possible to step outside all contexts. These cultural contexts are themselves products of overlapping networks of relations, and the boundaries of one context from another are never clear-cut. The 'thrownness' of humans limits the possibilities of making a sharp distinction between fate and will along the lines of biology (nature) and culture. It is

---

[6] Islamophobia's inexact origin as a term is not necessarily a sign of its conceptual weakness but a recognition of its newness, and the contested terrain it has to operate in.

[7] It would not follow that just because a form of identification is considered to be a matter of choice it should legitimately be the subject of unjust exclusionary practices.

as much a matter of fate to be 'thrown' into one particular context as another. For example, being a Kashmiri, or Chechen or Palestinian at a time of Indian, Russian or Israeli occupation is not a context which is determined biologically. Racialisation does not depend on biology to produce 'races'; rather it sees the construction of collective identities as a product of social processes. It does not follow that just because Muslims are not a 'race', or there is yet no Muslim gene, their subjugation is not racism.

To be fair to the Runnymede report of 1997, it was precisely because Muslims were not covered by the anti-racism legislation in Britain at the time, that its authors sought to address this omission arguing that Islamophobia was a serious issue of social injustice. However, by depending on a liberal conception of racism the Runnymede report was unable to articulate a category of Islamophobia in which the association of racism with Islamophobia would be axiomatic.[8] This can be seen very clearly in the way in which the report differentiates what it calls anti-Semitic racism from more generalised anti-Semitism. The impression given is that racism is dependent on the existence of a category of race (whether it is biologically or culturally determined). In this regard, anti-racism laws covered Jews and Sikhs since they were able to establish that they were religious as well as ethnic communities. From liberalism's point of view what exactly a Muslim is remains a problem. Muslims are clearly not reducible to one community of descent (however mediated); Muslims can be of European descent, of African descent, of Asian descent, not to mention descent of any combination thereof. Muslims also transcend the usual broad racial classifications that regulate the British ethnoscape: white, black, Asian etc. This distinction between identities which are ascribed and those which are chosen is seen as being crucial in determining what kind of limits can be placed on liberal freedoms (e.g. freedom to criticise) on the assumption that while there is no point in criticising a form of identification that is given—since no-one can really do anything to change it—identities which are chosen can be abandoned in the face of reasoned discourse. For Islamophobia to be articulated unambiguously as a form of racism, one has to address the specific process by which Muslim identity has become racialised. This is a task that the Runnymede report cannot accomplish, because it is unable to address the question: what exactly is a Muslim now?

[8] It is ironic that *Islamophobia: A challenge for us all*, is aware of 'liberalism's prejudices' against religion and Islam in particular, however, its philosophical mooring remains within liberalism's ambit in its vision of a society composed of individuals and shorn of antagonisms.

What follows, is an ontological interpretation of 'Muslimness' and this requires abandoning the primacy of ontic studies that posit an essence that underpins (and predetermines) any subsequent investigation (Thomson, 2005). It is often argued that being a Muslim is one of many possible forms of identification that an individual may embrace (the extent to which that 'embrace' is a matter of will or fate is, as we have seen, open to dispute). A correlative argument claims that the focus on Muslim identity erases the diversity within Muslim communities. Thus, assertions of Muslim identification often elicit the response that this is an homogenising and totalising label which privileges one identity option or subject position over others. More specifically, that it privileges a religious form of identification over other potentially more meaningful subject positions such as those offered by gender, class, nationality, among others. Muslim identifications, in other words, are considered superficial because they are 'religious'. This denial of Muslims as a meaningful category is not simply an epistemological exercise or academic enterprise, though it takes the form of such mere intellectual pursuits, but rather involves forging a framework which systematically excludes and violates Muslim agency. The polemical nature of the argument is often disavowed by deployment of a form of sociological reasoning which presents itself as simply the description of the world as it is. The difficulty, however, is not necessarily with Muslim identities but rather with conventional wisdom's inability to understand the nature of political identity. Political identities are central to any form of politics and can in principle be constructed around any set of social demands. The mobilisation of Muslims as Muslims is not an ersatz form of mobilisation, and Muslim identity is not less (or more) authentic than other forms of political identification.

At the heart of Islamophobia is not the prevalence of 'closed' rather than 'open' views of Islam but rather the maintenance of the 'violent hierarchy' between the idea of the West (and all that it can be articulated to represent) and Islam (and all that it can be articulated to represent). This colonial hierarchy has many homologies with the hierarchy that constitutes racism itself, that is, the difference between 'Europeanness' (note, not Europeans per se) and 'non-Europeanness'. The emergence of Islamophobia can be understood as a response to attempts to erode the West and non-West framework. Islamophobia can perhaps be defined as the disciplining of Muslims by reference to an antagonistic Western horizon. As such, Islamophobia manifests itself in a variety of debates—over multiculturalism, national and international security, literature, feminism—and in a variety of sites: America, Europe, Russia, India.

Its different inflections are partly a response to the difference between societies and histories that are narrated (and narrate themselves) as Westernising and those whose hegemonic constructions represent them as already Western. The idea of a Western telos towards which non-Western but Westernising societies can orient themselves does not require a geographical or cultural sense of the West, but only a concession to tropes that are hegemonically articulated with a particular reading of Western history—e.g. modernity. Such an understanding of Islamophobia rejects the view often taken by many well-meaning Muslims to understand it as a transhistorical phenomenon. That is, to consider every moment of Islamicate history where Muslims are marginalised or excluded an instance of Islamophobia. The first Islamophobes then would be found among the Makkan aristocracy who opposed the Prophet, making life for him and his early followers so difficult that they had to leave Makkah. Such an interpretation of Islamophobia (similar to perennially popular accounts of anti-Semitism as the 'longest hatred' taken to encompass all actions against those who are retrospectively and often unproblematically described as Jews including those initiated by Egyptians, Babylonians, Seleucids, Romans etc.) fails to pay due attention to the very different contexts in which antagonism to Islam and Muslims emerge.

Concepts emerge to address particular problems; whether they succeed or are re-articulated to other purposes does not alter the argument that their appearance is an attempt to deal with a particular issue at the time. What does Islamophobia describe that could not be adequately grasped by the concept of racism? There are three major ways in which Islamophobia can be distinguished from racism in general. Firstly, given the hegemonic understanding of ethnicity based around quasi–biological notions of race, discrimination against Muslims is deemed not to be racism since Muslims are not reducible to one ethnicity. Thus the concept of Islamophobia makes it possible to see that multi–ethnic groupings can also be subjects of discrimination. Secondly, Islamophobia transcends the boundaries of the nation-state—it arises partly from the crisis of the nation-state in which the figure of the Muslim comes to stand in for the relativisation of the nation-state and its inability to contain Muslim acts as a metaphor for the way in which the nation-state is less and less able to exercise control over its own destiny. Islamophobia bridges the separation which established colonialism and racism as distinct assemblages despite their homologous nature (see Hesse and Sayyid, forthcoming). Thirdly, Islamophobia paradoxically demonstrates the contingent nature of the Western enterprise. By seeing in the assertion of Muslim identity an existential threat to Western civilisation itself, Islamophobes inadvertently betray their anxieties about a future in which cultural, economic and military dominance of the West may not be sustained. The inability to project into the future the dominance that so many Westerners have taken for granted, transforms Western assumptions of superiority into a condition reflecting a particular set of circumstances rather than something intrinsic to Western nature itself.

The distinctiveness of Islamophobia has to be related to contemporary developments in the world. As such, it is structured by a postcolonial and post-Caliphate logic. The postcolonial logic raises doubts about the future of the world as being decipherable as an upscaled version of Western history. The narrative of 'Plato-to-NATO' that underwrites the destiny of the West seems to have been interrupted and its ignoble beginnings exposed, thus, enabling the development of an Islamicate counter-narrative that no longer needs to attempt to fill a West-shaped hole. This Islamicate counter-narrative takes its bearing from the post-Caliphate universe in which demands for justice in Mus-limistan (and subsequently the entire *ummah*) take forms in which moments of the institutionalisation of particular socio-economic order become con-tested. The conflict between Kemalists and Islamists generates an ever-widen-ing interpellation of Muslims as Muslims, and their recruitment into ranks of proliferating counter-narratives and language games that can be described as Islamese. That is, narratives that reject the structuring of history along the 'Plato-to-NATO' axis as being the destiny of the world, by articulating a series of sequences—the beginning of which can be symbolised by the Archangel Gabriel speaking to a forty-year-old merchant, or the flight of that merchant from his hometown of Makkah to Medina. The emergence of Islamophobia relates to the presence of Muslims qua Muslims in settings in which Islam can be described as an antipode of a Western horizon. In other words, Islamopho-bia emerges in contexts where being Muslim has a significance which is politi-cal. What Islamophobia seeks to discipline is the possibility of Muslim autonomy, that is, an affirmation of Muslim political identity as a legitimate historical subject. In this regard, it is interesting to note that the re-formulation and re-introduction of Islamophobia has its beginnings in a clearly marked British context. While this suggests that the processes that led to its formation point to peculiarities of the public policy making nexus between the state and civil society organisations that are specific to the United Kingdom, it also points to the relative political strength of the Muslim community in the U.K. It is possible to argue that Muslims in the UK are far more powerful than other Muslim communities in the Western plutocracies, and this despite the fact that it is not the largest or the wealthiest or the best educated of Muslim communities outside Muslimistan. It is purely to do with the way it has become the most politicised of Muslim communities and among the most politicised of ethnically marked minorities. This politisation reflects the way in which the Anglophonic world has been strongly influenced by the U.S. Civil Rights Movement and the way in which anti-racist and anti-colonial critiques have continued to circulate both at intellectual and popular culture level.[9] This combination of two critiques has been significant in problematising divisions that constitute national majority—ethnic minorities configurations that structure the postcolonial order. The difficulty in containing Muslims within a purely domestic context opens the possibility for the mobilisation of Muslims along with other political groups and organisations, which seek a liberating transformation of the current order. The marches against the invasion of Iraq and in support of Palestinians against Israeli attacks on Gaza did as much as purely local and domestic issues to entrench many Muslims in the critical public life of Britain. The relative political strength of the Muslim community in Britain helped create the conditions for the challenge to Islamophobia. The globalisation of the category of Islamophobia points to the way in which conditions which made it possible to name Islamophobia can no longer be seen as peculiarly British.

---

[9] For an elaboration of the centrality of the Civil Rights Movement and its articulation with anti-colonial national liberation movements in challenging racism, see Hesse and Sayyid (forthcoming).

3

ISLAMOPHOBIA AND THE CRUSADES

Jonathan Riley-Smith

Five days after the attacks of 11 September 2001, President Bush in a rather offhand remark compared the War on Terror he was launching to a 'crusade', and in so doing helped confirm the view held by large sections of the Muslim public that the War on Terror was an euphemism for war against Muslim autonomy. The idea that crusades can be a prime manifestation of Islamophobia owes much to the efforts of the Caliph-Sultan Abdulhamid II, who publicised his conviction that European colonial expansion into 'Muslimistan' was a new crusade. The pan-Islamic press took up this argument; the first Muslim history of the crusading movement, published in 1899, drew attention to the fact that 'our most glorious sultan, Abdulhamid II, has rightly remarked that Europe is now carrying out a crusade against us in the form of a political campaign'. Up to this point, Muslims had looked back on the Crusades with indifference and complacency. They felt that they had beaten the crusaders comprehensively, driving them from the Levant and occupying far more territory in the Balkans than the Westerners had ever held in Palestine and Syria. But as they began to take an interest in the historical parallels between contemporary and medieval Christian-Muslim interaction, they were confronted with Western rhetoric portraying contemporary empire builders as quasi–crusaders returning to complete the work their ancestors had begun. It was easy to gloss this with the view that Europe, having lost the first round in the Crusades, had embarked on another and that therefore the Crusades were an

THINKING THROUGH ISLAMOPHOBIA

authentic representation of Islamophobia. Such a view, however, is anachronistic both in relation to Islamophobia and the Crusades.

The Crusades were a form of Christian Holy War that came into existence in the late eleventh century, at a time when the Muslims were believed to be posing a serious threat to Christian Europe. Almost the whole of what is now Asiatic Turkey had been lost to the Seljuks and there had been a resurgence of Muslim power in the Iberian Peninsula. Fear of Muslims persisted and it was fuelled by the Ottoman invasions of Europe from the fourteenth century onwards. The last crusaders are to be found in Western armies trying to recover the Balkans in the late seventeenth century and in the Christian fleets operating out of Malta against North African corsairs in the eighteenth. So a motivating factor for crusading against Muslims was apprehension, although it should be remembered that they were only one of the enemies against whom crusades came to be launched.

The earliest crusaders knew very little about Islam, although many of them had had contact with Muslims, in Spain or Sicily or when taking part in mass pilgrimages to Jerusalem. Their descendants knew much more, but better knowledge did not make much difference to their attitudes. Convinced that the Christian religion embodied God's wishes for mankind, they considered that Islam posed a threat to God's providential intentions. They—or at any rate the more educated among them—knew that Christian war-theology forbade conversions by force and that the purpose of crusading was a defensive one: to recover any land lost to Islam, however far back in the past, and to protect Christendom from any further Muslim advance. Crusaders were supposed to leave the business of conversion to Christian missions, which is why one indirect consequence of the crusade movement was the Franciscan and Dominican mission to Asia in the thirteenth century.

The need to justify Christian warfare, as a necessary reaction to aggression was one reason why fear and loathing of Islam was a feature of crusader propaganda. Another was the fact that crusades had to be fought by volunteers. Of course the armies contained large numbers of men who had been conscripted or were mercenary, but the nucleus had to be men (and women) who had responded freely to the call, since they were expected to make vows, which were considered to be valid only when they were voluntary. If there were no volunteers, there couldn't be a crusade. The enterprises had, therefore, to be presented to audiences in ways that convinced them of their necessity and encouraged them to respond spontaneously to the call. To whip up their audiences, Crusade preachers portrayed the Muslims in exaggerated and highly coloured terms as wicked and intolerably aggressive. The propaganda certainly affected the attitude of newly arrived Westerners in the Levant and it was reflected in the edge that there could be to crusading violence.

On entering Syria and Palestine in 1098–99—and for about a decade afterwards—the earliest crusaders seem to have adopted a policy of terror with respect to every place of religious or political significance, with the aim of driving away all non-Christian elements, which they considered might threaten them. However, they subsequently decided that selective ethnic cleansing was counter-productive—it had never been applied to the generality of locations—and they developed a *modus vivendi* with the Muslim inhabitants, who may have been less numerous than has hitherto been supposed, because it is possible that Islamisation had proceeded quite slowly in Palestine. The statelets the Christians established found no difficulty in entering into defensive and offensive alliances with the petty Muslim powers in the region, which had come into existence in the eleventh century and were again to be found in the first half of the thirteenth. Both sides seem to have adhered to primitive 'rules of war'. If a town or fortress refused to surrender, it was sacked (such as Jerusalem by Christians in 1099, although the numbers massacred in that notorious event are now subject to modification; Vadum Jacob by Muslims in 1179; Acre by Muslims in 1291). Where surrender was negotiated (as with Jerusalem to the Muslims in 1187 and to the Christians in 1229) it was spared. The terrible sacking by the first crusaders of Ma'arrat in 1098, which shocked the Muslims, occurred after negotiations had broken down.

Once the new Western settlers had reconciled themselves to the indigenous Muslim presence, the principle of government adopted by them seems to have been based on existing Muslim *dhimma* regulations. These were lifted from local Christians, left on Jews and imposed on Muslims. So Muslims had to pay a special tax and suffered legal discrimination. On the other hand, they had their own courts for minor and communal cases. Mosques and shrines still flourished and although some of the great mosques in the main towns were taken over and turned into cathedrals, the new cathedral in Acre retained a *mihrab* and a part set aside for Muslim prayer, Muslims were still permitted to use part of the al-Aqsa mosque (now the Templar headquarters) and there was even a church-mosque at a site in Acre sacred both to Christians and, probably, some Muslims.

There was, of course, no toleration in the sense we understand it. This was a world in which the words *infideles* and *kuffar* denoted insurmountable obstacles. It was possible to trade and make treaties with those of another religion.

It was possible to be influenced by their culture and to admire aspects of it. It was possible to recognise that men and women of other faiths could be naturally good and to blame oneself for one's ill treatment of them. It was possible to have friendships with them that transcended the divide. But there could never be empathy and there was always suspicion. The arrangements put in place by the crusaders, in which the Muslims as *dhimmi* people remained in a subservient position, were pragmatic.

The same practical approach is vividly illustrated in the surviving letters from the leaders of the crusader settlements in the Levant back home. These men were the Christians most actively engaged in continuous war against Islam. Their knowledge of those aspects of Near Eastern politics relevant to the situation in which they found themselves was accurate and detailed within certain limits, but their correspondence is characterised by a restrained tone. Many of their letters were, of course, private, but even when they seem to have been intended for a wider circulation they were neutrally expressed. They must have believed that the kings, senior churchmen and great nobles in the West to whom they wrote appreciated unemotional language, since if they had been convinced that their correspondents, from whom they were, after all, soliciting assistance, would have been responsive to highly coloured rhetoric they would certainly have used it. The bulk of the correspondence from the West to the leaders of the crusader settlements has been lost, but circumstantial evidence suggests that senior figures in Europe must have written to them in the same understated way.

A neutral approach made sense in the circumstances in which they found themselves. Indeed the histrionics indulged in by Crusade preachers must have made it hard for those on whose shoulders the defence of the Christian Holy Land actually rested, because they were faced by unreasonable expectations and were inevitably blamed if a war on God's behalf turned against them. It is natural to wonder what was more typical of Western attitudes: the hyperbolic propaganda and the emotionally charged aggression of some newcomers to the Levant; or the cool matter-of-factness of the settlers' correspondence and their adaptation of a Muslim system of control when confronted by the need to deal with other religions under their rule.

4

IS THE ISLAM IN ISLAMOPHOBIA THE SAME AS THE ISLAM IN ANTI-ISLAM; OR, WHEN IS IT ISLAMOPHOBIA TIME?

AbdoolKarim Vakil

Only a fool would think it was enough to point to this misty mantle of illusion in order to destroy the world that counts as essential, so called 'reality'! Only as creators can we destroy! But we should also not forget this: creating new names and assessments and apparent truths is eventually enough to create new things. [Friedrich Nietzsche]

Naming alone is never enough to create. [...] For a name to do its creative work, it needs authority. One needs usage within institutions. Naming does its work only as a social history works itself out (Hacking, 2002, p. 8).

When can one speak of Islamophobia? The approach taken in this chapter is to ask not when the term Islamophobia was coined, but what political discourse was required for the concept of Islamophobia to be meaningful. With the Runnymede Trust, I argue that 'Islamophobia' '[was] coined because there [was] a new reality that need[ed] naming', and, more crucially, 'so that it [could] be identified and acted against (Runnymede Trust, 1997a, p. 4). Contrary to the Runnymede definition, however, what is most significant is not *what* it names, which is also not a centuries old fear and dread of Islam and Muslims (much less the 'unfounded'-ness of such hostility), but rather *that* it names; and in naming, the namer it bespeaks rather than the named. Quite the opposite of victimhood, then, Islamophobia is about contestation and the power to set the political vocabulary and legal ground of recognition and redress. It is about the contemporary subjectification of Muslim political subject(ivitie)s. What is called for, therefore, is not a history of Islamophobia but rather its genealogy: the conditions of possibility of its enunciation.

Words and Things

Of when is it legitimate to speak of Islamophobia? In a recent article on Leibniz's response to Islam, Ian Almond wrote:

Certainly, there is a standard essay on Leibniz and Islam that one could write; it would involve a Saidesque compendium of the thinker's largely negative references to the faith and its followers, his dismissal of Turks as undeveloped, cruel, and backward, his constant emphasis on Christian unity in the face of the Ottoman threat; in such an essay, the author of *Consilium Aegyptiacum* (the *Egyptian Plan*) would be foregrounded as an early, classical model for the modern intellectual of Empire. Leibniz's advice to Louis XIV, his attempt to persuade the monarch that an attack on Egypt would be 'to the profit of Christendom' (*pro profectu religionis Christianae*), appear almost to have been written with Gramsci and Said's analysis of the intellectual's complicity with imperialistic hegemony in mind. [...] The ultimate point of such an approach, predictably enough, would be to underline precisely how Christian the limits of Leibniz's Christian humanism actually were—how Leibniz's allegedly universal concern for "the welfare of mankind," with regards to Islam at least, never really moved beyond Belgrade and Gibraltar.

Paradoxically, such an essay would be both necessary and superfluous. 'Superfluous' because, as Joseph McCarney has already pointed out in another, quite different context, the collective damning of figures such as Leibniz or Kant for their Islamophobia and race-bias becomes quite meaningless in judging a vocabulary where terms such as 'Islamophobia' simply did not exist (Almond, 2006, p. 464).

The passage, though long, is worth quoting in full, for its argument goes to the heart of our question. Disentangling three interrelated strands of Almond's argument will help map out the problematic of this chapter.

The first strand concerns the citational deployment of McCarney as shortcut for a critique, which, though apparently crucial, he has rendered superfluous—namely, the invalidity of the charge of race bias, and by extension also of Islamophobia, on account of the anachronism of the term. This is puzzling in two respects. Firstly, because that is not at all the point of McCarney's argument in the critique of Bernasconi upon which Almond here draws. The closest

McCarney comes to such historicist absolution is in his claim that 'it is doubt-ful whether many European thinkers whose opinions were formed before, say, the 1970s would emerge unscathed' (McCarney, 2003, p.34). McCarney's own intervention on the question of racism and Enlightenment philosophy speaks rather to three very different and very specific questions: Bernasconi's misread-ing of his (and Hegel's) geographical materialism as a racist geographical deter-minism; the question of 'what belongs to the structure of philosophy and what does not', of what is biographically contingent and what is of the essence of their philosophical discourse; and whether such critiques as Bernasconi's, by the very fact of thickly laying out the obvious exclusionary nature of Western philosophy do not actually end up 'crushingly' reinforcing that very exclusion-ism. Hardly in respect of racism, then, a matter of the meaninglessness of a term not yet in existence, as Almond suggests. Secondly, it is puzzling because it strangely fails to even acknowledge, let alone deal with, Bernasconi's own reply and refutation of McCarney's fundamentally miscast critique (Bernas-coni, 2003a, p. 34). In short, and not without its relevance here, the main point of Bernasconi's article had been, as its very subtitle made clear (Bernasconi, 2003b, p. 13), the contemporary academy, the teaching machine and its prac-tices of reading, and perpetuating its readings, of the canon; not the racism of the historical authors themselves. Moreover, given Almond's explicit concern with historicism in his article it is all the more puzzling that in citing McCar-ney he should so entirely elide Bernasconi's deeper historicist objection that the historicist 'a child of his times' absolution more often than not proves but lazy apologism and selective historical reconstruction blind to the historically determined configuration of the extant past in contemporary archives (Ber-nasconi, 2003a, p. 35).

The second strand concerns the question of Orientalism. Even charitably assuming that the 'Saidesque' reading Almond so contemptuously dismisses is, as the suffix *esque* suggests, less an expression of his contempt for Said's *Orientalism* than for the caricatured applications it has bastardly spawned, the question nevertheless remains of the validity, if any, of the Saidian cri-tique. Almond's approach dwells on the irreducible ambivalences of the Leib-nitzian corpus: its 'epistemological subtlety' and 'polyphony', and the 'multiplicity of optics' that must be brought to bear in 'evaluating' Leibnitzian pronouncements on Islam (Almond, 2006, pp. 464, 465). The same irreduc-ible 'dissonances, complications, and paradoxes' of 'jarring voices' and 'different faces' are explored in Almond's more recent discussion of Herder (Almond, 2008, pp. 58, 74). In these historically and theoretically informed close and nuanced readings Almond does exactly what Bernasconi calls for, situating the explicitly negative comments in the contexts of the individual works, (off-)setting them against the corpus and general context while also threading out the different and contradictory strands which run through them. Yet, the question is whether in doing so, but settling for the sheer polyphony of the speaking voices and the shiftiness of the placing of Muslims, he does not in fact end up losing sight of the more fundamental aspects of Said's critique. First, it is less a matter of highlighting 'negative references to the faith and its followers', or merely exposing intellectual complicities with imperial designs, than of attending to the dynamic interplay of the manifest with the latent; the play of imaginative geographies in the performance of the dramatic boundaries by which the West both ontologises the difference between the West and the Orient, and thereby orientalises the oriental and Westernises itself (Said, 2003 cf. Prakash, 1995). Moreover, and more importantly, the question is whether—the ambiguities and ambivalences of each of the figures studied individually, and for their very exceptionality, notwithstanding—the economy of the archive, the consistent regularity enfolding of heterogeneity, is disturbed.

The third and final strand relates to Almond's identification of Leibniz's and Herder's figurations of Islam as transitional, dramatising the tensions between a theological and a secular enmity to Islam, in Leibniz, and a romantic and a Protestant Christian repulsion-attraction, in Herder. This illuminates a crucial step, which Said himself had emphasised in the emergence of modern Orientalism. In Said's argument, one aspect of this process was the restructuring of Orientalism from the prison of Christian theological categories into secular, historical, comparatist, classificatory and ultimately civilisational ones. The other was that this restructuring involves both the secularisation of categories, and their re-habitation by a 'reconstructed religious impulse' that Said, with recourse to M.H. Abrams, describes as a 'Natural Supernaturalism' (Said, 2003, pp. 116-122). Two points should be made in response to this. Firstly, while this is not the place to revisit the secularisation/reoccupation debate (cf. Jay, 1985, p. 184), alertness to its unresolved subsumption is crucial to a reconstructive critique of the limitations of Saidian Orientalism in respect of "Islam", and hence of how Islamophobia builds on the critique of Orientalism. For, as Hart incisively puts it, 'the religious-secular distinction is Said's Orientalism, the very way he produces otherness for his own uses' (Hart, W.D., 2000, p. 85). In effect, 'the invidious distinction between East and West, was the cultural common sense of those whom Said calls Orientalists. The invidious distinction between religion and secularism is part of Said's cultural common sense' (Hart, W.D., 2000, pp. 85, 86). Second, reading Leibniz and Herder with Almond invites us to think through this process more critically, as two crucial, fraught, and far from completed processes which do not so much clear the way but rather thickly lay the ground for the emergence of the contemporary Muslim: the de-theologisation of Islam, and the denial of coevalness (Fabian, 1983) in the structuration of eurocentrism. While it is essential to build on the discontinuity identified by Said, it is no less important to complicate it with reference to the fact that, as Hart succinctly puts it, Islam 'as an object of discourse, and certainly as a proper name, is a rather late development' (Hart, W.D., 2000, p. 84; see also Hughes, 2007; Devji, 2007, p. 64; Tayob, 2007). Different questions, and indeed temporalities, are at issue in this nexus of the making of 'Islam' as a 'Religion', colonial 'ethnicisation' and the emergence of 'Muslim communities', imperial conscription into modernity, and the struggle for the mastery of self-ascription. One such strand may usefully, and provocatively, be explored with reference to Gil Anidjar's claims that it was 'Hegel who invented the Muslims' (Anidjar, 2003, p. 133) and that it is to the Nazis that we owe the recognition of Islam as 'the paradigm of religiosity' (Anidjar, 2008, p. 19). By way of context they refer to the genealogy of the theological-political in European philosophical thought, and are alert to the particular figuration of the Muslim as the problem. Here, however, they attempt two things: to unsettle 'the Muslim' of our discussions out of unproblematic, naturalised religious and theological fixings and into the fray of discursive figurations, and to caution against a too rushed, or linear, 'periodisation' of what is involved in the process Said was getting at.[1]

Foregrounding the surreptitious transposition of the debate over 'race'/ism in Western philosophy into that over Islamophobia, and the silent displacement of the Saidian critique of Orientalism in Almond's historicism, usefully brings both questions back to the fore: what is the relation that can be established between them? From an avowed dismissal of Saidesque critique Almond moves seamlessly to rule out speaking of Islamophobia, and he does so, by extension of the objection to racism. What do these linkages, slippages and analogies imply about the relational configurations of the categories? Poignantly, it is the elided Bernasconi, evoked only as the silent critic refuted

---

[1] For a useful introduction to Anidjar's project in his own words, see the 'Introduction' to *Semites* (Anidjar, 2008) and the 2003 Q&A *Asia Source* interview now reprinted in Shaikh (2007, pp. 225–253).

by the named McCarney, whose questions prompt us to similarly interrogate Almond's practice: what is the point of his analysis other than nuancing the Saidesque reading of his own imagining? How does Almond's focus on the Saidesque, coming as it does in the context of a full blown revisionist backlash against Said's 'vulgar' worlding of the imperial complicities of scholarship, exactly when Orientalism is being redeployed in the War on Terror, play out beyond the question of Leibniz and Herder? The question, for us, is precisely that which Bernasconi raises of Enlightenment philosophy and racism: what, by analogy, is the relation of the anti-Islam of the texts, and their canonised, bracketed, institutionalised reproduction, to the Islamophobia in the present? (In fact, the very point of the Saidian rather than the Saidesque critique of Orientalism [see Asad, 1980, p. 648]). Our initial question, then, comes back to us transposed, not *of when* can we speak of Islamophobia but when can *we speak of* Islamophobia? Not a chronological, but a conceptual question.

Reading Othello in War on Terror Times

In a tribute to Edward Said written on the occasion of his death, Ania Loomba sought to retain the contemporary significance of a comment of Said's which spoke to the question of the relation of racism to colonialism. Namely, that 'racism repeats and appropriates certain images and tropes to the point where they take on a trans-historical flavor' (Loomba, 2003, p. 13). The point had originally been made to her by Said in an interview of 1997 in which she had put to him the charge levelled by critics that *Orientalism* wilfully disregarded the heterogeneities of imperialist conceptions of the Orient. In reply, Said had reiterated the argument already essayed twenty years earlier, in that very book, about the enduring deep structure of Orientalism, and the recurrence of its basic premise of ontologised difference. Said then illustrated that recurrence with an appropriate topical reference to the re-appropriation of the civilisational boundary-making in Huntington's *Clash of Civilizations*. The repetition and appropriation noted, Said immediately stressed the difference in repetition which recurrence carries, adding '[it's] been there all along, I mean, for hundreds of years', which 'doesn't mean it's the same' (Said, 1997, quoted in Loomba, 2003, p. 13. For the original full text see Said 1998, p. 84.). Recalling the point, several years later, in what was now intended as a eulogistic exploration of Said's legacy to postcolonial critique, Loomba went on to develop its significance in respect of the relation between racism and colonialism and its analogous repeating and appropriation of images and tropes. As in both her previous and subsequent work, Loomba did this by drawing on Etienne Balibar's discussion of 'neo-racism' (Balibar, 1991). Following Balibar's lead in tracing the prefiguration of cultural racism to the Spanish Inquisition, Loomba suggests that in this respect it is useful to go back to a consideration of Renaissance cultural stereotypes, and insists on the articulations between colour and religion in Renaissance England and wider European imperial circulations, to explore continuities and discontinuities of the kind a terminological historicism would foreclose. Interestingly, in regard of this point, Loomba adds that 'Balibar is thinking of contemporary anti-Semitism, but also of the rise of Islamophobia' (Loomba, 2003, p. 13). Balibar, both in the 1991 text cited and since, does refer to Arabophobia (and its confusion of 'Arabness' and 'Islamicism' [Balibar, 1991, p. 24]), but not to Islamophobia.

This redescriptive move in Loomba's reading of Balibar is suggestive. As the very term and strategy of postcolonialism and postcolonial critique entails, it proposes we eschew linear readings and the logics of contained periodisations in our approach to problematics such as racism and Islamophobia. For the project of a more comprehensive exploration of the genealogy of Islamophobia this means two things. Firstly, we do not merely extend back to a consideration of articulations of the exercise of power, categorisation and exclusion (telescoped through the workings of the successive formations of the medieval persecuting society; Renaissance 'encounters', conquest and Slavery; Early Modern state formation and Inquisitorial practices; Enlightenment 'universalism' and imperialism; up to nineteenth-century colonialism and scientific racism), but we also read them sideways, as a 'contrapuntal co-presence' to reading the contemporary.[2] Moreover, that we do so through different grids: if, with Loomba (see especially Loomba, 2005), we read race back to, and for, tropologies of difference (ideologies of otherness in 'ideas about skin colour, location, religion, rank and gender' [Loomba, 2002, Chapters 1 and 2]) in the Balibarian mirror of the naturalisation of culture; with Barnor Hesse, what we are tracing in race is, rather, following Fanon, colonial categories and techniques of social administration as a 'relationship of governance', and through the contraposition of this subaltern reading of racism, read for the 'creolisation' of 'political formations' (see Hesse, 2003; 2004). The difference, for us, can be put thus: with Loomba, 'race' is opened to

[2] The phrase is Ato Quayson's (2005), drawing on Said (though, oddly, race is entirely absent from his discussion of the postcolonial Middle Ages).

encompass the racialisation of religion; with Hesse, read in conjunction with Talal Asad (1993; 2003), 'religion' and 'the secular' are opened up to the articulations of governance which co-constitute them. In short, neither the foregrounding of 'Islam' in "Islamophobia", nor the imputed displacement of 'Muslim' from the name will stand unproblematically as a critique of its supposed privileging of 'religion' over 'race', or its repositioning onto an imputed neutral and level playing ground of secular contestation of ideas.

The fuller import of Loomba's (2003, p. 13) redescriptive move to the question with which we are concerned here, can be better brought out by returning to the text and context of the passage quoted:

Etienne Balibar has suggested that we are faced with the resurgence of neo racism (or what he calls 'racism without race') [...] In suggesting this, Balibar is thinking of contemporary anti-Semitism, but also of the rise of *Islamophobia* which since his essay was written, and *especially after 9/11*, has indeed become a global phenomenon. The language of such Islamophobia invokes the Crusades, freezes the Islamic world in a medieval past, and depends upon the recirculation of a very old repertoire of images, a division between "us" and "them" that does not reflect but seeks to manage a far more complex reality. Of course this division is not static and today it cannot be mapped onto a simple East-West binary as some of the most pernicious articulations of anti-Muslim sentiment is now to be found among Hindu fundamentalists (both in India but also elsewhere).

Two points are worth drawing out. The first concerns Loomba's use of the word 'Islamophobia' here. On the one hand, it is deployed re-descriptively to designate what Balibar himself refers to by other names or in different terms; on the other, Loomba's use of the term, the coalescing of the term in her own work is, like the increasing visibility of the phenomenon, 'especially' a 9/11 effect.[3] If, as I have been arguing, the genealogy of Islamophobia is that of the conditions of possibility for a performative speaking of the name, the re-description is what matters here. To a genealogy of Islamophobia, in other words, what is at stake is not whether Loomba is faithful to the 'spirit', let alone the letter, of Balibar's text, but Loomba's own re-descriptive use of the term. And re-description returns us to the dense structures and webs Bernasconi spoke

---

[3] Thus, reference to Islamophobia is absent from the first edition of *Colonialism/Postcolonialism* (Loomba, 1998), but appears in its second edition (Loomba, 2005, p. 217); it is absent from both the journal and book versions of one of her essays (Loomba, 1999 and 2000), but present in a 2002 book which otherwise recycles the exact same points and references (including to Balibar).

of. Two examples suggest the broader processes at work. Post 9/11, both individual scholars and disciplinary agendas, responded 'to being interpellated' either as Muslim (Ismail, 2002), or, as in Loomba's case, by the 'Othering' of Muslims, thus entangled in the twin processes of the Making of Muslims, and of the Muslim Question. It is of course the case that one must be wary of the complicity enshrined in exceptionalising the interpellative effect of 9/11 (Behdad, 2008). In crucial ways, however, the 9/11 US effect (and its global iterations) is significant. While both 1979 and 1989, that is the Iranian Revolution (and the siege of the American Embassy in Tehran in particular) and the Rushdie affair interpellated 'Muslims' into recognition as Muslims, thereby articulating the subject position, arguably they did so with significantly different internal splits in the configuration of that subjectivity, politically and otherwise. In 1989 left, Marxist, secularist Muslims, especially intellectuals and artists, positioned themselves in their responses to the Rushdie affair primarily in relation to the 'mullacracy' which lined them up with the Western discourse of aesthetics, freedom and rationality (however critical of Western imperialism) and therefore in terms of a Western articulation of autonomy which orientalised other (peasant/ignorant/fanatic book burning) Muslims; 9/11 significantly reshuffled the grids, re-aligning the internal split between resistance and identification (compare Qadri Ismail's responses to the Rushdie Affair [Ismail, 1991] and to 9/11 [Ismail, 2002; see also Ismail, 2008]). In this sense, the ways in which this internal reconfiguration within the category Muslim have taken place is more important than simply the notion that there has been a greater identification with the name Muslim by speaking out on Muslim issues or being spoken to as Muslim. Islamophobia is configured in these very articulations. An example of the micro-textures of the making of the Muslim Question can be found in the fact that 'Islamophobia' has made it as a bibliographical indexing 'keyword'. Like any classificatory category, the very fact of the name becomes productive and re-descriptive, enabling of the retrieval of a named corpus, generating its own academic niche and specialism, its own institutional centre of gravity, and materiality. Perversely, where a journal opts for it, even articles whose authors do their utmost to distance themselves from the use of the term can end up being indexed under it.

The second point which Loomba's comment on Said's reply invites, pertains to the destabilising problematisation that her last claim poses back to Said's opening response, and the space Said himself opened for difference within 'recurrence'. Said argued that the basic premise redeployed anew repeated the same basic gesture of mapping as ontological distinction between West and

East. Yet even while repeating this very claim in respect of contemporary Islamophobia's reiteration of anti-Islamic tropes, Loomba throws that mapping out of joint with the claim that a Hindu fundamentalist discourse of Islamophobia re-centres the lines of battle onto different histories, narratives, symbols and geographies. Two possible responses can be suggested: one, that Indian nationalist and Hindutva Islamophobia were, particularly in their historical narratives, grafted onto (though not reducible to) British colonial historiography of India,[4] and thus reproduce its ontologies. In this move, Hindutva Islamophobia slips into derivative discourse. The alternative is to take seriously the material geographies of Islamophobia's located historical forms. The challenge this is thought to raise, though, again miscasts the issue. To say that Islamophobia is differently configured through and around usable pasts, dominant ideologies and relations of power, that its dominant expressions reflect local histories of State-Religion relations, bio-politics, citizenship, immigration, narratives of identity and otherness etc., and that in this sense Islamophobia is diversely plural is to say something very necessary but insufficient. When it is reduced descriptively and analytically into nationally labelled Islamophobias it is more than that, to distort. While nation-building powerfully sought and seeks to nationalise frames of reference, recasting past and future in national cultural and statist terms, neither the histories nor the tropes mobilised in Islamophobic discourses ever quite fit the national. To say that Greek Islamophobia is structurally constituted in relation to Greek Orthodoxy, or that the Battle of Kosovo is a central reference of Serbian nationalist Islamophobia, that Turkish Islamophobia bears the fundamental imprint of Kemalism, or that francophone Islamophobia on both—French and Algerian—sides of the post-colonial divide betrays the traumas of both colonial and Islamist violence is a truism; but all four also immediately problematise simplistic national framings. The fact that the 'in-assimilability' of Muslims—which is currently the dominant trope of contemporary Islamo-

---

[4] Without necessarily endorsing its reading, see Misra's discussion of 'The legacy of British Historiography' (in Misra, 2004, pp. 189–224) for a brief overview of the texts and topics; Padamsee (2005) for a nuanced and critical reading of the impact of the 1857 Mutiny as a critical turning point in the making of a new 'Mussulmanophobia'; Wolfe (2002, p. 374) for a succinct statement of the point that colonial constructions continue to structure the terms of even such critical postcolonial interventions as Gayatri Spivak's; for how the colonial categories connect with the related extensive debate on the construction of communalism and Hindu-Muslim conflict in India, see Gottschalk (2007).

phobic discourse in Europe, the one most visibly exploited in nativist and rightist anti-immigration rhetoric—plays to the political 'common sense' of the cultural coherence of nationally bounded communities, reinforces the intuitive perception of national Islamophobias. But even here the transnational circulation of Islamophobic texts and tropes, the very real linkages between Islamophobes and movements, not to mention the Western or European civilisational battle lines of their rhetoric transcend national lines, and both through the 'Westcentric' agendas of globalised Western news and the re-description entailed by the franchising of the Global War on Terror, re-map and recode far beyond it. The alternative analytical typology proposed in this volume (see Sayyid, Chapter One) shifts the focus to the formations that configure both the problematisation of the Muslim presence, and the ways of being Muslim. Naming Islamophobia maps the global articulations between the different formations of the relation between the two.

The Beginning of History and the First Islamophobe

...to invoke the history of a concept is not to uncover its elements but to investigate the principles that cause it to be useful—or problematic (Hacking, 1990, p. 360).

Returning, yet again, to the question of the legitimacy of speaking the name of Islamophobia, we come now to a different prospection: first uses of the term 'Islamophobia'. First use, to paraphrase Bernard Bernasconi, depends on 'what one takes to be significant about the concept' and whether one believes what defines the moment it is introduced is 'the first usage of the word in the required sense or the definition that secures its status and influence' (Bernasconi, 2001, p. 11). Clearly, whatever weight may be attached to claims by some (such as Fuad Nahdi and Zaki Badawi)[5] to having coined the term, the case that may be made for the possible influence of Edward Said's use of the term in print in 1985, in three different print contexts reaching, crucially, both an academic and an activist anti-racist readership, in Britain and the U.S (Said, 1985a, 1985b and 1985c)[6] (coincidentally also the year the French use of the

[5] See Nahdi's and Badawi's Oral evidence to the *Select Committee on Religious Offences in England and Wales* (2003, II, p. 182, 23 Oct. 2002, Q.425); I am indebted to Jamil Sherif for this reference.
[6] For a sceptical take on Said's twinning of Islamophobia and anti-Semitism in the text referred (which, moreover, pits anti-semitism on the Zionist lines of a transhistorical hatred) as a rhetorical flourish with strategic intent, see Pasto (1998, p. 472).

term enters the English language academic literature on representations of Islam via the translation of Hichem Djait's earlier critique of Orientalism),[7] or its by now conventionally cited first use in wider readership media in 1991.[8] It remains the case that what secured its status in the present usage was its adoption by The Runnymede Trust Commission on British Muslims and Islamophobia, both in its name and terms of reference, in 1996, and, especially, in its Report, the following year.

While the Commission's use of the term secured its international currency, this does not, as Christian Joppke insinuates, make it the external imposition of 'a predominantly non-Muslim elite committee, which included the Bishop of London [...] and Britain's first female Rabbi' (Joppke, 2009a, pp. 90–91). Contrary to the impression suggested by Joppke, whose omission of the fact thus reinforces its external nature, the term emerged among Muslims. As the Commission's Chair, Gordon Conway (whose personal dislike for the 'ugly word' was several times publicly expressed)[9] acknowledges in his Forward to the Report (Runnymede Trust, 1997a, p. iii), the Commission 'did not coin the term Islamophobia. It was already in use among sectors of the Muslim community'.[10] Moreover, and reinforcing the point, Muslim mobilisation around the term (as even cursory perusal of the *British Muslims Monthly Survey* reveals) was immediate and widespread, finding expression in media monitoring, seminars, Muslim media focus on the Report, and the visibility given to the term by ordinary Muslims to name and denounce incidents and patterns of discrimination.[11]

[7] Dajit's text, originally presented at a 1975 conference was first published in its precedings (Djait, 1976, pp. 258–266), subsequently integrated into his 1978 book (Djait, 1978, pp. 60–64), which was translated into English (Djait, 1985, pp. 53–56).

[8] The conventionally cited reference, following the OED, being an article in the US magazine *Insight* of 4 February 1991. The first Gulf War was, in any case, a significant marker.

[9] See, for example, the interview with Conway in *Q-News* (3 Oct. 1997, p. 14), cited in BMSS (1997) 5:9 (Sept., p. 2).

[10] In the 'Introduction' to the Report (1997, p. 1), it is stated that the word 'was coined in the late 1980s'.

[11] See the *BMMS*, vols. IV and V in 1996 and 1997: examples include: the Muslim initiative launch of media monitoring in September 1996; a public meeting organised by the Wycombe Race Equality Council in March 1997; a seminar on 'Islamophobia—its features and dangers' organised by the Indian Muslim Federation

The repertoire of dismissive and critical responses to 'Islamophobia' can also be discerned in the immediate responses to the Consultation Paper and the Report: as exemplified by the Reverend Dr. Patrick Sookhdeo's repeated charge that it fails to distinguish between race and religion, and that it will be deployed to silence 'legitimate' criticism against Islam and Middle Eastern governments;[12] Fay Weldon's response, which, in a replay of her Rushdie affair polemics (Weldon, 1989) reduces the issue to fundamentalisms decontextualised of relations of power and racism and sees the Report's thrust as paving the way to stifling reasonable criticism;[13] and Polly Toynbee's infamous 'In Defence of Islamophobia' which, in addition to separating religion entirely from race, equates 'Religiophobia' with rationality itself.[14]

While the dynamic set off by consultations and fact-finding missions of the Commission's working group, the publication of the Report, and its reception, contributed positively and enormously to framing the realities of Muslim life through the concept of Islamophobia, the conceptualisation of 'Islamophobia' itself, was, and has remained 'undertheorised', as a number of constructive sympathetic critiques have already advanced (for example, Allen, C., 2007). One such weakness concerns the formulation and conceptualisation of 'phobic' views as 'closed views'. It should be noted, of course, that the Commission itself moved to strengthen areas of weakness of the original 1997 Report in its second incarnation, now for the Uniting Britain Trust and convened under the Chairmanship of Richard Stone. Thus, besides confronting the new realities of the post 9/11 and 'War on Terror' contexts and climate of Islamophobia (which includes acknowledging that 'combating Islamopho-

---

and the London Borough of Waltham Forest in May; a *Q-News* 'exclusive' on the Report's findings ahead of its publication in October 1997; a conference, the same month, organised by the Muslim Parliament bringing together Muslim leaders from across Europe to discuss the problem of Islamophobia; and the founding of the Islamic Human Rights Committee by the Muslim Parliament that year, to pursue cases of Islamophobic discrimination.

[12] Dr Patrick Sookhdeo in *Church Times*, (28.02.97), and the *New Christian Herald* (22.03.97), quoted in BMMS (1997) 5:2 (Feb., 2–3) and 5:3 (Mar., 1–2); virulently restated post 7/7.

[12] Weldon, cited in the *Independent on Sunday* (2 Mar. 1997).

[14] Polly Toynbee, 'In defence of Islamophobia' *Independent* (23 Oct. 1997), and consistently repeated, e.g. 'Last Chance to Speak Out', *Guardian* (5 Oct. 2001) with recourse to the authoritative pronouncements of Ibn Warraq, and 'Get Off Your Knees', *Guardian* (11 Jun. 2004).

bia within Britain necessarily involves engaging with the neo-Conservative views of world affairs'), the 2004 Report explicitly considers the notions of 'Institutional Islamophobia', and 'anti-Muslim racism', problematising the objections, particularly from the liberal left, centred on a distinction between race and religion. But discussion of these is minimal, and ultimately without consequence to the conceptualisation of Islamophobia or its workings which remains tied to the dichotomy of open and closed views and the bedrock of 'reasoned' vs. 'blind hatred against all of Islam' (Commission on British Muslims and Islamophobia, 2004, p. 21).

It is generally accepted that the international currency of the term 'Islamophobia' was established by the Runnymede Trust and debates in Britain; from here, it entered other national contexts and debates, both re-shaping and being shaped by its deployment in particular configurations of power, locally and nationally, including being adopted by international monitoring bodies. This raises some minor and some important questions, which, while beyond the scope of an overview to explore in detail, need noting. One concerns the sense in which the various transliterations of the term into other languages (e.g. *Islamophobie* in French, *Islamofobi* in Scandinavian languages, *Islamofobia* in the Southern European Romance languages, or *Islamofobya* in Turkish) or its semantic re-inscription where it already existed, and the concomitant processes of re-description it entailed. These come to re-articulate existing mobilisations of community activisms and anti-racist struggles and alliances (whose previous rallying terminology reflected both the vernacular anti-Muslim/Islamic and racist vocabularies, and colonial categories, and the layered terrain of national political, anti-immigrant, anti-clerical histories, and, not least, Muslim public voices[15]), with debates and agendas re-sited from the British context.

The importance of the narratives of origins and vernacular use of the term to the polemic over its uptake is probably best illustrated by the French case. Although the term has its longest sporadic history in the French language, sustained usage, in the contemporary sense, in the French context as elsewhere answers to the same recent conjuncture (see Gresh, 2004, Gardesse, [n.d.],

---

[15] Vincent Geisser's mapping of the French case, structured by French Republican laicism and fractured by the traumas of the two Algerian complexes, the colonial war and the Islamist civil war, featuring prominence walk on parts for the 'moderate', 'enlightened', 'arabophile but Islamophobe', native informant 'Muslim Islamophobes', or 'Muslim facilitators of Islamophobia', whose rabid 'islamistophobia' gives manifest expression to latent Islamophobia, is a good example; see Geisser (2003).

Ternisien, 2004 for brief overview). Tellingly, among its first uses in this context was by Tariq Ramadan citing Conway's Runnymede Report definition. No less tellingly, its Islamophobic contestation became entwined with French 'Ramadanophobia', routing and fixing the term in an alternative 'intégriste'/Islamist ideology which traced its origins to its purported coining in revolutionary Iran, where Iranian clerics are said to have used it as a strategy of delegitimising and silencing Iranian women critics as anti-Islamic, and to post-Rushdie London (which French critics of British toleration of Islamist movements would later label 'Londonistan') where al-Muhajiroun and the Islamic Human Rights Commission supposedly similarly deployed it to silence critics of its repressive morality (Fourest and Venner, 2003). Vincent Geisser's (2003) French recasting and proliferation of adjectived Islamophobias (summarised in English by Caeiro, 2006, p. 196) is, additionally, a good example not only of its uptake and conceptual stretching, but also of the asymmetries of global flow. Geisser's book has failed to feed back into the UK and Anglophone debate in much the same way that the analytically significant categories of 'Muslim Islamophobes' and of 'Islamistophobes' have failed to cross over from their francophone and Turkish contexts into British debates, whereas francophone laic and Turkish kemalist Islamistophobe tropes have.

Conversely, an excellent example of a contextual recasting which illustrates how the proliferation of stories of Islamophobia, analytical narratives of origins, conceptualisation and adaptation rather than weakening are a necessary part of the process of operationalising it, is Junaid Rana's 'The Story of Islamophobia' (Rana, 2007), which draws on a different genealogy for the term as part of putting it to work in the US and Black American context (see also Marable and Aidi, 2009), and which has now fed into the global debates on the story of Islamophobia.

Whether, neologism aside, in each context such reclustering through and around the Runnymede concept and agenda represents a move forward for Muslims is anything but given. The meaning of Islamophobia is, in each situated context, relationally configured in tension with the terms and conceptions it is privileged over and against (xenophobia, racism, intolerance, anti-Islam, anti-Muslimism, anti-Muslim racism, Muslimania, maurofobia, Arabofobia, etc.), and specifically so, in respect of the performative, and the enunciator it legitimates. In the British context, this work is currently fulfilled by the term 'Islamophobia'; elsewhere, it may be fulfilled by different words. But 'situated context' is not reducible to linguistic and spatially configured contexts, political or otherwise. The very resemblance of the term in its various transcriptions and dictions in different languages enshrines a conceptual and discursive articulation, which both subverts localised containment and establishes global articulations through the name.

The term Islamophobia was first employed in its modern sense in French ('*islamophobie*'), in the last days of the First World War and in its immediate aftermath. Several points are significant in respect of this claim.[16] Firstly, the term is used by its authors, Étienne Dinet and Sliman Ben Ibrahim, repeatedly, and consistently over a nearly twenty-year period. Initially in two closely related and complementary works—one a biography of the Prophet (on which Dinet had been involved since around the time of his taking the Shahada and the name Nasr-ed-din, in 1913), published in 1918; the other an important companion essay, conceived and announced at the same time, but concluded in 1921. And then again, in the last collaborative book by the same authors, completed a few months before Dinet's death, in 1929. Second, both authors were Muslims, and the works assume an explicitly Islamicate register. It is from a desire to produce a specifically Muslim perspective, free of Orientalist distortions, that *La Vie de Mohammed, Prophète d'Allah* (Dinet and Sliman Ben Ibrahim, 1937)[17] signifi-cantly dated as completed '27th Ramadan 1334/28 July 1916' (traditionally the night in which the first Revelation of the Qur'an is symbolically celebrated) results. And it is in the course of confronting such orientalist distortions, of de-legitimising the claims of critical erudition and scholarly neutrality of such authors by exposing at work rather a wilful negation of the Islamic perspec-tive—of the transcendence of the Qur'anic revelation and prophetic mission, no less than of the Islamicate traditional corpus—that the term Islamophobia is employed. Thirdly, the term, first employed in the Preface to *La Vie de Mohammed*, consubstantiates and is informed by the critique of such orientalist perspectives fleshed out in the essays of the 1921 companion piece, *L'Orient Vu de L'Occident* ([The Orient Seen from the West], Dinet and Sliman ben Ibra-

---

[16] Lopez (2009, p. 61) has meantime established an earlier first recorded print appear-ance of the term (Delafosse, 1912, pp. 211–12), though its sense, as in Bernard (1927) whom Lopez also cites, is nothing but the sum of its component elements, as is clear from the fact that in both it appears as part of a paired contrast between Islamophobia and Islamophilia (as native policies towards Muslims by the French colonial administration in the Sudan, in Delafosse; as literary and artistic Islamo-philia vs its Islamophobic opposite, in Bernard [1927, p. 115]).

[17] Originally published in French in 1918, translated into English as *The Life of Muhammad, The Prophet of Allah* (Dinet and Sliman Ben Ibrahim, 1918).

him, 1921).[18] It is but provocatively that Dinet and Sliman's *Critical Essay* has been compared, for its 'sainte colère' (righteous anger), to Said's *Orientalism* (Poillon, 1997, p.122), and it would be preposterous to suggest any comparisons in their respective critiques of Orientalism, but a critique of a textual Orientalism (of 'l'orientalisme qui travaille exclusivement *"sur le cadavre"'* [an orientalism which applies itself exclusively *"to the corpse"*]), it is. And (for all that it embodies a belated ethnographic Orientalism of its own) not only does Dinet and Sliman Ben Ibrahim's work write—and paint—back to Western Orientalist representations, it articulates these in an avowed and wider frame of political representation of Muslims, in connection with both Muslim loyalty and sacrifice in the cause of the Great War (staking a moral claim to practical assistance and advocacy on behalf of convalescing Muslims, and Islamic funerary observances for the dead, *La Vie* was dedicated '*A la mémoire des musulmans morts pour la France*').[19] And this advocacy, and the politicisation of the frustration over the French failure to recognise and translate recognition of Muslim sacrifices into parity of citizenship, while never leading to sympathy for the independence cause, found (mostly private but passionate) expression in criticism of France's colonial relations with Algeria.[20] In the later work by the two authors, essentially a reflective travel journal of their joint Pilgrimage to Makkah, the scope widens. Commenting on European hostility to Islam and its elite manifestation, they note, first, the role of certain 'Islamophobes', 'such as Gladstone,

---

[18] The 1918 English translation of *The Life of Mohammed* translates the reference in this French work to the planned pamphlet with the English title 'The East Seen from the West', but I have here used Orient as more in keeping with its explicit critique of Orientalism. The reference, which concerns the Jesuit orientalist Lammens, is in justification of its need to expose 'à quel degré d'aberration l'Islamophobie pouvait conduire un savant' (1921, p. 26) [to what degree of aberration Islamophobia can lead a scholar].

[19] 'To the Memory of the Muslims Who died for France'; a patriotic dedication which the English translation literally reinscribes and re-sites by rendering: 'This work is dedicated by the author and his collaborator to the Memory of the Valiant Moslem Soldiers particularly those of France *and England* who, in the Sacred Cause of Right, Justice and Humanity have piously sacrificed their lives in the Great War of the Nations' [emphasis added].

[20] In one biographer's words, 'Dinet est véritablement ulcéréré de l'ingratitude dont la France fait preuve vis-à-vis des musulmans qui se sont battu pour elle' [Dinet was truly dilacerated by the ingratitude which France demonstrated towards those Muslims who fought for her] (Brahimi, 1984: p. 140).

Cromer, Balfour, the Archbishop of Canterbury, and missionaries of all stripes' who stoke up the political traditions of hostility dating back to the Crusades (Dinet and Sliman Ben Ibrahim, 1930, p. 178). Besides these, and drawing on the previous works, the authors go on to describe what they call the 'pseudo-scientific Islamophobia' of the orientalists, and the 'clerical Islamophobia' of the missionaries (Dinet and Sliman Ben Ibrahim, 1930, pp. 176, 183). Considered together with Dinet's understanding of the *ummatic* dimension of Islam, dramatically represented (in terms of religious fraternity but not without political overtones)[21] in the culmination of the pilgrimage rites on the plain of Arafat, the coining of Islamophobia by these two authors acquires a deeper resonance: it is a performative speech act.

Such is the compelling consistency and fullness of Dinet and Sliman ben Ibrahim's use of the term Islamophobia that in her study of Dinet, his biographer, Denise Brahimi, comes to use it herself. Brahimi does so not merely to describe what she plainly grasps as the ideological standpoint of the project of *La Vie de Mohammed*, which, in characterising it as '*de récuser la fausse science islamophobe et l'erudition*' [of challenging the false Islamophobic science and erudition] she may be said to be merely paraphrasing in their words, but, more significantly she makes it her own description of Dinet at the end of his life, and of his politicised understanding of Islamophobic colonial relations.[22]

When Dinet and ben Sliman's *Life of the Prophet* was translated into English that same year of 1918, in the English translation 'Islamophobie' was rendered as 'feelings inimical to Islam', and thus failed to make it into English from the French. The first meaningful use of the word in print in English[23] is, arguably,

---

[21] 'Quoth the Prophet: "The Moslems are as one body: the pain in any single limb gives rise to fever and insomnia in the whole of the frame". On the Arafa, Islam has nothing to fear from enemy spies; it can make good its losses and prepare its future. Despite its disasters, it is more alive than ever!'. My reading of Dinet's discussion of the decline of Islam is considerably at odds with Roded's in her stimulating critique of Dinet and Sliman's gendered representations in *The Life of the Prophet* (Roded, 2002).

[22] See Brahimi (1984, p. 138, 154): the latter reads: 'Sur le plan politique, nous savons dejá qu'à la fin de sa vie, il n'a pas d'illusions. Il a pu se rendre compte, dés son retour à Alger, que l'islamophobie y régnait avec virolence' [At the level of politics we know that at the end of his life he had no illusions left. He had understood, since his return to Algiers, that Islamophobia here reigned virolently.'].

[23] Lopez (2009, p. 62) has traced its first appearance in print in English to a bibliographical notice by Cook (1923, p. 101) where Dinet and Sliman's 1921 Essay is

of francophone inspiration, but what is of interest, is its diametrically opposite deployment to that of the first two authors. It occurs in the context of an article by the Egyptian Dominican Islamicist (with long missionary experience in Algeria) Georges C. Anawati, engaging the work of Gustav von Grunebaum. What is of interest here, is that his use of the term recalls that by Dinet and Sliman, and its meaning, but inverted: it names not the fanatic orientalist assault on the Islamic corpus, such as that by Lammens which Dinet denounced, but a purported Muslim interdiction of legitimate orientalist scholarly textual critique, for 'what makes the task difficult, perhaps impossible, for a non-Muslim is that he is compelled, under penalty of being accused of Islamophobia, to admire the Koran in its totality and to guard against implying the smallest criticism of the text's literary value' (Anawati, 1976, p. 124). Between them, then, Dinet and Sliman ben Ibrahim's and Anawati's uses of the term already configure the current battles over the (il)legitimacy of the concept. To reiterate, what interests us, is neither the historical occurrence of the term, incidental, or otherwise, or its nominalistic usage, but its deployment in terms of a particular genealogy, one that bespeaks a Muslim subject. What Dinet and Sliman Ben Ibrahim gesture towards in and through their conceptualisation of Islamophobia is the permission to narrate (Said, 1984) a Muslim counter-narrative. But theirs is a position which, necessarily of its time, remains structured both within a universalised metropolitan French citizenship and by the geopolitical and racial logics of the Red and Yellow perils (Dinet and Sliman Ben Ibrahim, 1937, pp. 174–175). What separates Dinet and Sliman ben Ibrahim's Islamophobia from its contemporary articulation, is the condition of possibility of 'articulating the post-Western' (Sayyid, 2006a, p. 178).

The Labelled Story

Said Adrus' painting 'The Labelled Story' ('Black European 1' and 'Black European 2' [1989], reprised as 'The Labelled Story' [1990]), depicts three mug shot style heads side by side on canvas inscribed with the graffiti: 'Not Long Ago They called us colored; then came the term Immigrant; and by 1992 somebody said Black European'. As both a reflexive intervention in the field of rep-

---

sympathetically reviewed, but this literally takes the form of a translated citation of the word by itself (rather than its its use by Cook, or by the authors), whose sense readers are left to deduce from the sentence: 'Certain writers in particular are blamed for their "Islamophobia".

resentation and a visually interpellative one Adrus' 'Labelled Story' speaks powerfully to the dynamics of hetero and self ascriptive identities, ethnicities and identity politics in specific determined relation of the bureaucratic State practices of border controls, surveillance and identification, which his earlier work on Identity Papers obsessively revisited. In this, it usefully reminds us of the nexus between visuality and technology, power and resistance in processes of governmentalisation and subjectification. Unwittingly, it also reminds us of the shifting dynamics, complex and worldly webs of redescription. And not only by what it does on the canvas. Dating from the years 1989–90, Adrus' 'Labelled Story' is exactly of its time. It draws, on the one hand, on the legacy of his involvement with the British Black Arts movement and the 'problem space' of the 1980s masterly described by Stuart Hall (2006). It anticipates, on the other, the European foreclosure of 1992. After 1989 both the categories of Black political identity and the politics of anti-racism to which it speaks would unravel. Post 7/7 Adrus' continuing prospection of the questions of identity, diaspora, colonialism and postcolonialism, inclusion and exclusion has come to focus on the presences and absences of BrAsians (Sayyid, 2006b, pp. 12–31) and Muslims in British memorialisation of the past, as symbolised by the 'Lost Pavillion' of Brighton which lies at the centre of his recent installation work (see Malik, A., 2006). Adrus' Muslims, now brought to the fore and retrospectively rendered conspicuously absent from his own earlier 'Labelling Story' and 'Identity Papers' series, mirror the emergence of Muslims out of the categories of 'Coloured', Black and Immigrant.

The historical nominalism and ontology which underpins this process of visibilisation and identification of Muslims is crucial to the genealogy of Islamophobia. The point is not, as Kenan Malik would have it, that Muslim identification represents an atavistic, religiously communitarian narrowing of broad, secular, anti-racist political solidarities of pre-Rushdie Affair days. Of a time when, Malik argues, 'young Pakistanis and Bangladeshis were so open-minded about their origins and identity that they were quite happy to be labelled "Indian", notwithstanding the turmoil and bloodshed of Partition. But while they were happy to be labelled "Indian", it never entered their heads to call themselves "Muslims"' (Malik, K., 2009, p.50). Malik appears here to be blind to the ascriptive nature of the identities which his purportedly descriptive labelling imputes to the youths: primordially 'Pakistani' and 'Bangladeshi' but open minded enough to also comfortably wear an 'Indian' identity.[24] Yet, there

[24] To say nothing of the contradiction involved in supporting the claim that BrAsians

is of course nothing more given in the first than voluntary in the second. Nor are post-Rushdie "Muslim" self-ascriptions any more, or less, historical, constructed or invented, than 'Indian', 'Pakistani', or 'Bangladeshi' identifications. Nor, for that matter, is the shift from ethnic or immigrant labels and identities into Muslim identities a shift from secular to faith identities, to religiosity, or a betrayal of politics into theology which the chapter title 'from street-fighters to book-burners' is intended to denounce. Multiple, globally articulated processes of dynamic nominalism (Hacking, 2007, p. 294) have gone into the making of Muslims. In particular contexts this has involved primarily racialisation, in others culturalisation, and in others still politicisation. In all of these there is self-fashioning, and none is possible outside the global articulations forged through successive struggles for autonomy, both political and epistemological, including the many dead ends along the way.

There is an intrinsic relationship between Islamophobia and the Making of Muslims. Contrary to what is sometimes affirmed, however, it is not that of Islamophobia reactively producing Muslims. It is, rather, that the making of Muslims involves the epistemological repetition of the foundational gesture of remaking the world with universalising claims: Islamophobia, as with Dinet and Sliman ben Ibrahim's moment of Arafat, is its stamp.

---

did not call themselves Muslims by reference to Tariq Mehmood's comment about how racists did not use the word (Mehmood, cited in Ramamurthy whose argument Malik here traduces along with the quote (Malik, 2009, p. 50; cf. Ramamurthy, 2006, p. 39; also p. 58 for his more nuanced argument).

5

THE PROBLEM WITH PARABLES

Katherine Butler Brown

There is a famous story told about the last great Mughal emperor of India, Aurangzeb, probably the best-known story of his reign (1658–1707). Aurangzeb was a strict (many would say fanatical) orthodox Muslim. In 1668, so the story goes, he began a purge of 'un-Islamic' customs and practices in the Mughal Empire, which had hitherto enjoyed peaceful and respectful relations between its majority Hindu and minority Muslim populations. Legendarily, one of the practices Aurangzeb banned was music. In response, the court musicians, perceiving what a threat this was to the emotional well-being of the body politic, not to mention their own livelihoods, staged a public protest in the time-honoured form of a funeral procession. Carrying coffins, wailing and crying at the death of one so dearly beloved, the cortège wended its way through the crowded streets of Delhi towards the foot of the imperial fortress. Slowly but surely the sound reached Aurangzeb's ears, and when the clamour grew so great beneath his feet that he could no longer ignore it, he put his head over the parapet and shouted down, 'Why are you making such a terrible noise?' In anguish, the musicians cried back, 'Music is dead! We have come to bury her.' Aurangzeb replied implacably, in a cold-hearted sentence that has echoed down through the centuries: 'Then bury her so deep under the earth that no sound of her voice will ever be heard again' (Khan, K., 1977, p. 245).

This popular tale continues to be repeated widely today by historians, journalists, and ordinary people alike, and is believed to be true amongst the global

45

community of scholars as much as in the Indian popular imagination. More importantly, it is almost always used as a cautionary tale for today's world about the threat of political Islam, not just to music, but to all that makes life worth living (Jairazbhoy, 2001).

But the story is, in fact, not true—neither literally, nor in its apparent import for the ongoing health in Aurangzeb's India of cultural practices not strictly sanctioned by Islam. On the contrary, Aurangzeb was widely known at the time as the most knowledgeable and dedicated connoisseur of North Indian art music since Akbar (1556–1605). Although he himself renounced his practice of listening to music in 1668 for reasons of personal piety, Aurangzeb continued to allow his sons and noblemen to enjoy music unhindered until his death in 1707 (for a full discussion, see Brown, K. B., 2007, pp. 77–121). That the story is nonetheless still asserted as truth, and promoted as a parable (Delvoye, 1994, p. 118) of the dangers of extremist Islam, says something profound about global misunderstandings of the place of music and pleasure in Islam, as well as the role they play in misrepresentations of Muslims themselves.

It is a popular misconception that music is forbidden in Islam. This impression is not alleviated by the pronouncements and actions of ultra-orthodox groups like the Taliban, whose widely publicised disembowelling of audio cassettes and burning of instruments when they came to power in Afghanistan in 2000 were strikingly prefigured in Niccolao Manucci's heavily embellished retelling of the story of Aurangzeb's ban on music (c.1700) (Baily, 2001, pp. 36–39; Manucci, 1907, p.8). Nor is it, unfortunately, assuaged by the admirable activities of anti-censorship organisations like Freemuse,[1] whose laudable attempts to publicise acts of music censorship by states and religious organisations worldwide sometimes serve to give the impression that the powers-that-be in Muslim societies are particularly prolific offenders in this regard.

It is indeed the case that music has traditionally been controversial in Islamic discourse. Musical instruments in particular are the subject of a number of *hadith* (al Faruqi, 1985, pp. 19–21), and the musical arts are a major topic of legal discussion in relation to the Sufi practice of *sama'* (listening to musical sounds as a means of enhancing communion with the Divine). Yet Muslim societies have also given the world such musical giants as Youssou N'Dour, Nusrat Fateh Ali Khan and Umm Kulthum, who have inspired and fostered the great art music traditions of Indonesia, North India, Iran and al-Andalus, and have challenged the status quo of many modern political entities through

[1] http://www.freemuse.org [Last accessed on 13 Jan. 2009].

the popular mediums of rai, arabesk and hip-hop. Moreover, certain Islamic practices that sound like music, such as the melodic recitation of the Qur'an, are integral to the devotional experience of all Muslims and are entirely beyond reproach. How can these facts possibly be reconciled with the idea that Islam 'forbids' music?

One of the main causes of misunderstanding concerns the way the term 'music' is used in Arabic and other languages of Muslimstani societies. The word 'music' in English has an unusually wide range of meaning, incorporating all 'humanly organised sound' (Blacking, 1973, p. 10) from the high technical complexity of a Beethoven symphony to accidental sounds of coughing and ambulance sirens as long as they are *heard* as music. The word '*musiqa*' in Arabic,[2] on the other hand, while derived from the same Greek word, is only ever applied to certain secular genres, some of which may be associated with morally suspect social situations (al Faruqi, 1985, p. 6). '*Musiqa*' thus excludes a vast amount of 'humanly organised sound' that is enjoyed regularly in Muslim societies and even positively commended as an enhancement to religious life.

Pre-eminent amongst these valued 'non-music' sound-art genres is the recitation of the Qur'an, which any Muslim may be called upon to do, but which may equally be masterfully elaborated by professional reciters using the same modes as 'secular' classical music (Marcus, S. L., 2007, pp. xvi, 5). Other genres commended generally in religious practice include the call to prayer (*adhan*) and hymns on the life of the Prophet and other religious topics, such as *nasheeds*. But equally, a number of ostensibly non-religious genres, such as lullabies, work songs, military band music, and wedding songs, have also been very widely endorsed as morally acceptable forms of sound-art (al Faruqi, 1985, pp. 10–11)—even the Taliban have recorded songs mythologising their military exploits.[3]

What these genres have in common is, firstly, that they all perform a function (i.e. they are not 'art for art's sake') in specific social or devotional situations that Muslims universally regard as beyond reproach, and, secondly, that they are all, with the exception of military band music, vocal genres unaccompanied by musical instruments except, in some cases, drums. In other words, they valorise the human voice insofar as it acts as a vehicle for words of significance and wholesomeness in social contexts considered *halal*.

[2] *Musiqi* in Persian.
[3] Baily, C.D. These can be listened to via the Freemuse website: http://www.freemuse. org/sw1106.asp [Last accessed on 13 Jan. 2009].

One recent refinement of the term 'music' in British Muslim discourse is illuminating. A remarkable recent phenomenon in the UK has been the rise of professionally produced *nasheed* singers and groups, such as Sami Yusuf and SHAAM, who are enormously popular amongst British Muslim youth, and whose songs are often in English and use Western pop harmonies. Media outlets dedicated to Islamic devotional sound-art tend to divide the *nasheeds* they distribute and promote into the categories 'music' and 'no music', in which the category 'music' is solely associated with tracks that include musical instruments, other than percussion.[4] Sami Yusuf, for example, recorded two versions of his album *My Ummah*, a 'no music' version that only uses percussion instruments to accompany the vocal lines, and a 'music' version that has full instrumental accompaniment.[5] That the vernacular meaning of 'music' today is thus reduced just to 'melody instruments', at least amongst English-medium virtual communities, clearly opens up a wide range of sound-art practices for Muslims to enjoy freely as part of their devotional practices. That these media outlets and at least some artists nevertheless promote both 'music' and 'nonmusic' genres as potentially legitimate, even for religious contexts, points to something more significant—the continuance of a longstanding, legitimate debate amongst Muslims as to whether or not listening to 'music' itself can sometimes be acceptable. The question has often been answered positively.

A sizeable proportion of Muslims throughout history have considered listening to *musiqa* acceptable, as long as the time and place of performance and the company in which one listened to music were morally blameless (al Faruqi, 1985, pp. 17–18). This was and still is considered applicable to serious artmusic genres, and especially to songs and vocal music with 'noble' lyrics. The more closely a 'secular' genre approximates the stylisations of Qur'anic recitation, the more acceptable it is to a greater number of people—one of the reasons for the unsurpassed success of the Egyptian 'secular' singer Umm Kulthoum was her extensive training in *tajwid* (the rules of Qur'anic recitation) (Danielson, 1987, pp. 26–45). Furthermore, Sufis have long argued that all music is legitimate as long as its themes are pure, the heart of the listener is pure, and listening to that music inclines the heart towards God (Hasan, 1663, Mus. 8 f. 2b). Only musical performances associated with activities legally pro-

---

[4] For example, http://alifmusic1.homestead.com/radio.html [Last accessed on 13 Jan. 2009].

[5] http://www.samiyusuf.com/albums/album02_myummah.htm [Last accessed on 13 Jan. 2009]. Sami Yusuf himself is an accomplished violinist, pianist as well as a singer.

scribed as *haram*, such as drinking alcohol or extramarital sex, are universally condemned (al Faruqi, 1985, pp. 12–13). Another precept widely observed in Muslim history has been that of balance: listening to music may be acceptable and even commended—but only as long as the listener does not become too attached to it, and thus become distracted from more important worldly and religious duties (Fazl, 1902, p. 211).

As Freemuse points out, music censorship exists everywhere; all cultures 'ban' some music, at some point, to some degree. In 2003, a large number of country-music radio stations in the US banned the airplay of Dixie Chicks' songs, and organised rallies at which, like the Taliban, their CDs, cassette tapes and other fan material were burned and crushed, because the Dixie Chicks publicly opposed George W. Bush and the Iraq War (Krugman, 2003). Would this therefore suggest that music is forbidden in Christianity? To say that music is forbidden in Islam is equally inaccurate. Muslims should be extended the courtesy of recognition that the issue of music's place and value in Islamicate cultures worldwide is equally complex. It is the contexts in which music is performed, and its effects on the individual listener, that determine whether or not music is permissible for each particular Muslim listener, on a case-by-case basis. Aurangzeb's personal renunciation of music makes most sense in this context—a genuine concern, based on past experience, that his personal attachment to music was potentially so excessive that it might pose a threat to his duties as emperor (Brown, K. B., 2007, pp. 110–113). But he never did ban music.

6

ISLAMOPHOBIA

FROM K.I.S.S. TO R.I.P.

Chris Allen

It might come as something of a surprise to realise that just five years ago both the term and concept of 'Islamophobia' had little discursive relevance or value across much of Europe. Today however, the same could be no further from the truth. Contemporarily, Islamophobia emerges from some of the most bi–polar extremes across Europe: from those who decry and denounce any criticism whatsoever of Muslims or Islam as being Islamophobic to those who actively and openly espouse the vitriolic hatred of Islam and Muslims founded upon a premise of various ideological justifications. Because of this, neither clear thinking nor expression rarely—if indeed ever—comes into the equation as regards usage or understanding. From the high profile murder of Theo van Gogh in the Netherlands and the backlash against Muslims that ensued through to complaints about irresponsible parking at mosques during Friday prayers, these myriad and disparate events and incidents are—whether rightly or wrongly—regularly and repeatedly incorporated into the discursive landscape of Islamophobia. Islamophobia therefore is at times little more than an indiscriminate and all-encompassing term that is employed to satisfy or appease a vast spectrum of commentators, actors and perpetrators in varying different measures.

This situation has not necessarily been the same in the UK. Here, October 2007 marked the tenth anniversary of the publication of the groundbreaking and possibly most influential document of its kind, the highly influential Runnymede Trust report, *Islamophobia: A challenge for us all* (Runnymede Trust, 1997a). Produced by the Commission for British Muslims and Islamophobia, the report stated in its opening pages that, 'Islamophobic discourse, sometimes blatant but frequently coded and subtle, is part of everyday life in modern Britain'. It went on, 'in the last twenty years...the dislike [of Islam and Muslims] has become more explicit, more extreme and more dangerous' (Runnymede Trust, 1997a, p. 1). Who, on the Commission at that time, given subsequent events that have unfolded since the report's publication would—or indeed could—have predicted the situation today?

Back in 1997, the report spoke of how 'Islamophobia'—'the shorthand way of referring to the dread or hatred of Islam—and, therefore, to fear or dislike of all or most Muslims' (*Ibid.*)—was necessitated by a new phenomenon that needed naming. Nowadays however, that same term is far from new where it is always seemingly lingering in the murky underbelly of our public and political spaces. Yet despite its wider usage, it remains questionable as to whether the debates concerning Islamophobia today and the way we use the term is any more informed than it was ten years ago. Increasingly the debate about Islamophobia sees one side pitted against another, where claim and counter-claim, charge and counter-charge dictate what we know and more crucially, how we know and subsequently voice 'what is' and 'what is not' Islamophobia.

Why then, despite the Runnymede report being so influential, are we still simplistic in the way that we speak about and understand Islamophobia? Why has a more nuanced usage of the term failed to evolve? And why, ultimately, has Islamophobia failed to be addressed let alone begin to go away? With hindsight the answer, it seems, can be found in the Runnymede report itself.

At the heart of the report's notion of Islamophobia was the recognition of what it set out as 'closed' and 'open' views (Runnymede Trust, 1997a, p. 3). So important were these views that the report changed its definition of what Islamophobia was: soon after the preceding definition, the Runnymede version of Islamophobia became the recurring characteristic of closed views and nothing more. Conceived by the Commission, the closed views of Islamophobia were seeing Islam as monolithic and static; as 'other' and separate from the West; as inferior; as enemy; as manipulative; as discriminated against; as having its criticisms of the West rejected; and where Islamophobia was ultimately becoming increasingly natural. All of which are useful in being able to identify Islamophobia in certain given situations—for example, in the media—but how, for example, might the closed views offer any explanation or even relevance in other equally important situations, in explaining how Muslims are discriminated against in the workplace, in education or in service provision, for instance?

In doing so, the Commission failed to offer a clear explanation as to how this might be possible, preferring instead to focus on how, say, Pakistanis or Bangladeshis were discriminated against rather than Muslims per se. Not only did this completely overlook the central tenet of what any Islamophobia must surely be, what with existing equalities legislation rightfully affording protection to those groups such as Pakistanis and Bangladeshis, but also the argument for a specific anti-Muslim, anti-Islamic phenomenon was weak and any immediate legislative or other response could be deemed somewhat unnecessary. Thus, whilst those who held the power to make the changes were far from impressed, a precedent was set that negated the reality of Islamophobia as a very real and dangerous phenomenon, and as something that was distinctly different from other forms of discrimination and prejudice.

Because of the emphasis upon closed views, the report established a simple premise from which those who wanted to detract from or dismiss Islamophobia could easily do so by merely suggesting that if 'closed views' equalled Islamophobia, one must presume that 'open views' equalled *Islamophilia*. Those who wanted to argue against Islamophobia therefore suggested that the only solution being put forward by the Commission was an abnormal liking or love of Islam and Muslims (philia). The black and white duality of the love or hate of Muslims and Islam were therefore the only options available thereby ignoring all those grey areas that exist. Since 1997, then, all that which has fallen within that grey area has been given licence to gain momentum and form the basis upon which more indirect forms of Islamophobia have found favour. So for example, to what extent has a 'grey' Islamophobia been underlying the more recent debates about the need for better integration, the 'death' of multiculturalism, the *niqab* as a barrier to social participation, the need for universities to 'spy' on the students and the need to look for the 'tell-tale' signs of radicalisation? What scopes the establishment and subsequent unfolding of the entire community cohesion programme?

It is these unaccounted for grey areas that have contributed to a climate where those such as the British National Party (BNP) have found favour and gained an increasingly listened to voice. One result of this was that in the 2006 local elections, the BNP won eleven of the thirteen seats they contested in Barking and Dagenham—making history through being the first time that a far-right political party has ever been the official opposition in any council chamber in Britain. On the evening of the first Barking and Dagenham council meeting attended by the BNP, an Afghan man was repeatedly stabbed outside Barking tube station, his body left on the pavement draped in the union flag (Bragg, 2006). How might the 'closed' views offer any explanation of this?

Since 2001, the BNP has become increasingly sophisticated and nuanced in the way it has spoken about and referred to Islam and Muslims. Unfortunately, the same has failed to occur as regards Islamophobia and so in the Commission's last report published in 2004 there was little change in evidence, persisting instead with existing notions of Islamophobia, using the same language, ideas and meanings throughout. Continuing to refer to Islamophobia in such simplistic terms is therefore detrimental to understanding. More worryingly, the dualistic 'either-or' system of closed and open has reflected how Muslims have increasingly become understood in wider society. Whether 'mainstream' or 'extremist', 'moderate' or 'radical', as Ziauddin Sardar noted shortly after 9/11, Muslims have since been seen in one of two ways: either as apologists *for* Islam or terrorists *in the name of* Islam (Sardar, 2002, pp. 51–56). Take this further and the closed and open, apologists and terrorists, easily fall into that simplistic trap of being either 'good' or 'bad'. As such, if you're not a 'good' Muslim—moderate, mainstream and 'open'—then you can only be 'bad'—radical, extremist and 'closed'. What is known and understood about Islamophobia therefore rests upon the naïve premise that 'Islamophobia is bad only because it is' and nothing more.

As noted at the outset, the Runnymede report's views of Islamophobia were at their most useful in the media. Despite the report's apparent usefulness in its ease of identification in the media, and its associated recommendations to better the media's representation of Muslims and Islam, the situation has since the publication of the report, dangerously deteriorated. If research published by the GLA in 2007 is anything to go by, the amount of coverage in a 'normal week' relating to Muslims and Islam in the British press has increased by almost 270 per cent in the past decade. Just over 90 per cent of this dramatic increase is entirely negative and typically rooted in stories relating to war, terrorism, threat, violence and crisis (INSET, 2007). If this is where the report was most useful, where then has the Runnymede report achieved its impact?

Underpinning the discourse and rhetoric of Islamophobia, exists a highly fluid, protean and largely inconsistent phenomenon that, as yet, has failed to be adequately captured. As Marcel Maussen critically highlights, 'Islamophobia groups together all kinds of different forms of discourse, speech and acts, by suggesting that they all emanate from an identical ideological core, which is an "irrational fear" (a phobia) of Islam' (Cesari, 2006, p. 6). With so many disparate events, activities, actions and attitudes either emerging from or being expressed as a consequence of Islamophobia, simplified discourses, definitions and terminologies that even include the term Islamophobia itself fail to properly and adequately provide enough explanation or understanding to a phenomenon—whether real or otherwise—that has had such a dramatic impact on both Muslim and non-Muslim communities here in the UK and beyond across the continent.

Given this recognition, how then do we move towards a better means of defining and conceptualising Islamophobia? How do we stop 'keeping it simple and stupid'?

The constraints of this particular volume do not allow for this question to be addressed with the depth and clarity that is now urgently required. However it does allow for some consideration to be given to what exactly it is that is known about Islamophobia and to set out a foundation upon which further questioning may begin to be undertaken. One way of doing this is to look at two fundamental questions: what is Islamophobia and, what do we know about it?

It might appear nonsensical to fundamentally question ten years on what Islamophobia is. But given the flawed nature of the Runnymede model and its inability to substantiate or explain Islamophobia, it is indeed quite valid and somewhat necessary if greater clarity and insight are to be offered. From the Runnymede report, a largely ambiguous phenomenon emerged, at times indistinguishable from other similar phenomenon, both nondescript and indistinct. Rarely did it argue either a 'Muslim' or 'Islam' element as its catalytic essence, where inappropriate and inaccurate evidence was repeatedly cited as indicative and substantive of Islamophobia, undermining the necessary separateness or distinctiveness that Islamophobia must have.

There is, however, some evidence to suggest that anti-Muslim and anti-Islamic phenomena are apparent even though they may not have necessarily been properly pinned down or theoretically explained. To evidence this, a quick look back over 'the first decade of Islamophobia' highlights this. If focusing on the post-9/11 period for instance, data relating to anti-Muslim incidents were collated by a number of different organisations. Unfortunately, this was not systematically undertaken by any governmental institution or national network and so some problematic 'holes' do become apparent. So for example, whilst the Islamic Human Rights Commission (IHRC, 2002) claimed that

674 attacks on Muslims were recorded by them following 9/11 (IHRC, 2002, p. 8) and that this amounted to 'concrete proof of Islamophobia', there are some potential problems with this. The IHRC are a primarily London-based organisation and is clearly not seen by many external commentators as sitting within the 'mainstream', acknowledging the inappropriateness of the terminology being employed. Because of this, their evidence is attributed with little credibility and so remains open to criticism.

Another organisation, the Forum Against Islamophobia and Racism (FAIR) also drew similar conclusions from its monitoring programme, reporting that the number of Islamophobia incidents increased by a staggering 600 per cent immediately after 9/11.[1] As with the IHRC, FAIR too was a largely London-centric organisation with little substantive permeation outside the capital. Consequently, despite two sets of data being put forward to substantiate Islamophobia, empirically and methodologically they can only realistically be seen to be indicative, especially when one considers that neither organisation appeared to have any baseline criteria of what might reasonably be deemed or categorised as 'Islamophobic'. Both datasets therefore fail to provide the necessary statistical evidence at least required to prove a distinct anti-Muslim, anti-Islamic phenomenon. Making such a statement neither diminishes nor derogates the work of either organisation, but it does make an observation about the data and the methodologies employed.

An unpublished document that drew extensively upon these datasets however was the now defunct Commission for Racial Equality's (CRE) second monitoring report for the European Monitoring Centre for Racism and Xenophobia (EUMC).[2] With much of this data being geographically specific, the

---

[1] Statistics taken from unpublished documents made available by FAIR between the period October 2001 and August 2003.

[2] Commission for Racial Equality, 2001. Collated between the period 14 September 2001 and 19 October 2001 inclusive, the report was the second in a series of five that the EUMC required each of its National Focal Points (NFPs) produced—the CRE being the British NFP—to monitor any changes in attitude and/or acts of violence or aggression towards ethnic, cultural or religious minorities especially Muslim communities in the wake of the 9/11 attacks. Whilst the report in its entirety was never published, its findings, data, evidence and conclusions would have been a part of the final UK report produced by the EUMC and available to download at the website http://www.eumc.eu, as indeed it would have featured in the final, EU-wide synthesis report that incorporated a section on each of the various national contexts.

CRE sought to counter this by broadening its context, incorporating media reports as well as incidents that were reported through their own regional offices. Resultantly, a more balanced, if not necessarily complete,picture was constructed even though the report itself was largely inconclusive, being far too broad at times and far too sporadic at others. Under 'Physical Attacks', for example:

In the Northeast of England a 20 year old Bangladeshi man suffered from a broken jaw after being beaten by a gang of youths...'; '...a 19 year old woman wearing the hijab was beaten around the head with a metal baseball bat by two white men in Swindon. Prior to the attack one of the men was reportedly heard to say "here's a Muslim" (Commission for Racial Equality, 2001, p. 2).

As was too often apparent in the Runnymede report, whilst the second example acknowledges a 'Muslim' marker as a catalyst, the first does not, leaving doubts about how Islamo- or Muslim-specific the incidents were. Of all the alleged Islamophobic incidents cited by the CRE, a third failed to acknowledge any 'Muslim' or 'Islamic' markers, fluctuating from serious examples of a seemingly distinct anti-Muslim, anti-Islamic nature to those that were vague and indistinguishable from more traditional forms of racism based on the colour of skin. Consequently, it is difficult to substantiate or conclusively identify a distinctive Islamophobia from the evidence purported.

Broadening the focus to Europe and that which the CRE's report contributed to, the EUMC's monitoring of Islamophobia post-9/11 provides some interesting insight and context to the consideration of whether Islamophobia exists (Allen and Nielsen, 2002). Being quick to acknowledge the impact of international events at both local and national levels, on the 12 September 2001 the EUMC implemented a monitoring mechanism across its fifteen member states, much of which has been documented in some detail elsewhere (Allen, C., 2004, pp. 1–25). However, in providing a comparative analysis of the reactions and changes in attitudes towards Muslim communities across the EU, the findings noted that, 'Muslims became indiscriminate victims of an upsurge of both verbal and physical attacks following the events of 11 September.'[3] Anti-Muslim and anti-Islamic attitudes and responses permeated various different social and political strata, from street discourse to national and European governance across all fifteen member states. Irrespective of the variation between each of the countries, the report's most significant finding

[3] Press release from the EUMC at the launch of the report's publication (14 May 2002).

was that incidents were motivated or initiated as a response to the recognisable and visible traits of Muslims and Islam. Motivating the incidents appeared to be the assumption that the victims were legitimate because of their 'Muslimness', sometimes even irrespective of whether they were Muslim or not. Unlike that which had gone before, the EUMC report therefore recognised and acknowledged the very distinct and equally necessary, 'Muslim' or 'Islamic' factor essential and integral to Islamophobia. The report therefore was—quite surprisingly—the first time that the recognition of 'Muslim-ness' or 'Islamicness', or at least which was perceived, and accredited with being both necessary and catalytic.

The synthesis report established a firm basis upon which a distinct anti-Muslim, anti-Islamic phenomenon was apparent, tempering its evidence and thinking in preference of making inflationary claims or conclusions. As it stated:

These explanations are neither exhaustive nor conclusive but attempt to clarify some of the common trends and themes that were apparent in the wake of 11 September. No single explanation can completely account for the events that followed those in the US, but this does allow an insight to certain identifiable phenomenon. In this respect therefore, the explanations must be considered both in isolation, largely as they have been presented here in the text, but also as corroborative contributions as well. What many of them do highlight however is the deep-seated nature of Islamophobia. Expressions of Islamophobia have certainly in some instances been a 'cover' for general racism and xenophobia, in some countries offered legitimacy by the statements of politicians and other opinion leaders. However, there have also been instances in which such expressions have been selectively targeted at visibly perceived manifestations of Islam. In general terms, however, anti-Muslim sentiment has emanated from a vast array of sources and taken on a range of manifestations building upon premises that were already pre-existent to the events of 11 September and may even have been strengthened by them (EUMC, 2002, p. 49).

Importantly, the report acknowledged an anti-Muslim, anti-Islamic phenomenon that was pre-existent to and subsequently strengthened by the events of 9/11, one that was at times indistinguishable from more traditional forms of racism but also at times, quite distinct and discriminate, manifesting itself in a myriad of ways and emanating from an equally myriad range of sources. Similarly, the report noted that its findings were neither exhaustive nor conclusive, leaving open questions about how this phenomenon was distinct from other similar and inter-related phenomena, making it incongruent as a phenomenon defined and conceptualised through over-simplified means.

A clear understanding and argument, that were both grounded and realistic, for the existence of an Islamophobia was therefore being established. Whilst the evidence in the synthesis report was methodologically inconsistent,[4] the report did not make claims beyond its findings, setting out and acknowledging its limitations and weaknesses, but at the same time identifying what it saw as a distinct phenomenon, one that had a firm and necessary 'Muslim' or 'Islamic' component to it but without conflation or claims to authority whatsoever. The report therefore categorically and justifiably concluded that a 'certain identifiable phenomenon' was evident (Allen and Nielsen, 2002, p. 49). In this context, that same 'certain identifiable phenomenon' could only have been Islamophobia. In doing so and in opposition to previous conceptualisations, the report differentiated between the manifestations or forms that the phenomenon acquired and what might possibly be the phenomenon itself, neither concluding nor making the assumption that the manifestations or forms of that 'certain identifiable phenomenon' were either that which constituted it or in any way subsequently defined it. The report was therefore clearly different in its conceptualisation of Islamophobia than those that had gone before. Does this recognition therefore address the criticisms and dismissals that recur throughout society about the legitimacy and reality of Islamophobia?

Many such dismissals typically appear in the press—identifiable in the writing of Toynbee (2001) and Burchill (2001) to name but two—although consideration should not be limited to these more traditional forms of media. The internet-based periodical *Spiked* for example boasts a number of articles that question the existence of Islamophobia (see Appleton, 2002; Hume, 2003; Appleton, 2004). Employing the very evidence that was put into the public domain in an attempt to 'prove' Islamophobia, referencing both the IHRC and FAIR, Josie Appleton unequivocally states that, 'a popular anti-Muslim racism did not happen' (Appleton, 2002). As with earlier observations about this particular data, Appleton stresses the unconvincing nature of the evidence, abruptly dismissing it as an 'over-sensitivity' on the part of Muslims. Whilst it is difficult to agree with her claims of 'over-sensitivity', what Appleton does justifiably highlight is that the given for Islamophobia is largely inconclusive and limited: a situation reflecting the inconclusive and limited nature of knowing what Islamophobia is a decade on from Runny-

[4] For a fuller exposition and critical analysis of the data collection processes and methodologies employed by both the EUMC and its NFPs, see Allen, C. (2002).

mede. The result is that Islamophobia—whether arguing for or against it—is indeterminably subjective.

As Richardson has since written, easy dismissals and rejections can be made against almost any data, incident or event because of the subjectivity inherent in defining Islamophobia through the Runnymede model (Richardson, 2004, p. 24). When Islamophobia is defined as 'unfounded', immediately the evidence, manifestations and consequences of such are subjected to an interpretive understanding: what is unfounded to one may not necessarily be unfounded to another thus resulting in a situation where individual, group or communal subjectivities prevail over a somewhat invisible and difficult to establish objectivity. Take for instance those refraining from travelling on the London underground following the bombings on the 7 July 2005 ('7/7'). The decision not to travel on the underground is therefore founded on the argument that because bombs had been detonated and people had been killed by Muslims, this could happen again. Consequently, the decision not to travel is founded rather than unfounded. This is not to say that being founded is necessarily the same as being reasoned. As such, this decision—which may not even be founded upon the dislike or hostility towards Muslims or Islam per se—is founded upon the actions of a handful of Muslims and its consequences, something that may have the possibility of being projected onto and thus detrimental to all Muslims without differentiation. Because this is founded, any detrimental consequences for all Muslims may not necessarily be Islamophobic using the Runnymede model.

Through subjectivity, clarity never exists thus rendering the phenomenon invalid within individual, group or communal interpretative frameworks, all of which must be arguably accepted. Thus whether Islamophobia is dismissed by Burchill, Appleton or the BNP, that it is defined and categorised as unfounded allows for detractors, irrespective of the criticisms and dismissals they put forward, to argue them as subjectively valid, and by consequence, founded. Existing understandings of Islamophobia therefore have little, if indeed any grounding in reality or objectivity, and can, resultantly, be either appropriately or inappropriately dismissed or countered, thus rendering the phenomenon invalid and illegitimate, if not entirely objectionable. It is this situation and the resultant processes that leaves wider society unconvinced of the existence of an Islamophobia that is distinct, separate or 'real'.

This sense of being 'unconvinced' not only underpins what Maussen was voicing but might also underlie the findings and conclusions of a number of projects and reports undertaken in recent years, where the argument or infer-ence of a distinct and separate Islamophobia is not evident. Thus the question of what is Islamophobia is an entirely legitimate one, but not, as yet, adequately answered—not least because of the 'K.I.S.S.' approach to Islamophobia that has been in evidence for more than a decade now.

In responding to this, the EUMC report did recognise that a 'certain identifiable phenomenon' was in evidence. This identification and recognition therefore does not suggest that the products, manifestations or consequences of that largely ambiguous, widely interpretive and entirely subjective Islamophobia, that have been posited previously and established as the concrete and static basis for all understanding equates to this 'certain identifiable phenomenon', but instead merely reiterates—and confirms—that a 'phenomenon' exists. In acknowledging this, such an assertion is neither overblown nor unfounded but instead grounded in the research and evidence available. What has previously ensued is the putting forward of a phenomenon that has neither been empirically proven nor has it stood up to critical analyses of its concepts, theories or function in practice, thus establishing a phenomenon that is easily derogated and dismissed by way of its own weaknesses and subjectivities.

Reflecting what has been described as the 'anti-racism problematic' that Stuart Hall acknowledges regarding racism, simplistically imposing positive images over negative ones will never combat anything, 'since the binaries remain in place, meaning continues to be shaped by them. The strategy challenges the binaries—but it does not undermine them' (Hall, 1997, p. 274), hence the reason why Islamophobia remains weak and unconvincing in the public and political spaces is because it was never accredited with any substance or theoretical underpinning that went beyond the merest of positive images. If a 'certain identifiable phenomenon' is therefore acknowledged, based only upon the evidence and research at hand, assuming that this is 'Islamophobia', the logical step must be to use this to better explain what Islamophobia is, or if that is too difficult, what constitutes Islamophobia.

In terms of the Runnymede model, the use of 'open' and 'closed'—based upon the work of Milton Rokeach—was described by Leyens, Yzerbyt and Schadron as being 'not content-free...' where 'the instrument does not measure up to the theory' (Leyens et al., 1994, p. 37). Regarding the 'K.I.S.S.' approach to Islamophobia, the same is brutally true: the instrument for identifying Islamophobia neither measures up to the theory nor is it entirely content-free. In referring back to Hall et al., what we already know about Islamophobia does not have the ability to counter the 'race relations problematic' and so convince of the reality and existence of an Islamophobia. For Hall, if this is not achieved, a situation will emerge where the acceptance and subsequent deployment of such theories become overwhelmed and obfuscated by phoney and patronising definitions that simultaneously over-inflate, homogeneously accuse, and wallow in the negativity of reminding everyone 'just how bad Islamophobia is' but without making a conclusive justification about why. In other words, failing to go beyond the somewhat naïve and immature argument that Islamophobia is 'bad because it is' (Hall et al., 1978). In this way, any answer to 'what is Islamophobia?' must ensure that it is neither over-inflationary, accusatory nor merely regurgitating positive stereotypical frames and arguments, all of which can have little grounding or apparent justification. If this is not overcome, then any acknowledgement or under standing will continue to be rendered largely meaningless.

What then do we know about Islamophobia that is both grounded and to some degree, objective enough to be able to construct a firm foundation upon which further exploration can be undertaken? What exactly is it that we know about Islamophobia at the end of its first decade? Firstly, it would seem that Islamophobia—the 'certain identifiable phenomenon'—is neither consistent nor uniform, neither in the way in which it is manifested nor in the way that it is defined. It may even be that a plurality of 'Islamophobias'—or more so a multiplicity—rather more than a single, all encompassing entity is that which exists. Secondly and despite being asymmetrically shifting between notions of anti-Muslim and anti-Islamic, Islamophobia seemingly overlaps with other similar phenomena—such as racism by colour, anti-Semitism or xenophobia— that either may or may not be acknowledged as distinct or differentiable. Thirdly, both the nature and manifestations of Islamophobia would appear to be shaped and determined by the national, cultural, geographical and socio-economic conditions within which any Islamophobic phenomena is identified: being different in Germany where it might be informed by experiences of significant Turkish communities whereas in Britain that same phenomenon might be more informed by experiences and interaction of South Asian communities. Fourthly, Islamophobia would appear to have the possibility of having a historical legacy from which it draws information, relevance, under standing and meaning. Fifthly, it would appear essential that a distinct 'Muslim' or 'Islamic' identifier or identification process be present and underpinning, albeit explicitly or implicitly, direct or indirect, either expressly acknowledged or not. And finally, it would appear that despite the discursive prevalence that the neologism Islamophobia has attained, Islamophobia has significantly failed to permeate all settings and contexts, and even where it has achieved greater social and public permeability.

Recognising and acknowledging the need for these seven factors to be inherent within any 'certain identifiable phenomenon' is not merely a new simplistic or substitutive set of criteria against which to identify whether or not a given discourse, act or event is Islamophobic or not. Instead, it is the setting out of the factors that are evidentially substantiated from which a better albeit as yet suitably defined or conceptualised model and definition of Islamophobia might be established. Whilst these may be employed to inform and give meaning, they are in themselves not an attempt to define or conceptualise. They are merely the first step necessary in a potentially long and laborious process of furthering and developing the limited theoretical foundations upon which existing discourses and understandings of Islamophobia have been founded. In other words, they are the first steps towards dismantling the 'K.I.S.S.' (Keep It Simple and Stupid) approach to Islamophobia that has been so detrimental to understanding and subsequently addressing Islamophobia in the contemporary setting.

As has been the case over the first decade of Islamophobia, broad definitions and meaningless conceptualisations become over-inflated and remove any concretised or empirical grounding. So when overly simple definitions and conceptualisations are put forward, overly simple—and overly inadequate—solutions to the problem ensue, culminating in the situation that is apparent at the end of the first decade. One where both definitions and purported solutions obscure the multi–dimensionality, specificity, depth and at times, complexity of what is necessary to fully understand Islamophobia, thus undermining, hindering and even negating the problem and enhancing the contestation.

Without doubt, the Runnymede report and the model of Islamophobia established through this by the Commission on British Muslims and Islamophobia, is the seminal source from which the most common and widespread definitions and conceptualisations about Islamophobia have evolved. So much so that it could be argued that it had provided and established *the* definition and conceptualisation of Islamophobia. Yet possibly because of the report's authoritative status and subsequent almost blind acceptance, little critical analysis or engagement has since been applied to it. Few have been willing for whatever reason to posit what appears to be both the totally justified and entirely legitimate criticisms at it that it clearly deserves. What must now be understood as the definition and conceptualisation of Islamophobia must be recognised—and duly relegated—to being the definition and conceptualisation of the first decade of Islamophobia alone. It cannot be the definition and conceptualisation of the here and now: the first throes of Islamophobia's second decade.

A decade on from the publication of the Runnymede report and a climate of ever worsening mistrust, misunderstanding and misrepresentation can be easily witnessed. In 1997 the Runnymede report stated that Islamophobia was becoming 'more explicit, more extreme and more dangerous'; in 2008 the same phenomenon has become more natural, more normal and because of this, far more dangerous than ever before. The need for a new approach to tackling Islamophobia is therefore clearly required, as indeed is a new language and greater knowledge to both explain and respond to the subtleties and nuances of Islamophobia that are at present overlooked and subsequently allowed to take root and flourish. This exploration adds little to what already exists although it does set out what is already known about Islamophobia and what factors must be recognised in any further research that is undertaken. In many ways, this particular consideration is a consolidation of the first decade of Islamophobia as a premise or foundation for undertaking the second.

Given that the Commission on British Muslims and Islamophobia is once again in the process of reforming, so the need for a much more radical approach to Islamophobia is required, going beyond the 'K.I.S.S.' approach of its previous reports. If the Commission—and indeed Muslims and wider society alike—fail to do this, then it is highly likely that in another ten years we will be speaking at the end of another decade without having made any advances whatsoever, whether in understanding and defining Islamophobia or indeed, even beginning to address a potentially more virulent Islamophobia. Now is the time to be much bolder and braver, addressing Islamophobia for what it is now and not what it was then. K.I.S.S. approaches have already failed: there needs to be no more time given over to considering these or any similar approaches. Islamophobia—and more importantly the victims of its ever-widening arc—cannot wait another decade for everyone else to recognise this.

7

THE VOYAGE IN

SECOND LIFE ISLAMOPHOBIA

Yakoub Islam

Second Life (SL), an award-winning online virtual world owned by Linden Lab, opened to the public in 2003. As of September 2008, the so-called 'meta-verse' boasted a membership of over fifteen million. Unlike other massively multiplayer online role-playing games (MMORPGs), SL's content is predominantly generated by fee-paying users and its gaming functions are therefore limited only by its continuously evolving technology and commercial access. At the same time, the CEO of Linden Lab and SL's leading visionary, Philip Rosedale, has drawn much inspiration from post-Chicago School neoliberal theorists in building what he believes is an online nation, a cultural perspective that arguably has implications for Islamophobia 'in-world'.

Members of SL are represented by 3–D figures called avatars who can edit their physical appearance, move around, shop, interact and even have virtual sex with each other. Its cultural possibilities has inspired novels and works of anthropology (Boellstorff, 2008) and SL has been used as an educational tool by over 80 per cent of British universities (Kirriemuir, 2007). Sweden and Columbia have official national embassies in-world. People have married 'virtually' and in real life through meeting in-world, and avatar adultery has led to at least one real-world divorce. SL has also attracted the interest of religious groups and organisations, including Muslims, and in 2007, Egyptian-owned

IslamOnline supervised the construction of a virtual Makkah as an educational tool for Muslims and non-Muslims alike.

IslamOnline's presence largely post-dates my own involvement in Second Life as an independent autoethnographic researcher interested in the relationship between my own Muslim identity and community, and the possibilties of developing a non-sectarian virtual *ummah*. This vision of a broad-based virtual Islamic community was made possible by circumstances unique to the metaverse at the time. One continuing wonder was the incredible and growing diversity of Muslim citizenship, both in terms of nations of origin and sectarian allegiances, with Muslims logging-in from PCs on every continent. The potential for community between SL's Ahl as-Sunnah wa Jamaat, Ithna Ashari, Ahmaddiya, Salafi and progressive Muslims was also facilitated by the fact that the owner of Second Life's then sole mosque—a beautiful reproduction of the Cordoban *Mesquita*—was 'neutral' and non-Muslim.

During my initial involvement with Second Life, Islamophobic racism constituted little more than an occasional nuisance as far as most Muslims were concerned. Most attacks took the form of 'griefing', a term used to describe aggravation and harassment of SL players, and focused on the *Mesquita*. Griefing varied from avatars sitting naked on the virtual Qur'an to attacks using 'scripts' that temporarily restricted mosque access. LGBTIQ groups and the SL synagogue were also victims of similar casual racist attacks. Things changed during the run-up to the French presidential elections of April-May 2007, with the arrival in-world of the *Front National* (FN), the far right party led by Jean-Marie Le Pen, whose anti-Muslim policies included a call for the cessation of Mosque building in France. The subsequent huge upsurge in attacks on the mosque ironically forged a more coherent identity for the in-world Muslim community, after the owner formed a defence committee, delegating to selected Muslim players the power to summarily ban griefers from the mosque.

Despite our more organised response to alleged FN attacks, facilities to confront racist organisations remained limited. SL community standards reproduced 'light touch' neo-liberal regulation, focusing primarily on the use of 'derogatory' anti-religious language reported by individual gamers. Anti-fascist groups thus felt unable to campaign for neo-Nazi organisations to be permanently excluded from Second Life, merely hoping individuals expressing racist views would be banned. Even the success of complaints could never be properly gauged because Linden Lab refused to release specific details of actions taken against griefers. As Channel 4 News reported on the war against the FN, however, our increasingly visible community began to experience more sophisticated speech and text attacks, representing Islam as monolithic, inferior, separate and threatening (see Runnymede Trust, 1997b).

As de facto spokesperson for the emerging virtual community during this period, I was at the forefront of facing off such abuse. Probably the most prominent assault was instigated by veteran avatar Taras Balderdash, who features in Second Life's official guide (Rymaszewski et al., 2007). Balderdash, whose pipe-smoking sagacious image was the icon of his syncretic interfaith in-world religious group, the Avatarians, provoked an outcry after describing Islam as an inherently 'intolerant religion'. Many Avatarians committed to interfaith dialogue immediately distanced themselves from his comments and a leading SL Buddhist charity placed a bar on his donations. Despite being compelled to resign as Avatarian leader, Balderdash retained a cohort of sympathisers and my response, deconstructing his essentialist representation of Islam, was depicted by one supporter as 'dangerous'.

The combination of Second Life's liberal ethos and its imaginative possibilties also invoked new and disturbing forms of anti-Muslim offence. Perhaps the most distressing took place in the wake of the *Jyllands-Posten* Muhammad cartoons controversy. Not only were these cartoons reproduced inside SL, but one enterprising user designed an avatar in the form of the most offensive drawing, which he then put on sale. For a small sum, griefers were thus able to visit the mosque resembling the cartoon depicting The Prophet with a bomb-shaped turban. When a member of the sado-masochistic 'Gorean' sect, renowned for their use of Orientalist imagery, transferred a Quranic aya onto a pornographic mat outside of his shop for passing avatars to walk on, the owner dismissed our politely expressed concerns with irate contempt: 'I can do what the hell I like!'. Complaints to Linden Lab came to nothing.

Frustratingly, expressions of support for such imaginative liberalism within SL's own diverse Muslim community, killed all hopes and ambitions for an inclusive virtual *ummah*. A pair of fractious Progressive Muslim converts declared that nobody ought to be offended by anything inside the metaverse on the grounds that 'none of this is real'. In order to assert their ontological cause, they staged a noisy protest outside the mosque holding virtual pigs. Exasperated by their interminable oppositionalism, the defence committee barred them from the mosque indefinitely.

8

THE RACIALISATION OF MUSLIMS

Nasar Meer and Tariq Modood

Conditions for Muslims in Europe must be made harder across the board: Europe must look like a less attractive proposition. And of course it should go without saying that Muslims in Europe who for any reason take part in, plot, assist or condone violence against the West (not just the country they happen to have found sanctuary in, but any country in the West or Western troops) must be forcibly deported back to their place of origin... Where a person was born in the West, they should be deported to the country of origin of their parent or grandparent.

Douglas Murray, Director of the Centre for Social Cohesion, Civitas

It has been argued that there are currently two dynamics shaping hostile attitudes toward Muslims in Europe. The source of the first is located squarely in contemporary agendas of counter-terrorism (and associated anxieties that may fuel a securitisation of ethnic relations more broadly). The second, it is argued, has been inherited from an ideological-historical relationship with the Orient, one that is intertwined with legacies of imperialism (Geisser, 2005). Neither dynamic is discrete and both can be seen to overlap in the public discourses of a variety of European political discourse. Amongst these we might include statements by the Austrian Freedom Party on the prospect of Turkey's accession to the EU, the Flemish Block's insistence that 'Islam is now the no. 1 enemy not only of Europe but of the world' (see also Fadil, this volume),

French National Front literature on the 'Islamisation of France' (quoted in Bunzl, 2007, pp. 1–47), as well as the way in which the Swiss People's Party has recently sought office with electoral posters depicting veiled Muslim women under the question: 'Where are we living, Baden or Baghdad?' (Spritzer, 2009). Parallels can also be found in the leading, but much less mainstream, far-right British National Party (BNP), which frequently campaigns on what it describes as 'the Muslim problem' (see Meer, 2007, pp. 112–116).[1] These macro political sentiments coalesce with the findings of some European attitude surveys which report the worrying trend that more than half of a representative sample of Spaniards and Germans state that they 'do not like' Muslims (Pew Global Attitudes Project, 2008). In Poland and France, meanwhile, the number of people holding unfavourable opinions of Muslims is reportedly 46 per cent and 38 per cent respectively, against which it is perhaps some comfort that 'only' one in four Britons expresses attitudinal hostility to Muslims (Pew Global Attitudes Project, 2008). In his meta-study of British opinion polling, Field has confirmed this trend and characterised the prevalence of negative perceptions of British Muslims as an increase in 'Islamophobia' (Field, 2007, pp. 447–477).

Whilst such findings perhaps reflect a social and political climate marked by various 'crises' involving Muslims, Field nevertheless draws our attention to the need to unpack conceptual issues surrounding this term (Field, 2007, pp. 447–477). For as the opening extract from Douglas Murray betrays, there appear to be several components in contemporary anti-Muslim sentiment, which any concept of Islamophobia should seek to capture. For example, in his prescription for 'dealing with Muslims', Murray relies upon an essential idea of Europe that is closed to Muslims, and where, concomitantly, Muslims' civil and political rights are less meaningful, while their ethnic origins serve as important means of ascertaining where they really belong. His anti-Muslim sentiment, therefore, simultaneously draws upon signs of race, culture and belonging in a way that is by no means reducible to hostility toward a religion alone, and compels us to consider how religion has a new sociological relevance because of the ways it is tied up with issues of community identity, stereotyping, socio-economic location, political conflict and so forth.

On the one hand, and especially given that religious discrimination in most Western societies does not usually proceed on the basis of belief but perceived

---

[1] For examples of less flagrant, more coded, but equally alarming comments made by British politicians and intellectuals, see Meer (2006, 2008), and Meer and Noorani (2008).

membership of an ethno-religious group (e.g. Catholics in Northern Ireland, Muslims in the countries of former Yugoslavia, and Jews in general), Murray's account is consistent with an established tendency of targeting religious groups and communities as opposed to beliefs and opposition to beliefs. For as his extract illustrates, this phenomena need not be pure 'religious discrimination' but one which also traffics in stereotypes about foreignness, phenotypes and culture. As such there are obvious similarities between forms of anti-Semitism and anti-Muslim sentiment that remain under explored (Meer and Noorani, 2008, pp. 195–219) but which may herald important differences as well as similarities (Bunzl, 2007, pp. 1–47). Of course how Muslims respond to these circumstances will vary. Some will organise resistance, while others will try to stop looking like Muslims (the equivalent of 'passing' for white); some will build an ideology out of their subordination, others will not, just as a woman can choose to be a feminist or not. Again, some Muslims may define their Islam in terms of piety rather than politics; just as some women may see no politics in their gender, while for others their gender will be at the centre of their politics.

The question that is nevertheless posed for any contemporary concept of Islamophobia is whether it can, amongst other things, (i) analytically capture the contingent racial and cultural dynamics of the macro-historical juxtaposition between 'Europe' and 'Islam'; (ii) sufficiently delineate the racialising component of polemics such as Murray's, from a potentially sedate critique of Islam as a religion; and (iii) more broadly summon enough explanatory power to stipulate how long established organising concepts within the study of race and racism may, in some Hegelian fashion, be developed and formulated in a sociologically convincing manner. This raises the broader point of how it is striking to note the virtual absence of an established literature on race and racism in the discussion on Islamophobia.[2] This chapter makes a tentative contri-

---

[2] Whilst it would be easy to state at the beginning that the *idea* of race is used under 'erasure' as in Derrida (1976), or rejected outright in the manner preferred by Miles (1989), it will instead be argued that since all categories including ethnicity, age, gender and class are unstable and contested; subject to potential reification and essentialism, the implication of 'race' as more 'real' than other social categories is dismissed at the outset. The idea of race should instead be understood as a social construction that nevertheless serves as a potential vehicle for subjective and attributed identifications. Rather than offering a post-race account (Gilroy, 2004; St. Louis, 2002), this chapter will elaborate on the *social reality* of race and racism, and ways in which these can be combined and interlinked with religion and culture.

bution to overcoming this disconnection by exploring what purchase the ideas of 'racialisation' and 'cultural racism' can bring to bare on the conceptualisation of these matters. To examine the entanglements between race and religion as they apply to Muslims, the first part of the chapter explores the theoretical and normative issues raised by these questions, while the second half discusses the reaction from intellectuals to the novelist Martin Amis' controversial comments about Muslims as a means to apply the preceding discussion and evaluate the explanatory power or Islamophobia.

Conceiving Islamophobia

The origins of the term Islamophobia have been variously traced to a pair of critiques of Orientalist scholarship published by Etiene Dinet and Sliman Ben Ibrahim in 1918 and 1922 (see Vakil, this volume), 'a neologism of the 1970s' (Rana, 2007, p. 148), an early nineteen nineties American periodical (Sheridan, 2006, pp. 317–336), and, indeed, to one of the present authors (Birt, 2006a). What is less disputed is that the term received its public policy prominence with the Runneymede Trust's Commission on British Muslims and Islamophobia (CBMI), *Islamophobia: A challenge for us all* (Runnymede Trust, 1997a). Defined as 'an unfounded hostility towards Islam, and therefore fear or dislike of all or most Muslims' (Runnymede Trust, 1997a, p. 4), the report conceived of eight argumentative positions[3] to encapsulate its meaning, and through which the members of the commission sought to draw attention to their assessment that 'anti-Muslim prejudice has grown so considerably and so rapidly in recent years that a new item in the vocabulary is needed' (Runny-

[3] 1. Islam is seen as a monolithic bloc, static and unresponsive to change.
2. Islam is seen as separate and 'other'. It does not have values in common with other cultures, is not affected by them and does not influence them.
3. Islam is seen as inferior to the West. It is seen as barbaric, irrational, primitive and sexist.
4. Islam is seen as violent, aggressive, threatening, supportive of terrorism and engaged in a 'clash of civilisations'.
5. Islam is seen as a political ideology and is used for political or military advantage.
6. Criticisms made of the West by Islam are rejected out of hand.
7. Hostility towards Islam is used to justify discriminatory practices towards Muslims and exclusion of Muslims from mainstream society.
8. Anti-Muslim hostility is seen as natural or normal.

mede Trust, 1997a, p. 4). This, of course, was before global events had elevated the issue to a prominence previously only hinted at, and which resulted in a second sitting of the commission which heard testimonies from leading Muslim spokespeople (in this instance, Baronness Uddin) of how 'there is not a day that we do not have to face comments so ignorant that even Enoch Powell would not have made them' (quoted in Commission on British Muslims and Islamophobia [CBMI], 2004, p. 3).

What the commission perhaps did not fully anticipate was how the term would be criticised from several quarters for, amongst other things, allegedly reinforcing 'a monolithic concept of Islam, Islamic cultures, Muslims and Islamism, involving ethnic, cultural, linguistic, historical and doctrinal differences while affording vocal Muslims a ready concept of victimology' (Ozanne, 2006, p. 28; Afshar, Aitken and Myfanwy, 2005). To others the term has neglected 'the active and aggressive part of discrimination' (Reisigl and Wodak, 2001, p. 6) by conceiving discrimination as a collection of pathological beliefs, inferred through the language of '-phobias'; with the additional complaint that the term does not adequately account for the nature of the prejudice directed at Muslims. This complaint is advanced in Halliday's thesis and is worth examining because Halliday accepts that Muslims experience direct discrimination as Muslims. He nevertheless considers Islamophobia misleading because:

It misses the point about what it is that is being attacked: 'Islam' as a religion *was* the enemy in the past: in the crusades or the *reconquista*. It is not the enemy now [...] The attack now is not against *Islam* as a faith but against *Muslims* as a people, the latter grouping together all, especially immigrants, who might be covered by the term (Halliday, 1999, p. 898, original emphasis).

So in contrast to the thrust of the Islamophobia concept, as he understands it, the stereotypical enemy 'is not a faith or a culture, but a people' who form the 'real' targets of prejudice. Halliday's critique is richer than many others, particularly more journalistic accounts (a good illustration of which can be found in Malik, 2005).[4] What it appears to ignore, however, is how the

[4] For example, in a television documentary Kenan Malik has argued that 'the Islamic Human Rights Commission monitored just 344 Islamophobic attacks in the twelve months following 9/11—most of which were minor incidents like shoving or spitting. That's 344 too many—but it's hardly a climate of uncontrolled hostility towards Muslims. [...] It's not Islamophobia, but the perception that it blights Muslim lives, that creates anger and resentment. That's why it's dangerous to exaggerate the hatred

majority of Muslims who report experiencing street level discrimination recount—as testimonies to the 2004 Runnymede follow-up commission (CBMI, 2004) bear witness—that they do so more when they appear 'conspicuously Muslim' than when they do not. Since this can result from wearing Islamic attire it becomes irrelevant—if it is even possible—to separate the impact of appearing Muslim from the impact of appearing to follow Islam. For example, the increase in everyday personal abuse since 9/11 and 7/7 in which the perceived 'Islamicness' of the victims is the central reason for abuse, regardless of the validity of this presumption (resulting in Sikhs and others with an 'Arab' appearance being attacked), suggests that discrimination and/ or hostility to Islam and Muslims is much more interlinked than Halliday's thesis allows (and, in all fairness to Halliday, may not easily have been anticipated at his time of writing). In contrast we contend that, instead of trying to neatly delineate social tendencies that are inextricably linked; they should instead be understood as a composite of 'racialisation'. This requires some elaboration.

Muslims and Racialisation

The idea of racialisation boasts a long pedigree even if the term itself does not, and although it was perhaps first encountered in British sociology through the

---

of Muslims. Even more worrying is the way that the threat of Islamophobia is now being used to stifle criticism of Islam' (transcript of 'Are Muslims Hated?', 30 Minutes, 8 Jan. 2005, Channel 4). Malik is not alone in holding this view and there are several problematic issues that arise in his analysis that may also be evident in others' (Joppke, 2009; Hansen, 2006). For example, it is easy to complain that Muslims exaggerate Islamophobia without noting that they are no more likely to do so than others who might exaggerate colour-racism, anti-Semitism, sexism, ageism, homophobia or many other forms of discrimination. That is that his claim remains a political rather than a comparatively informed empirical claim. Secondly, and more importantly, Malik limits Islamophobia to violent attacks and ignores its discursive character in prejudicing, stereotyping, direct and indirect discrimination, exclusion from networks and so on, and the many non-physical ways in which discrimination operates. Thirdly, Malik draws upon data gathered prior to the events of 7/7, following which, according to the same source (the Islamic Human Rights Commission) and using the same indices, there were reported to be 200 Islamophobic incidents in the first two weeks after the bombings.

work of Michael Banton, arguably in his *Race Relations* (Banton, 1967), it was Robert Miles (1982; 1984; 1986; 1988; 1989; 1993) who for a long time offered its most sustained exposition. Reminiscent of a Du Boisian tradition in which the psychic and the social are intertwined, Miles' conception of racialisation (Miles, 1989, p. 75) sought to capture the ways in which racial processes can attribute 'meaning to somatic characteristics' in a way that 'presumes a social psychological theory which explains the nature and dynamics of the process' (Miles, 1989, p. 75). As a Marxist, of course, Miles anchored his conception of racialisation in an account of material relations and an ideologically driven conflict borne of the contradictory impulses inherent to circumscribed nationhood and labour migration (Miles, 1982, pp. 170–173). What is important for our discussion, however, is that Miles never insisted that processes of racialisation must be premised upon a 'biological inherentism' (an issue elaborated below) and which informed his resolve that scholars 'must not restrict the application of the concept of racialisation to situations where people distinguish one another by reference to skin colour' (Miles, 1982, pp. 170–173; see also the discussion of Miles in Modood, 1996). More specifically, what he maintained that we should be studying instead are the ways in which 'signifying processes' interact to 'construct differentiated social collectives as races'. (Miles, 1989, p. 79).

To facilitate such inquiry, and because he recognised that the social dynamics of racism can in practice be mixed-up with a host of different kinds of '-isms', such as nationalism, ethnicism and sexism and so forth, Miles (1989, p. 87) put forward a conceptualisation of 'racial articulations'.[5] He did so to preserve the analytical clarity of racism while recognising that in social life exclusionary discourses and prejudices are rarely discrete and, to the contrary, frequently overlap in 'sharing a common content or generalised object which allows them to be joined together or interrelated, to be expressed in ways in which elements of one are incorporated in the other' (Miles, 1989, p. 87). This is an astute conceptualisation and a good contemporary illustration of its explanatory purchase may be found in the summary report on Islamophobia published by the European Monitoring Centre on Racism and Xenophobia shortly after 9/11. This identified a rise in the number of 'physical and verbal threats being made, particularly to those visually identifiable as Muslims, in

---

[5] See also Grossberg's (1993, p. 31) idea of how racial articulations can contain 'a multiplicity of ways in which different meanings, experiences, powers, interests, and identities can be articulated together'.

particular, women wearing the hijab' (Allen and Nielsen, 2002, p. 16). What is of particular note is that despite variations in the number and correlation of physical and verbal threats directed at Muslim populations among the individual nation-states, one overarching feature that emerged among the fifteen European Union countries was the tendency for Muslim women to be attacked because of how the *hijab* signifies a gendered Islamic identity (Allen and Nielsen, 2002, p. 35). Indeed, and to return to the earlier point concerning the distinction between antipathy toward Muslims and antipathy toward those appearing to follow Islam, these overlapping and interacting 'articulations' of anti-Muslim and anti-Islamic prejudice can also be illustrated further in the attitude polling of non-Muslim Britons one year after 9/11. This showed that:

...there could be little doubt from G-2002e [31 October–1 November, YouGov, n=1,890; The Guardian, 5 November 2002; http://www.YouGov.com] that 9/11 had taken some toll. Views of Islam since 9/11 were more negative for 47%, and of Britain's Muslims for 35% (almost three times the first post-9/11 figure in G-2001f [8–10 October, NOP, n=600; Daily Telegraph, 12 October 2001]). [...] Dislike for Islam was expressed by 36%, three in four of whom were fearful of what it might do in the next few years. One quarter rejected the suggestion that Islam was mainly a peaceful religion, with terrorists comprising only a tiny minority... (Field, 2007, p. 455).

If these examples and the preceding discussion begin to make manifest a number of confusions contained within contemporary references to racial and religious antipathy toward Muslims and Islam, then—as debates concerning racism and other religious minorities, not least with respect to anti-Semitism, betray (Meer and Noorani, 2008, pp. 195–219)—this is not uniquely problematical in the conceptualisation of anti-Muslim sentiment.

Religion and Racialisation

More precisely, the interactions between racial and religious antipathy can be helpfully drawn out through Modood's description of anti-Semitism as 'a form of [ethno-]religious persecution [which] became, over a long, complicated, evolving but contingent history, not just a form of cultural racism but one with highly systematic biological formulations' (Modood, 2005, pp. 9–10). This should not be read as an endorsement of the view that all racism can be reduced to biological inferences. Indeed, in the example above, modern biological racism has some roots in pre-modern religious antipathy—an argument that is supported by Rana (Rana, 2007, pp. 148–162). Moreover, while racism in modern Europe took a biologistic form, what is critical to racialisation of a group is not the invocation of a biology but a radical 'otherness' and the perception and treatment of individuals in terms of physical appearance and descent. The implication is that non-Christian religious minorities in Europe can undergo processes of racialisation where the 'otherness' or 'groupness' that is appealed to is connected to a cultural and racial otherness which relates to European peoples' historical and contemporary perceptions of those people that they perceive to be non-European (Goldberg, 2006). This means that how Muslims in Europe are perceived today is not un-connected to how they have been perceived and treated by European empires and their racial hierarchies in earlier centuries (Gottschalk and Greenberg, 2008). This is because their perception and treatment clearly has a religious and cultural dimension but, equally clearly, bares a phenotypical component. For while it is true that 'Muslim' is not a (putative) biological category in the way that 'black' or 'south Asian' (aka 'Paki'), or Chinese is, neither was 'Jew'. In that instance it took a long non-linear history of racialisation to turn an ethno-religious group into a race.[6] More precisely, the latter did not so much replace the former as superimposed itself because even though no one denied that Jews were a religious community, with a distinctive language(s), culture(s) and religion, Jews still came to be seen as a race, and with horrific consequences.

As Bunzl maintains, 'the move from Judenhass (Jew hatred) to anti-Semitism marks a crucial turning point of the late nineteenth century. It was understood both by contemporaries and later observers as marking a momentous transformation, characterized by the rise of an organized political movement as well as a shift in alterity from religion to race' (Bunzl, 2005, p. 537). Similarly, Bosnian Muslims were 'ethnically cleansed' because they came to be identified as a 'racial' group by people who were phenotypically, linguistically and culturally the same as themselves. The ethnic cleanser, unlike an Inquisitor, wasted no time in finding out what people believed, if and how often they went to a mosque and so on: their victims were racially identified as Muslims (Modood, 2006, pp. 51–62).

---

[6] See the case study of Incitement to Religious Hatred legislation in Meer (2008), and Modood's rejoinder in his discussion of the Danish Cartoon affair in Modood (2006).

Biological and Cultural Racism

Race is not just about biology or even 'colour'; while racialisation has to pick on some features of a people related to physical appearance and ancestry (otherwise racism cannot be distinguished from other forms of 'groupism') it need only be a marker, and not necessarily denote a form of determinism. This is illustrated in the conceptualisation of cultural racism as a two-step process (Modood, 1997). While biological racism is the antipathy, exclusion and unequal treatment of people on the basis of their physical appearance or other imputed physical differences, saliently in Britain their non 'whiteness', cultural racism builds on biological racism a further discourse which evokes cultural differences from an alleged British, 'civilised' norm to vilify, marginalise or demand cultural assimilation from groups who also suffer from biological racism. Post-war racism in Britain has been simultaneously culturalist and biological, and while the latter is essential to the racism in question, it is, in fact, the less explanatory aspect of a complex phenomenon. Biological interpretations have not governed what white British people, including racists, have thought or done; how they have stereotyped, treated and related to non-whites; and biological ideas have had increasingly less force both in the context of personal relationships and in the conceptualisation of groups. As white people's interactions with non-white individuals increased, they did not become necessarily less conscious of group differences but they were far more likely to ascribe group differences to upbringing, customs, forms of socialisation and self-identity than to biological heredity. The interesting question arises as to whether it could be one-step racism: could colour racism decline and fade away and yet cultural racism remain and perhaps even grow?

One can certainly imagine a future in which a group could continue to have their culture vilified while colour racism simultaneously declined, and the distinction between what might be called racism proper and 'culturalism' is commonly held and continues to be argued for (Blum, 2002; Fredrickson, 2002). Yet while it appears that to discriminate only against those perceived to be culturally different might be borderline racial discrimination, where cultural essentialism and inferiorisation may be involved it would certainly share some of the qualities of what we know of racist stereotyping and practise today. Even then, however, it may still be regarded as a cultural prejudice or cultural exclusionism rather than racism per se, so that if persons are targeted only on the basis of their behaviour and not on the basis of their ancestry, then might we not have something we should call culturalism rather than racism?

While this is an interesting question it appears to go against what we should expect from communities and social dynamics, since cultures and cultural practices are usually internally diverse, containing and omitting various 'authentic' elements, and adaptations and mixes. It follows then that the culturalised targeting could very easily be expansive, rather than purist, and so in one way or another catches most if not all cultural minorities in that group. For example, a non-religious Muslim might still be targeted as a cultural Muslim or Muslim by community, which means Muslim by background, which means birth and ancestry. Hence it is not clear that culturalism, where it is associated with distinct communities, can really be distinguished from racism in practice, even if it can be in theory. But if we accept that racism does not necessarily involve attributing qualities that inhere in a deterministic law-like way in all members of a group, then we do not have to rule out cultural racism as an example of racism. This means that cultural racism is not merely a *proxy* for racism (Barker, 1981; Gilroy, 1987; Solomos, 1991) but a form of racism itself, and that while racism involves some reference to physical appearance or ancestry it does not require any form of biological determinism, only a physical identification on a group basis, attributable to descent. As such we should guard against the characterisation of racism as a form of 'inherentism' or 'biological determinism', which leaves little space to conceive the ways in which cultural racism draws upon physical appearance as one marker, amongst others. As such, we maintain that formulations of racialisation should not be solely premised upon conceptions of biology in a way that ignores religion, culture and the like (cf. Miles, 1989).

Permissible Discourse on Muslims

We proceed with the view that terms such as anti-Muslim sentiment and Islamophobia, as well as indeed anti-Semitism, should nest in conceptions of racialisation and cultural racism. This is not least because neat and categorical delineations within terminology are made implausible by variations in the social phenomena that they seek to describe and understand, so that a more nimble and absorbent nomenclature is preferred. These theoretical concerns can be applied to the reaction to comments about Muslims made during an interview with the *Sunday Times* in September 2006 by the celebrated British novelist Martin Amis:

They're also gaining on us demographically at a huge rate. A quarter of humanity now and by 2025 they'll be a third. Italy's down to 1.1 child per woman. We're just going to be outnumbered... There's a definite urge—don't you have it?—to say, 'The Muslim community will have to suffer until it gets its house in order.' What sort of suffering? Not letting them travel. Deportation—further down the road. Curtailing of freedoms. Strip-searching people who look like they're from the Middle East or from Pakistan. Discriminatory stuff, until it hurts the whole community and they start getting tough with their children (quoted in Dougary, 2006).

When the tenor of these comments is coupled with Amis' notoriety, it is perhaps surprising to learn that they went largely unnoticed until a year later when Terry Eagleton (2007) criticised them in the preface to a revised edition of his book *Ideology: An Introduction*. This prompted a robust defence from Amis himself who characterised his comments as an experiment in the limits of permissible thought or 'adumbrations', and which in turn invited separate but over-lapping charges from the film-maker Ronan Bennett (2007) the journalists Yasmin Alibhai–Brown (2007) and Peter Wilby (2007) the satirist Chris Morris (2007) and the novelist Pankaj Mishra (2007) that Amis was sanctioning a form of racism.

Taken together, the objections to Amis derived, firstly, from his attribution to all Muslims of pejorative group characteristics; specifically an irrational desire for violence. Secondly, the perpetuation of fears concerning a demographic challenge posed by Muslims to 'native' (non-Muslim) European populations. Thirdly, the championing of discriminatory surveillance of people who 'appear' Muslim—'strip-searching people who look like they're from the Middle East or from Pakistan'—on the grounds that there is an essential Muslim appearance and that it correlates with the risk of terrorism. Fourthly, that Amis was advocating a form of collective punishment according to which all Muslims must bare responsibility for the actions of the few.

Despite these clusters of criticisms, Amis nevertheless received strong support from several leading intellectuals who endorsed his anxieties, if not his exact framing. Indeed, even *The Guardian* ran a leader entitled: 'In Praise of... Martin Amis' stating that while 'his writing on Islamist terrorism has made him enemies...we should prize him—for his engagement as well as his gifts' (*Guardian* Leader, 2008). *The Independent* (2007), meanwhile, applauded his 'right to stand up for the right, in a culture of free speech, to think aloud'. These examples appear to confirm Bennett's (2007) conclusion that:

Amis's remarks, his defence of them, and the reaction to them were a test... we failed that test. Amis got away with it. He got away with as odious an outburst of racist sentiment as any public figure has made in this country for a very long time. Shame on him for saying it, and shame on us for tolerating it.

It is important then to examine the discursive content of Amis' defenders' arguments in a way that can add to our understanding of the relationship between racialisation, cultural racism and Islamophobia, in order to evaluate on what grounds the racialised content in such discourse is permissible when discussing Muslims. For example, *The Times* columnist David Aaronovitch argued that 'it was fairly obvious that Amis wasn't advocating discriminatory action against Muslims, and that his views on responsibility were far more nuanced than the 'urge' he described' (Aaronovitch, 2008, p. 5). While this nuance is not apparent in Amis' comments, quite the contrary in fact, the greatest concern for Aaranovitch is to recognise how 'Amis's conclusion [was] that an ideological struggle must be waged, in which the proper values of the West are championed' (Aaronovitch, 2008, p. 5). There are several assumptions informing this characterisation, which are by no means specific or unique to this columnist (see Aaronovitch, 2004), and that are elsewhere displayed by 'Left' and 'Right' alike (cf. Cohen, 2007; Anthony, 2007; Phillips, 2006; Gove, 2006).

These include the assumption that politically assertive religious Muslims in Europe look upon Western societies as 'heathen' and 'degenerate'. Or that any Muslim identity politics that are critical of Western foreign policy, harbour subversive, anti-democratic and revolutionary aspirations (Parekh, 2006). In meeting these compelling dangers with a combative response ('until the whole community gets tough with their children', to use Amis' words), the finessed thoughts and contemplations expected in normal discourse may on occasion be forfeited. It is on these terms that the author Ian McEwan (2007) excuses Amis, for 'when you ask a novelist or a poet his or her view of the world, you do not get a politician's or a sociologist's answer'. McEwan (2007) does not rest there, however, but takes issue with the charge that:

...because religion is 'also about identity, background and culture, and Muslims are overwhelmingly non-white', to criticise this thought system is 'Islamophobic', and therefore racist. This is an old ploy, familiar to the extremes of the political left and right, of attempting to close down debate...

While some may challenge the competencies of Amis' grasp of aspects of Islamic history, politics and cultural traditions and so forth (Dalrymple, 2008)—his critique of these do not inform the general charge of racism against him (the slippage between race and faith is frequently invoked and returned to below). The criticisms of Amis have instead focused upon the four tendencies elaborated from his comments, and concern the mechanisms of racialisation, which proceed through 'a process of categorisation, a representational process of defining an Other (usually, but not exclusively) somatically' (Dalrymple, 2008; Miles, 1989, p. 75). McEwan's complaint returns us, then, to Halliday's argument discussed earlier, and supports our analysis that the ambivalence attributed to anti-Muslim sentiment reflects a commonly held narrow definition of racism which assumes that the discrimination directed at conventionally, involuntarily, conceived racial minorities cannot by definition resemble that directed at Muslim minorities (Meer and Modood, 2009). Such views are premised upon the assumption that Muslim identities are religious identities that are voluntarily chosen. So it is frequently stated that while gender, racial and sexuality based identities are ascribed or involuntary categories of birth, being a Muslim is about chosen beliefs, and that Muslims therefore need or ought to have less legal protection than these other kinds of identities. What this ignores, however, is that people do not choose to be or not to be born into a Muslim family. Similarly, no one chooses to be born into a society where to look like a Muslim or to be a Muslim invites suspicion and hostility, and this logically parallels the kinds of racial discrimination directed at other minorities as discussed above.

*Islam*ism*ophobic futures?*

The defence of Amis draws our attention to a new front of entanglements between race, religion, and politics, one which is hitherto subject to sufficient ambiguity so as to further license the attribution to all Muslims of pejorative group characteristics; specifically an irrational desire for violence. For example, Amis himself has insisted that while we ought to 'respect' Islam as 'the donor of countless benefits to mankind, and the possessor of a thrilling history... we do not respect Islamism' (Amis, 2008, p. 50). In so far as it assumes that there is no relationship between the psychic and the social, or that an individually held identity can be de-coupled from the way in which that identity is referred to and represented at a more societal or macro level, Amis' distinction is a permutation of the insistence that we can freely choose to live within discrete identity boundaries. Or as Kundnani puts it: 'a great deal hangs on the three letters separating Islam from Islamism and the two can easily be conflated or linked together structurally' (Kundnani, 2008, p. 43). This was already much in evidence with Amis' conflation of 'the Islamists' with 'the Muslims' during his insistence that 'they are gaining on us demographically' (as discussed above). It is perhaps unsurprising therefore to hear him maintain: 'No doubt the impulse towards rational inquiry is by now very weak in the rank and file of the Muslim male' (Amis, 2008, p. 89). It would require some stretch of the imagination to conceive this as a principled contestation of a social or political discourse, instead of a rehearsal of the types of syntheses between race and culture that are projected upon and intertwined with religion. So just as our discussion of Douglas Murray compels us to seek a terminology that can simultaneously explain the reliance upon signs of race, culture and belonging, in a way that is by no means reducible to hostility to a religion alone, so our discussion of Amis and newer racialised cleavages surrounding Islamism requires us to pursue the same.

In this chapter we have tried to show how anti-Muslim sentiment simultaneously draws upon signs of race, culture and belonging in a way that compels us to consider how religion has a new sociological relevance because of the ways it is tied up with issues of community identity, stereotyping, socio-economic location, political conflict and so forth. The sociology of race and racism possesses a powerful repertoire of explanatory concepts to address this topic that makes it all the more striking to find so little by way of application. Chief amongst the concepts we identify are those of racialisation and cultural racism, for these can explain how religious discrimination in most Western societies does not usually proceed on the basis of belief but perceived membership of an ethno-religious group. We have argued that the arithmetic of Islamophobia, like anti-Semitism, shares much with this formula in a way that is strikingly illustrated in Martin Amis' characterisation of Muslims. Amis employs a form of cultural racism which trades on pejorative characterisations of religious groups and communities, as opposed to beliefs and opposition to beliefs, and so it is not a pure 'religious discrimination' but one which traffics in stereotypes about foreignness, phenotypes and culture. We therefore maintain that conceptions of Islamophobia must draw analytical weight from those of racialisation and cultural racism.

9

NO INNOCENTS

MUSLIMS IN THE PREVENT STRATEGY

M. G. Khan

In April 2007, Community Secretary Ruth Kelly announced the Government's new action plan to 'isolate, prevent and defeat violent extremism': Preventing Violent Extremism (PVE). Given the almost complete identification of the contemporary violent extremist with Muslim, and the homegrown Angry Muslim Young Man in particular, this chapter proposes to contribute to the discussion of Islamophobia by asking what the Government's PVE agenda, its workings, assumptions and underlying conceptualisation of extremism can bring to a critical conceptual understanding of Islamophobia. Moreover what, conversely, an approach informed by the concept of Islamophobia can bring to the critique of PVE. It argues two things: first, that Islamophobia and PVE are both structured by iterated polarising dichotomies of good and evil, with us or against us, part of the solution or part of the problem, fighting the good war against terror or enabling terror's warmongering. Second, that Community Cohesion discourse laid the foundations in both public opinion and public policy for the acceptance of the Islamophobic strategies employed by the Prevent agenda, and the assumptions that underpin PVE in turn went on to lend credence to fear of Muslims (and to realising Muslim fears).

Islamophobia finds expression at an institutional and organisational level in relations with both individuals and collectives, whether in the hiring, employment and deployment of Muslim staff, or in the approach by institutions, organisations and professions in their work with the Muslim community. They are experienced in the micro detail of the transactions of everyday life: walking down the street, shopping, driving the car, taking the underground, carrying a rucksack, in the work place, socialising after work, at school, at university, at a restaurant, passing through customs and immigration, watching TV, reading newspapers, etc.

The recent events—terrorism and 'disturbances'—that drive the Prevention agenda also structure Islamophobia. Power, and powerlessness, is central to them, as it is to the cluster of questions and perceptions around them. The response made by the Muslim Youthwork Foundation (Khan, M.G., 2006) was that policy responses to issues affecting young Muslim, should be based on the detail of their lives rather than on political imperatives reacting to events. This is theoretically and practically sensible, but it may be politically naïve when dealing with a system with a long history, institutional infrastructure and a conceptual language for managing dynamics of race, ethnicity and faith (Husband, 2003). Government strategies, experience suggests, rarely come to a freely assessed realisation of their faults until forced into it. Detail is rarely a feature of policy responses to events, and rarely tolerated.

The Preventing Violent Extremism agenda emerged out of the Preventing Extremism Together task force (PET) that was set up after the 7 July bombings in 2005 to develop practical recommendations for tackling violent extremism. Due to the relatively short time frame imposed on it, that first process seemed to almost by default end up picking up from and continuing the conversation on the merits and implications of the concept of 'community cohesion'. Put forward by Ted Cantle following the urban disturbances of 2001, community cohesion was a concept based on the fear of religiously segregated towns and cities. Preventing Violent Extremism Together added extremism to the perception, if not charge, of self-segregation in Muslim communities.

This representation of Muslims as something of a congealed mass, both impenetrable and inassimilable, which informs both the discourses of Community Cohesion and Preventing Violent Extremism (part of the CONTEST Strategy which is managed by the Office for Security and Counter Terrorism in the Home Office) also informs the Terrorism Act 2006 which is in turn a local articulation of the global 'with us or against us' of the War on Terror launched by George W. Bush. This seamless interrelatedness has been further woven together by a political consensus built on a party-political ratcheting up of securitarian agendas. Collapsing together issues of terrorism, immigration, belonging, 'Britishness' and British values, identification and loyalty, proliferating discourses circulating in different registers have coalesced to lend seemingly graspable content and meaning, to the otherwise 'slippery notion' of Community Cohesion.

The problem is compounded by the fact that these communities are poorly legible to the State (Scott, 1998). These are communities that overwhelmingly tend to use informal networks and structures of association, dispense with paper trails, or are suspicious and distrustful of organisations and bureaucracies. Seen through the lens of the policing and criminalising machinery legislatively rolled out, the activities and financial flows of self-help groups, charity drives, aid fund and immigrant remittances, can all too swiftly be turned from undocumented good intentions to 'kafkaesquely' unprovable innocence (Khan, M.G., 2007). As civil liberties groups have argued, the Terrorism Act 2006 casts offences such as encouragement to terrorism and dissemination of terrorist publications so broadly as to not actually require any intention to incite others to commit criminal acts to be found guilty. The Act has moved liability from the realm of actions to the realm of ideas and associations. Whether it is its objective or not, its effect has been to disrupt the nature of community and the relations of recognition, solidarity and exchange that create the ties that bind communities. Specifically, it particularly seeks to break 'overly cohesive' communities that Cantle argues are a threat to Community Cohesion.

Collaterally or otherwise, these agendas criminalise communal forms of life. It leaves professionals working with young people, such as youth workers, in a precarious position. Youth workers require the trust and confidence of young people to establish associations and relationships for meaningful conversations. These conversations may serve the purpose of letting-off steam, testing boundaries, counselling, or support but, as Banks (1999) states, young people will only have these conversations if they are confident that the worker is not going to report them to the police, their parents or their school. But youth workers are now expected to notify the police, and can be charged under this legislation if they do not inform on young people who manifest extremist views or are in danger of being radicalised. However, as many youth workers attest, being extreme is not that same as extremism: for young people it is a rite of passage, a form of resistance, and young Muslims have clearly figured out what will shock the sensibilities of those they may feel most aggrieved by. It is their version of punk, and according to Aki Nawaz (2004) 'Islam is more punk than punk'.

Anecdotal evidence suggests that youth workers employed by the Youth Offending Service's YIP (Youth Inclusion Programmes) are particularly prone to pressure from the police to reveal names of young people they are working with. These are often young people with offending history who are in what the Department for Children, Schools and Families (DCSF) term as NEET (Not in Employment, Education or Training). Such mono perceptions of Muslim communities and 'Muslimness' allow random connections to mark out a young offender with conviction for theft as a potential terrorist, even though the terrorism offender profile—according to leading criminal law advocates—suggests otherwise. With the reversal of the burden of proof and the with us or against us logic of the War on Terror which informs the Prevent strategy, challenge, contestation, resistance, or refusal to work on PVE agendas results in Muslim youth workers themselves being seen as part of the problem, 'radicalisers' rather than 'de-radicalisers'.

Through the introduction of NI 35 'Building resilience to violent extremism', a new national performance directive for local authorities and other key service providers, the government has sought to 'mainstream' the War on Terror. This performance indicator was devised to measure how effective local services are in building resilience to violent extremism and is part of the drive to equip the 'home front' in the War on Terror. Organisations such as An-Nisa Society and Muslim Youthwork Foundations have alerted to the dangers of misjudgement from staff due to the lack of experience and knowledge of Muslims, especially in a context where Islamophobic assumptions are expressed with ever increasing confidence. In particular, by staff more readily predisposed to internalise anti-Islamic sentiments wrought through the association of values with professional approaches, and those working in the service sector are particularly prone to this in their desire to make a difference, or as Davis put it, to 'save and salvage'—save for God and salvage for the economy (Davies, B., 1999). In the shift from the global to the local that NI 35 effects, as the reach and impact permeate the minutiae of the every day existence in the lives of individuals, communities and neighbourhoods, the conflation between Islamophobia and PVE threatens to become more insidious.

Mehmood Naqshbandi (2006) has suggested that what is needed is to stop the low-level petty abuse of Muslims which is an everyday fact of life. Though it is hard to pin down and hard to prove, Muslims 'feel it', yet precisely because respect, self-esteem and dignity are intangible factors, they often remain unexpressed, particularly when doing so merely appears to feed into the onslaught of right wing pundits such as Melanie Phillips (2006), who seek to present minority ethnic communities as 'victim cultures'.

The notion of micro inequity, as advanced by feminist thinkers such as Sandler (1986), with reference to the ways in which individuals or groups are singled out based on unchanging characteristics such as race or gender—and to which we should add religion—is useful here. Micro inequities can assume many forms—a gesture, a change in language or tone of voice, or whether one is heard when one speaks. But they have several things in common: they are subtle, almost imperceptible; they are ephemeral, and by their very nature difficult to prove, and often the victim is left looking overly sensitive, whilst it is possible that the perpetrator can be unconscious of what they are doing and therefore will not acknowledge the behaviour.

Micro inequities inhabit the gap between the rhetoric of equality and fairness, and the reality lived by the victim; the more confident the Islamophobia the bigger the gap, the more obvious its manifestations. Micro inequalities increase and multiply in expression and intensity as they cohere more seamlessly with Community cohesion, PVE and the War on Terror. Such reinforcing coherence is manifest in cases such as the arrests of the so-called 'Manchester terror plotters' on 10 April 2009. Eleven Pakistani students were arrested and then faced trial by media (Bhattacharryya, 2009) yet none were subsequently charged, and still their visas were revoked. The statistics reeled

out by Louise Christian (2006) support her description of the logic of 'fishing expeditions' at work: '895 arrests for terrorism offences, 23 convictions, 138 charged under the Terrorism Act, 156 under other legislation, 496 no further action' (Christian, Groombridge and Peirce, 2006, p. 4). Moreover, they support her contention that the net effect of such policing and legislation is to feed a sense of injustice and fear, alienate people, and ultimately is counter-productive.

The reinforcing logic of Islamophobia and PVE inheres in a self-referential circulation of assumptions, which both places Muslims under suspicion and denies their sense of grievance the kind of moral recognition by the wider community which is extended to victims of injustice. It also, and very fundamentally, works through ambivalence. The afore-portrayed picture illustrates the point. It is the image that appears on the cover of the Government's *Preventing Violent Extremism—Next steps for Communities* 2008 Report.

What is the picture supposed to be saying, and to whom, in the context of this document? Is it saying the way forward is to work with young people (and perhaps young women in particular)? Is it saying the way forward is to Westernise young Muslim women? Is it saying life for these young Muslim women needs to be more challenging and enjoyable, full of fun activities; that fulfilled lives are the key to integration, or that channelling aggression is the key to de-radicalisation? Is it just a happy picture of two young women who are having fun, without a care in the world? They don't look like they are thinking about violent extremism. Or are they? Is it perhaps suggesting that anybody can have information or contact with violent extremists? Is it saying that we need to be talking to more Muslim women; the men cannot be trusted? Is it saying that we need to talk to younger people, as the older generation cannot be trusted?

The point is that rather than judging the book by the cover, we start judging the cover by the book. In this case, the image of these two young women can be seen through the lens and the logic of the Prevent strategy. In this, the image is perhaps iconic of the insidious relation between Islamophobia and Prevent. It encodes the interwoven strands of the global War on Terror and its Steps for Communities where there are no innocents.

Reference is often made to consultations and task groups as part of the processes of policy making, and in the legitimising and pitching of policies and programmes thus devised, as was the case with the Preventing Extremism Together, or with the establishment of women's and young persons advisory groups. Muslim communities already feel poorly catered to and invisible in public policy except when the issue is community cohesion or PVE. The danger of such consultation methods and the NI 35 approach is that it will further distance Muslims from core services as well as create a level of cynicism towards consultation that they, and young people in particular, will come to see little benefit in responding to invitations to contribute and 'have their say'. Cynicism, in turn, works to reverse civic engagement. PVE and Islamophobia legitimise one another whilst desensitising the wider public by portraying Muslims as 'self harmers'. PVE, with its targeting and criminalising of an entire community would be difficult to sell without the conceptual foundation provided by a confident Islamophobia given currency by the discourse of Community Cohesion.

10

'FLOODING THE EMBANKMENTS'

RACE, BIO-POLITICS AND SOVEREIGNTY

David Tyrer

It is useful to consider the relationship between Islamophobia and representations of the 'moderate' Muslim. On the one hand, these representations move beyond rendering Muslims invisible or fixing them as 'extremists', and by apparently giving them voice, imply a refutation of racist principles. On the other hand, the sudden emphasis on representations of 'moderates' has emerged at a time many feel is marked by increasing levels of anti-Muslim racism (for example, Hagopian, 2004). In this context, many of the ideologues whose works inform the current global strategy on combating 'extremism' and promoting 'moderacy' have been accused by some of only cynically recognising, in order to blur, the distinction between 'moderates' and 'extremists', so that Muslims can be represented as a generic, undifferentiated threat (Youmans, 2004, pp. 120–121.).

Throughout this chapter I will speak of 'moderate' Muslims, but do not do this in reference to real, empirical subjects. I am not concerned with 'moderate', 'extremist', 'terrorist', 'pacifist', 'Islamo-fascist', or any other strain of Muslim. Rather, I am concerned with the ways in which various 'types' of Muslim subjects are represented, the relationship between this process and broader questions of governance, and what we can learn about contemporary forms of Islamophobia by considering these complexities. The frequently stereotyped representation of

Muslims in terms of 'extremism' has often been recognised in terms of its role in anti-Muslim racism, particularly in media and film (for example, Poole, 2002; Shaheen, 2001). In this chapter I consider how stereotyped representations of 'moderacy' are also bound up in this process and explore how analysis of this can assist us in unpicking the relationship between race and governance today.

Debates concerning Muslims have taken a decidedly categorical tenor, as it has become increasingly difficult to ignore the broad trend away from identifying primarily in terms of ascribed 'traditional' racialised markers of difference recognisable to the modern disciplinary state, and toward self-identification primarily as Muslims. How we determine to fix these identities (as purely 'religious' or somehow 'ethnicised') has a direct bearing on how we understand Islamophobia (as racism or merely religious discrimination). Meer (2007, pp. 114–118) contends that the central problems in addressing Islamophobia through legislation are difficulties about categories. But the categories themselves are at once arbitrary and contingent; the problem is not the categories into which we shoehorn human subjects, but the logic of this binary categorisation itself and the role it plays in constituting them as subjects. In the case of Muslims, the question of categorisation has come to be a racial question, so that even when Islamophobia is not incorporated into legislation on racism (Meer, 2007, pp. 114–118), this is justified largely on grounds that re-centre the idea of race as real and immutable. Toynbee's (2005) rejection of Islamophobia on the grounds that Muslims are not a bounded 'race' is typical of the *a priori* assumptions about race that persist in shaping debates on Muslims, even when the argument being made ostensibly concerns religion, rather than race. Such assumptions, which begin with implicit refutation of all that we know about the socially constructed nature of race, serve only to reify race.

I contend that these questions are not, in fact, centrally about which category is best applied, but rather concern the way in which race fixes subjects into classifications, and how it works across and between these categories to throw up such ambiguities as a seemingly 'religious' group experiencing racism, or representations of the 'moderate' Muslim that unsettle the binary 'them'/'us' configurations of race that we might traditionally have expected. That these questions are central to this chapter is largely because they are not simply abstract, conceptual debates, but involve questions about the extent to which racialised subjects can choose how they identify. Meer (2008) and Modood (2005, p. 16) note that when Muslims identify *qua* Muslims, this 'choice' is often invoked to justify further opposition to requests for legal protection against Islamophobia. This question of choice does not merely concern the constraints on identification that are internal to the experiences of racialised minorities (e.g. 'how much choice does one really have over one's religion?'), but are fundamental questions concerning the constraints imposed by race and racism on the choices racialised subjects can make about self-identification. In other words, 'to what extent do members of a racialised group have choice over their racial signification?'.

This is a key question, for when Muslims do self-identify as Muslims, they can often find themselves expressing a sense of identity that jars with, and disrupts, the normative grammars of 'race' that were central to the modern disciplinary state, and which form the ideological and practical basis of many of the ways in which people are categorised and subjectified. For a considerable time, the difficulties this posed to accounts of Muslim identities were frequently reflected in the application of binary logics of absence/hyper-differentiation as public expressions of Muslim identities were often either denied as inauthentic and incomplete in themselves without the supplement of an ascribed racial identity, or hyper-differentiated as 'extremism' (or as surface evidence of this). These modes of rendering Muslims invisible or holding them in radical alterity served to re-centre modern, disciplinary notions of race since they typically re-authorised the grammar of race: either Muslims were absent because their identities were incomplete in themselves by dint of not being purely racial, or they were hyper-differentiated because their identities reflected an extremist interruption of purely racial, authentic identities.

But contemporary Islamophobic representations are qualitatively different, as is shown by the proliferation of representations of 'moderates'. Rather than denying the persistence of Muslim identities based on appeals to older notions of biological 'race', contemporary Islamophobia recognises Muslims *qua* Muslims, but on the terms of racism (i.e. as though a discretely ethnicised group [see, for example, Kundnani, 2007a, p. 126]). This marks an important development to the ways in which Muslim identities have been problematised. Contemporary Islamophobia involves a move beyond the previous logic of absence/hyper-differentiation; now the emphasis is on a broader frame linked to different intensities or registers of alterity, and different modes of representing these registers of difference and differentiation. As Sayyid (2004) notes, racism works through the alternate ascriptions of exotic and banal characteristics to racialised groups. One instance of this is the radical differentiation of Muslims (as 'extremists') and their relative de-differentiation (as 'moderates'). In other words, if Muslims provoke crisis it is because of their racial indeterminacy and the crisis in racialised governmentality that they provoke as racialised subjects who interrogate the terms of their subjectification. Contemporary Islamophobia mimics this effect by coding into its representation of Muslim figures who appear specifically indeterminate (e.g. 'moderate') but whose indeterminacy is in fact a central facet of the very different logics of 'race' in societies of control. The categorical questions that seem to infuse discussions about Muslims are perhaps more fruitfully understood as tensions within the modern disciplinary logics of race itself, and illustrate problems posed by the large-scale expression of Muslim subjectivities, and changes to the nature of racism. In this chapter I am therefore concerned with the ways in which seemingly benignly racialised representations act as registers for new forms of racialised discourse. I term this discourse Islamophobia, and in this paper suggest that it is an archetypal form of control racism, drawing from the conceptions of racism offered by Hardt and Negri (2000) and Deleuze and Guattari (2004).

Race, 'Extremists' and the 'Moderate'

One frequent contradiction in discussions of Muslims is that between the classification of Muslims as a purely religious group, on the one hand, and the representation of Muslims in racialised terms, on the other. This is not only manifested in the re-centring of race in the terms of these debates, but also through depictions of Muslims in which physical racial markers are replaced by 'culture' and 'clothing'. For instance, the following appeared in the *Daily Mail* during the aftermath of the botched Forest Gate anti-terrorism raid that was launched on the basis of information provided by a criminal serving time for dishonesty offences (*Independent*, 2008) in which an innocent man was shot:

We are told that the two brothers now in police custody had become 'radicalised' after 9/11, grew beards, adopted extreme Islamic dress and were fond of spouting jihad against the west.

Growing a beard is not yet a hanging offence, though give [then Home Secretary] John Reid a chance. But it's fair to say they had put themselves on offer (*Daily Mail*, 2006).

This racialised representation of Muslims reflects the linkages between Islamophobia and representations of the 'extremist'. These links work on a number of levels, but most obviously through the importance of stereotypes about 'fundamentalism' and 'extremism' in anti-Muslim racism. Another manifestation of these links is the problematic association between expressions of Muslim rights and the influence of 'extremists'. The assumptions underlying this have in turn informed, and drawn inspiration from, the wider attack against multiculturalism, and unite some on the political far right with others on the secular left, albeit for very different reasons. The May 2008 launch of British Muslims for Secular Democracy, for instance, saw discussions about the need to support 'moderates' couched in criticism of Muslims for 'opting out' by dint of the legal protections they have accrued and what many Muslims see as the rights-based campaigns in which they have been involved (for instance, in relation to women's dress rights). Thus, some (Bhatt, 1998; Yuval-Davis, 1992) have suggested that 'extremists' and 'authoritarian' religious leaders have prospered from multiculturalism. Others (such as Tibi, 2007, p. 41), that Orientalism and Islamophobia are 'charges often made for propagandistic purposes', while 'the multiculturalism of post-modern cultural relativism also opens the gate for Islamists to Europe. It is this combination of a lack of integration and the 'anything goes' ideology of multiculturalism which smoothes the way for Islamic fundamentalists to establish safe havens (Tibi, 2007, p. 49).

These close associations between Islamophobia and representations of the 'extremist' are strengthened by the tendency to focus on 'visible' manifestations of Muslim identity. This can often bring to the fore, particular modes of Islamophobia experienced by certain 'types' of Muslims (see, for instance, Allen and Nielson, 2002; Sheridan, 2006). The emphasis on Muslim visibility is also problematic since representations of the 'extremist' tend to emphasise Muslim visibility. Jack Straw's suggestion in 2006 that 'the veil' is 'a visible statement of separation and difference' is an obvious example of this in a context in which separateness and difference have been coded as 'extremist'.

Precisely because of what has often seemed to be a fixation with the most observant 'types' of Muslims, the 'visibility' of Muslims, and questions about 'extremism', it is far less straightforward to unpick the relationship between Islamophobia and representations of the 'moderate' that have been traced out during the War on Terror. The most obvious way in which this link manifests lies in the suppressed racism that is frequently played out in the insistence upon classifying the innumerable expressions of Muslim identities into a comparatively narrow set of 'types'. This necessarily essentialises, particularly when the range of types most frequently deployed is as narrow and ill defined as 'extremist'/'moderate'. Another obvious connection between representations of 'moderates' and Islamophobia is the ravelling together of the relative, normative notions of 'moderate' and 'extremist', which render any reference to either as a means of inscribing the other. 'Moderate' is moored in opposition to 'extremist' and gains its meaning from this coupling, notwithstanding the frequent stereotyping of Muslims as 'extremists'. In this light, it is perhaps unintentionally revealing that the 'moderate' organisation 'The Radical Middle Way' is so allusively and ambiguously named.

Despite these linkages, it can often be difficult to acknowledge the links between Islamophobia and representations of the Muslim 'moderate' because the comparatively recent emergence of the 'moderate' in official discourse on Muslims seems to be an entirely positive development which entails formal recognition of Muslims on terms with which they increasingly self-identify, rather than on the grounds of ascribed race. It also avoids previously dominant binary logics of absence/hyper-differentiation, or monolithic Muslim other/the West, entailing, rather, a softer mode of alterity that ostensibly signals social inclusion and political agency of Muslims. Thus, Abbas (2007, p. 440), for example, speaks of 'gains' and 'positive engagement' associated with the empowerment of a professional, middle class body of Muslims (the clearly classed dimension of this, though falling outside the scope of this chapter to consider, should be noted).

Connecting representations of the 'moderate' to Islamophobia is also displaced in commonly articulated assumptions that these representations merely reflect a specific form of Muslim subjectivity that emerged as an entirely natural process. This implies that the atrocities of 11 September 2001 created the opportunity for an assumed singular pre-existing Muslim subjectivity to articulate in new ways with membership of the national polity to produce the 'moderate' (see, for example, Geaves, 2005, p. 76), and thus ignores that the ways in which moderates are represented may at times be problematic or essentialist. This approach acknowledges that the 'moderate' has only really been spoken of seriously by states and the media as an ideal subject in the context of the War on Terror, but it elides what that means to racial bio-politics. In order to be able to take seriously the possibility of a link between Islamophobia and stereotyped representations of Muslim 'moderates', we need to be able to acknowledge that such representations can play a key role in signifying stereotyped notions of extremism, and acknowledge that there is frequently a disjunction between the behaviour or beliefs of Muslims and whether or not they are ascribed 'moderate' status in others' representations of them. In this light, although the very term 'moderate Muslim' appears as muted Muslimness, in fact it is not, despite the ways in which representations of moderacy position moderates as being less different, and mimic the racial indeterminacy of Muslims. This is because the 'moderate' is also always used as a way of inscribing harder forms of Muslim alterity even if s/he is represented in terms of indeterminacy. This central tension in representations of moderacy is one reason why those represented as moderates not only still experience Islamophobia but also find themselves de- and re-classified in alternative terms (usually, 'extremist') with relative ease. Such subjects are not represented as 'moderate' once-and-for-all, but momentarily, and remain open to re-signification as 'extremist' whether by the state, by racists, or even by other Muslims. Finally, the 'moderate' is notably recognised in her/his own terms rather than on the grounds of some prior racial marking, so that while the logic of most representations of 'moderacy' implies a muting of Muslimness, this is not a final operation but one in a series of modulations that are central to the exercise of power in contemporary Islamophobia.

It is also important to recognise that representations of 'moderate' Muslims in the press and among politicians did not necessarily naturally emerge in response to some sudden transformation among Muslims, but in response to a number of moral panics about them. The *casus belli* for the War on Terror was provided by a handful of murderous psychopaths. However, the fears and anxieties that materialise the various Muslim 'types' of contemporary Islamophobia are alternately amplified, attenuated, reduced through their mediatisation, and take their precise forms by mingling with a range of anxieties that pre-date the mass murders of 2001. Thus, fears of terrorism articulate with a range of other anxieties: 'swamping'; 'multiculturalism gone too far'; 'the enemy within'. When Muslims interrupt 'race', their challenges to established systems of racialised classification are bound up with the (ongoing) crisis of the disciplinary institutions with which these anxieties are concerned. The contemporary panic over 'multiculturalism gone too far' is an over-determination of a set of other basic concerns about crises in the modern disciplinary 'race' project and its associated institutions. It is not just a backlash against Muslim self-identification that transgresses 'race'; it is framed by the inescapability of racial crisis in the institutions of disciplinary racism (it is not merely coincidental that contemporary notions of 'multiculturalism gone too far' emerge in the context following the MacPherson enquiry's recognition of institutionalised racism in the police). What allows these various anxieties to take their recognisable shapes is not that those who would murder (or support murder) are common enough among Muslims, for there is no evidence to suggest this to be the case, but rather that the lines of flight with which the emergence of Muslim identities are bound up do not just interrupt 'race' as an abstract system of categorisation but rather at a founding point of the modern disciplinary state. It is in this way that the banal expressions of a countless multiplicity of 'ordinary' Muslim subjectivities interrupt race, and in turn find themselves materialised through fear as ciphers for 'the non-place in which all disciplinary barriers are destroyed and all embankments flooded' (Agamben, 1999, p. 48). It is in this context, then, at a time of heightened anxieties and increased racial tensions, that representations of the Muslim 'moderate' have, alongside the related notion of the 'extremist', emerged as the two most common positions used to fix representations of Muslims. Indeed, it is in this context that the National Security Council earmarked $1.3 billion in 2003 for 'transforming Islam from within' (Mahmood, 2006a, p. 330).

Disciplinary Racism, Control Racism

Agamben's (1999) *Muselmann* acting as a cipher for the camp invites us to consider a time, and a mode of regulating life, in which the logic of the camp is generalised throughout society. The traditional Giddens-ian, essentialist, notions of social inclusion and exclusion as they might conventionally be called upon to figure our analysis of distinctions between incorporated subjects like the 'moderate' and radically differentiated subjects such as the 'extremist' are of strictly limited conceptual value: gone with the declining legitimacy of many of the disciplinary institutions (Clough, 2003; Gandy, 2006), is the hard inside/outside distinction (Hardt and Negri, 2000, p. xii). In its place are smooth spaces of control (Clough, 2003; Diken and Laustsen, 2002), zones of indistinction (Agamben, 1998; Diken and Laustsen, 2002) in which even the disciplinary enclosures appear to us in terms of their dispersal in exteriority (Deleuze, 2006, p. 51) and in the context of which the production of 'bare life', included solely in order to be excluded, is the 'essential function of modern politics' (Agamben, 1998, p. 8). Amid these shifts from discipline to control, the dispersal of power away from 'traditional' disciplinary institutions concerns a:

never ending modulation of moods, capacities, affects, potentialities, assembled in genetic codes, identification numbers, ratings profiles and preference listings...bodies of data and information...The production of normalization is no longer simply trusted to the family kin groups or other institutions of civic society: it also is a matter of the investment in, and the regulation of, a market-driven circulation of affect and attention (Clough, 2003, p. 360).

Amid the shift to control, affect (Clough, 2003) and action-at-a-distance possibilities afforded by the media (Lazzarato, 2006) are as central to bio-politics as the factory, school or army were in a disciplinary society. The interplay between Islamophobia and shifts to control society work on a number of levels, through various modalities: the centrality of affect, and the constant modulation of Islamophobia as it disperses across various sites of anxiety and institutions of control, and as it acts through re-/de-/differentiations, its 'otherings' and 'mutings', are examples.

Two differing instances exemplify the distinction between modern, disciplinary representations of 'moderacy' born from colonial, disciplinary racism, and those of contemporary imperial racisms of control societies. Following a meeting with Mohammed Ali Jinnah in November 1921, Lord Reading described Pakistan's future founder as being an 'extremist', then as being between 'moderate' and 'extremist', and finally as an implied 'moderate' by dint of identifying other nationalist figures as the real 'extremists' (Sayyid and Tyrer, 2002, pp. 62–63). Despite the contesting of 'moderacy' and 'extremism' in this account, under the terms of modern colonial racism, Jinnah was still recognisable in terms of his pure alterity, even when he appeared to be a 'moderate'. 'Moderacy' was defined here solely in relation to 'extremism', with both accounted for in terms of hard alterity as the colonial other. The colonial education project as outlined in Macaulay's infamous minute on Indian education was precisely to prise away, or recuperate within this absolute alterity, colonial others who could intervene between coloniser and colonised by being more 'like us' without losing their fundamental alterity.

In contrast, contemporary Islamophobia constructs 'moderacy' in terms of apparent sameness and intimacy between the 'moderate' and the white male universal self. This operating logic is instructively illustrated by an interview prior to the 2008 London Mayoral elections in which Ken Livingstone made a weak attempt to justify his engagement with the Islamic theologian Yusuf al-Qaradawi, who has been repeatedly embroiled in controversy over homophobia (Hari, 2008). Despite Livingstone's reputation as a 'pro-Muslim' candidate (Butt, 2008a) the interview with Hari implied essentialism and othering ('us all outside denouncing, will do no good at all...so you engage with the better ones'). Two features distinguish this from the racism of the modern, disciplinary society and locate it within the logic of Islamophobia: first, 'them' was not a reference to all Muslims but to specific 'types' of Muslim subjects; second, this distinction was softened by the introduction of degrees of sameness in relation to 'us'. Thus, Islam is 'actually where we were seven hundred years ago', but the presence of 'progressives' eats into the boundaries between 'them' and 'us', given their greater proximity (and similarity) to 'us'. Livingstone's response to a question about Qaradawi's homophobia began with the defence that Qaradawi 'was absolutely clear—he said nobody should physically attack homosexuals'. Should the essentialist reduction of homophobia to physical violence fail to establish Qaradawi's liberal credentials, his closeness to 'us' was cemented through the claim that Qaradawi 'was the first imam to issue a fatwa about oral sex—recommending it. An imam can't be all bad if he's recommending oral sex'. The implicit suggestion was that even if the broader defence failed to repudiate Qaradawi's homophobia, then at least he is unmistakeably heterosexual. This logic positions Qaradawi within a frame of 'heteronormativity' increasingly central to new formations of 'race' and nation during the War on Terror (see, for example, Puar, 2007).

Islamophobia codes the Muslim other in terms of degrees of difference from the universal white male, rather than through the hard logic of pure alterity. This is increasingly reflected in the temporalisation of Muslim difference which blurs binary categories of alterity not only through the introduction of additional terms such as 'moderate' but also by essentialising representation of Muslims through a repertoire of moments from white Western histories (for instance, 'Islamo-fascism'; 'backwardness'; 'pre-modern'; 'medievalism'). This operation is central to the differentiation of Muslims in terms of alterity as difference from sameness; those Muslims more radically differentiated ('fundamentalists') tend to be represented as being further from Western presents than those who are de-differentiated ('moderates'). That moderates are increasingly referred to as 'progressives' is significant in this context. It is not merely coincidental that the racialised project of reducing the huge diversity of Muslims into just two camps (extremists and moderates) is closely associated with the logics of representing Muslims as incompletely realised by dint of not having passed through Western histories, and therefore in need of undergoing key stages from European history (most commonly, Reformation and Enlightenment). As Mamdani notes, Muslims are frequently even denied a history, and Muslim culture is increasingly represented as though having 'petrified into a lifeless custom' (Mamdani, 2002, p. 767). Neither is it coincidental that the distinction between 'moderates' and 'extremists' is often expressed as an opposition between 'traditionalists' and 'modernisers' (see, for example, Fattah and Butterfield, 2006, p. 50). These modes of speaking about key features of 'moderates' are bound up with the central logic of Islamophobia, which constructs Muslims as inadequate, or incompletely realised or racialised white male subjects.

The Islamophobic representation of Muslims as incompletely realised subjects is also illustrated by some of the wider tensions around representations of 'moderates'; in a powerful account, Brown writes of the differential repre-sentation of Muslims in terms of cultural distance, as heavily gendered:

For the government, British Muslim women are witnesses to a moderate and liberal Islam, and are through their daily lives engaged with issues of rights and 'Britishness'. This is because they, more than their male relatives, have benefited from becoming 'British', as they are liberated from backward, cultural practices...Support for women's access to mosques is seen as a way of shoring up the 'radical middle' of liberal Islam... [the] underlying assumption is that British Muslim women are by their nature not radical and by their circumstances most likely to support 'mainstream' Islam. If their dress or behaviour appears radical (such as wearing a niqab or jilbab) then it is because of undue pressure from male relatives and community 'culture' (Brown, K., 2008, p. 481).

Islamophobia's logic is framed by a wider series of shifts associated with post-modernity. Here, I am most concerned with the shift from modern disciplinary society to societies of control. Implicit to my argument is also recognition of the epochal significance of decolonisation (Sayyid, 1997). The apparently increased porosity of borders, globalisation, the increasing centrality of the diasporic condition to postmodern life, and postcoloniality, shift the emphasis from 'race' as empire to struggles over the meanings of 'race' as nation (Hesse, 1997) and are bound up with the dislocating effects of what Sayyid (1997) views as the decentring of the ideological project of 'the West' that underpinned mod-ern colonial expansion. These shifts are accompanied by a proliferation of dif-ferent ways of articulating identities within and across borders in the range of ways that defy the range of expectations associated with the modern, disciplin-ary project. Through their association with the crises of disciplinary institutions, and the ways in which they interrupt the modern disciplinary project of 'race', they come to require new forms of regulation of life. The increasing choice by many Muslims to identify themselves as Muslims rather than as members of a traditionally defined ethnic or racial group is an obvious instance of this. One way of expressing the effects of these shifts is to suggest that the 'regime of con-finement' which has characterised the modern-era disciplinary society is threat-ened by the proliferation of differences which occurs (Lazzarato, 2006, p. 177) but which can no longer be held beyond the margins nor contained through the traditional systems for classifying difference and subjectifying the governed. There are different manifestations of this: for example, the distinction between the assimilatory nature of disciplinary societies was based on the premise of fairly clean-cut inside-outside distinctions and the normalisation of immigrants through a predictable range of institutions (education, policing, etc). In contrast, the community cohesion of contemporary control society is equally aimed at citizens born in this country, and moves beyond the clean inside-outside distinction both in this respect and in respect of the use of disciplinary institutions such as schools and control techniques such as action at a distance, public opinion, CCTV, etc. Whilst assimilationism was premised around a binary distinction between immigrants and white Britons, community cohesion deals with the nation as inescapably heterogeneous and is premised around dealing with indeterminacy.

The relationship between 'extremist' and 'moderate' only appears as a binary distinction when framed by a modernist conception of racism. In the context of Eurocentrism's emergence not as a descriptive term but rather as an ideological project concerned with the re-centring of the modern, Western disciplinary project, the two terms work differently across each other, effectively marking and measuring degrees of closeness to the universal white male self. Contemporary tropes of temporalised Muslim difference which are closely bound up in debates about 'moderacy' and 'extremism' in the War on Terror follow the same logic, referring to different points on an implied scale of difference from sameness. But while this frames contemporary Islamophobia temporally and distinguishes it from Orientalism, it still fails to resolve the tensions presented around the relationship between Islamophobia, 'race' and racism.

The central logic of contemporary Islamophobia is a logic of 'race' that moves beyond the binary distinctions of inclusion/exclusion, and self/other of modern disciplinary societies. Bound up with the postmodern, postcolonial condition, and closely associated with the crises in the institutions of disciplinary societies, this racism is a racism of its time. Although this is not to deny the persistence, recoding and recirculation of older modes of racist discourse, it is the dominant form taken by Islamophobia and locates Muslims as indeterminate people, racialising them on the basis of degrees of difference from the white male universal self, and even racialising them as incompletely racialised—that is, as purely religious—subjects. Within the terms of this racism, then, representations of the 'moderate' do not necessarily signal the suspension of racism, but are, rather, often signs of its successful re-emergence. This mode of racism closely relates to the imperial racism outlined by Hardt and Negri (2000, pp. 190–194), as a racism that appears not to be based on race, which centres on the integration of racialised others and 'rests on the play of differences and the management of micro-conflictualities', rather than the clear boundaries of modern, disciplinary racism. This conception of racism is derived from that of Deleuze and Guattari:

European racism as the white man's claim has never operated by exclusion, or by the designation of someone as Other: it is instead in primitive societies that the danger is grasped as an 'other'. Racism operates by the determination of degrees of deviance in relation to the White-Man face, which endeavours to integrate nonconforming traits into increasingly eccentric and backward waves, sometimes tolerating them at given places under given conditions, in a given ghetto, sometimes erasing them from the wall, which never abides alterity (it's a Jew, it's an Arab, it's a Negro, it's a lunatic...). From the viewpoint of racism, there is no exterior, there are no people on the outside. There are only people who should be like us and whose crime it is not to be. [...] Racism never detects the particles of the other; it propagates waves of sameness until those who resist identification have been wiped out (or those who only allow themselves to be identified at a given degree of divergence) (Deleuze and Guattari, 2004, pp. 197–198).

This definition of the racism of control perfectly encapsulates the logics of Islamophobia, which is the archetypal form and mode of control racism.

Legitimacy, Moderacy, Sovereignty

Dominant modes of speaking about Muslims increasingly refer to differentiation; both articulations of Muslim identities and Islamophobia in their different ways burst through the disciplinary boundaries of modern racism's seemingly perfect, binary logics and institutions. Meeting these analytical challenges involves reconsidering the association between 'race' and control. But the usefulness of notions such as 'moderate' and 'extremist' lies in their relative nature, which makes them useful in a continual, modulating play of subjectification (since they have no fixed meaning). Yet this is also their chief weakness, leaving them unable to produce stable, unambiguous meanings. In practice this means that while it is relatively straightforward to signify (or re-signify) a particular individual as 'extremist' or 'moderate', the exercise appears largely rhetorical—as is illustrated by the debates over al-Qaradawi noted earlier.

The difficulties of unpicking 'moderacy' are heightened since it is one among an extensive, shambolic, array of vaguely defined floating signifiers and essentially contested concepts (Jackson, 2006). The number, and the contested nature of these pose the question of what it is they are ultimately reducible to. This question is important since the multiplication of markers of difference does not necessarily constitute the erosion of racism, but merely the multiplication of ways of invoking racism. Or, to phrase it slightly differently (after Sayyid, 1997), merely adding a plural suffix to an essential monolith is not the same thing as de-essentialising (rather, this logic produces multiple, syncretic, iterations of the originatory essential monolith). The surface inscription of 'types' of Muslim subjects does not in itself support the claim that the terms of racism have been breached, for this superficially 'positive' move is another way of coding race and the logic of reducing Muslims to 'types' (benign or not) is a racial project. For instance, as Elia (2006, p. 158) notes, the way in which Muslim women have been represented as 'harmless and redeemable' since 9/11 simultaneously represents Muslim men as 'perennial enemies never to be trusted', while invoking the racially gendered trope of Muslim women as lacking in agency (see also Steans, 2008). What superficially appears as a positive representation of Muslim women has often been problematic; this kind of deployment of 'moderate' is not necessarily fixed by particular qualities innate to any particular actors, but rather it is anchored by race and gender.

Some, therefore, have approached the question of what it is representations of the moderate are ultimately reducible to by acknowledging racism's construction of 'good' and 'bad' types. There is, for instance, an increasing focus in the literature on the reducibility of representations of Muslims to a 'good'/'bad' Muslims binary.[1] This recognises that the increasingly differentiated representation of Muslims does not mark a rejection of racism but an alternate mode of racialisation, and acknowledges the normativity of reducing Muslims to ideal 'types'. However, although the UK government has sponsored and supported a range of Muslim groups, it has neither taken to describing them as 'good Muslims' nor begun speaking of extremists as 'bad' ones. Even a group such as *al-Muhajiroun*, which was banned on account of its lengthy, and rather vile track record of involvement in hate crimes and its vociferous expression of unsavoury views about terrorism, was not described as 'bad'. 'Good' and 'bad' are not directly used because, while governance entails the formation of subjectivities based around ideal types, it does not entail broadly validating particular subjects as 'good'. To argue otherwise misunderstands bio-politics, which is centrally concerned with normative questions of becoming. To validate a subject as having 'become' (in this case, become 'good') would obviate governance. 'Good' does not account for the representation of moderates, while 'bad' understates how extremists are represented.

But this analysis does suggest that the good/bad binary exists in tension with other labels, by noting that it sets the threshold for distinguishing between 'genuine' Islam from 'extremist' Islam (Mamdani, 2002, p. 767). This reflects the government's emphasis on distinguishing between 'true Islam' and the 'new

---

[1] For a US perspective see, for example, Mamdani (2002; 2004); for a British focus on Muslim religious leaders see Birt (2006).

and deadly virus' of the 'extremist' 'perversions' of Islam (see, for instance, Lyon, 2005, p. 80; Jackson, 2006). Emerging from this has been the single distinction that underpins all contemporary representations of Muslims: that between legitimate and illegitimate (as Spalek and Imtoual, 2007, p. 186 note). Categorising Muslims as il/legitimate is not merely an exercise in weeding out groups such as *al-Muhajiroun* or the terrorists and their supporters. This is in part because those ends are in any event met through terrorism legislation, which means that the differentiation of Muslims into moderates and extremists—the soft expression of il/legitimacy—is not per se a way of dealing with those who are breaking the law (the terrorists), but a means of classifying Muslims generally. Moreover, as noted earlier, extremism has often been signified in relation not to criminality but to rights-based campaigns and the extent to which multiculturalism stands polemically charged with benefiting Muslims and eroding national unity.

The distinction between moderate and extremist is, therefore, a question of how one captures the huge diversity of Muslim subjectivities and fixes them into an increasingly complex array of stratified, and often indeterminate types, which tend to be deployed as a way of marking degrees of Muslim difference. Many of these superficially appear benign but all play bio-political roles. These are cemented through their reducibility to either 'legitimate' or 'illegitimate', and by their consequent service in the exercise of sovereign power. To understand this, we need not only to acknowledge the intimate relationship between governance and racism but also to refine our conception of racism—or, more accurately, bio-racism. Noting the writing of racism into the structures and machinery of modern state power, Terranova (2007, p. 135) suggests that racism selects those who can live or die, and therefore deals with a basic bio-political question that emerges from 'the relation of war'. This places racism as central to the very structure of sovereignty, where 'the sovereign sphere is the sphere in which it is permitted to kill without committing homicide and without celebrating a sacrifice' (Agamben, 1998, p. 83). But if this point forms the crucial link between sovereignty, the regulation of life, and Islamophobia, it runs counter to Hardt and Negri's formulation of imperial racism from which I have drawn in this chapter. This is because Hardt and Negri's definition of empire is based on the assumption that sovereignty has changed and is no longer concerned with the 'useless domination' they associate with Schmittian analyses (Negri, 2003, p. 58). This reading is problematic, however, since it ignores that absolute power is exercised. Even ignoring the high-profile instances such as the case of de Menezes or the Forest Gate shooting, Sivanandan (2006, pp. 2–3) sketches out an image of the daily grind of sovereign power where 'anyone whose face is not quite the right shade, who does not walk in exactly the right way, who does not wear the right clothes for the season, can be taken as a suicide bomber [...] And if you are recognisably Muslim (or just believed to be Muslim), you will be subjected to official stops and searches by the police and to unofficial racial attacks and harassment in the community' (Sivanandan, 2006, pp. 2–3). Race is grounded in accounts of the ways in which Muslims are often represented as an existential enemy within (for instance, Murray, N., 2004; Morlino, 2004), while Dillon and Reid (2001, p. 42) remind us that 'global bio-politics operates as a strategic game in which the principle of war is assimilated into the very weft and warp of the socio-economic and cultural networks of bio-political relations'.

Negri (2003, p. 57) further objects that Agamben views the ban as central to sovereignty and the state of exception. But the classification of Muslims as legitimate or illegitimate closely follows the structure of the ban and marks this as a sovereign sphere thanks to its role in maintaining the state of exception. To Agamben (1998, p. 18), the structure of sovereignty is defined by the inclusion of the outside through banning, and by the 'suspension of the juridical order's validity'. Thus, 'he who has been banned is not, in fact, simply set outside the law and made indifferent to it but rather abandoned by it, that is, exposed and threatened on the threshold in which life and law, outside and inside, become indistinguishable. It is literally not possible to say whether the one who has been banned is outside or inside the juridical order' (Agamben, 1998, pp. 28–29). The inscription of legitimacy maintains this indeterminacy, occurring outside the scope of juridical process, but implying legality. Representation of the 'moderate' as 'legitimate'—and the related representation of others as 'illegitimate' that completes the unity of this act—implies a binding over of 'moderate' and 'extremist' to an alternative, religious, juridical order, particularly since this increasingly mimics theological argument and is presented as a theological move. But while the turning over of the subjects to this order demonstrates the sovereign power to deliver the banned 'over to its own separateness' (Agamben, 1998, p. 110), that this juridical order carries no legal weight within the UK underlines the indeterminacy. If the banned figure is 'not, in fact, simply set outside the law and made indifferent to it but rather abandoned by it' (Agamben, 1998, p. 28), then the subject deemed 'legitimate' under these terms is as much abandoned by the law as the subject designated 'illegitimate'. These subjects find themselves in a position analogous to that of the banned, 'consigned to the mercy of the one who abandons it—at once excluded and included, removed and at the same time captured' (Agamben, 1998, p. 110).

If the state of exception as suspension of the stable juridical order is increasingly paradigmatic of government (Agamben, 2005, p. 2), then it is bound up in the crises facing disciplinary institutions both as the underpinning logic of the camp and, as such, on account of the increasingly normalised role of the logic of the camp, generalised throughout society. The power to suspend the law is a sovereign power, and thus the state of exception is closely connected to sovereignty. The current context represents a continual state of exception, as a consequence of the extension of sovereign power and the increasing difficulty of distinguishing between rule and exception during the War (see also Thoburn, 2007). Agamben (2005, p. 3) cites the USA Patriot Act (2001) as an example of the paradigmatic nature of the exception, which produces 'a legally unnameable and unclassifiable being'. The logic of 'moderate' as 'legitimate' may work differently, but its central indeterminacy ensures that this marking suspends the 'moderate' subject in a state in which classification breaks down; the categories themselves lack weight and, given the continued lack of legal recognition of Islamophobia as racism on the one hand and the ongoing War on the other, their main function is to fill the void left by the lack of a legal classification, status or name for these subjects. 'Being outside, and yet belonging' is, writes Agamben (2005, p. 35) 'the topological structure of the state of exception', and this is the definitive status of the 'moderate' as 'legitimate' subject.

If the figure of *homo sacer* is a threshold at the suspension of law and creation of sovereignty (Agamben, 1998, p. 27), then s/he has come to be central to modern racism. As Agamben (1998, p. 32) notes, modern states increasingly focused on 'natural life, discriminating within it between a so-to-speak authentic life and a life lacking every political value' ['bare life'] in response to the crisis which, by the end of the First World War, had severed the founding link between birth and nation. The production of bare life is thus tied to sovereignty and closely related to questions around 'race'. Attempts to draw this bare life into politics at the same time can expose it to new forms of bio-politics (Clough, 2003, p. 361). Thus, the racism we can term Islamophobia occurs both as a response to the emergence of new forms of Muslim agency in self-identifying by rejecting the natural order of disciplinary race, and through the paradox of exclusion as incorporation and inclusion. The changing forms of bio-politics are underscored by the shifts from discipline to control (which do not occur in a vacuum, but intersect with postcoloniality and globalisation). Written through them are changing notions of 'race' in which distance from the white male same rather than hard modes of alterity dominates, articulated around increasingly stratified racialised populations, often cut through with variegation and de-differentiated in a way that implies de-essentialisation (though only if one remains rooted in a modernist, disciplinary conception of 'race'). Islamophobia therefore comes to be the defining form, and mode, of control racism. Of course, the work of the disciplinary institutions continues, and disciplinary conceptions of 'race' circulate, intersect with, and often inflect contemporary control racisms; bio-politics is the logic that encompasses both discipline and control. But there is a dual logic at work here that we can no longer ignore, and one that presses us to rethink questions about 'race' and the regulation of life.

To think through Islamophobia, as the title of this collection encourages us to do, involves meeting a number of conceptual and empirical challenges concerning the nature of Islamophobia. I would like to suggest, then, that the problem of dealing with anti-Muslim racism is not a difficulty of categories—whether 'racial' or 'religious'; 'extremist' or 'moderate'—but rather a tension within the underlying logics of racialised classification. The case of Islamophobia reveals to us, *par excellence*, the forms of control racism that have emerged, and in so doing points to a racism that can make do without race; a governance that no longer relies on enclosure within traditional disciplinary institutions but thrives in exteriority from them; a mode of racialisation in which the seemingly perfect binaries we might expect of modern racism are in fact markers of degrees of difference (rather than hard alterity). It is unsurprising that Islamophobia has proven difficult for policy makers and academics to define or counter. But perhaps the most striking feature of contemporary Islamophobia is this: despite the difficulties of defining anti-Muslim racism, most people who describe themselves as Muslim appear to know what it is, notwithstanding the ways in which Muslims can be represented as being 'closer' to a white male ideal. This is because if they recognise the racism of casting subjects out on the grounds of their radical alterity (as stereotyped extremists), they also understand that it is racist to incorporate subjects because 'they are just like us'. It is increasingly the case that our focus on exceptionalised forms of racism (e.g. the far right; institutional racism etc.) obscures the daily grind of racialised governance that orders these and links them to the most mundane instances. Recognition of the nuanced nature of contemporary anti-Muslim racism problematises the cynical reason of this neo-Liberal racism since its challenges lie not in the easily exceptionalised cases, such as the crude representations of Muslim beasts, but, rather, in its subtleties.

11

SEXUALISING THE 'WAR ON TERROR'

Adi Kuntsman, Jin Haritaworn and Jennifer Petzen

Gender and sexuality are often overlooked as moral underpinnings in the 'War on Terror' and the backlash against multiculturalism. Yet, both gendered and sexualised as well as feminist and gay images and ideas are closely intertwined with the contemporary currency of Islamophobic discourses.

From the de-veiling of Afghani women or migrant Muslim women in Europe (Moors, this volume), to the Orientalising of domestic violence as 'honour crimes', from the hyper-visibility of sexual transgression in Abu Ghraib, to the 'sexiness' of the warfare itself, gendered images of Orientalism are spectacularly globalised and proliferated. At the same time, they are mobilised differently in diverse local and national settings. Alongside 'security' and 'democracy', women's and gay rights have functioned as key legitimating factors for the racism and imperialism we are currently witnessing. But this is hardly a new phenomenon: notions of 'progress' and 'liberation' have long been used to justify colonial enterprises and constitute ideas of Western superiority.

The challenge, then, is twofold: to identify what, if anything, is unique or distinctive about the current mobilisation of Islamophobia, and to do so as an issue of political urgency while also fully attentive to the import of its histories, and to account for the globalisation of gay and lesbian Islamophobia while remaining attuned to its local geo-political figurations.

In Britain and Germany, gay activists have drawn on existing notions of 'Muslim sexism' in order to mainstream a new discourse on 'Muslim homophobia.' (Haritaworn, 2008; Haritaworn et al., 2008; Petzen, 2005). In both countries, the enfranchisement of a (certain) gay subject has coincided with the disenfranchisement of the racial/religious 'Other'. As national 'traditions' and 'core values' are re-invented as pro-gay and pro-feminist, individual gay leaders are invited onto the political mainstream political stage as mediators and consultants.

Gay and lesbian activists in Germany, for example, have inserted themselves into the debates on Muslim 'honour crimes'. By describing these crimes as an outcome of perverted Islamic gender relations, a Muslim migrant masculine subject is simultaneously produced, condemned and held responsible for posing a violent threat to European culture and values. Sexual and gender equality is suddenly claimed by gay and lesbian activists to be the mainstays of European civilisation: the natural outcome of the Enlightenment and its role in shaping a modern European identity. These same activists now want to claim a leadership role in the taming and integration of 'migrant queers' into European gaydom.

Gay and lesbian activists are reflecting the broader, entrenched racist rhetoric in debates on integration. This rhetoric creates an essential Muslim masculine 'Other' in order to highlight European gays' and lesbians' commensurability with white, bourgeois heterosexual normativity. As white European gays and lesbians 'move up the ladder', they are able to become more politically influential, as long as they buy in to the neo-liberal politics of the European project. To stay politically viable, they have chosen to stand behind the rhetoric of European Civilisation—a relic that has somehow withstood sixty years of post-war soul-searching in Germany. In the post 9/11 age of War on Terror, these activists suddenly find themselves in profitable political position when compared to the gender terror of Islamic fundamentalists.

In Israel, one can find similar links between GLBT (Gay Lesbian Bisexual Transgender) rights discourse and notions of 'Progress', 'Civilisation' and 'Democracy'. These became particularly apparent in the debates about Pride Parades in Jerusalem, first as a national event and later as a home for World Pride. In these debates the Israeli Occupation and Palestinian national struggle were simultaneously co-opted into the rhetoric (which used universal terms of respect and tolerance among all groups, nations and colours), and eliminated altogether, because gay and lesbian visibility were constituted as a sign of political superiority, recycling Zionist colonial discourse of Israel as 'the only democracy in the Middle East'.

Orientalism has long been used to constitute Israeli colonial nationhood as European, by defining its internal 'Other'—the *Mizrachi* (Oriental, Heb) Jew and its enemy—the Arab. These colonial figurations have a profound effect on past and contemporary queer imagery. In early Zionist cinema, for example, Jewish settlement was often imagined through sexual encounters of masculine Jewish colonisers with homo-passive, feminised Arab men (Yosef, 2002). Militarising the national self and 'homo-sexing' the enemy received a new twist during gay claims of citizenship in the 1990s, when Israeli gay men envisioned the Israeli Defence Forces as a site where they could prove their national belonging through military violence. 'Let's prove that we, too, can serve in *Golani* [elite infantry/combat unit] and shoot Arabs between the eyes', suggested the author of an essay in the nation-wide free distribution GLBT newspaper (Kener, cited in Kadish, 2001, p. 17). The participation of gay men in violent military acts towards Palestinians was proudly represented as proof of their national loyalty. 'Shooting Arabs between the eyes' held a promise of national masculinity unthreatened by effeminacy; at the same time it figured as a guarantee of gay men's citizenship.

These new formations of gay citizenship were excitedly embraced by many queer 'repatriates', who arrived in Israel from the former Soviet Union since the early 1990s, welcomed by the Israeli 'Law of Return' which grants citizenship to all Jews and their families. Some of them have explicitly adored the image of the Israeli soldier precisely for the military violence he embodies. Such adoration came hand in hand with Orientalising Palestinians as both inherently passionate objects of queer sexual fantasies, and as repressed, homophobic and outside of Western, 'modern' gay and lesbian 'subjecthood' (Kuntsman, 2008a; 2008b). Many representations of Palestinians as simultaneously dangerous and inferior at times conflated race and religion, but often were explicitly Islamophobic (for example, by suggesting that it is only the Muslim Arabs that are terrorists, but the Christians 'are OK').

This immigrant's embrace—and queering—of Israeli militant nationalism, Haritaworn (2008) coins 'loyal repetition to the nation'. In Britain, homosexuals were traditionally banned from the army. This ban harked back to sexologist understandings of homosexuality as effeminacy or 'inversion', as well as a moral threat to 'normal' masculinity. In gay culture, this exclusion from masculinity has been reworked through ironic performances of military masculinity. This tradition of performing military hyper-masculinity in a context of criminalised, pathologised and feminised male homosexuality can be theorised as mimicry and a subversive performance. But this context changed radically in 2001, at least in Britain. The lifting of the ban on homosexuality in the army coincided with the wars on Afghanistan and Iraq. *Pink Paper*, the biggest free paper catering to the gay community, celebrated this reform as a dual human rights victory. At home, gays gained inclusion into a homophobic institution; abroad, 'we' were liberating gay people in the countries under attack. Colonialism, once described by Gayatri Spivak (1988) as 'white men saving brown women from brown men' is rewritten, in this moment of gay assimilation, as 'white (straight and gay) men saving brown women (and gays) from brown men'.

War and colonialism, as the analysis of both the British and Russian-Israeli contexts suggested, are central to struggles for gay citizenship, constituting militarism and racism as invaluable capital in both the national and global economy of Western superiority and the War on Terror. For white gays in Britain the 'War on Terror' becomes an entry ticket into new political subjecthood, formed in the globalised war with the Orient. For Jewish immigrants in Israel, Orientalism functions as a way of negotiating their place in local hierarchies of ethnicity and class, and eventually becomes a way of national belonging through violence. Gay and lesbian politics in Germany, similarly, shows how colonial ideas of race and the civilising mission are still viable discourses that legitimate positions of power.

For white gays in Britain the War on Terror became an entry ticket into new political 'subjecthood', formed in the globalised war with the Orient. For Jewish immigrants to Israel, Orientalism functions as a way of negotiating their place in local hierarchies of ethnicity and class, and eventually becomes a way of national belonging through violence. Gay and lesbian politics in Germany, similarly, shows how colonial ideas of race and the civilising mission are still viable discourses that legitimate positions of power.

Joseph Massad (2007) shows that sexual imperialism has become globalised through the growth of an 'international' (i.e. Northern) lesbian, gay, bisexual and transgendered human rights movement, which targets Southern, especially Muslim countries. Adopting a Saidian frame, Massad argues that 'the Orient'— both the old, homophile one, and the new, homophobic one—has long been an object of fascination for white gays, which continues to inform their investments in it.

Theoretically, we have a wealth of postcolonial feminist writings at our disposal to make sense of these developments; for example, authors, such as Chandra Talpade Mohanty (1991) or Meyda Yeğenoğlu (1998) have focused on the complicity of Western feminism within colonial knowledge and politics. Queer studies have been slower to pick up on this, with Judith Butler commenting on some of them in 2007. Jasbir Puar (2007) in her book, *Terrorist*

Assemblages, has gone furthest in explaining the convergence of the war and sexual citizenship by proposing the concept of 'sexual exceptionalism': the ideology of the West as the pinnacle of gendered progress, which justifies the state of exception. When looking at the simultaneous expansion of liberal gay politics and its complicity within the US War on Terror, Puar calls our attention to the 'differences between queer subjects who are being folded (back) into life and the racialised queerness that emerge through the naming of populations', often those marked for death. Puar notes an important political shift from queers as those left to die (through HIV/AIDs or denial of reproduction and parenting), to queers that reproduce life, and asks: 'Which queers are folded into life? How do they give life? To what do they give life? How is life weighted, disciplined into 'subjecthood', narrated into population, and fostered for living?' (Puar, 2007, p. 36).

Puar's analysis is predominantly focused on the US context (although her book also offers important insights on both the UK and Israel), and her notion of sexual exceptionalism (Puar, 2005; 2007) is arguably less central to European self-identities. Nevertheless, colonialism from the start had a sexual script, which has travelled intertextually across different parts of 'the West'. Despite striking—and disturbing—similarities, we are not arguing for a universal queer Orientalism, of which particular national formations are only a variation. Rather, we propose that there is a need for a careful and detailed examination of queer complicities in the globalised formations of the War on Terror, complicities that have simultaneously national and globalised effect. We call for scholarly attention to the ways local gay and lesbian politics become 'Westernised', 'Europeanised' and globalised precisely through Islamophobia, Orientalism and war, but also to the ways such transnational formations can open a way to anti-racist coalitions across borders.

12

GOVERNING MUSLIMS AFTER 9/11

Yahya Birt

In contemporary times, it is arguable that Islamophobia has been manifested primarily as the fear of Muslim political agency; in fact, the term comes into use (at least in English) with the ending of the Cold War, religious revival in the Muslim world, and Muslim political mobilisation in Europe. But what precisely is 'feared' in Muslim political agency? It is primarily a fear of reversal: Muslim political agency is feared because it is imaginatively linked with Europe's own pre-modern Christianity and its history of violent sectarianism, the Crusades and the Inquisition (Werbner, 2005). Muslim political agency, or Islamism—simply put, is the engagement of Muslims with modern politics, mobilising Islamic discourses, symbols and practices—and contains many possibilities within itself, but it is construed largely as retrogressive and atavistic, as a vicious combination of the pre-modern religion and modern totalitarian politics. For the Islamophobe, Islamism's victory would be the reversal of the European story of Progress, Reformation and Enlightenment, a winding back of the clock, and the loss of hard-fought freedoms from religious tyranny. In fact, opposition to Islamism has become the litmus test for authentic liberalism and 'Europeanness' (Kundnani, 2008a). More broadly, Islamophobia also encapsulates the fear of Muslim agency in terms of the display of religious symbols and the public expression of Islamic values, things that might not normally be construed as political in a conventional sense, but which nonetheless have become heavily politicised. Similarly claims once made for public recognition of Islam under the logic of European multiculturalism have been reclassified as tendentious and divisive within a national setting (Modood, 2008a; Parekh, 2008, pp. 99–129). Bhikhu Parekh summarises the main liberal objections to Muslim identity politics well: it is undemocratic in spirit, democratic institutions are not properly respected, loyalty to the *ummah* (the Muslim 'supernation') takes precedence over that owed to the nation, and it is illiberal and collectivist, opposing freedom of expression, secularism, critical thought, personal autonomy and individual choice, and dismissive of gay and other minority rights while asserting its own (Parekh, 2008, p. 103).

If this reaction constitutes the substance of the 'moral panic' about Muslims in Europe, the question arises: how is perceived potential reversal to be contained and combated? Certainly the years after 9/11 have provided a myriad of measures to govern Muslims, yet Muslim scare stories in our twenty-four hour global media news culture are so relentless and pervasive and the scope and variety of various state policies so various and wide-ranging that mapping them, and thereby making some sense of them, constitutes a genuine challenge. It is the contention of this chapter that the application of governmentality theory provides some illumination with regard to the contemporary rhetoric and practises of Islamophobia.

In his discussion of governmentality, or 'the conduct of conduct', the techniques of state governance that direct behaviour, Michel Foucault (1991, p. 102) identifies the following repertoire that emerged in his analysis of Europe between the sixteenth and the eighteenth centuries:

(i) *sovereignty*: 'a discontinuous exercise of power through display and spectacle, law as command, sanctions as negative and deductive', applied to 'the thin moral subject of habits...'
(ii) *discipline*: 'the continuous exercise of power through surveillance, individualisation and normalisation', applied to the individuated normal subject of constitution, character and condition (or the social subject of solidarity or of alienation and anomie);
(iii) *governmentality*: 'maximising the forces of the population collectively and individually', applied to the autonomous 'deep' subject of choice and self-identity or to the citizen subject of rights and obligations in regimes of social welfare and social insurance.

These modes could either be applied to the individual body ('discipline') or to collectivities ('bio-politics') (Rose, 1999, pp. 23, 45–46). Subsequently a new field of governmentality studies has emerged that has applied Foucault's insights to fields like the use of statistics, political economy, the professions, psychoanalysis and the 'policing' of family life, and consumerism (Miller and Rose, 2008).

The recent work of Giorgio Agamben has strengthened the point that the repertoire of governmentality remains operative; in particular, he has stressed the continued presence of sovereign power in modern democratic and non-democratic nation-states, whereby constitutional restraints on executive power are suspended with regard to a class of persons stripped of all legal rights (*homo sacer*) under a 'state of exception'. In this regard he makes a recent example of detainees in Guantanamo who had no legal status either as criminals or Prisoners of War to whom the Fourth Geneva Convention did not apply (Agamben, 1998; 2005, p. 3). Agamben (2005, pp. 86–88) differs from Foucault (1991, p. 101) in that he does not think that sovereignty can be disciplined by law, and so 'bio-politics' is truly defined by 'the state of exception' or violence and coercion rather than by law and rights.

These three modes of governmentality—sovereignty, discipline and governmentality—have been applied to Muslims within and beyond 'the West'. Historically, the liberal state was not solely concerned with the individual but with the promotion of empire and free trade; in the post-colonial setting, and its artificial forms of closure between the colonial past and mass migration to the metropole, racialised migrants were set within the boundaries of an assimilative process or an 'immigrant imaginary' (Hindess, 2004; Hesse and Sayyid, 2006). Forms of racialised governmentality are applied to Muslims both inside and outside the nation-state, and unpacking this is essential to the question of defining Islamophobia. One of the quandaries in so doing is to distinguish between the slippage between rhetoric and law and policy, whereby Muslims in the West were simultaneously being wooed, berated, disciplined and, at the margins, coerced while their brethren were being bombed abroad; this disjuncture coincided with the erosion of state sovereignty alongside a reformulation of global order. It has been a matter of debate as to whether this global order may be characterised as an unfinished project led by a conglomerate of core Western democratic states against authoritarian non-Western states or whether it has now transcended all nation-states to be a truly dispersed global Empire in which all conflicts have become internalised (Negri, 2008; Shaw, 2000).

Islamophobia is a discourse that is simultaneously assimilative and exclusionary, that attempts to domesticate Muslims within the nation-state by means of the contrast between 'good' and 'bad' Muslims (Mamdani, 2004). If this process of stigmatisation by distinction arguably places Islamophobia as part of a post-colonial national project, it may usefully be contrasted with *neo-Orientalism*, with its distancing metaphors of spatial segregation, echoing an earlier age of imperialism. A neo-Orientalism, which—with two wars in Afghanistan and Iraq, two proxy ones in Lebanon and Somalia, and a threatened attack on Iran—is now part and parcel of today's neo-imperialism in the Muslim world. After the Cold War, 'the West' led by the US has sought to expand into post-Soviet areas of influence, including much of the Muslim world, in order to stamp a uni–polar ascendancy on the globe, partly in order to outflank the emerging Asian powers, most notably China. Neo-Orientalism provides the rationale to allow for the massive reordering of what is portrayed as the anarchic non-West periphery, dealing with 'failed' or 'weak' states. Rhetoric and policy has indeed been caught in an oscillation between characterising the enemy as a global and consolidated Islamist terrorist threat that has made inroads into Western Muslim minority populations and an attempt at disaggregation to decouple global or international terrorism from local insurgencies and grievances that might be re-inscribed within a crumbling 'Westphalian' order of nation-states. How else is the huge reaction to 9/11 to be construed, in which al-Qaeda has been essentially a second-order threat and one that paled into insignificance in comparison with the mutually-assured destruction of the Cold War era?

Therefore it might be proposed that governmentality in an Islamophobic register works both nationally (and perhaps in the case of Europe, federally) and globally, using all of its three major modalities of sovereign power, discipline and governmentality. A preliminary attempt to provide a framework by which to categorise the disparate ways by which Muslims may be governed is set out in rudimentary tabular form.

While it is beyond the scope of this short chapter to discuss all these strands in detail, some indicative examples of them will be given, with a particular but not exclusive focus upon the bio-politics and discipline of Islamophobic governmentality, taking Britain as a case study. However, an overarching point about the application of governmentality theory to Islamophobia and neo-Orientalism should be spelled out here. Namely, that political control is rendered through *separation*, the aim of which is to counteract Muslim political agency in a prejudicial Islamophobic form. This separation is expressed in three ways through:

(i) *modalities* (sovereignty-discipline-governmentality) applied to Muslims respectively as terrorists/Islamists, conservatives and liberals;

(ii) *applications* (biopolitics/collectivities-discipline/individuals) applied to Muslims respectively as subjects of policy/law and rhetoric;
(iii) *domains* (nation-state-global order) applied to Muslims respectively as subjects of Islamophobic national domestication or global neo-Orientalist pacification.

Modality/ Subject	Islamophobic Governmentality (National)		Neo-Orientalist Governmentality (Global)	
	Bio-politics	Discipline	Bio-politics	Discipline
Sovereignty/thin moral subject	Anti-Terrorism Legislation/ Policing	Combating extremist ideology	War/Occupation/State of Exception	Combating extremist ideology
Discipline/ individuated subject	Reform of conservative Muslim institutions/ communities	Reform of conservative Muslim practices	Promotion of neo-colonial or client political order	Reform of conservative Muslim practices
Governmentality/citizen subject	Self-Regulating Muslim Communities	Promotion of liberal Islam	Self-governing pro-West political order	Promotion of liberal Islam

Of course no such a schema of control can ever be wholly consummated, primarily because Muslim agency in this case mainly consists of denying the process of separation of modalities, applications and domains through political and religious solidarity. The binary division into 'moderates' (liberals) and 'extremists' (Islamists/terrorists), often expressed as a ternary division with an ambiguous and intermediate category of 'conservatives', is resisted by calls for unity, allied with protest at differential *modalities* of coercion, exclusion, reform of Muslim institutions, customs and mores, and endorsement in favour of equitable and fair treatment. The slippage between rhetoric designed to garner Muslim support for policies and laws (or *applications*) directed discriminately or disproportionately at Muslims is also contested. Finally, transnational Muslim support for the anti-war movement against the invasions of Afghanistan and Iraq conflates the distinction between national and global *domains*. In fact agency rests in reintegrating and mobilising a political identity founded in Muslim solidarity and empowerment for which otherwise massive effort is being expended to either deny its very existence (there is no such thing as the Muslim community or Muslim *ummah*) or to depoliticise it. However the aim of this chapter is not to chart the dynamic between stigmatisation and agency, or between Islamophobia and Muslim identity politics, which I have explored at length elsewhere (Birt, 2009),[1] but rather to present what is a structural and therefore rather static snapshot of Islamophobia in one recent historical moment, or what might be called 'the Bush years'.

The re-emergence of a legal state of exception is a prime example of sovereign power applied discriminately to Muslims, and one that does most to confute the careful rhetoric made to distinguish between what is done 'at home' and 'abroad' in the name of democracy. This has many features, including internment without trial, the sanctioning of torture, extra-judicial kidnapping or 'rendition' and other deprivations of basic human rights. The state of exception has gone hand in hand with the racialised securitisation of Muslim communities, held to be collectively responsible for dealing with the causes and symptoms of 'Islamic terrorism' and therefore subjected to discriminatory parallel legal or extra-legal provisions. Evidence has emerged for instance of British personnel being either present or complicit in the torture of British detainees at the US military base in Guantanamo, Cuba, or in torture 'outsourced' to third-party countries like Morocco. In Guantanamo, stress techniques were used like forced standing, hooding, starvation and thirst, sleep deprivation, the 'frog crouch', the Israeli *shabeh* and extreme noise, techniques that were designated by White House lawyers as not constituting torture in 2002. These leave no visible marks but inflict excruciating muscle pain. Binyam Mohammed, a British resident, was tortured in Morocco, including the infliction of cuts to his genitals, with the complicity of the British intelligence services (BBC News, 2009). Similarly the withdrawal of habeas corpus for a dozen British residents in 2001 who were to be held for an indeterminate amount of time without charge or legal access to any evidence the state held on them has driven eight of them into mental

---

[1] It should also be noted, as alluded to in the opening paragraph, that Islamism is the search for Muslim empowerment through *all* forms of modern politics, and therefore I would reject Saba Mahmood's insinuation that a consonance between Islamic reformers and a post-Kantian liberal outlook would *ipso facto* constitute a fatal entanglement with what she describes as a long-term aim of American Empire: the production of a 'religious subject who is compatible with the rationality and exercise of liberal political rule' (Mahmood, 2006, p. 344). Rather, it is the commitment to Muslim empowerment in the broadest sense that is at issue here, and not a commitment to a particular form of hermeneutics of the text.

illness. Four of these were transferred from Belmarsh Prison to Broadmoor, the high-security psychiatric hospital, suffering from florid psychosis. Although the House of Lords overruled internment in 2005, the men concerned have remained under strict control orders and highly debilitating conditions since (Pierce, 2008 and Brittain, 2008). What of course allows such derogations from fundamental human rights to occur is not a trade-off between freedom and security as such but between 'our' security and 'their freedom': the state of exception applies to 'them' because they are not us. As securitisation is racialised, so Islamophobia is directly implicated in rendering the Muslim terrorist as *homo sacer* (Blick, Choudhury and Weir, 2007, p. 12).

An example is the application of 'discipline' to the regulation of Muslim identity politics in Europe. One influential form of Foucauldian discipline is to initiate Muslims into the concordat model, based on the historical settlements reached between the Churches and the State in European nation-states of Catholic heritage in particular. With historical precedent, this provides a formula of official recognition in exchange for the delimitation of the role of religion to civil society and its confinement to prescribed institutional pastoral roles, e.g. in prisons, hospitals and interfaith relations.

In theory at least, governments aspire to the idea that interfaith processes should play some role in redirecting Muslim politics through the lead of the Churches, not only into theology, but also to affect a separation as any true political integration of Muslims must come through party politics and not through religious lobbies. In the concordat model the state explicitly sets out the nature and parameters of the dialogue (usually an official platform) in the pursuit of the delimitation of Islamism, the corralling of conservative elements into designated civic society roles, and the promotion of liberal alternatives. Whom to talk to and why should be strictly regulated. Rather than seeking to mediate between interests, which has been a hallmark of the British approach in the past.

State-level 'dialogue' with Muslim communities should not involve mutual interaction but asymmetric discipline through four main features, according to one very frank report put together by veteran European and American politicians (Lawrence, 2007):

(i) the state sets the terms of debate;
(ii) official Islam platforms must be separated from the political process;
(iii) the accommodation of religious practices must seek their banalisation, or separation from identity politics, and not their 'recognition' if that means that it feeds into identity politics;

(iv) the selection of Muslim participants must fit in with the state's agenda, and remain 'diverse'.

Historically, the post-war British state, with the exception of an established Church of England, did not consider the promotion of interfaith or indeed official national platforms to be important or desirable in policy terms until the late 1980s. However the Church was encouraged to play a brokering role through interfaith in terms of organising the recent 'faith communities' that had begun to emerge in a more organised fashion in the eighties and early nineties, as this seemed pragmatically to be the most effective way to access communities in the poor inner cities; the Church of England had at the same time revived its interest in social mission. The whole process got much more attention after the fallout from the Satanic Verses Affair of 1988–89 (Weller, 2009), which helped to pave the way for an official form of religious multiculturalism at state level in the 1990s, through which a centralisation of local religious communities was encouraged, and that led to the formation of national umbrella bodies like the Muslim Council of Britain in 1997. The emphasis here was on the promotion of social cohesion among faiths and some public funding of inner city regeneration projects through faith organisations. Yet while the MCB was patronised between 1997–2006, it fell out of favour, mainly for its oppositional stance to the wars in Afghanistan and Iraq after 9/11 and was then seen as too 'Islamist', and the government 'rebalanced' its agenda to put counter-terrorism at the forefront in its relations with Muslim communities after 7/7. Subsequently, government has supported a plethora of liberal and Sufi groups, provided local and national funding to preferred Muslim interlocutors, and set up some advisory boards—for imams, young people and women—to promote 'unrepresented' elements amongst British Muslims (Birt, 2005; 2006b).

Imams were then of no particular interest to the British state: the process of incorporating them into prisons, hospitals and universities was largely left to Muslim communities themselves working through the brokerage and facilitation of the Church of England, a relatively minor issue given the small numbers involved. The emphasis on 'civic religion', which in nineties Britain meant a focus on multi–faith inner-city regeneration, was largely disconnected from issues of the formation of religious authority among Muslim communities.

However after the London bombings of 2005, the training of imams—along with the regulation of chief religious institutions—became seen as an important means by which to contain violent extremists and Muslim identity politics more generally. The provision of local imam training, which in many cases in mainland Europe has been given over to universities to provide (whereas in Britain the preference seems to be for the accreditation of existing seminaries) has come near the top of the agenda, and is linked explicitly with the goals of combating extremism and fostering cultural (and note, not political) integration. The imam is to provide the right sort of discipline to his young, unruly flock. The criteria for employment of foreign imams, widely seen as disconnected from young Muslims, has been made more stringent, and significant numbers of radical preachers have been banned from entering Britain (Birt, 2006b; Birt and Lewis, forthcoming).

The new counter-terrorist imperative has led the British government to overturn its secular tradition to intervene much more directly in the core religious institutions—the mosques, the supplementary Qur'an schools and the religious seminaries. Politically, the purpose of the new Mosques and Imams National Advisory Board (est. 2005) seems to be the redirection of 'Islamists' and 'conservatives' into mosque management, interfaith dialogue and tackling extremism. There is similarly a rollout of citizenship education to the supplementary schools to teach shared values. All this intense activity is a good example of institutional discipline under governmentality theory, and prejudicial inasmuch as Muslims are construed as abnormal, undisciplined and, as non-liberals, in need of disciplinary reconstitution of their character so as to be remade as true moral persons, in short, as liberals (Asad, 1993, p. 276).

Finally after 2005, there has been the political patronage and funding of a younger post-'Islamist' generation of Muslim technocrats whom, it might be surmised, would reasonably be expected over time to eventually lead in the development of liberal self-discipline of Muslim communities. Like with the transition from anti-racism to equal opportunities in Britain during the early 1980s where activists were supplanted by local government managers, the marking of the transition between Islamism and 'Britslam' is partly a question of transferable career skills, and not just of politics. This new generation is now expected not only to lead the rhetorical charge against extremism and Muslim conservatism but to imagine more liberal, more patriotic, futures as fully-realised citizen subjects.

While some legal and policy examples of bio-political coercion, institutional reform and liberal self-discipline have been outlined, more might be said of individuated 'discipline'. It is important perhaps to remark that this has been significantly gendered, between 'dangerous Muslim men' who are the exemplary subjects of sovereign power and 'imperilled Muslim women' who are to be saved from Muslim patriarchy and conservatism (Razack, 2008). These rhetorical constructions not only drive perceptions but policy and law, and mark Muslim men and women out in distinctive ways. In Britain and France, the debate about agency and choice with regard to the wearing of the headscarf and/or the face-veil has oscillated between explanations of passive oppression, delusional choice or defiant self-expression. In 2006, in Britain, British politicians started a debate about the face-veil that a few Muslim women wear; one government minister, Harriet Harman, said that she wanted to see the face-veil go from Britain, as it was a bar to integration and a denial of equal opportunities. Three years later the French President Nicholas Sarkozy proposed that the face-veil be banned, as it was not of the Republic; the French intelligence services had gone to the trouble of counting up French *niqabi*s, coming to a grand total of 367, as *Le Monde* reported in July 2009. The French approach is redolent of nineteenth-century techniques of disciplinary rule used to create the law-abiding citizen, with the assumption that new laws must be crafted to regulate behaviour to accord with French Republican norms. The British approach seeks to regulate desire with rhetoric of shared national values, rather than of rule of law, which appeals to notions of liberal self-discipline that reached their fruition in the late twentieth century in advanced capitalist societies (Miller and Rose, 2008).

Another instance of British liberal disciplining and reform of Muslim behaviour can be seen with the integration debate after 9/11. After the riots in the North of England in 2001, a new view had solidified on the left that Muslims self-segregated for reasons of cultural aversion, rather than for reasons of industrial decline, 'white flight' and institutional racism, and therefore cross-community projects were refocused on encouraging 'community cohesion' rather than addressing inequality. The political left's onus on tackling inequality had been replaced by a focus on the Right's trade-off between diversity and solidarity, which marked a more assimilative turn in that cohesion was premised more clearly on shared values, which has been allied with an attack on multiculturalism manifested as a muscular liberalism that now saw conservative and extremist Muslims as its main target (Goodhart, 2004; Kundnani, 2007b; Modood, 2008a; Parekh, 2008).

The usefulness of this schema of Islamophobia in terms of 'governmentality' theory is to redress the formal dissonances created by the effort to compartmentalise prejudicial rhetoric, policy, law and the state of exception at home and abroad, applied to individuals and collectivities from the sense of the experiencing Muslim subject for whom, at all levels—existentially, socially and politically—this has felt like a vast simultaneity, and the years of the War on

Terror have felt like a war on Islam. The contention argued here is that governmentality theory provides a useful means to discern where these separations
and exclusions take place not only in terms of rhetoric, but in terms of policy,
law and indeed the absence of law. While much remains to be done the schema
outlined here provides some clues to understanding how Muslim political
agency might work to contest the discipline and bio-politics of the post-9/11
world.

13

NEOCONSERVATIVE NARRATIVE AS GLOBALISING ISLAMOPHOBIA

Cemalettin Haşimi

The relationship between neoconservatism and Islamophobia is anything but straightforward. Neoconservatives did not invent Islamophobia, and Islam and Muslims per se have hardly been an integral part of their agenda in their history, which stretches back to at least the late 1960s.[1] Thus Lynch (2008, p. 185), for example, refrains from examining the Islamophobic stance of neo-conservatism, and Halper and Clarke (2004, p. 41) refer to 'staunch defence of Israel', harsh criticisms of detente and radical anti-communism as the defining features of early neoconservative figures. However, beginning from the late 1990s, and especially after 9/11, neoconservatism, with its powerful political investments (think-tanks, journals, websites, campaigns) and through its tremendous impact on the Bush administration (Bacevich, 2005, pp. 94–5) has become the mouthpiece of a machine that normalises Islamophobia. This transformation of neoconservatism around Islam calls for an examination of the ways in which it has inflected and intensified Islamophobia.

The interaction between Islamophobia and neoconservatives begins as a derivative of the post-Cold War quest to define the United States' mission in the New World Order. A mission which, because of 'its military supremacy,

[1] On the history of neoconservatives see Halper and Clarke, 2004 and Friedman, 2005.

THINKING THROUGH ISLAMOPHOBIA

and moral confidence' (Kristol and Kagan, 1996, p. 23), some came to see as the twenty-first century's 'white man's burden'. In this quest, questions and assumptions about the nature of Islam and the political landscape and regimes of the Middle East constitute major aspects of the narrative.

In regard of the first, this turns out to be a desire and expectation to change 'something in the religion itself' (Podhoretz, 2002, p. 27). Regime-change and the prevention of the emergence of any strong state (other than Israel) in the Middle East characterised the second (Falk, 2005, p. 21). The calls for intervention in Iraq, the priority given to Israel and the insistence on the US's 'inescapable mission to fight for the spread of democracy' had already been part of neoconservative agendas well before 9/11 (see Ledeen, in Abrahms et al., 2000, p. 36; see also Kagan, Kristol and Cohen in the same exchange, and Kristol and Kagan, 1998). The attack on US soil basically facilitated an already-ongoing process.

Alongside the invasion of Iraq and Afghanistan, the neoconservative project has been executed through the setting up of organisations aimed at fostering paranoid suspicion of the Islamicate world, the implementation of 'New American McCarthyist' tactics to instil fear and intimidation, turning Muslims into 'usual suspects', surveillance strategies, and the criminalisation of their political activities (Islam, 2006, p. 82). A new imperial structure in the making was exercised through violence (physical and symbolic) upon Muslim politico-cultural and territorial bodies. The Muslim substantiates the 'personification of the enemy civilization' which in turn legitimises military actions on Muslimistan (Miles and Brown, 2003, p. 167), and the Middle East becomes the embodiment and source of evil in the world, today named terrorism. Underpinning and legitimising it all is an Islamophobic language and a cultivated prejudice against Islam and Muslims.

One of the most crucially effective manifestations of Islamophobia in the neoconservative literature is the delegitimisation of Muslim representation. This is at its most visible in the invention of 'Islamo-fascism' as the enemy in the War on Terror. The latter, it was argued, was too vague and abstract (Pipes, 2002a, p. 22). Recourse to older and variant terms (such as 'militant Islam' or 'Wahhabis') in defining the enemy did not cease, but 'Islamo-fascism' produced an indispensible opportunity for the popularisation of the neoconservative outlook (Schwartz, 2002 and 2006a; Podhoretz, 2002; Scruton, 2006; Hitchens, 2007). It was employed several times by US president George W. Bush, particularly from 2006, and its deployment has enabled neoconservatives to configure new public events such as 'Islamo-fascism Awareness Week' orchestrated by David Horowitz (Hess, 2007). The term owes its effectiveness, not to its consistency but to its cache of familiar and ready-drawn consensual historico-political resonances of fascism.

Not least, the term enabled neoconservative literature to seemingly differentiate and demarcate between 'ordinary majority Muslims' and 'militant Islam', and reveal the 'distortion' of Islam by the 'Islamo-fascists' (Pipes, 2002a and 2006; Schwartz, 2005 and 2006a; Podhoretz, 2004; Frum and Perle, 2003). Yet, as even a cursory glance at the neoconservative texts would compel us to conclude, virtually all prominent Muslim organisations or figures are hijacked by the ghostly power of Islamo-fascism (Pollitt, 2006). Alongside the usual suspects, the figures or movements that are said to be infected, directly or indirectly, by 'Islamo-fascism' include figures such as Yusuf Islam (Cat Stevens), Tariq Ramadan, the prime minister of Turkey Tayyip Erdogan and organisations such as ISNA, CAIR, MSA or MPAC, all prominent mainstream Muslim organisations in the US and Canada (Gaffney, Jr., 2006; Schwartz, 2004, 2005 and 2006b; Pryce-Jones, 2004, p. 33). Criticism of this homogenising stance is readily countered with the historically loaded charge of appeasement by apologists and collaborators (Coulter, 2007). Real and significant differences between virtually all figures and movements are simply ignored as they are all reduced into a single, homogeneous position, which in turn legitimises a credible threat. There remains only a voiceless Muslim majority waiting to be rescued by the US. At the same time, contradiction notwithstanding, the presence of 'moderate Muslims' is reduced into a historical exception in the experience of Islam (Pipes, 2006). Popularisation of certain gestures such as 'not all Muslims are terrorist but...' (Podhoretz, 2002, p. 27), assumes an explicitly reinforcing relationship between Islam as a religion and 'terrorism' (Alam, 2006). All compounded by the neoconservative obsession with notions such as *jihad*, which essentially meant to imply that the real problem lies in Islam, not only in its representation.

Neoconservative literature appears to be characterised by a distinction, and tension, between the essence of Islam and the experience of Islam. But one in which it would appear that 'pure Islam' is an Islam without Muslim representation, and that where there is Muslim representation there lurks either an actual or a potential enemy. It is not an accident that virtually all examples of 'good Muslims' in these texts speak through neoconservative sensibilities. This, rather than any 'Muslimness', is what earns them their presence. The result of the deployment of Islamo-fascism in short, is the disqualification, when not the criminalisation, of the major forms of Muslim subjectivity and of criticism against the US.

A similar process, in more intense form, can be seen at work in the neocon-servative agenda on democratisation. The agenda enables neoconservatives to claim a moral superiority to *realism* and to assume a distinct position in the field of International Relations (Williams, 2005, p. 324; Lynch, 2008, p. 189). Democratisation, promising to 'drain' the political, cultural and structural sources of 'terrorism', becomes a constitutive aspect of neoconservative. How-ever, the relationship between democratisation and neoconservatism is more complex than this suggests.[2]

Firstly, the response toward democratisation is heavily subjected to a divi-sion of pro and anti American distinction rather than any unequivocal 'moral priority' accorded to democracy. A cynical tendency prevailed in the responses: democratisation was meant to produce pro-American positions not essentially representation of popular will. So when, on 1 March 2003, the Turkish Grand National Assembly rejected the military resolution that would have enabled the US and UK to attack Iraq from the North, despite the democratic legiti-macy of the decision, Paul Wolfowitz criticised the Turkish Army for not tak-ing 'the leadership role' (Brewin, 2005, p. 104). Similarly, Hamas's election victory met with intensification and further attempts at the de-legitimisation of Palestinian political movements. Second, the priority given to democratisa-tion is an outcome of the desire to control the potential consequences of an already-ongoing process of transformation and political impasse in the Middle East. It was the inability of the 'status quo' in the Middle East to contain the rising challenges which led neoconservatives to invest in the narrative of democratisation, not the contrary. The aim, in short, has been to employ the most efficient means to reconstruct the stability and the well being of the *status quo* in the Middle East, not democracy, which is no different from the consti-tutive logic of the previous configurations. This is quite crucial as it disrupts the moral superiority claimed by the neoconservative narrative, and reveals the moral claim as an instrumental propaganda tool. Nonetheless, the role attrib-uted to democratisation and the de-stabilisation it brought the Middle East has tremendous implications. First, it afforded a historical opportunity to employ a radically instrumentalist use of democracy in the policy of regime change. It essentially enabled neoconservatives to lay the ground to prevent

---

[2] See Lynch (2008), for the prospects of democratisation in the Middle East and its different expressions among neoconservative figures. The threat of militant Islam, though, and its relationship with Islam as a religion is a cross-cutting sensibility among virtually all neoconservatives.

the rise of any strong state in the Middle East, either through direct military action or through indirect pressure. Second, it enabled neoconservatives to claim the moral-political leadership in the process of a potential transformation in the Middle East. It seems that there is something crucial in the neoconservative instrumentalisation of democracy.

Since, according to Pipes (2005a), in the Middle East only Islamists have enough 'energy ... talent ... devotion ... and organizational skill' to win elections, an interesting entwining of the two strands of neoconservative discourse is apparent here. Just as Islam is said to have been hijacked by 'Islamo-fascists', democratisation would appear to be fated to the same course at the hands of Islamists. The first, as we saw, was resolved by an investment into an Islam without Muslim representation and the delegitimising of all major representations of Islam. The second would appear more of a conundrum, since democratisation is both supposed to be the only path to counter militant Islam yet paves the way for Islamists to hijack it (Pipes, 2005b). But the problem goes deeper than a matter of organisational skill or energy. It goes to the very question of legitimacy. Where does their legitimacy come from?

The neoconservative answer is clear: 'there is *something* in the religion itself' which legitimises militant Islam, such as the 'belief in jihad' (Podhoretz, 2002, pp. 27–28). But then all that bad stuff in the Islamicate world does not seem to be the product of distorted Islam but the consequence of translating the 'pre-modern', 'barbaric', 'offensive' and 'militaristic' nature of Islam into the modern world. Pipes (2002b, pp. 20–21) is quite clear on this point: Islamists' understanding of 'jihad' is concordant with its meaning and usage 'through fourteen centuries of Islamic history' and with the majority of contemporary Muslims. Islam, not only Muslims, suffers from the same trouble of being caught in a pre-modern and militaristic historical constant.

The resolution of this problem crystallises the neoconservative vision of and project for Islam: 'reform and modernization of Islam' (Pipes, 2002b, p. 28), 'forced injection of Western liberal values into the Middle East' (Bacevich, 2005, p. 92), 'challenging the threat *inherent* in Islam ...by changing its nature...' (Lynch, 2008, p. 196). All other moments of neoconservative investment were but stages of 'clearing the ground' for the successful realisation of this mission. Since the threat is nothing but the very real and authentic expression of Islam, the response must be to change the nature and essence of Islam. Democratisation, both as an end and as a means, emerges as a necessary process in laying the ground for the salvation of Muslims, who are waiting to be rescued from certain aspects of Islam itself. In the neoconservative outlook, in other words, there is not only historically but also contemporary compelling foundation for 'fear of Islam' both as a religion, and as a culture or tradition. Islamophobia here is not only a product of ascribing an absolute homogeneity to the whole history of Islam and Muslims but also of the way in which that continuity is deployed to explain violence in Islamicate contexts. The legacies of colonial orders, the politics of forced Westernisation, and the political economy of imperialisms are simply abstracted from the picture. What remains, as a plausible explanation, is the demonstrated tendency of Islam and its heritage to violence. The trouble with Islam is Islam.

Projecting threats and dangers onto the Islamicate world and ascribing them to the inadequate modernisation of Islam has long been part of Orientalist and colonialist discourses. Race and racism has likewise always been effective in the construction of world orders. In this sense, the neoconservative narrative is continuous with previous experiences of colonial and imperial interventions in the Islamicate world. The difference would seem to lie in the distinctive features underpinning the neoconservative narrative: the US' power and ability to order the world in a new political order formed through a complex relationship between globalisation and military technology. Nonetheless, the neoconservative narrative has also contributed distinct new inflections. Its vision and projection of Islam and the Middle East has helped shape and popularise both a language and sensibility of fear, threat and urgency, and policy recommendations, which in turn cultivate and are legitimated by those fears while seemingly uniquely addressing them. This explains how and why Islamophobia has been intensified, globalised, and comes to the fore in the reconstruction of a new global order in the last decade. It becomes a matter that pertains to the ordering of the world. Therefore, a decline in the neoconservative narrative will not necessarily mean a decline in Islamophobia. An essential 'return' from this condition would require not only the political defeat and retreat of neoconservatism, but a substantial combat against Islamophobia.

14

ASKING THE LAW QUESTIONS

AGENCY AND MUSLIM WOMEN

Samia Bano

From the standpoint of structure, conceptions of legal subjectivity (identity) act as modes of selection—of exclusion and inclusion—of the relations that inform entities. The seemingly universal legal subject is in fact a social and historical figure, whose abstract characteristics function to instantiate a political and moral order and to exclude alternative and competing voices and claims (Norrie, 2005, p. 151).

The legal regulation of migrant communities has of late received considerable scholarly attention. Issues such as forced marriages, the right to veil, anti-terrorism, the accommodation of Sharia law and the limits of religious practice in the public sphere have led to a renewed focus on Muslims living in Western societies and the relationship between law, religion and culture. The logic of such discussions, which focus on the strict separation between Western democratic values and principles of human rights versus the legal cultures of Muslim immigrant communities—which are framed as being 'neither based on Western democratic principles nor [...] sensitive to Western standards of human rights' (Banakar, 2008a, p. 73)—underpins the increased critique of multiculturalism in Western European states. In this way, discussions on multiculturalism, citizenship and the law frequently focus on questions of how the state should manage cultural and religious difference in civil and political society and whether in fact this is simply now a failed political project. Unsurprisingly the persistent presentation of Muslim communities as homogeneous and mono-cultural means that debates on the types of legal accommodation of religious difference in English law remain framed around various attempts to delineate clear cut boundaries between the public and private spaces. In the public sphere all citizens irrespective of cultural and religious difference are expected to operate as undifferentiated citizens who all embody universal notions of 'Britishness' and what it means to be British. Such views recognise the right of individuals to freely belong to, identify and express their difference as part of complex networks of families and communities in the private but with limits to such practices in the public spheres. This distinction between public/private serves as the yardstick for liberal legality and the basis upon which cultural and religious difference is deemed acceptable/unacceptable. In this way the state is able to define the limits of religious practice in the public (and permeate the private in order to protect those it deems vulnerable and justified by public policy considerations). These tensions between the public/private have of course been well documented but remain at the forefront of social and political thinking and the sphere of law and legal relations has increasingly occupied an important position in the regulation, surveillance and management of specific religious communities in British society.

In this chapter I ask how a critique of current legal developments can contribute to our conceptual understanding of Muslim women's subjectivity and agency, whether this can further our understanding of how Muslims are being framed in English law, and how this process contributes to our understanding of Islamophobia. Razack (2008, pp. 86, 125) argues that Europe has long had a legal fascination with the Muslim woman's body as a culturally different body. I draw upon this work and start from the fairly common premise that traditional notions of legal objectivity and legal neutrality simply do not exist, and that the operation and effects of law cannot be understood in isolation from the social, moral and political context in which law operates. The diversity in critical legal thinking is neither new nor exhaustive, and I draw upon these critiques to better understand how specific ideas of Muslim women are mediated through the law to produce the dialectical representation of Muslim women both as agents and victims of their communities. How does this specific version of Muslim female subjectivity contribute to our understanding of a type of Islamophobia in Britain today? Two questions posed by Banakar (2008b, p. 38) in his recent work on Muslims and the Law may be cited here by way of succinctly outlining the ground of enquiry. Firstly, 'which factors influence the interface of legal cultures, where one legal system is operating within the jurisdiction of the other, and, thus, is subject to its conception of legality and moral standards?' Second, 'to what extent is the acceptance or rejection of the legal culture of the 'other' a function of an assessment of the actual compatibility of the cultures in question, that they can or cannot coexist in the same social space, and to what extent is it the outcome of legal ideologies and transient socio-political interests?'

A Critique of Liberal Legal Ideology

Critical legal scholars point out that at its most basic, the liberal legal framework simply operates to maintain and ensure the existence of the hegemonic social and political order, consolidating the power of the state and operating as a closed and autonomous system of rules, norms and regulation (Kelman, 1987). Over the past two decades modern and postmodern critical scholarship has critiqued the positivist postulations of law challenging the three key modernist claims which underpin it: individual rationality as the single source of values; the formal or abstract universalism of the law, and the centrality and meaning of state justice. This critique informs us that the law must be understood as a specific, historical and socio-political practice which operates in a social field of complexity, fragmentation and conflict and thus law can only ever be understood as a specific form of historically constituted sociality. Furthermore and perhaps most importantly at the heart of these debates lie questions of justice, citizenship and rights.

Positivism in English law can be traced back to the nineteenth century, with scholars such as Jeremy Bentham (1996 [1798]) and John Austin (1995 [1832]) who focused on the questions of law and morality and jurisprudential questions on precisely what the law was for. As Alan Norrie (2005) points out, this period in jurisprudential thinking was based upon the need to control, maintain and stabilise bourgeois industrial society.

'Once the conditions for industrialisation had been achieved, it was more important to consolidate "what is" than to dream dangerously about what might be in an ideal world of metaphysical abstractions. What "ought to be" should be no more than a deduction based upon the facticity of what had already been achieved' (Norrie, 2005, p. 21). This shift from the moral standpoint of the individual to a positive theory of law led to the pursuit of a coherent, logical and rational legal system. But 'Law's importance is only seen in the light of a general metaphysical stance on the nature of the social and political order. Law is seen in terms of an ethical other, is always understood in the first place in terms of its *heteronomy*' (Norrie, *ibid.*).

In his seminal work, *The Concept of Law*, Hart (1994) re-established the links between law and philosophy and developed a form of legal jurisprudence in which legal concepts such as command, rule, sovereignty and sanction are analysed to better understand the ways in which law is formed and how legal relations take shape. This analysis was closely followed by Dworkin's (1986) critique in *Law's Empire*, where a positivist understanding of law—one based upon rules and procedure—was replaced by developing the idea that judges do not make law but simply determine the outcome of the cases by applying legal principles. In his work Dworkin accepts that there is substantial disagreement about what the law 'really' is, and that the production of meanings is achieved by the interaction of the interpreting subject and the object of interpretation (Davies, 2002, p. 64).

Modern and post modern theories of law share the perspective that law is 'embedded in its respective socio-cultural context, taking many different forms' (Menski, 2006, p. 103). Theories of legal pluralism critique the positivist interpretations of law and redefine the parameters of law as just one part of the existing social milieu within all societies (Griffiths, 1986 and 2002). In particular Moore's concept of the semi–autonomous social field illustrates how law is simply a part of social life and should therefore be treated as such. Menski (2006, p. 108) sums up the value of this contribution: 'Moore's seminal work shows that, in any given legal system, a variety of sub-systems exercise limited autonomy in the construction and application of socio-legal norms. An understanding of law that is narrowly focused on state law and national legal systems is therefore too rigid'. Law, therefore, emerges as a social fact which operates alongside many other social facts in any particular society.

In turn the sociological approach to the study of law stresses the autonomy of the individual and how legal specificity emerges within 'certain social relations and mediating them' (Fitzpatrick, 1992). Socio-legal scholarship in this way focuses on the social dimensions of law and this often takes place as part of law-in-action critiques with a focus on the question of justice. This approach has been subject to criticism for its focus on the Western legal polity but it does contribute to our understanding of the emergence of different legal forms specific to particular historical periods. For example, Derrida (1990, p. 41) advocates a deconstructionist critique of law, 'a critique of juridical ideology, a sedimentation of the superstructures of law that both hide and reflect the economic and political interest of the dominant forms of society'. Western law operates on the need to maintain the 'fixed legal subject' and what becomes clear, however, is the fact that this move towards a sociology of law coupled with a postmodern idea of law and legal relations has increasingly focused on questions of immigration, cultural diversity, integration and the management of ethnic difference. Legal scholars such as Prakash Shah (2005; 2006) and Werner Menski (2006) draw upon the concept of legal pluralism to re-evaluate the concept of law 'in a culturally diverse, plural society' (Shah, 2005, p. 1) and explore the relation between cultural diversity, legal pluralism and state response to conflicts generated by the settled diasporic communities and their continued practice of cultural/religious norms and values. In particular it is the family and wider kin groups that are presented as the two key sites upon which such legal conflicts are based.

For many legal scholars the underlying questions addressed by historical and socio-legal approaches focus on questions of justice and morality. In his seminal critique of Western liberal legality Norrie argues that liberal law is inherently contradictory, and that justice is a form of ethical judgment that lies outside the boundaries of positive law. For Norrie the contradictory elements of law are partly created by, and remain linked to, attempts to guide action by reference to abstract ahistorical criteria, while the institution of law remains tied up to socio-historically defined social relations. Law has to ignore and deny the relevance of its socio-historical ties, if it is to appear as an internally coherent system of rules, doctrines and decisions. That is why positivistic theories of law describe the totality of law in terms of legal rules and doctrine that are to guide the practice of law, while ignoring broader social contexts in which rules and doctrine need to be interpreted before they are transformed into legal practice. By overlooking the significance of the broader social and historical context out of which emerge not only legal practice but also institutions of law, they obscure and mystify the relationship between legal practice and the societal context of law (Norrie, 2005, pp. 28–31). To unpack this, Norrie refers to the idea of 'legal subject as a responsible agent' which is represented by such doctrines as *mens rea* and *actus reus*. He argues that liberal theory, which underpins the subjective principles of criminal law, 'affirming the need for intention, foresight, knowledge and belief concerning actions and their consequences', are highly individualistic and atomistic (Norrie, 2005, p. 53). Not even the atomised liberal understanding of human action can completely ignore society, which is why the above account of social action is restricted by recognising the need for mutual cooperation. Liberal law abstracts the agency from 'the context of social conflict and deprivation which generates crime' and excludes 'that context from the judicial gaze' (Norrie, 2005, p. 30). Instead, it provides a partial and mystified image of the individual and society that allows it to justify an individualised relationship between legal and moral judgment. This critical reassessment not only challenges the ontological premises which frame the formalist definitions of law but also explores the relation between law, religious identity and the move from individual notions of identity towards a communitarian identity. For Banakar (2008) the question of liberal legality raises critical questions regarding the accommodation of minority religious and cultural demands and the law must engage with the idea of justice and ask whether positive law is capable of delivering the form of justice that is required in a plural society.[1]

Contemporary liberal thinkers, shaping the terms of liberal values in Western societies and the postcolonial world have been able to advance a rather conservative agenda in and through liberal rights discourse not in opposition to it (Kapur, 2005, p. 19). For many of these thinkers the focus on Muslim women serves as a yardstick to consider the conflict between community rights and the rights afforded by the liberal state. As Razack (2008, p. 86) points out, 'Women's bodies have long been the ground on which national difference is constructed. When the Muslim woman's body is constituted as simply a marker of a community's place in modernity and an indicator of who belongs to national community and who does not, the pervasiveness of violence against women in the West is eclipsed. Saving Muslim women from the excesses of their society marks Western women as emancipated'. We can see that the current presentation of a cultural clash in the West is organised around the idea of the Muslim 'Other'—essentially in conflict with and disloyal to the values of liberalism and the liberal state—and, in Razack's (2008, p. 124) words, producing a form of cultural 'European superiority'.

Muslim women belong to many diverse communities and their lived experiences must therefore be understood as complex, strategic and at times contradictory (Afshar, 2005; 2007). Over the past three decades feminist theorists have grappled with the question of how to reconcile Western interpretations of sexual equality and the autonomy of women's agency with cultural and religious difference.[2] Debates have largely been focused on a clash of values scenario where liberal notions of equality, free will and choice have been deemed

[1] In Britain, church and state are firmly established which has led to vociferous debates on the privileged status of the Church of England and its dominance in the law-making process.

[2] The concept of agency is often understood in relation to concepts of the individual, the person and the self; discussion of these questions falls outside the scope of this chapter.

'progressively modern' and open to all, whereas the continued adherence of women belonging to minority communities to religious and traditional ties is presented as illiberal, backward and a barrier to the enhancement of women's rights. In these debates the law and juridical liberalism (for example, anti-discrimination legislation) serve as the starting point to enhance the rights of all women. Admittedly this dichotomous approach of Western liberalism versus traditional practice and the universal applicability of 'Western modernity' with the ideas of Enlightenment to non-Western traditions and in non-Western contexts has been the subject of intense critique. Post-colonial theorists such as Gayatri Spivak (1988) and Chandra Mohanty were among the first to challenge the historically over-generalised constructions of Muslim women as members of minority religious communities. Rooting themselves in both a post-colonial and feminist critique they challenged the epistemological roots of Western scholarship that focused on the subordinated position of women belonging to minority, ethnic and religious communities. Going against the grain of traditional Western feminism Spivak (1988, p. 25) highlights the hierarchical positions of power that Western feminists occupy and the need to critique feminist 'subject positions', the failure of which renders many arguments simply inadequate and limited.

Perspectives like these also emerge in the scholarship on agency. By framing the question of individual agency in terms of the extent to which Western democratic principles can be applied to and within those in non-Western societies (and the idea of human rights interconnected to Western liberal democracy) raises the rhetoric of a 'clash of civilisations'. A key debate in human rights literature is the conceptualisation of cultural human rights. Purkayastha (2009a, p. 290) points out that:

The notion of cultural human rights has gotten mired, almost exclusively, on debates about the hijab, honour killings, stoning rape victims (along with genital mutilation, forced marriages, and polygamy). Cultural human rights were developed to protect minority cultures from extinction in the midst of a powerful majority culture. The world's indigenous people, for instance, have sought cultural human rights protection to revive and sustain their identities. Yet most of discussions of cultural human rights do not focus on organized attempts to promote cultural extinction. Nor do many 'transnational' feminist activists who claim to speak for 'global women's rights' systematically consult with local groups that actually work on these issues.

However, providing cultural rights is not simply a matter of making provisions for multiple sets of 'personal and family' civil laws based on the idea that religions and cultures are unchanging and non-diverse. These same laws have been used by men to repress women in their communities (see Purkayastha, 2009a, p. 292).

In the UK a number of legal issues have been addressed and policy measures introduced which have a particular relevance for Muslim women. Most prominent among these have been the right to veil at school, to wear the *jilbab* at the workplace, policies against forced marriage, and debates on the introduction of Islamic law in the UK. Underpinning each of these debates is the question of consent versus social coercion and the extent to which Muslim women are able to express their autonomy and agency living within Muslim communities. For example, women's apparent consent to marriage in the face of coercive social, cultural, and structural forces has often been broadly interpreted as acquiescence to patriarchal authority, whereas agency is equated with women's declared resistance (Goddard, 2000, p. 3), often through the strategy of exit. Others have argued that the very idea of choice in the context of more overarching systems and networks of power and domination is problematic (Wilson, 2006). Inter-generational changes among British Asian communities in the UK have also been interpreted as evidence of the rational exercise of agency by young British Asian women through strategic maneuvers, and through compromise and negotiation within structural constraints (Samad and Eade, 2002).

The complexity of women's actions in different contexts can be understood in multiple ways. Wendall points to the role of structural inequalities while retaining a strong sense of respect for women's agency and responsibility to act within the constraints and possibilities presented by their context (Wendell, 1990; Chetkovich, 2004). That this agency, which has been defined as 'the socio culturally mediated capacity to act' (Ahearn, 2001, p. 112), can emerge in particular situations and places and at particular times has been noted in research that has examined the impact of education, employment, class and the perception and reality of racism on women's marriage choices (for example, Bredal, 2005). However, there has been far less exploration of how personal histories, emotions, motivations and institutional arrangements, as well as practical concerns such as access to information and perceived access to services, all have a bearing on women's agency and the language they use to talk about it. How women perceive their situation (and their choices), and thereby exercise their agency, may indeed change over time, as the configurations of the various forces that effect their decision-making change.

Furthermore, not all Muslim women seek to exercise their agency as understood by Western feminists in order to enhance Western feminist interpretations of their autonomy. Within the context of a patriarchal system, women will often act to uphold gendered norms, such as beauty culture, or adopt disciplinary bodily technologies like elective cosmetic surgery (Frank, 2006). Most feminist celebrations of women's agency are in service of the politics of emancipation, and such accounts interpret women's lack of autonomous impulses as acquiescence to patriarchal power structures, and see women's desires as informed by 'oppressive norms of femininity' (Morgan, 1991; Wolf, 1991). Waggoner examines the question of ethics in discussions of agency and draws upon the notion of 'ethical embodiment'. As he puts it: 'The idea it preserves is that a strong model of agency (as radically autonomous) is a fiction, since subjects are always formed and shaped by conditions not of their making, but there is nonetheless more to subjectivity than those conditions and their effects alone. Causal conditions are capable of giving rise to undetermined moments of self-reflection, self-interrogation, openness to the unforeseeable...' (Wagonner, 2005, p. 239) One argument that does not conceptualise agency as oppositional has been voiced in Saba Mahmood's (2006) account of the women's piety movement in the mosques of Cairo, which uncouples agency from liberatory politics. In this important study we learn how Muslim women not only engage with the mosque movements but actively create new spaces and hence create new meanings of faith, freedom and belonging. For Mahmood the imperative for all feminists is to consider the terms of these women themselves, both their understanding and relationship to God and how they are able to negotiate this. In this way she challenges traditional liberal philosophy, which emphasises individual choice as of primary value. She describes these Egyptian Muslim women's strong desires to follow socially prescribed religious conventions as 'the potentialities, "the scaffolding" [...] through which the self is realized' (Mahmood, 2006, p. 148), not the signs of their subordination as individuals. She argues that their desire to take the ideals and tools of self-reference from outside the self (in Islamic religious practice, texts, and law) challenges the usual separation of individual and society upon which liberal political thinking rests. Mahmood's analysis reinforces the critical thrust towards questioning the (modern American) distinction that underlies most liberal theory between 'the subject's real desires and obligatory social conventions' (see Abu-Lughod, 2002).

Research on the marriage practices of BrAsian Muslim women in Britain has also uncovered instances where young women have spoken about their need to uphold certain traditional norms out of a positive need to assert their belongingness within a community under siege (Bredal, 2005). In her study, Bhimji (2009) examines the ways in which British born South Asian Muslim women engage with Islam through study circles. She argues that the religious spaces within which the women participate allow them to assert various identities, as well as agency, as they collectively search to comprehend Islam. In traversing these religious spheres, women transform them from male dominated sites to spaces wherein feminine, political and cosmopolitan identities are expressed.

The practice of forced marriage has over the past decade gained national and international attention partly due to increased media coverage of high profile cases[3] but also due to the campaigning work of community and feminist activists who have demanded state protection—in all its forms—to victims of forced marriage. Over a long period of time such activists have, in the name of gender equality, organised and represented not only the experiences of victims of forced marriage but demanded state accountability in failing to tackle the problem of forced marriage. Most recently the issue of forced marriage has been addressed at a national and increasingly international level.[4] In Britain the recent murders of young women who had been killed for refusing to marry[5] has mobilised a 'multi–agency' approach to tackling the problem. Thus the connection between crimes of honour (such as forced marriage) and honour killings (murder in the name of honour) illustrates the problems in conceptualising differences between consent, coercion and force that can ultimately lead to murder.

In her work, Ahmad (2006) notes how terms such as arranged marriage and forced marriage continue to pathologise marriage practices within BrAsian Muslim communities as 'backward' and 'traditional' where the individual agency of Muslim women as active participants in the arranged marriage process is constantly questioned and challenged. She points out that the term 'Arranged marriages' is 'commonly abstracted as a metaphor for BrAsian life-styles' (Ahmad, F., 2006, p. 273) and 'since "love marriages" [...] are often pre-

---

[3] In Britain the case of Rukhsana Naz is often cited as the catalyst for this interest. There have been a number of high profile cases most recently that of Shafilea Ahmed.

[4] In August 1999, the Home Office established a Working Group to investigate to what extent forced marriage was a problem in England and Wales and to make proposals for tackling it effectively. In its report, a forced marriage is defined as a marriage conducted without the valid consent of both parties and where duress is a factor. In January 2004 the Metropolitan Police set up a Taskforce to deal with the practice of 'Honour Crimes'.

[5] Including, Rukhsana Naz in 1999; Heshu Yones in 2003, and Shafilea Ahmed in 2007. See The Guardian (17 Mar. 2004).

sented as the polarised opposite of "arranged marriages", the underlying assumption is that the choice of one or the other is in some way reflective of cultural or religious conformity and conservatism and also symbolic of the degree of integration into, and influence of, Western lifestyles'. The portrayal of 'arranged marriages' as oppressive and traditional continues to shape discussion on forced marriages where the homogeneity of communities is presented as fixed and unchanging.

Today we have a number of legislative and policy initiatives which seek to eradicate its practice. At the heart of these policy and legal initiatives lies the experience of women as victims of forced marriage—within the wider framework of dealing with violence against women. It is interesting to note that strategies to challenge forced marriages also include initiatives designed to explore the psychological motivations of the offender's behaviour and to understand the complex ways in which forced marriage manifests in the family, home and community and to understand its relationship to cultural practice and religious ideology (in this case principally Islam). Yet the wider debates on conceptualising a generic definition of a forced marriage and its articulation within different communities has proved both contentious and problematic. Perhaps more importantly the culturalist approach adopted by the state has led many to argue that the debate on forced marriage stigmatises Islam and Muslim communities as key perpetrators of forced marriages, which reinforces the logic that there is an irreconcilable clash between Islam and the West. For Muslim diasporic communities living in the West such understandings are not without consequence, particularly as they both confirm and draw upon culturalist and securitarian Islamophobic discourses which question their loyalty to the state and the failure of Muslims to integrate within Western democratic societies, while seamlessly mapping onto debates on immigration and border controls. Compounding it, is the growing literature on the experiences of Muslim women as victims of forced marriage and Razack (2004, p. 107) describes the 'hyper-visibility of the Muslim women's body' that have led to the extraordinary measures of stigmatisation, surveillance and control.

The Marriage Act 1949 and the Matrimonial Causes Act 1973 govern the law on marriage in England and Wales. The minimum age at which a person is able to consent to a marriage is sixteen years old; a person under the age of eighteen may not marry without parental consent. Marriages conducted abroad in accordance with the proper formalities required by that country's laws are generally recognised in England and Wales, provided both parties have the legal capacity to marry. Section 12c of the Matrimonial Causes Act 1973 states that a marriage shall be voidable if 'either party to the marriage did not validly consent to it, whether in consequence or duress, mistake, unsoundness of mind or otherwise' (see Herring, 2009).

There have been a number of UK initiatives on forced marriage. In 1999 a working group on forced marriage was set up by the home secretary to investigate the extent to which forced marriage was practiced in England and Wales. In the same year the Community Liaison Unit was set up by the Foreign and Commonwealth Office (FCO) which was given responsibility of dealing with the international dimension of forced marriages (see below). In 2000 the working group published the report *A Choice by Right*, and this report focused on clarifying the arranged/forced marriage distinction and providing clear guidelines to public bodies such as the police, schools and social services as to what can be deemed a forced marriage. In 2002, police guidelines were issued by the Association of Chief Police Officers to better equip members of the Police force in dealing with forced marriage (Phillips and Dustin, 2004, p. 535).

Most recently the introduction of the Forced Marriage (Civil Remedies) Protection Act 2007 was passed to provide specifically for people at risk of being forced into marriage. The Act enables the court to make 'forced marriage protection orders' to protect the individual being forced into marriage. In deciding whether to make an order, the court must have regard to 'all the circumstances including the need to secure the health, safety and well-being, the court is to have regard to his or her wishes and feelings (so far as reasonably ascertainable) and giving them such weight as the court considers appropriate given his or her age and understanding' (Herring, 2009, p. 66).

In their work Anitha and Gill (2009) note that case law on forced marriage reveals that agency continues to be framed in terms of the individual's ability to choose freely and it is this issue of consent that is used to differentiate between forced and arranged marriages. By considering the social and cultural construction of personhood, and especially womanhood, among BrAsian communities, she argues that a considerably less clear-cut and far from dichotomous perspective on consent and coercion emerges. She points out that consent and coercion in a marriage can be better understood as two ends of a continuum (arranged and forced marriage) between which lie degrees of cultural and social expectation, control, persuasion, pressure, threat and force. Within these constraints, BrAsian women exercise their agency in complex and contradictory ways, which are not always recognised by the existing exit-centred state initiatives on this problem.

The cases of *Mahmood v Mahmood* 1993, *Mahmud v Mahmud* 1994, and *Sohrab v Khan* 2002 have involved acceptance by the courts that emotional pressure can take a variety of forms, from being made to feel responsible for bringing about a loved one's death to threats of suicide made by the coercer. Anitha and Gill (2009, p. 67) point out that:

judgements indicate some engagement with the cultural contexts within which emotional pressure or threats are used to coerce. However, despite the extension of the
definitional ambit of coercion to include such hazily defined 'grey areas', the notion
of 'free will' remains central to the legal discourse on forced marriage in the UK,
which is underpinned by opposing the concept of self-constituting, free individuals
entering into a consensual marriage to that of a marriage contracted through coercion.
The courts have long recognized the coercive power of direct threats of force, whatever
their source, and have more recently been willing to accept that emotional pressure
can also be coercive. But in either case, the fundamental issue at stake is the individual's free will. The problem is that this pre-occupation with the concept of 'free will'
obscures the contexts in which consent is constructed and the process through which
this is done, especially in the absence of explicit threats: simply put, many coercive
forces go undetected.

Each of these initiatives focuses on the question of individual agency and the option of exit for vulnerable women being forced into marriage. Moreover, community attempts to persuade the state to adopt a dialogue-centred approach via the use of mediation services have been met with resistance from women's organisations.[6] It is argued that in practice women's attempts to rec-oncile with families can lead to undue levels of social pressure to do so in the face of a continued threat.

Yet such non-oppositional demonstrations of agency have implications for the exit-centred state response to the problem of forced marriage. The primary state response to the problem of forced marriage is the criminal justice one, which has three aspects to it: a range of civil responses to protect women who have presumably left their abusive family or are seeking to do so; to render marriages based on coercion null and void, and to punish perpetrators under a range of existing law. Women's groups have long recognised that not all women seek to leave abusive families through exit, and that an even smaller number want to initiate criminal or civil proceedings against family members

---

[6] For example, the women's organisation, Southall Black Sisters resigned from the working group on forced marriage in protest against the recommendation of media-tion to reconcile victims of forced marriage with their families.

in cases of forced marriage. However, current state response is geared towards criminal justice intervention over any other, and the recent legislation on forced marriage has not been accompanied by any additional funds for specialist domestic violence services, which face mergers and closures in the current shift in state policy towards 'community cohesion'. The right to exit is, at heart, an extension of the idea of the reasonable alternative—it suggests that women can only express their agency by fleeing from their own cultures, just as the normative white female might be expected to do. Yet, as we have seen, women may choose not to take such a course of action, which is, to many of them, often not a legitimate course of action at all. We need to give more support to those women who wish to express their subjectivity within the framework of the communities of which they perceive themselves fundamentally a part.

Women exercise their agency in complex and often-contradictory ways, as they assess the options that are open to them, weigh the costs and benefits of their actions, and seek to balance their often-competing needs with their expectations and desires. While there remains a need to recognise gendered power imbalances at the same time there also remains a need to respect women's exercise of agency.

The debate on veiling in the UK and other European countries, mirrors political and human rights debates that focus on 'women's bodies and attire to discuss how traditions impinge upon and impede modernity and freedom' (Purkayastha, 2009a, p. 288). Such discussions underpin the question of whether Muslim women are able to freely express their autonomy and agency when choosing to veil (see Moors, this volume). Most commonly, they are predicated on the idea that Muslim women have little choice but to veil, which displaces any consideration of notions of autonomy and personal decision-making when choosing to veil. Cultural human rights issues are often discussed in the context of women's human rights discussions and the *hijab* and veiling has become the symbol of enforced traditionalism (Okin, 1999). Speaking of the French context, Scott (2007, p. 17) points out that terms like Muslim, or Veil:

evokes associations of both inferiority and menace that go beyond the objective definition of the word itself: 'Muslims' are 'immigrants', foreigners who will not give up the signs of their culture and/or religion. Invariably too, the religion they are said to espouse is painted as 'fundamentalist', with incontestable claims not only on individual comportment but on the organization of the state. In this discourse the veil denotes both a religious group and a much larger population, a whole 'culture' at odds with

French norms and values. The symbolism of the veil reduces differences of ethnicity, geographic origin, and religion to a singular entity, republican France (2002, p. 57).

It is precisely the use of democratic ideals of human rights to construct the subjectivity of Muslim women who choose to veil as powerless that promotes the very idea of a clash of civilisations. Barlas (2002, p. 57) points out that the veil 'has become so overinvested with meaning that one can no longer speak of it in any simple way'; in many Western societies the Veil has become a 'Muslim cultural icon'. For some Western feminists the right of Muslim women to veil must be defended as an authentic expression of a particular culture and their 'lived experience' and their expression of agency. Such discussions immediately raise conceptual difficulties both in regard of the term 'Muslim women' and of the question of in whose name such claims are being made? As Mojab (2006, p. 345) points out, 'the notion 'Muslim women' ignores the heterogeneity of women in Islamic societies and constructs them into a universal category shaped by one particular characteristic, a common religion, Islam. The imagined Muslim woman is so unique that she cannot share anything—demands, rights, politics, ideals—with Western women'. Similarly, 'The veil has had multiple and changing meanings throughout history. One of the myths about veiling is that it is worn by the majority of Muslim women. It is often ignored, both in the West and in Iran, that most women, Muslims and non-Muslims, have never put the Islamic veil on their faces and bodies. Women, with and without the cover, lived side by side for centuries, and the clergy either failed or did not care to impose it on all women' (Mojab, 2006, p. 352).

Two recent high profile cases in the UK, both involving Islamic dress code for Muslim women and the use if the Human Rights Act 1998, best illustrate this conflict between Islamic religious practice and public space. In Begum v Denbigh High School Governors,[7] the House of Lords ruled that the exclusion of Sabina Begum for her unwillingness to comply with school uniform requirements was not in violation of Article 9 of Human Rights Act 1998. The claimant, Shabina Begum, a young Muslim woman, sought the right to wear a *jilbab* as part of her school uniform. Her insistence on wearing the *jilbab* meant that she contravened official school policy and was excluded from her local school, Denbigh High school. Claiming that the school was in breach of Article 9 of the ECHR—the right to freedom of thought, conscience and religion—she challenged the decision of her school. The majority judgment, though, found that her right had not been infringed on the basis that in the interests of social

---

[7] 1 A. C 100 (2006) UKHL 15HL.

cohesion, the school had legitimately infringed her right to wear the *jilbab*. Relying on the Grand Chamber of the Strasbourg court's judgment in *Sahin v Turkey* (2005) 19 BHRC 590, the majority recognised:

[T]he need in some situations to restrict freedom to manifest religious belief; the value of religious harmony and tolerance between opposing or competing groups and of pluralism and broadmindedness; the need for compromise and balance; the role of the state in deciding what is necessary to protect the rights and freedoms of others; the variation of practice and tradition among member states; and the permissibility in some contexts of restricting the wearing of religious dress (*Begum*, paragraph 32).

A second case, of *Azmi v Kirklees* (2007) WL 1058367, involved a Muslim woman who worked as a school teaching assistant and refused to follow an instruction not to wear a full-face veil when in class with pupils assisting a male teacher. She had been suspended and brought claims for direct and indirect religious discrimination and harassment on the ground of religion or belief. Again, the appeal was dismissed as the tribunal found no indirect discrimination and the local council's ways of achieving its aim was proportionate.

These findings have led to increased debate on questions of Islam, identity, belonging and citizenship in multicultural societies. Western commentators and legal scholars now discuss at length the limits of religious practice and belief and many query the need to accommodate and respect cultural and religious diversity in Western societies. For some the politics of multiculturalism and the recognition of cultural difference have led to a rise in the politics of cultural separatism, but for others the liberal principles of justice, equality and human rights justify the protection of all cultural and religious minority communities.

There has been much discussion in academic literature also, on this court decision and the conflict between an individual's choice of religious dress and the uniform policy of a school. In these cases, there is an explicit desire to protect social harmony and pluralism from religious extremism, which the jilbab and *niqab* have come to represent in the social imaginary. Culture, race and religion are all at play here, but the UK is seen as a defender of difference for those 'reasonable' Muslims who fit within the limits of British tolerance (Bhandar, 2009).

In her work the anthropologist Lila Abu-Lughod (2002, p. 786) illustrates the diversity of meanings, which Muslim women living in Muslim societies attach to the veil. Drawing upon her work in Bedouin societies she points out that veiling cannot be associated with a lack of agency but more importantly reflects the ways in which Muslim women are able to negotiate and strategise in their lived social realities. The thrust of her point is of immediate relevance to contemporary debates on veiling in all contexts, Islamicate or not.

The Sharia Debate in Britain

The recent controversy surrounding the comments made by the Archbishop of Canterbury on civil and religious law in England reflect the current consensus among many Western commentators that Islam and its legal principles (Sharia) threaten the very foundations upon which Western democratic societies are built. Liberal commentators were quick, for example, to point to the consequences of demands made by Muslims for the introduction of parallel legal systems into English Law. It was claimed that the consequences of this 'imposed Islamism' threatened not only the social and legal foundations of liberal legality but the very Enlightenment values—democracy, reason, equality, autonomy and individual choice—upon which Western legal systems are based. Underlying this argument was also the claim that Islamic law is unreasonable and patriarchal whereas Western law is both secular and egalitarian. Unsurprisingly perhaps these tensions were expressed via the site of gender and gender relations and the 'subordinating' effect Islam has upon Muslim women. Western women were presented as 'enlightened' and bearers of liberal legal ideals such as equality and non-discrimination; the Muslim female subject as the 'other', a victim to cultural and religious practices and thus in violation of her human rights. Law thus became the site upon which constructions of Muslims as the 'Other' took shape, where internal traditions of dissent within Islam were sidelined, and Islam deemed anathema to Western intellectual thought and reason. Islamic legal tradition and human rights are presented as incompatible, in opposition, or at best in uneasy tension.[8] Indeed the very idea of Islam and Islamic thought as embodying the principles of human rights, justice and equality, remains at odds with its presentation in much of mainstream multicultural and political theory as a culturally relativist ideology which features the impossibility of individual free will, consent and reason. In this way the current totalising of Islam is not only dangerous in its explicit Islamophobic tone but for many Muslims themselves the relationship between religious practice and law cannot be neatly fitted into the trajectories of integrated/ separated, public/private currently presented.

---

[8] This is not of course to underestimate the wealth of literature challenging such interpretations. See for example Abduallahi Na'im (1987), Ali–Sadar (2001) and Mayer (1999).

It is important to strike a note of caution concerning calls for the recognition and/or accommodation of Sharia into English law. Apart from the significant practical difficulties in giving legitimacy to Shariah Councils the narratives of Muslim women must underpin such discussions. Therefore debates regarding the accommodation of Sharia must place the experience of Muslim women—the primary users of Shariah Councils and the ones most likely to be affected by any accommodation reached—at their very centre.

Typically there has been much discussion on the motivations behind the lecture and much of this relates to what some commentators identify as a real desire to enhance a greater role for Christianity in public life.[9] Others, such as Tariq Modood (2008b), argue that a new form of 'practical multiculturalism' must allow 'for a nuanced understanding of the inter-relationship of 'secular' and 'religious' notions in civic life'. Modood supports the accommodation of Sharia in the form of recognition of Shariah Councils as official arbitration bodies as long as they are consistent with English law, human rights, gender equality and child-protection legislation. Yet even such thoughtful responses must contend with the position of Muslim women who are reluctant for such bodies to be formally accommodated in English law.

The Archbishop should be applauded for tackling a complex and difficult topic and for his thoughtful insight into the heterogeneity of Muslim communities settled in British society and the complexity of Islamic jurisprudence and Sharia as evolving and dynamic rather than as fixed and prescriptive. The lecture critiqued the cultural essentialism inherent in state law and articulated a sophisticated understanding of the ways in which power and dominance have shaped the ideals of 'equality before the law' and the rule of law such as to legitimate dominant social and political discourse and practice which may exclude individuals and communities from equal access to the law and forms of justice. However I also believe that this spirit of complexity and heterogeneity which underpins the lecture is somewhat undermined by assumptions that most if not all Muslims are in favour of accommodation of Sharia into English law and the implicit presentation of a unified Muslim community, the Muslim *ummah*. Clearly this is not the case and what such arguments succeed in doing is privileging a particular religious practice as part of a specific Muslim identity. The problem with this approach is that it tends to ignore the possibility of alternative narratives within the Muslim community. Clearly there is a sense of belonging to a Muslim community but descriptions of belonging and community were

[9] For a range of interesting interventions see the Open Democracy (2008) forum on the Archbishop's Lecture/Sharia question.

articulated in different ways. Some women had been marginalised, others occupied a closer position to the acceptable dictates of community expectations and such discussions must therefore recognise the complex lived reality that Muslim identity entails. To simply analyse the relationship and conflicts between secular law and religious practice in relation to Sharia misses out the key issues of conflict, change and diversity within the Muslim communities in question. The Archbishop was clear in his understanding of an Islamic law embodying traditions of reason, critique and pluralism over the past 1,200 years. However, we must be cautious in not conflating developments surrounding Sharia in Muslim countries with how such processes develop and operate within minority diasporic communities as part of multicultural British society. Such conflation, however limited, also runs the risk of not understanding how these religious laws and cultural customs are reformulated within a British context to suit the specific needs of the Muslim community in question.[10]

Religious arbitration bodies may provide spaces for new forms of governance to resolve marital disputes away from the context of a Western secular framework but this does not imply that these local settings predetermine a more suitable outcome for the parties involved. For example, religious and socio-cultural terms of reference often marginalise women. Furthermore the space(s) inhabited by these bodies is neither distinct from local communities nor in totality separate from state law, rather, it is a space that intersects with contested sites of local communal power and state law, an in-between or third space of diasporic formation. Understanding these socio-legal processes requires a critique of the underlying power relations within the family, community and state and to recognise that dialogue is often imbued with power relations. The dichotomous approach, that posits 'law' and unofficial law as opposite and in conflict, consequently fails to explore these spaces 'in between', the sites of resistance and change. Furthermore as Sunder (2005, p. 896) points out 'more and more people on the ground are challenging traditional cultural and religious leaders to incorporate norms of equality, reason and liberty into the private spheres of religion and culture' but this does not itself mean that Muslim women wish to formalise these bodies. This space is only used to obtain a Muslim divorce and the women were fully aware of the need to, in parallel, utilise state law to deal with issues concerning access, custody and financial settlements.

The angry reactions sparked by the Archbishop's lecture have also led to discussions on ways in which constructive dialogue can be developed with

---

[10] Similarly discussions on the Muslim '*ummah*' and the presentation of a community of believers simply does not exist in the uniform way in which it was presented.

those representing the Muslim faith. Although in favour of such developments, we need to include Muslim women in such debates and this requires a critique of the underlying power relations within family, individual and community bodies. We must recognise that dialogue is often imbued with power relations and is constituted in relation to controlling family and communal boundaries, and thus must strive to develop an inclusive dialogue that includes the narratives of minorities within minority groups. As Anthias (2002) points out, 'effective dialogue requires an already formulated mutual respect, a common communication language and a common starting point in terms of power'. It is the 'common starting point in terms of power' that raises the dilemma of the multicultural question of 'how then can the particular and the universal, the claims of both difference and equality be recognised?' (Hall, 2000, p. 235). We must also address the potential conflicts and tensions that arise in different and at times conflicting social contexts, including intra-family relations. Muslim women have complex views about who they are and thus identity cannot be understood as a dichotomous variable of insider/outsider, muslim/non-muslim or resistance versus victim. Instead the narratives produced by the women themselves justify closer attention to their participation, interaction and outcomes with these 'unofficial' bodies.

Undoubtedly we need to address these issues in the light of empirical findings rather than solutions based upon abstract theoretical discussions. We need to incorporate debates on complexity, difference and diversity to understand the realities of Muslim women's lives. Women feel the contradictory pulls that these forces exert but their narratives must be heard. Some are happy to conform, others are not, some trade identities but for others there is the primacy of a Muslim identity. Many are suspicious of state interventions which challenge cultural norms deemed oppressive because the state has not historically acted as the neutral arbiter of disputes (Hall, 2000). Furthermore some women view 'themselves strictly bound to submit to the dictates of Islamic law and the commands of the authorities charged with its execution' (Mayer, 1999, p. 35) and we must recognise this as their lived experience. The real conflicts are over power and how those competing voices for power and representation ignore the internal voices of dissent and change, most often the voices of women.

The concern of this chapter, which closely reflects my own intervention in the debates referred, has focused on three key issues: firstly the claim that seeing culture and forms of religious practice as a mode of legitimating claims to power and authority dramatically shifts the way we understand the universal-

ASKING THE LAW QUESTIONS: AGENCY AND MUSLIM WOMEN

ism-relativism debate. Thus the view that Muslims increasingly seek the freedom to live under Sharia law is not only problematic but fails to capture the
complexity of British Muslim identity as fragmented, porous and hybrid.
Secondly, anthropological scholarship points to the importance of locating
gender and gender relations as key to the debate, of seeing the ways in which
Muslim women engage with Shariah Councils in Britain and how processes
and concepts of Sharia law are mobilised, adopted and transformed: in other
words, of recognising Muslim women's agency. Underlying this process are
power relations that define the nature of the interaction, define meanings of
Sharia within the Shariah councils and constructs the possibilities of change
and action. Finally an essentialised understanding of Muslim religious practice does not reflect the experience of Britain's Muslim women. A more
dynamic understanding of British Muslim identity is needed which does not
label the needs of Muslims to accommodate Sharia as fixed but rather understands this process as historical and as a process, shifting from cultural to
religious practice and vice versa.

Conclusion

In the UK, the boundaries of tolerance of cultural, religious and racial difference reflect and define the character of British nationalism. The controversies
over the rights of girls and women to wear various forms of the veil in educational contexts, along with the proposed recognition of limited Sharia arbitration tribunals, sparked a renewed desire to define common British values. The
anxiety and fear that created a general equivalence between any expressions of
Muslim identity and terrorism and religious extremism led to a tightening of
the limit of acceptable difference; difference was tolerable only insofar as it
was palatable to the majoritarian British sensibility. This sensibility, of course,
is underwritten by racial, religious and gendered formations that emerged with
a modernity deeply rooted in the colonial encounter. Difference is fine, as long
as it exists as a differentiated unity, with the unitary whole being disciplined
into shape by a sovereign juridical order which itself emerges out of a Christian
political heritage. As Bhandar (2009) points out:

Despite their ostensible differences as political ideologies, both multiculturalism and
secularism are deployed as techniques to govern difference. This difference is at once
cultural, religious, gendered, and mired in the history of colonial encounters that
shaped the emergent political consciousness of the subject of Enlightenment Europe.

155

Differences that challenge the boundaries of the sovereign political subject are perceived as a threat to be contained and managed.

An awareness of the social, political and cultural context of BrAsian communities is crucial to understanding the agency of Muslim women. In other words, a new discourse of personal freedom and agency to encapsulate the actual experiences of Muslim women is required. In so doing, the hope is to begin to reformulate the reductionary binary conceptions of agency versus coercion. In the current context populist discourse on forced marriage takes place within essentialist explanations that stigmatise Muslim communities and feed into racist responses. The dominant media discourse on forced marriage comes to what may superficially seem like a similar conflation of arranged and forced marriage and views them both through a culturalist lens which overwhelmingly portrays such women as passive victims of an 'overly patriarchal and inherently uncivilised' culture (Razack, 2004, p. 107) and devoid of any agency.

Through this conflation of arranged and forced marriage, the veiling, and Sharia law debates, the media naturalises coercion as a condition of belonging to Muslim communities, as 'just the way things are' (Razack, 2004, p. 142), rather than unpack the context of belonging and the exercise of agency. According to this logic, Muslim women who opt for exit strategies are lauded as heroines for having resisted the patriarchal structures within their communities, managed to escape their control and successfully reconfigured themselves as completely autonomous individuals existing outside their communities. The category 'Muslim woman' in English law constructs a unidimensional woman whose consciousness or identity is shaped by one factor only—religion. Yet, struggles for equality from within the framework of the Qur'an's teachings, such as advocated by the Muslim scholar, Asma Barlas, go unrecognised. Within the liberal paradigm informing both current legal discourse and the wider public debate on Islam, women and family law it is Muslim women's agency as Muslims which has been framed out.

15

FEAR OF SMALL NUMBERS?

DEBATING FACE-VEILING IN THE NETHERLANDS

Annelies Moors

In *Fear of small numbers*, Arjun Appadurai (2006) analyzes the darker sites of globalisation that have led to large-scale cultural violence. *Fear of small numbers* also condenses much of the public concern about face-veiling in the Netherlands.[1] Whereas the number of women who (partially) cover their faces in public is extremely small—Estimates of the total number of face-veiling women range from 100 to 400 for the whole of the country, or less than three in 100,000—face-veiling women have not only attracted tremendous media attention, they have also become a major target of politicians. In 2005 the Netherlands became the first country in Europe where a parliamentary majority voted for a resolution 'to prohibit the public use of the *burqa*'.

How have such a small number of women been able to attract so much attention and what have been the consequences? Let me start with tracing how the media hype on face-veiling has emerged. Up until late 2008, there have

---

[1] This contribution draws on Moors (2009), which provides a more extensive analysis of debates about face-veiling in the Netherlands. It is based on a discourse analysis of newspapers articles, official documents and political talk as well as on ethnographic fieldwork with all parties concerned, including policy makers and face-veiling women.

been four main peaks in media attention.[2] The first emerged in January 2003, when a school in Amsterdam banned three students wearing face coverings, the second occurred in December 2005, when Geert Wilders tabled his resolution in parliament to prohibit the *burqa* in all public space, the third in November 2006 when the Cabinet debated how to enact this resolution, and the fourth in February 2008 when the Cabinet sent a letter to parliament about its plans to enact a number of functional bans on face-veils. This indicates that, with the exception of the first case, these media hypes were the result of statements made or actions undertaken by Members of Parliament or the Cabinet itself. Rather than responding to major public concerns, in other words, politicians have been a driving force in attracting attention to this issue. What turns out to be particularly striking is how rapidly public policy has changed with respect to the face-veil.

The first media hype started when three sixteen and seventeen-year old Moroccan-Dutch students came to school (a large institution for vocational training and adult education) wearing a face veil. After some teachers complained about their presence in the classroom, and when attempts to mediate did not work out, the girls were refused entry to the school grounds. Two of them decided then to raise a complaint with the Equal Treatment Commission (CGB), claiming that they were discriminated against on the basis of religion.[3] The school, however, argued that this was not the case as its ruling prohibited the wearing of any type of face covering. In the end, the Equal Treatment Commission agreed with the school's point of view.

The ruling against wearing face-veils at school and the decision of the Equal Treatment Commission to uphold it, gained wide public support. Virtually all secondary schools in Amsterdam, including the Islamic College Amsterdam, were in favour. Spokespersons for a wide variety of Muslim organisations, including the Turkish Milli Görüs, and the Union of Moroccan Mosques, as well as those protecting minority rights, such as Forum and the National Office

---

[2] The peaks are calculated on the basis of the total number of articles about face-veiling in the Netherlands in four Dutch national newspapers that had an equivalent of the term 'face-veiling' in their headlines. The four newspapers are *De Volkskrant* and *NRC* (both more upscale), *Trouw* (Protestant) and *De Telegraaf* (right-wing populist).

[3] CGB case no. 2003–40 (see www.cgb.nl). This Commission monitors compliance with the Dutch Equal Treatment Act, which prohibits discrimination in education and employment on grounds such as religion, sex, race, and political orientation. It does so by responding to complaints in the form of a non-binding ruling, which is, however, taken seriously in court cases.

against Racial Discrimination, agreed with the prohibition. Politicians were also satisfied. Neither those on the right nor those on the left were in favour of enacting legal measures at the national level. All agreed that it was up to individual schools to include a ban on face-coverings in their regulations. In order to support schools that wanted to do so, the Ministry of Education published guidelines on dress codes in schools, which included the possibility of banning face-coverings for reasons of communication, security, and access to internships.

Still, by the end of 2005, a parliamentary majority of centre and right-wing political parties supported Wilders' resolution to prohibit the public use of the *burqa*. What had happened in the meantime? Had there been major issues with face-veiling women that could not be solved locally making national legislation necessary? There had indeed been some media attention focused on face-veiling, such as when three universities also decided to prohibit face-coverings in the classroom. But the most remarkable aspect of those cases was that at one of the universities only two girls wore a face-veil, while at the other two universities no students at all engaged in this practice. This turned out to be a recurrent pattern. When politicians later proposed to ban face-veiling women from public transportation, the public transport sector itself stated that face-veils were not a problem. When the Ministry of the Interior issued a letter prohibiting civil servants from wearing a face-veil, the very same letter also acknowledged that there were no known cases of civil servants wearing a veil. While there were, indeed, a few cases of face-veiling women who applied for unemployment benefits, the number was again very small, and existing legislation was available to deal with this.

Why then this sudden politicisation of the face-veil in 2005? In a word, because face-veils turned out to be a topic that politicians could score points with. After 1989, and the fall of the Berlin wall, a few mainstream politicians started to express the view that particular forms of Islam (or even Islam generally) were incompatible with European values. The Netherlands themselves witnessed a very rapid growth of anti-Islam right-wing populism from the late 1990s, and the late Pim Fortuyn—who in 1997 published his book *Against the Islamization of Our Culture*—in particular, attracted a huge following and changed the Dutch political landscape. The attacks of 9/11 in the USA, the invasion of Afghanistan and the lead up to the Iraq War further polarised the relations between Muslims and non-Muslims in the Netherlands. The ruling against face-veiling at the Amsterdam school in 2003, then, as the school director herself explained, needs to be seen within this context. Such a reading is further supported by the fact that in a very similar case in 2000, the Equal Treatment Commission had ruled that there were no legitimate grounds to prohibit wearing a face-veil, and, at least as notable, that at the time it generated no media attention.[4]

In the course of 2004 and 2005, polarisation escalated. One crucial moment was the airing of the film *Submission*, produced by Ayaan Hirsi Ali and Theo van Gogh, in August 2004 during a three hour long television programme with Hirsi Ali as the only studio-guest. The main argument of the film was that Muslim men maltreat their women because the Qur'an tells them to. To drive this message home, in the film Qur'anic verses are inscribed on women's scarred bodies, visible through their transparent dresses, while their faces were partially covered by face-veils. In the same year well-established academics such as Herman Phillipse and Paul Scheffer were publishing long articles in prominent newspapers with titles such as 'Stop the tribalisation of the Netherlands' (Phillipse, 2004) and 'The discomfort in Islam' (Scheffer, 2004).[5] Both reproduced the well-worn dichotomy of a liberal, democratic West versus an oppressive and violent world of Islam that utterly lacks any self-criticism. Although Scheffer acknowledged that Muslims cannot collectively be held responsible for terrorism perpetrated in the name of Islam, he simultaneously argued that Muslims have a particular responsibility to publicly distance themselves from terrorism. Such arguments were amplified after the political murder of Theo van Gogh in November 2004 by Muhammad Bouyeri, a young Dutch-Moroccan man who explained that he had killed van Gogh for religious reasons. In short, Muslims need to prove their loyalty to the nation, at the very moment that the nation became increasingly defined in ethnic-cultural terms.

It was in this context that on 20 December 2005 Geert Wilders tabled his resolution and was able to obtain the support of a parliamentary majority.[6] He had already announced that he intended to table such a resolu-

[4] CGB case no. 2000–63. The Commission argued that wearing a face-veil 'leaves sufficient possibilities for communication' (also non-verbal), and commented that the school should take into consideration that 'in a multicultural society like the Netherlands not all groups in society show their feelings through facial expression.'
[5] Scheffer is a prominent member of the Labour Party, whose much quoted article 'The multicultural drama' (2000) considered Islam a major cause for the failure of the integration of minorities.
[6] Wilders did so as an independent Member of Parliament as he had left the right-wing Liberal Party about a year earlier because this party did not categorically refuse any negotiations about Turkey's EU-membership.

tion a month earlier during a parliamentary debate about the radicalisation of Muslims. Moreover, he had started to draw attention to his desire to ban the face-veil in an interview with *De Telegraaf*, the largest populist right-wing newspaper in the Netherlands, on 10 September 2005. With no obvious cause available to start a campaign against the face-veil, the newspaper turned to Belgium where the municipality of Maaseik had banned the public use of the *burqa*. In an—at least for this paper—extraordinary long article about the successful struggle of Maaseik 'against the Muslim mask', *De Telegraaf* drew a strong connection between the *burqa* and terrorism. The article stressed that the only woman unwilling to take off the *burqa* was the wife of a terror suspect, adding that black is, according to some Islam experts, 'the colour of Al-Qaeda', and that the *burqa* 'points to the subjection of women in the Afghanistan of the Taliban'. In the interview, Wilders expressed his strong appreciation of these municipal measures and announced that he would soon present a resolution for 'a national prohibition of the *burqa*' in the Netherlands. Note that the newspaper itself added, 'Up till now there has not been a debate in the Netherlands about the face-veil in the streets'.

Two days later, the face-veil had become an issue, at least for some readers of *De Telegraaf*, when this daily made the face veil the topic of its 'Statement of the Day' internet poll. An article summarising the results the next day, concluded: 'If our readers were members of Parliament, Wilders' resolution would be immediately accepted.' According to the article 90 per cent of the respondents supported a prohibition of the *burqa*, with many pointing to the dangers of terrorism because it is impossible to see who is hiding underneath. Hence, 81 per cent said that the *burqa* causes fear. The article also mentioned that 43 per cent saw the *burqa* as a symbol of oppression and disdain for women, 35 per cent agreed that it is a sign of fundamentalist politics and only 18 per cent consider it as standing for a religious conviction.[7]

Looking closely at how the face-veil was turned into a national concern, it is worthwhile zooming in on some seemingly minor points. First of all, the use of the term *burqa* is far from innocent. When in 2003 newspapers reported on the ban of face-veils at the school in Amsterdam, a variety of terms ranging from the Dutch equivalent of 'face-veil' (*gezichtssluier*) to terms such as '*niqab*' or '*chador*', was used to describe what the students were wearing.[8] In the course

---

[7] *De Telegraaf*, (13 Sept. 2005).

[8] The term face-veil describes quite adequately what the women wear, a piece of cloth covering (part of) the face; *niqab* is the term the women themselves use; and *chador*

of the following years, the term *burqa* largely replaced these alternatives. After Wilders used the term *burqa* in his resolution, *burqa* also became the main term used in parliamentary debate.

The shift to the term *burqa* is remarkable as face-veiling women in the Netherlands mostly cover the lower part of the face with a thin piece of cloth, often leaving the eyes visible. This is far more similar to an Arab Gulf style than to the Afghan-style *burqa*, an all-covering light coloured garment with a mesh in front of the eyes. What matters most, though, is that in 2001 and 2002 the *burqa* had already become a common-sense term to the Dutch public referring to the outfit women had to wear under the Taliban (as also in the newspaper article mentioned above). In and of itself, in other words, the term burka alone already evokes with it the imaginary of a regime, which had by then come to represent a singularly repressive regime for women (Mahmood and Hirschkind, 2002; Abu-Lughod, 2003). While tapping into existing feelings of uncertainty and unease, the use of this term then further contributed to the production of fear, dislike and even disgust, uniting large sections of the population against a very small number of face-veiling women (Ahmed, 2004, p. 82).

Secondly, the use of web polls also has particular effects. Whereas such polls usually do not work with a representative sample, the media tend to present the result of such polls as 'the view of our readers'. Quick surveys and polls have become widely popular after 9/11. In one instance, shortly after 9/11, a survey was held on the question whether 'Muslims who approve of the attacks should be expelled from the Netherlands'.[9] This question draws the line between Muslims and non-Muslims, suggesting that it is possible to denaturalise Muslim citizens, while assuming that non-Muslims would not hold such opinions or that, if they did so, no measures would need to be taken. The questions posed in polls about face-veiling reveal similar assumptions at work. In the case of the poll mentioned above, the main motivation cited by face-veiling women themselves—that wearing a face-veil is a form of devotion or the enactment of a religiously recommended practice—is not even included as a possible answer. In another poll the question was posed whether women should be allowed to

---

sounds quite similar to the term used in Afghanistan for another style of all-covering dress, *chadari* (although in the Dutch context the use of the term *chador* is confusing, as it usually refers to the all-enveloping cloak that women in Iran wear, which does not cover the face).

[9] *De Volkskrant*, (26 Sept. 2001).

wear a *burqa* inside the house; 53 per cent of those taking part answered 'yes'.[10] Such a question suggests first that women wear a *burqa* inside the house and secondly, that it is possible to legislate what styles of dress people are allowed to wear in private.

It is remarkable that politicians, such as Wilders, propose measures they know are unconstitutional. In 2003, the Amsterdam school purposely employed the neutral term face-coverings rather than a term referring to Islamic face-veils in order to avoid being accused of infringing on the constitutional freedom of religion. Wilders, in contrast, employed the term *burqa* to explicitly target face-veiling Muslims, in spite of the fact that this would make it virtually impossible to implement his resolution. In a similar vein, the media produce polls that ask people's opinion about measures that are discriminatory and hence unconstitutional. Proposing measures that cannot be implemented produces further anger and resentment.

As the above suggests, politicians do not take up the issue of the face-veil because it is an important societal problem, but because it is a convenient topic to attract public attention, to give the impression that action is being taken, while distracting from more serious and pressing societal problems. Precisely because they are such a tiny minority, face-veiling women function as an easy target for scapegoating. To anti-Islam politicians face-veiling women embody everything that is wrong with Islam, including women's subjugation, radicalisation, fundamentalism, and a refusal to integrate. For Muslims, expressing a dislike of face-veiling works as a means to prove their belonging to the Dutch nation. Mainstream politicians who take a tough stance on face-veiling can show that they are not 'soft on Islam' and are willing to draw the line.[11] Expressing discomfort and dislike about the presence of a very small number of face-veiling women is, however, not without consequences. It further contributes to the circulation of feelings of fear, dislike and resentment and has resulted in widely exaggerated estimates of the number of face-veiling women in the Netherlands. In 2008, almost half of the respondents of a youth web panel estimated the number of women wearing a face-veil at 5,000 or more and

---

[10] *De Telegraaf*, (7 Feb. 2008).

[11] A strong case is an interview by Wouter Bos, the leader of the Labour Party, in which he argued for a prohibition of the *burqa* as part of a larger argument in favour of polarisation in politics (*De Volkskrant*, 1 Mar. 2008). At the time Wilders' Party for Freedom had made strong gains at the elections, and Rita Verdonk's new political movement 'Proud of the Netherlands' (also right-wing populist, with strong statements against the *burqa*) was doing very well in election polls.

almost 17 per cent thought that more than 20,000 women in the Netherlands wear a face-veil.[12]

In *Fear of small numbers*, Appadurai points out that globalisation has undermined the control of nation-states over their territory and has caused a widely felt uncertainty about national belonging. When anxieties about globalisation are actively displaced onto national minorities, their sheer presence may come to be seen as threatening the existence of the majority, especially if such minorities can be imagined as part of a far larger global community. The efforts by Dutch politicians to ban the face-veil from public space have had the paradoxical effect of contributing to feelings of being under threat.

[12] This poll was held on 9 September 2008 by Top-X, the youth (aged 12–24) panel of the Dutch television programme EénVandaag (OneToday) (www.top-x.nl).

16

A SHORT GENEALOGY OF RUSSIAN ISLAMOPHOBIA

Madina Tlostanova

In contemporary discussion of inter-cultural and inter-religious relations and of the interpretation of otherness and diversity, the collapse of the Soviet Union acted as an important divide after which Islamophobia became globally the central xenophobic discourse. At first sight the connection between the unraveling of the Soviet Union and relations between the West and Muslimistan may not be immediately obvious. But it is becoming clearer today that the shift from the major ideological enemy of the Cold War to the new Muslim enemy does in fact betray a continuity of sorts. That continuity, this chapter will argue, can best be understood within the rhetoric of modernity and the logic of coloniality.

The shift from Cold War enmity was most clearly expressed in Samuel Huntington's (1996) now infamous book, *The Clash of Civilizations*. In the euphoric post-Soviet era the remnants of the empire and the defeated enemies populating its ruins appeared overnight to turn into old news, while the focus of attention shifted to the new Islamic 'other'. However, the defeated and the current enemy unexpectedly merged when it became clear that after the collapse of the Soviet Union there emerged from it several new Muslim states, entertaining different relations with Muslimistan. At the same time, moreover, came the realisation that Russia itself is home to not only ethnic Russians and Orthodox Christians but to several million Muslims, with their own needs and subjectivities, and that they did not quite fit in either with the simplistic image of Russia as a mono-ethnic nation-state, or into the newly entrenched global dichotomy of the West vs. Islam. Against this context, the former Sovietology in the West was forced to reorient itself into so called Eurasian area-studies, signaling a corresponding shift from the previous ideological markers of 'otherness' to the new cultural-religious ones. It is not by chance that the financing of Russian studies in the West has declined of late while the interest in the Caucasus and Central Asia has seen tremendous expansion in the last two decades.

Relations between Russia and Islam present a historically unique and still insufficiently studied model, largely ignored under the shadow cast by the rhetoric of Soviet modernity. Today, these relations are going through cardinal changes and coming closer to Western Islamophobia, in Russia proper, and to the self-Islamophobia of 'Muslimistani' countries, in the internal colonies of Russia and the post-soviet Muslim states.

I

Before turning to the question of Russian Islamophobia, it is necessary to first briefly sketch the genealogy of the discourses of 'othering' in Western modernity so as to see how Islamophobia fits into the historical and contemporary modes of interpreting the other. Following the stance of the de-colonial project, I argue that the fundamental discourse which gives birth to all other forms of modern xenophobia is Eurocentrism (Dussel, 2000; Quijano, 2000), while the main strategy of its realisation is racism. Eurocentrism is the dominant structure of knowledge in modernity from the sixteenth century onwards. In the first (Christian) modernity it acted as a theo-politics of knowledge; in the second (Secular) modernity it changed its face to an ego-politics of knowledge that masked the geo- and body-political grounds of knowledge as a real place where knowledge is created and a real body through and by which it is articulated, by presenting the Eurocentric rhetoric of modernity as a universal disembodied and de-contextualised knowledge (Mignolo, 2007; 2006). Eurocentrism as a structure of knowledge helped to build racism as a specific system of classification ranking all peoples and regions in the world in terms of their relation to Western Christianity, Europe, the White race, etc. Eurocentrism is a real and discursive space from which racism, as its instrument, makes the Eurocentric affirmation possible and normative. By means of these assumed racial classifications, Eurocentrism constructs a hierarchy of human beings in the world. Europeans classify, while the non-European peoples, newly tagged Blacks, Indians, or later Orientals, lose their right (and ability) to classify, and become the classified.

In the first (Christian) modernity Eurocentrism constructs racism as purity of blood within the frame of religious discourses, while in the secular modernity purity of blood transmutes into skin colour. Religion does not disappear altogether, but it acts in complex union with nationalism and secularised racism, it acts through them so that national or ethnic characteristics are used as the main signifier and it is through them that otherness is coded. The transition from purity of blood to skin colour goes hand in hand with the switch from religion to secular reason. As Walter Mignolo points out, 'in "Modern space", epistemology was first Christian and then White. In "enchanted places", wisdom, and not epistemology, was first non-Christian [...] and later on of color. Islam, for instance, became a colored religion while Christianity, and particularly Protestant Christianity, became Whiter after the reformation' (Mignolo, 2002, p. 935). Mignolo uses the concept of the locus of enunciation to define this Eurocentric mode of interpreting the world. I prefer to use a modified version of Bakhtin's metaphor of ventriloquism (Bakhtin, 1986): it is the voice of Western modernity that is being masked by its ventriloquists as if it were an objective de-contextualised and de-historicised universal voice of authority per se. And it is crucial to de-masque the hidden voice of the seemingly missing actor as the voice of Eurocentric modernity.

Outwardly it seemed that in the second modernity the religious factor was pushed aside and replaced with race, culture or biology. But in fact its Western Christian foundations remained, it is just that within the frame of the dominant discourses of secular modernity religious difference as such no longer figured as a serious enough argument, a relevant proof of otherness. Different, pseudo-scientific and rational grounds were required instead. Religion had to be translated into race, culture, national character or ethnicity. Thus the expelled Moors, for example, reappeared in the eighteenth century as Arabs. A good example in this respect is offered by Kant's classification of national characters in his *Observations on the Feeling of the Beautiful and the Sublime*, of 1764, where the assumed religious differences between Islam and Western Christianity are translated into national characteristics. One can also trace here not just the secularised racism but also the emerging Orientalism at work and as, among other things, an anti-Islamic discourse of this specific period of the European nation-state, and nationalist propaganda. Orientalism in this context is a type of racial classification that is superimposed on racial distinction based on skin colour. By the time Orientalism comes to full bloom some Orientals were already coded as yellow, but with others (like the Arabs) it was different forms of racism that came to the fore, most importantly, those based on religious difference, within which Muslim equaled non-White.

Kant says about the Arabs: 'If we cast a fleeting glance over the other part of the world' (that is, outside of Europe), 'we find the Arab the noblest man in the Orient, yet of a feeling that degenerates very much into adventurous. [...] His inflamed imagination presents things to him in unnatural and distorted images, and even the propagation of his religion was a great adventure' (Kant, 1960, p. 109). In other words, for Kant the Arabs lack reason and rationality, and therefore do not belong to Modernity and thus are deficient human beings. Drawing analogies, as was typical of the philosophic discourse of the time, he calls the Arabs 'the Spaniards of the Orient', while the Persians, on account of their refined taste and love for poetry and their mild interpretation of Islam (for they are not crude and blind followers of Islam), are for him 'the French of Asia' (Kant, 1960, p. 110). In Kant then, the clearly defined construct of the Orient with its predominant anti-Islamic mood is already at work, even if he speaks of Arabs and not of Muslims. In any case, as early as the eighteenth-nineteenth centuries Islamophobia in Europe often translates into Arabophobia and the term Arab is used to define any Muslim (even if in reality he is a Turk or a Persian, to say nothing of the 'exotic' Muslims of Central Asia of whom Westerners are, even today, often unaware). The focus on national characters does not cancel the underlying anti-Islamic tendency, which vacillates, as all phobias, between hatred and fear. However, within the Enlightenment world with its rather simplified social optimism and blind Eurocentrism (in spite of occasional doubts in civilisation) Islam is regarded as a religion whose days are numbered and Islamophobia acquires a tint of disdain rather than fear or hatred—disdain for a model doomed before the triumphant march of modernity that no longer presents any danger to European superiority. Islamophobia would become a real phobia again much later, when the West again started to see Islam as a real threat, and not just an exotic 'lagger' to modernity. During the Cold War and even some time after, the classifications of humankind in the West (and in the Socialist world) were largely based on a national and linguistic model, whereas religious difference was hidden: race equalled nation (Balibar and Wallerstein, 1991).

The return of religious markers in the interpretation of the European/Western other are often associated with 11 September 2001, although this was rather the projection of an already widely circulating discourse (which culminated in Huntington's work) into mass consciousness, as a result of which Arabs again started to be seen predominantly as Muslims. But secular modernity's legacy of coding religion through ethnic/racial and national differences was also preserved, so that while Arabs became Muslim again, in the West Muslims continued to be coded as mostly Arabs. The return of religion after the collapse of the ideological stage of modernity was only seemingly novel. The difference was that during the Cold War behind the ideological differences there hid the same Western modernity in its two variants—the socialist/statist and the capitalist/liberal, with coloniality of being, knowledge and power intact in both cases. In other words, it was an internal difference; while after the collapse of the Soviet Union the internal difference turned into an external one as the West started to look to the enemy outside modernity, once again, in the enchanted spaces associated with another religion and with the concept of tradition as an invented binary opposition to modernity.

In this context it is not surprising that most of the Western discourses turned to a tantalising quest for a re-territorialising on some non-discredited philosophical and intellectual grounds. But where were the Western ex–left and ex–right to look for such grounds? In Eurocentric modernity. Some, such as Slavoj Zizek (2000; 2002), find it in the predictable discourses of Europeanism, Christianity and epistemic racism; others turn to Orthodox Marxism trying to root it, once again, in Western Christianity (Hardt and Negri, 2000); still others, like Huntington (2004) himself, turn to xenophobia, nationalism, Protestantism and racism. Neither the Western right nor the left ever question the rhetoric of modernity itself, which does not leave them many alternatives— they are bound into pointless efforts to make peace with the European and Christian legacy.

In the present opposition of Islam and the West the phobia has once again become a real hatred and fear (not just the disdain for the has been) that, in a way, is a rollback to the time when the dominance of Modernity was not absolute. Paradoxically, at the time of its seemingly complete totality and power, Western modernity is most vulnerable to the discourses that contest it, refuse to speak in its terms, and question its fundamental logic. Islamicate protest is one such contestatory discourse, but not the only one. There are also the indigenous movements in South and Central America, non-Western Women's movements throughout the world, and many others engaged in struggles to decolonise from modernity and its discourses.

Scholars still cannot agree on when exactly Islamophobia as a concept emerged in the political, academic, or media discourse. Some think that it entered into wide circulation in 1997, after the publication of the Runnymede Trust's (1997a) *Islamophobia: A Challenge For Us All*. Others, drawing on the coining of the term by Muslim activists, attribute the crucial role in the formation of the discourse on Islamophobia to earlier stirrings in 'Muslimistan'. The latter would place the discourse on Islamophobia among the Islamicate reactions in Islam to the challenge of modernity, which started emerging in the late nineteenth century out of the modernising efforts within Muslim states such as the collapsing Ottoman empire, the future Iran, Afghanistan, etc. In other words, in modernity no one can avoid the necessity of defining oneself against or within its frame as the only legitimate point of reference. Islam is no exception. The self-consciousness of Muslim thought in the last 150 years at least could only be fashioned through a dispute, a dialogue, a rejection or an acceptance of Western modernity. Muslim philosophies emerging from the mid nineteenth century were marked by the double burden of their inferiority in relation to their own great past (the golden age of Arabic philosophy) and to Western modernity. The alternative models advanced to break out of this inferiority were based on the acceptance of modernity, the radical break up with modernity, or a fusion of modernity and (Islamic and Islamicate) authenticity, but none could avoid the imperative to define their attitude to modernity.

Who, when and in what context launched Islamophobia as the main phobia of the Western world, however, is actually unimportant. Far more important is to retrace the basic internal and external circumstances and features of Western modernity that made it possible, that naturalised Islamophobia in the global frame, and to understand what needs to be changed and how, in order to make the disavowal of Islamophobia truly effective. In this respect the genealogy of Russian/Soviet/post-Soviet Islamophobia turns out to be very useful because it borrows from Western modernity, but as a distorted reproduction which copies but exaggerates particular features of its interpretation of others, including the Muslim other, thus rendering more crudely visible that which in the European and the U.S. discourse is more subtle. How, then, does the Russian/Soviet/post-Soviet modernity differ from the Western model described above in its interpretation of the Muslim other?

II

In the case of the Russian Empire, the USSR, and post-Soviet Russia the genealogy of Islamophobia was different due to the specific subaltern role of this empire in modernity and the imperial difference between such subaltern empires and the capitalist 'winners' (France, Germany, England, the USA today). If for Latin America or India it is the colonial difference that plays the crucial role, for Russia, as well as for Spain—which was relegated from dominance within the second modernity—it is the imperial difference that comes to the fore (Mignolo, 2002; Tlostanova, 2005). However on the global scale we can say that the imperial difference mutates into the colonial, as is clearly seen in the case of the Ottoman Sultanate and Russia. The latter is an example of external imperial difference. Its imperial populace is Slavic, i.e. rather remote from Western Europe; Orthodox Christian; even its alphabet does not correspond to European expectations of an imperial language and literacy.

The Russian Empire was never seen by Western Europe as one of its own; it remained an Asiatic, racialised empire. Czarist Russia made the fatal error of choosing the catch-up model, which was impossible to realise, and the objective of 'out-Westing' the West (Tlostanova, 2003). In the case of the Ottoman Sultanate this complex gave birth to self-Islamophobia. In the case of Russia it generated the complex of the second class European ('a Tatar dressed as a Frenchman' in V. Klyuchevsky's [1937, p. 214] words). In the Muslim colonies of Russia it generated the self-orientalisation, which remains alive even today, leading to the stagnation of any alternative political and social movements and actors. Russian imperial discourses, particularly in the nineteenth century demonstrate the Janus-faced nature of this empire which, while it always felt itself a colony in the face of the West, at the same time half-heartedly played the part of the caricature 'civiliser', moderniser and real European in its non-European and particularly Muslim colonies. In a way we can say that Russia has always been in the condition of coloniality vis-à-vis the West, and not direct colonialism. This coloniality, while it has not been obvious, has been ubiquitous, manifesting itself mainly in the spheres of being, of knowledge and of thinking.

The Soviet empire in its subaltern imperial nature was not essentially different from the Czarist one, though it reformulated the main developmentalist slogan in a more powerful way—'to catch up and leave behind', while also escalating its global geopolitical designs. As for the relation to the Muslim colonies, the Soviet tactic did not change much—it became even more cruel and refined, based on methodical elimination of all alternative thinking and being, especially if it was linked to Islam, one of Bolshevism's greatest nightmares from the beginning to the end (with very short lived exceptions of the tactical solidarity with the *Jadids* and the cynical use of inter-confessional conflicts within Islam to Soviet benefit, and the briefly entertained idea of 'Muslim communism' soon rejected [Khalid, 2001, pp. 145–162]).

The historical evolution of Islamophobic discourses in Russia was marked by a combination of internal and external factors. Islamophobia did not start in the second modernity, it certainly existed before. But at the same time, it acquired particular new features after the eighteenth century, which made Islamophobia a more openly racist discourse. This shift was linked to Russia's turning into a subaltern empire. The external factor that influenced the shaping of Islamophobia was that of Western modernity in both its Christian (borrowed from the Byzantine Empire and Orthodox Christianity) and, later, secular forms. The internal factor was based on the specific experience of the Russian opposition to the nomads of the Eurasian Steppe and, later, the Mongols who colonised Russia in 1237–1480. The combination of these factors shaped the stable negative interpretation of the East (later, the Orient) and Islam as a constant threat and a religion of violence and intolerance in the Russian collective unconscious. Thus, before the active intellectual colonisation of Russia itself by the discourses of Eurocentric modernity (from the late seventeenth century onwards) there was already this local negative experience of the Muslim nomads superimposed onto the early Christian resentment. The original word used for the nomads was *pogany* (from the Latin *paganis*), however, in Russian *pogany* meant 'vile' or 'base', thus replacing the religious characteristic with a moral one, and later it was used to define the Muslim people of the East who also acquired a new name in Russia—that of the *busurman* (a distortion of *Musulman*) a negative and offensive term used derogatively of Muslims but often also of all non-Christians, and sometimes even Christians if they were Catholics or Protestants.

Before 1453 it was fear that dominated Russian Islamophobia. After the fall of Constantinople, hatred gradually replaced fear. Particularly important in this respect was the doctrine of Moscow as the third Rome (following the fall of the second Rome, Constantinople), a messianic imperial orthodox Christian discourse that dominated the Russian imaginary until the eighteenth century and, in transmuted form, is still in circulation today. Starting from Ivan the Terrible, the growing Russian Empire focused its colonising efforts more and more on its diverse Muslim neighbours; Russian xenophobia was expressed mainly in the Islamophobic form. At the same time it is true that the Moscow tsars between the sixteenth and the eighteenth centuries often continued their tactical alliances—military, political and even matrimonial—with Muslim peoples to use them in the struggles against the more powerful Muslim enemies such as the Ottoman Sultanate. In keeping with the logic of the first modernity purity of blood was for them more important than skin colour, and though of the wrong religion (Islam), this was not yet seen as a fundamental deficiency in their human nature as such. Conversely, adopting Orthodox Christianity was a way in for many Muslims, to attain belonging (however incomplete). Here we have to take into account the clear difference between, on the one hand, relations with Muslim states: such as the Ottoman Sultanate (which becomes the main target of Russian expansionism in its goal of turning Istanbul into Tsargrad—literally, Tsar-city—and placing the Orthodox Cross over Hagia Sophia), or the Crimean and Volga khanates and the Caucasus before they were conquered. And, on the other hand, internal Islam and later the Muslim colonies. Russia could flirt with the Khans and often talk them into joining the empire voluntarily, but afterwards the nascent empire invariably turned to forceful Christianising, strangling the many revolts, giving advantages to the ex–Muslims who became Orthodox Christians and co-opting the local elites by granting the aristocracy (the Murzas) rights equal to the Russian gentry in return for oaths of loyalty. In comparison with the second modernity and its more and more absolute rejection of Islam, Russian relations with the Muslim people in the sixteenth to eighteenth centuries were more complex and nuanced.

Islamophobia in Eurasia can be regarded within the following logic: the stronger the influence of Western modernity became, together with the intellectual self-colonisation of Russia, the stronger (though not always consciously) became the elements of Islamophobia in its cultural and political imaginary. This happens because adopting modernity cannot be a partial process, one cannot borrow only its better parts and leave out the worse ones.

A constitutive part of modernity is coloniality and hence racism, Orientalism and Islamophobia. The specificity of the Russian case in this regard is that all of the above mentioned discourses were here not original but copied from the West, though with many distortions, and inflected by the constant realisation of Russia's Janus-faced nature (in Dostoyevsky's words: 'In Europe we were hangers-on and slaves, in Asia we will come as masters'). As a result we find in Russia the second hand, *othered* forms of Eurocentrism, racism, orientalism and Islamophobia, which are always balancing on a carefully hidden inferiority complex that is being compensated for in an exaggerated way. These *othered* forms of Eurocentrism, racism, orientalism and Islamophobia played out differently within each particular model of Western modernity copied in Russia at each particular time—from the European enlightenment, through socialism, to today's neo-liberalism. As the focus on purity of blood was turning into that of skin colour in the interpretation of race, religion was also becoming more and more a racial indicator.

Islamophobia in today's understanding is a part of the wider phenomenon of racism and the coloniality of being as the instruments of Eurocentric modernity. This is directly related to secularisation, the emergence of the nation-state discourses in Europe and rising nationalism as a part of the Western package of modernity, which has been hurriedly adopted in the non-Western spaces, including Muslim ones (Turkey, Afghanistan, Persia, pre-Soviet and early Soviet Turkestan, the Russian Tatars in the late nineteenth century, e.g. the *Jadids*, etc.). It is precisely nationalism and the nation-state that stand at the beginning of the emergence of modern Islamophobia in its racist understanding. A crucial part here was played by science (instead of theology), which from the mid nineteenth century on has offered an array of pseudo-proofs for the essentialist frozen interpretations of Islam as ethnicity and a convenient rationale for Islam's racialisation. In Russia and its colonies in the last 200 years Islam has gradually transmuted into ethnicity (race). As this transformation has been taking place, the main form of relations with Muslim populations became that of physical annihilation and very selective assimilation (particularly in the Caucasus and in certain regions of Central Asia).

The second modernity in Russia was characterised by a partial and relative secularisation due to the specificity of Orthodox Christianity. The Russian imperial discourse was highly contradictory in this respect as in the eighteenth and even in the nineteenth century the state carried out particular policies in relation to religious and not ethnic-cultural communities. Czarist Russia had specific laws restricting the rights of certain religions, banning the conversion from Orthodox Christianity into any other religion, and differentiating the rights and duties of various groups in accordance with their religious belonging. Officially the way the Muslim community was treated depended on its loyalty to the regime (Krymin and Engelgardt, 2003), but in reality everything was more complex, because the Russian mind was strongly affected by the Western discourses of the second modernity which clearly coded Islam as a non-white religion and ultimately as a deficit in humanity, presenting the Muslims as fallen out of history, violent and cruel (Gatagova, 2006).

The secularisation went hand in hand with the formulation of the national discourses as imperial and the birth of the new category of otherness—that of *inorodtsy* (a term usually translated into English as 'aliens' but which literally means those who were *born others*). In the special *inorodtsy* law and in the way the meaning of the term was changing throughout the nineteenth century, acquiring a more and more negative meaning and spreading to eventually cover all non-Russians and particularly Muslim colonials, it is clear to see how the religious element mixed with ethnic-racial and civilising ones. The first Inorodtsy Act was issued in 1822 and was officially in use until 1917 (Slokum, 2005). A closer look at the rights of the Oriental *inorodtsy* and the Jews (who also belonged to this category) shows a mixture of borrowed racism and the civilising discourse with the preserved Russian imperial phobia of Islam as a possible unifying factor, in the context of the failed attempts at the forceful russification of the Oriental peoples who were actively developing their national consciousness and anti-colonial sentiment at the time. The crucial difference between the two types of *inorodtsy*—the Jews and the orientals— was that the category of Jews was determined not only ethnically but also religiously. A Jew who adopted Christianity, ceased being regarded as a Jew or a 'born other' in the eyes of the law. While, belonging to the Oriental *inorodtsy*, on the contrary, was determined by ethnic (racial) origin and the degree of civilisation and not by religion as such. Adopting Christianity for the Oriental *inorodtsy* could not save them from this status—they remained of those who were born others. The ethnic racism always triumphed, as the oriental *inorodtsy* remained non-White and ultimately impossible to civilise in Russian eyes.

In the nineteenth century during the period of active colonisation of the Muslim territories by the Russian Empire the Orient became an ideological concept and was gradually replaced with the word 'Asia' and 'Asiatic' with negative connotations. The Russian concept of the Orient referred mainly to the Muslim peoples and was divided into the real (European) Orient and a secondary (Russian) one (Tlostanova, 2008). Its demonising elements were always stronger than the 'exoticising' ones. Asia was opposed to civilisation which Russia saw itself to be the manifestation of. Clearly it was a collective inferiority complex of a subaltern empire compensated by exaggerating the difference with the demonised Muslim Orient. It was needed for the unconfident Russian coloniser who could not forget that the Europe that he so much longed to belong to saw no difference between him and the peoples of the Caucasus or Turkistan which he conquered. Lord Curzon (1967, p. 392) called the Russian colonisation of Central Asia, an annexation of Asiatics by Asiatics, thus drawing a clear line between Western colonialism based on a confident racial status and its Russian mimicry, hiding its own unstable racial origins.

Hence the instability and vagueness of the Russian imperial ideology, in relation to race and religion. Trying to retain both the Orthodox Christian element as a source of Russia's exceptionalism and a hastened adaptation of the

European civilising discourses, the Russian empire carefully hid the religious factor in its conquest of the Caucasus or Turkistan. The Czarist ideologues always sought to present the existing political power in the territories to be conquered as an evil for the local people so that Russia could be whitewashed and presented in its favorite image of a liberator. At the moment of colonisation the religious beliefs of the local people were not criticised. This came later, with the emergence of anti-colonial revolts that by the end of the nineteenth century started to be expressed in the form of pan-Turkism and pan-Islamism. As a result, in the Russian imperial discourse there emerged a contradictory mixture of the theo-politics and the ego-politics of knowledge, which would survive in a slightly altered form into the USSR. Both forms in the end collapsed into the physical annihilation of the other. The loyalty to the empire of the Muslim internal other could not guarantee his human rights either in Czarist Russia or today. In the minds of the elites, the imperial ideologues, the Orthodox Christian clergy and the common people, it was Eurocentrism and militant racism as its instrument that determined in the long run the relations with Islam.

The predominant annihilation strategy of nineteenth century Russian imperialism resulted in the genocide of Muslim and wider aboriginal populations of the Caucasus and Central Asia. The wider world still has no access to the true figures of this massacre as well as the circumstances of the forced massive deportations such as of the Caucasus peoples exiled to the Ottoman Sultanate. However, these activities were not aimed particularly against Islam as a religion. The Russian empire was not largely interested in the religious preferences of the peoples who were to be removed from the lands that it wanted to incorporate. The non-European populations of the colonies were not the objects of active christianising either. Many Russian 'Westernisers', who urged the lazy empire to copy the Western means of religious and civilising conversion, lamented this passivity of missionary activity (Sahni, 1997, p. 60).

The cooptation of the local elites into the empire was not a very lively process either, although it was always publicised by imperial propaganda. In the nineteenth century they mostly came from the local aristocracy and later were transformed by education in the Russian military institutions. Many of them became Orientalists with a decidedly pro-Russian orientation. However, they were always reminded of their true place by having their religion (even if they refused it themselves) translated into race (which they could not overcome). For the civilising modernising paradigm they remained half-wild 'Tatars', even if they became Orthodox Christians and wrote in perfect Russian. The term

'Tatar' was used to define a Muslim of any ethnicity, which was a Russian equivalent of the parallel European process of the 'ethnisation' of Islam mentioned above—the stereotypical image of the Arab in the sense of a Muslim. Thus from *busurmanin* the Muslim became a *Tatar* in the nineteenth-century Russian imaginary, and today simply the *Black*, completely replacing the religious difference with the racial one.

In the closing years of the Russian Empire, Islam was ready for a dialogue. It strove to fight for its political and social ends using the newly acquired legitimate means. As A. Rorlich points out, it is not the diversity of definitions and practices of citizenship in the Russian empire that comes as a surprise. What is surprising is the resilience of the racial marker of identity as a boundary of otherness that, at times, could not be obliterated even by religious otherness. Even for Russian Christian religious scholars and missionaries, race superseded religion as the defining identity marker of non-Russians (Rorlich, 2004, p. 40). After the proclamation of the Decree on Religious Toleration in 1905, many Muslims began to accept the compatibility of their racial/ethnic and religious identities with their civic identity. The slackening of religious imperial control came at a time when the Muslim communities themselves had already started the process of critical evaluation and came up with their own models of modernisation such as the integrationist grass-roots Jadidism with its claim to its own opinion. But their ideas were not accepted by Russian missionaries, scholars and government officials who used racial, theological and civilisational arguments proving the incompatibility of Islam and modernity (Rorlich, 2004, p. 42). Any efforts of the Muslims to reconcile their Islamicate identity with their loyalty to the empire (Rorlich, 2004) or Russia as a nation-state (Jamal, 2004) have always been rejected at all levels, while the empire remained safely within its lazy self-contentedness, seasoned with a large dose of Orthodox Christian messianism. Its main politics in relation to Islam remained that of neglect, discrimination, black PR and—at the smallest pretext—genocide.

III

The Soviet Union attempted to bring to life the marginal and seemingly contesting model to Western modernity—that of Socialism. While the Soviet empire chose to present itself to the world as the empire of affirmative action (Martin, 2001), it was marked by a double standard where the actual dominance of racial discourses was always masked and complicated by a more intricate ethnic and religious configuration. The Bolsheviks first used the Muslim progressive forces to win power and later destroyed these very people to make sure that any possibility of Islamic revival was strangled. In spite of its outward tendency towards atheism, the regime tended to smuggle into the collective unconscious the idea of the superiority of the Russian Orthodox church over all other religions, even if in the masked form of Russian national traditions, and rejected any Islamic thought and Muslim organisations—again, masking this tactic as a battle with 'bourgeois nationalism'. Note that no ethnic Russian was ever sentenced for this crime in the Soviet Union. Early Soviet anthropological and racial studies never dealt with Russian peasants but rather made expeditions to the non-European parts of the empire to investigate the biological, social, and intellectual patterns of Tadjiks or Chukchas using an argumentation that always betrayed its racist biases. The Bolsheviks were against the Western style of racism, but they were for a Soviet style of racism (Weitz, 2002). They were not going to erase the unbridgeable gap with the Muslim people, or with any other 'born others' for that matter. There also was and still is the well known process of taming the Islamic clergy to make them serve the empire which today is expressed in the paradoxical forms of Russian Islam which is a mode of state control by means of the inculcation of the Muslim community with state power missionaries presumably turned Muslim.[1]

Islam, even in its everyday and symbolic forms, remained one of the major anxieties of the Soviet empire which systematically eliminated all its signs as a part of, a wider campaign of erasing the indigenous cosmologies, religions, languages, histories, and replacing them all with the self-degrading slave mentality which is very hard to get rid of today. A good example was the forceful

---

[1] Russian Islam, and particularly revolutionary Russian Islam, is a far-going political project, based on the technology of wrapping the Eurasian revivalism and will to revenge into the packaging of a localised Islam. Hence such concepts as Geidar Jamal's Islam-Intern—the unification of all revolutionary Islamic organisations into one planetary union with the leaders from the Russian Caucasus Diaspora (Jamal, 2004, p. 296). The future Islam-Intern (Islamic International) would lead the total jihad against the world system of tyranny and injustice. Yet the final goal of Russian political Islam is nothing else but the (re)creation of the future Eurasian empire. It would include the former Russia, the Old and the New Europe and in fact, the whole continent of Eurasia. Jamal's liberation of Islam is sharp in the criticism of modernity and its rhetoric, while his efforts at envisioning the future global state under the auspices of reformed Islam are questionable at best, especially in view of his sexism and universalist pretensions.

'Cyrillisation' of all Turkic languages, which deprived them of the continuity of their traditions and of the possibility of a dialogue with others of similar religious or linguistic heritage. Other examples include the elimination of mosques in predominantly Muslim localities of the empire and the profanation of the sacred elements of Islamic architecture in Soviet public buildings.

The following correlation from early Soviet times demonstrates the merging of anti-Islamic and racist propaganda. In the process of forceful nation/ethnicity building in Central Asia the Soviet empire needed a permanent negative image, which would symbolise simultaneously the religious, the nationalist, the bourgeois or medieval and any anti-modern harmful survival, and on top of that could be redeemed in the process of Soviet social engineering. Such an image was found in the Oriental Muslim woman (Northrop, 2004). She was accused of backwardness, lack of hygiene, disease and illiteracy, and defined by the newly created Soviet taxonomy of national tags: Uzbek, Kyrgiz, Tadjik, Kazakh, Turkmen, etc. This woman was supposed to be modernised by the 'Great Russians' with the grandiose idea of making everyone finally fit the future standard of the new Soviet citizen—a racially mixed atheist, brought up on the ideas of Russian cultural superiority and manifesting theatrical multicultural traits in cuisine, singing, dancing, fiction, theater, national costume, etc. This tactic had a lot in common with the nation-building discourses in Turkey and several other Muslim countries, where women also played a crucial part as symbols of modernisation and emerging nation-state discourses (Göle, 1996). The national or nationality projects in the Soviet Union were self-negating and contradictory at birth. Because, if dirt, moral degradation, disease and religious fundamentalism were associated with newly invented nationalities, then the zombified locals would quickly learn to associate these nationalities with exclusively negative traits and would try to get rid of them a soon as possible, assimilating to the Russian norm. The association of Islam with diseases and dirt, clearly expressed in the anti-fetish of *paranjee* (a central Asian form of *hijab*), was also manifested in the refusal of the Soviet system to see the Muslim ritual ablutions as a legitimate cleaning. Piety could only be coded as a symbol of dirt, backwardness, or moral deficiency, whereas cleanliness was not just the lack of dangerous infections but a system of values and a synonym of loyalty to the empire and its order.

As in Czarist times an ex–Muslim intellectual could buy a place in the Soviet nomenclature only by betraying his people, his faith, his culture, his language and cosmology. By the 1960s this forced Russification and self-Islamophobia reached an almost automatic point when the people did not even have to make a choice anymore. Local languages, history or culture turned into exotic, archaic curiosities and no one who wanted to get a good education and an established place in Soviet society would be interested in them or even find many traces of it left. Before 1917, the local intellectual was simply ignored if he did not subscribe to Russian modernisation, in the USSR such an intellectual, particularly with an Islamic or ethnic-national bent, would now not simply be ignored but imprisoned, executed, or bought off, as is the case today.

The subhuman slave status of the majority of the colonial people in the Caucasus and especially Central Asia did not change from the Czarist Empire to the Soviet one. The Soviet division of labor was racist and indirectly anti-Islamic.[2] The hierarchy of colonial economies within the Soviet Union was not openly framed according to racist discourses, but through a mediated and blurred Eurocentric rhetoric, so that the more European Soviet colonies (the Baltic states, Ukraine) were also less mono-economic, while the Caucasus or especially Central Asia were deliberately caught into the vicious circle of dependency that is reproduced today on the global scale in their being completely thrown out of the world system. Their condition reproduces in the next stage, the imperial-colonial hierarchy that was shaped in modernity: the colonies of the second-rate empire turned third-rate.

In the Soviet Union we have also to take into account such a concept as 'ethnic Muslims', i.e. people whose ancestors were Muslim but who, due to their Soviet upbringing, were forced to become atheists at least externally, and yet remained suspicious to the empire. Even a merely ethnic Muslim, in the Soviet and post-Soviet society has remained a second-class citizen by several exponents. What we see at work here is the logic of modernity that justifies the sub-human status of particular groups of people and any violence against them. Nelson Maldonado-Torres (2007) aptly calls this a misanthropic scepticism linked to the ontological difference. It was clearly at work in the way the Soviet government treated the so-called enemy-nations, most of which were Muslim. As E. Weitz (2002, p. 23) points out, 'in relation to particular populations Soviet policies rested on the notion that ontology determined politics'.

IV

The post-Soviet time has brought a number of new nuances into this configuration. The previous Soviet project of redeeming and converting others into

---

[2] The Soviet division of labor was expressed, for example, in the Uzbek, but not Russian, children spending many months in the cotton fields instead of studying at school and the Uzbek peasants getting genetic diseases and dying massively because of the chemicals sprinkled on the cotton and its pickers from the air.

the communist faith is gone, while the total rejection and radicalised 'othering' prevails. The main element in Islamophobia has become once again that of hatred and not fear. This is clearly seen in the sphere of gender, where there has been a striking shift from Soviet redemption to today's repression of Muslim women, who became one of the most feared stereotypes of the *Homo Postsoveticus* (e.g. the openly Islamophobic Russian Ministry of Internal Affairs operation *Fatima* which prescribed to search all *hijab*-wearing women as possible terrorists in 2003).

The stubborn preservation of the biological idea of nation and ethnicity in post-Soviet Russia contributes to the racialisation of Islamophobic discourses today. The previously hidden racism surfaces in its primordial forms and is quickly linked with Western racism, no longer mediated by Soviet modernity. Besides, there were several internal and external events in the last two decades that contributed to the decidedly anti-Islamic face of racism in today's Russia. The sharp deterioration of living standards in the 1990s, and the rapid emergence of oligarchic capitalism that made the ruling powers divert attention towards an enemy—a Muslim migrant enemy in this case,[3] the wars in Chechnya, the mass migrations from the Muslim ex–colonies of the Soviet Union and the international anti-Muslim campaign after 11 September 2001 and in Russia itself—after several explosions and hostage situations. Russian people discriminate against many other religions and ethnicities, but anti-Muslim sentiment is the strongest today. Moreover, it is aimed at people who have lived in many cases for centuries in the Empire as its internal 'others'. The incomplete dismantling of the Russian/Soviet Empire complicates this situation. It still retains certain colonial territories (Northern Caucasus), while discriminating against their inhabitants who technically are also Russian citizens, but are nevertheless marred as 'Blacks' and Muslims and told to go back home, even if that home is also Russia.

The post-Soviet period has been marked with pragmatism and cynicism in the relations between the state and Islam. On the one hand, the authorities allow for the existence of Islamic centers, the building of the new mosques, the Muslim festivals, etc. On the other hand, the same authority pretends not to notice the organisations, parties and politicians who openly demonise Islam as a part of today's wider Russian xenophobia (a good example is an Islamophobic internet site *Orthodox Christianity and Islam*). On top of that, there

[3] Islam.ru. Independent Islamic Informational Channel, http://www.islam.ru/ [Last accessed on 4 Aug. 2003].

are clearly more calculated efforts to control the cultural-political unconscious and preserve dominance by flirting with Islam in fear of possible non-systemic organisations and leaders, which the authorities in Russia see as a potential danger.

The configuration of Russia vis-à-vis Islam today is different from that of Europe vis-à-vis its ethnically marked and immigrant Muslims, because the Russian Muslims are not newcomers, as they have sometimes lived on their territory since long before the ethnic Russians arrived. Among other things it means that they are already assimilated by the Russian and Soviet culture to some extent and used to being seen as 'internal others'. This Soviet linguistic and cultural commonality should be stronger than the religious and race differences, but in the mind of a modern Russian xenophobe Islam is seen as an invader, as something coming from outside. The ethnic Muslims are stigmatised by Russians mainly because of their language, appearance and behaviour, which are all conglomerated into the Russian concept of Islam as a colour of skin. The revamped biological racism does not see religion, or interprets it as race so that all dark skinned individuals regardless of their linguistic, religious or cultural belonging become 'Blacks'. The Muslim-Christian divide continues to play a symbolic part but is systematically distorted, which is clearly seen in the fact that the Orthodox identification with the Christian part of the Caucasus does not work, giving place instead to the most primitive racist principles of dividing sameness from otherness. Russians tend to see the Orthodox Christian Georgians or Armenians as Muslims.

The most elementary rights of all national minorities, and especially the Muslims, are being systematically and openly violated. This refers to the right to work, to medical help, education, social security, the right to leave the country, to property rights and even the right to live. A contemporary Muslim in Russia suffers from this lack of most fundamental rights on at least three levels—as a Russian citizen, as an internal other and also globally. For example, for a Chechen it is equally difficult to get a passport with a registration in Moscow, to find a job in any part of Russia or a visa to Europe (Sokolov, 2002).

The trajectory of Islamophobia from Czarist to post-Soviet Russia can be defined as a transition from the internal (relative) to external (absolute) otherness. The latter is directly linked with today's lack in Russia of any mediation of Islamophobic discourses in the previous Soviet forms. The collapse of the Soviet Union made Russians themselves face the painful problem of identity. As their national self-image is largely reduced to spatial dimension ('we are the biggest nation and have the largest territory'), the loss of almost half of the land that they considered their own was interpreted as disloyalty and an infringement upon their national identity. In contemporary mass Islamophobia, the external factors merged with the internal Russian national sentiment of resentment and a need for revenge. Islamophobia thus is closely linked with the identity re-structuring processes going on amongst the Russians themselves. Following the centuries old traditions, they take place in the form of total isolationist rejection and demonising of everything non-Russian and non-Orthodox Christian. At this point Russians can integrate and unite only *against* somebody else and this somebody most often is a Muslim.

The monopoly of Western knowledge in the form of Russian or Soviet mediation (and today in the form of direct borrowing from the West or choosing a more attractive mediator than the losing Russia, as it happens in case of popularity of the Turkish model in the Muslim ex– and present colonies) remains the main manifestation of coloniality and also the main impediment for the development of indigenous movements and indigenous agency among the post-Soviet Muslims. The ethnic elites of the newly independent states continued the economic, social and cultural discrimination of their own people, hiding behind the neo-liberal or ethnic-nationalist slogans and continuing to practice the self-deprecating intellectual dependency on the Western modernity. It is a result of the external imperial difference with its secondary Eurocentrism as the constitutive element that spreads over the colonised as well as the colonisers.

V

What are the possible ways out of today's 'zoological Islamophobia' (Jamal, 2004) as an outcome of a particular local history of the Russian/Soviet Eempire and its aftermath? They would have to be closely linked with the epistemic decolonisation of the Muslim peoples of the post-Soviet world, and with the building of a viable agency that would successfully negotiate a critical bordering stance in between the neo-liberal state and Muslim subjectivity (however vague and insufficient this concept might be), and in the long run, would manage to dismantle Islamophobia as a contemporary manifestation of the rhetoric of modernity. What is needed is not a scientific definition of Islamophobia within the existing terms, but rather, in Gordon's (2006) words, shifting the geography of reason, and revealing the geopolitics of knowledge to show the power epistemic relations between the West and the rest. We need to understand Islamophobia in a wider context of modernity/coloniality and the goal of changing the thinking in order to make Islamophobia or any other xeno-phobia impossible. This process of epistemic decolonisation and liberation from the myths of modernity is in full swing today, including in certain Muslim locales, and is starting even in the ex–Soviet Muslim colonies where for centuries there existed the traditions of trans-cultural 'tricksterism' and 'adaptive and creative resistance' which allows them to embody the project of 're-appropriation of the spirituality which is rooted in the soil' (Marcos, 2006).

An epistemic revolution is possible in the Muslim (ex) colonies, but to initiate it, it is necessary to combine the local and the global levels, to stop thinking in the limits of our own countries or even continents, to dismantle the chronically peripheral position of the peoples of Central Asia or the Caucasus in the world, to let them be a part of the informational and political space of alternative thinking and being on the global scale. In the conditions of the continual zombification of the people, the extreme poverty, the lack of basic human rights and informational isolation, we cannot really hope that this will happen in any foreseeable future. Yet we cannot ignore the way the people who live in these (ex) colonies see and feel the world. Their mentality still carries the traces of other thinking and the ideal of other trans-cultural world of harmonious and just social relations. Today, as before, this sensibility has no political manifestation, being restricted to the allegorical language of the arts, to the sphere of an *'other'* non-rational knowledge, and to gender discourses. This gives a small hope that the voices of around 40 million Central Asians and about the same number of non-Russians in Russia (including around 30 million Muslims) will at some point be heard in the global dialogue of others, that they will finally gain the right to true participation in deciding the future of the world and their own future in this world.

17

CULTURALISM, EDUCATION AND ISLAMOPHOBIA IN CHINA

Lin Yi

The global rise and prominence of Islamophobia as a defining feature of the start of the twenty first century is generally either attributed to the 11 September attacks or associated with the increased presence of Muslims in the Western world (Ben and Jawad, p. 111; Vertovec, 2002, pp. 32–33). In this light, focal insurgencies and other 'little wars' waged on Muslims across the globe have both made claim to and been explained as localised iterations of the War on Terror. Less straightforwardly, prejudice and discrimination against Muslims and polemics around them have similarly referenced cultural and religious factors around loyalties, integration and citizenship. But how Eurocentric in derivation and applicability is Islamophobia as a phenomenon and as a concept? How useful, for example, is it to the analysis of China's policies in East Turkestan or Uyghuristan, which the July 2009 crackdown on the Muslim Uygur riots in its Xinjiang Uygur Autonomous Region (Province) brought to unprecedented media spotlight? This intervention addresses the larger question of how well Islamophobia travels by exploring its relevance to the Chinese context. It proposes three primary criteria with which to identify whether or not, or to what extent, the Western based conception of Islamophobia may be relevant to China. Firstly, is there prejudice or discrimination against Islam or Muslims in China? Secondly, is there a specific 'phobia' against Islam or Muslims which is distinguishable from a general xenophobia against other ethnic minorities in China? Finally, is China's War on Terror an intrinsic part of the worldwide US-led War on Terror? These criteria are brought to bear through three further historical and/or current perspectives that are interrelated with one another: Chinese culturalism, the relationships between Muslims and political regimes, and the everyday discursive practices of the dominant Chinese Han towards Muslims in comparison with that towards other ethnic minorities.

Alongside the Chinese Han, there are fifty-five officially identified ethnic minority groups in China, comprising approximately 8 per cent of the whole population. Of these fifty-five groups, ten are committed to Islam. These Muslim groups can be basically divided into two blocs: those mainly concentrated in Xinjiang (Kazak, Kirgiz, Tajik, Tatar, Uygur and Uzbek), in the far West, and those across China but especially residing in the Gansu-Qinghai–Ningxia (GQN) borderland areas (Bonan, Dongxiang, Hui and Salar), in the northwest. Today the Muslim population is officially given as 20,320,580, accounting for 1.65 per cent of the population of China (National Bureau of Statistics and State Ethnic Affairs Commission, 2003). The Uygur (8,399,393) and the Hui (9,816,805) are the largest groups in the two blocs (*Ibid.*), and have a correspondingly high socio-cultural profile in China. Consequently, this article concentrates on these two Muslim groups. The former are indigenous to Xinjiang and has its own language (a kind of Turkic), however the latter are mainly the descendants of local people and of Muslims who, largely for business reasons or in the wake of war, migrated to China from the 'Middle East' or Central Asia between the seventh and fourteenth centuries. This latter group eventually adopted Chinese as their common language (see below).

Chinese Culturalism

Prejudice or discrimination against ethnic minorities as a whole is ingrained in China's ancient culturalism and manifests itself through shifting discursive repertoires depending on the differing historical circumstances. It is through these repertoires that the Chinese Han majority attempts to maintain control of legitimacy. Central to this culturalism is the belief that China was the only true civilisation, and this belief had remained undiminished even under military occupation and threats of alien invaders or migrants as other nationalities were perceived to be 'backward'. Furthermore, this culturalism requires that rulers should be educated and must govern according to Confucian ways of the universal values. Such culturalism is also applicable to aliens as the alleged

Han Chinese superiority is attributed to the 'civilising' effects of education, which also has the power to legitimise non-Chinese (James Harrison, 1969, cited in Townsend, 1992, pp. 98-99). This culturalist idea made it possible for non-Chinese to become Chinese and vice versa, dependent upon whether they behaved in Chinese ways as set out in the Confucian classics that advocated the rule of rites and traditional morals (Chen, 1989; Xiao, 1995). In other words, Han Chinese, as the name of a people(s) versus non-Chinese, reflected the fluidity of the boundary between Chinese and non-Chinese, and has resulted in the category of 'Chinese Han' being problematic in itself (Fei, 1989; Gladney, 2004).

Fundamentally, while the dominant group sets rules and standards, these are specifically designed to create 'others' and, from the outset, set the 'outsider' groups at a disadvantaged position. What matters then is not if the 'others' are aliens to Chinese society, but rather, if they are capable of transforming themselves into 'non-others'. This helps to explain the alien nomadic peoples' 'willingness' in acquisition of Chinese culture after entering the middle and lower reaches of the Yellow River, where allegedly the meticulous Chinese agricultural civilisation emerged (Fei, 1989). Ebrey (1996, p. 23) also infers from the fact that so many non-Chinese people have sought to claim descent from Chinese migrants that either, in looking down upon other non-Chinese, they truly wanted to believe it, or that it was in their interest to do so, for local politics or for social prestige.

Similarly, Confucians did not seem to practice the exclusion of various non-Chinese peoples from the Chinese group, as Confucius himself believed that *yuanren* (literally 'people from afar') could be attracted to its 'universal' culture or morals. In other words, those who were unwilling to accept the universal values set out by Confucians would therefore exercise self-exclusion from Chinese society. By the same token, when talking about rulers from different backgrounds, Chinese or otherwise, Mencius argued that they would be similarly accountable so long as their behaviour accorded to Chinese ways. Therefore, culturalism has determined ethnic boundaries and cultural membership in history (see particularly, Yi, 2005). Furthermore, whilst the supposed superiority of Chinese civilisation ran through all the dynasties of Chinese or non-Chinese rulers, this ideology was not only premised on an abstract concept, but had been institutionalised through, principally, the establishment of the civil service examinations of imperial China (*keju kaoshi*) (see Elman, 2000), and reinforced through the continuity of the examinations system lasting almost uninterrupted for thirteen hundred years before it finally came to an end at the end of the imperial era (1904) (Schirokauer, 1981, p. 7). The examinations system held up and reinforced the classics of Confucianism as a standard, and eventually became essential for the establishment of imperial autocracy in late imperial China (Elman, 2000).

One of the main reasons why this system could survive for thirteen hundred years was closely connected with the first emperor, who standardised the Chinese writing system, Chinese characters (*hanzi*), which became the official writing system of imperial China. This is because only with a uniform writing system would it become possible for the state and elites to gain control and exercise power over the masses (Lewis, 1999). In unveiling the association of writing with authority in early China (the Warring States period), Lewis (1999, p. 4) states that writing was employed to create the entire world, a world that 'provided models for the unprecedented enterprise of founding a world empire'. In doing so, the elites 'who composed, sponsored, or interpreted' this world gained authority on the one hand, and on the other, 'secured the longevity of the imperial system and led to the omnipresence of the written graph in Chinese culture'. This standardised system enabled the literary-based civil service examinations to be conducted across this vast country, where languages in different locations, to a varied extent, were mutually unintelligible. As a result, *hanzi* not only functioned as the conveyor of the classics, but also evolved a highly sophisticated form of art—calligraphy. To acquire Chinese characters is therefore necessary for people to become literate, and furthermore, to access 'universal' morality and high culture. As a consequence, Chinese characters became both the most basic and the most important symbol of Chinese (high) culture, and those who fluently master this system were considered highly respectable.

As a consequence, Chinese culturalism eventually resulted in education being technically closely related to the acquisition of Chinese characters, which is symbolically associated to one's 'cultural level' (*wenhua shuiping* or *wenhua chengdu*). This has resulted in 'wenhua', or 'culture', being the preferred vernacular expression in public discourse. Indeed, this preference for 'culture' complies with the traditional conception: acquisition of Chinese characters, and the whole package of knowledge it conveys (including sciences). In this light Islam, like all cultures other than Chinese, is regarded as a lower civilisation as they have not acquired Chinese characters. In his illustration of the conception of 'culture' in the Chinese context, Gladney (1999, p. 59) describes an elderly Muslim Hui Hajji who did not think that he had culture despite the fact that this Hajji had spent twelve years living in the Middle East, was a master of the Islamic natural sciences, and was fluent in Persian and Arabic, but not Chinese. Lipman similarly demonstrates that in imperial history, 'Chinese officials could not possibly regard texts in Arabic and Persian, or even Muslim texts written in elegant Chinese, as civilized' (Lipman, 1997, p. 213). This idea is actually reflected in the two characters of the Chinese word *wenhua* itself. *Wen*, translated as 'literary, literature, script, inscription', is the 'central part of the idea of culture', and *hua*, translated as 'change, transform', is the process of culturing people (Gladney, 1999, p. 59).[1]

Muslims and Political Regimes

Under these historical circumstances, the Muslims who migrated to China from the West or Central Asia experienced dramatic changes in their relationships with the political regimes and/or Chinese society. In the Tang and Song dynasties of Chinese regimes (618–1276) when these Muslims started to move to China, their influence in Chinese society was restricted to the economic and business arenas, without access to wider Chinese culture. Under the Yuan Dynasty of the Mongolian regimes (1279–1368), in spite of the somewhat privileged socio-political status with which they were endowed by the Yuan rulers, largely for political purposes, and sinicisation among some Muslims, as a consequence of their distinctive religious faith and corresponding life style, Muslims were still subject to specific regimes of control and disengaging from the dominant Chinese culture around them. Their socio-cultural status was much more seriously threatened with the succession of the Ming Dynasty (1368–1644) when the Chinese regained political power. The Ming rulers re-established Confucianism as the official ideology and implemented an assimilation policy towards Muslims, which inhibited Muslims from wearing their traditional clothes, speaking their own languages, using their surnames, or even marrying their co-ethnics. This cultural assimilation directly resulted in the loss of the diverse languages of these different Muslim groups and a gradual decline in a distinct identity. Their Islamic faith and (to a lesser extent) related life style and cultural habits became their only distinctive feature. This

---

[1] However, today *wenhua* can also be used in *shaoshu minzu wenhua* (ethnic minority cultures). *Wenhua* in this context does not contain the same meaning as it does in 'having (no Chinese) culture', but rather, refers to the historical heritage of ethnic minorities and so is thought to be static and should be kept in museums (also see Gladney, 2004, especially chapter three).

was the major force driving these differential Muslim communities to eventually adopt Chinese as their common language, and form into one group: thus emerged the modern Hui ethnic group.

The sinicisation of the Hui enabled a number of its scholars to interpret and explain Islamic faith and tenets in Chinese. While this facilitated Chinese understanding of Islam as well as Muslim absorption of Confucian cultural and moral values, this intellectual endeavor was unable to bridge the cultural gap between the Chinese and the Hui, especially at the grassroots level where a large number of Muslims (and Chinese too) were illiterate in Chinese and Muslim practice appeared alien to atheist Chinese (or even, to a lesser extent, to Buddhist Chinese or those from other religious groups). This cultural gap between the Muslim community and the larger society resulted in vendettas between Hui and Chinese people in some regions, and was in particular exacerbated by serious conflicts between the Manchurian Qing regime of the last Empire (1644–1911) and the Muslim community, despite the fact that it started from conflicts between Islamic sects within the Hui community. The Muslim Hui began to be seen and treated as rebels, and hence the Qing regime lost its interest in guaranteeing their lives and faith (Lipman, 1997; Songben and Matsumoto, 2003). Lipman (1997, pp. 219; 255) insightfully points out both that 'rebel' must be seen as a state-created category in most of these conflicts, and that it is fundamentally the theme of 'home' that lies at the core of these rebellions. All of this revealed a serious lack of communicative mechanisms between the Hui and the wider society, which has led Lipman (1997, pp. xxx; xxxii) to argue that, in 'Chinese writing about Muslims over the past 300 years, one theme overrides all others—that of violence'—a theme which has been articulated by Confucian, nationalist and communist alike.

Thus, in spite of the idea supported by the Nationalist Party (with the aim of making a single Chinese nation) that the Hui, as Chinese speakers, are Han Chinese believing in Islam, the Hui possess distinctive cultural features in comparison with the Chinese Han (Songben and Matsumoto, 2003). Further, they are not a homogeneous group, especially in terms of their diverse origins. In their attempt to subvert the dominant definitions of 'Chineseness', to resist homogenisation, and to remain different but present, (Hui) Muslims came to be the 'familiar strangers' to Chinese society (Lipman, 1997, p. xxxv). Under these circumstances, Hui survivors of elites from the Qing dynasty in the Nationalist Republican era (1911–1949 in Mainland China) started exploring how to address Han biases (Qing was not ruled by Han though) and thus to safeguard their lives and freedom of religion. Furthermore, they reconciled their attempts to revive their religion and to make a contribution to the Chinese revolution. This reconciliation was promoted and strengthened by their awareness that they were unable to overwhelm the Chinese, and hence that it did not make much sense to seek to establish their own regime. Consequently they became co-operators with the Chinese Han (Songben and Matsumoto, 2003).

The latest regime of the Communist Party tends to be suspicious of religion as responsible for political or ideological wars between the religious communities and the party-state, and as a threat to the party's regime. Concomitantly, based on its Marxist-Leninist oriented evolutionary ideology, the party regards secularism as a progressive or modern culture (a different version of culturalism?). Consequently, atheist Chinese Han top the evolutionary league table, and thus bear an obvious responsibility for 'civilising' less civilised minorities (Harrell, 1995 and *Zhongguo Lishi*, 1995, pp. 187–189). The perceived political threat and cultural inferiority of ethno-religious minorities in combination have resulted in the strict exclusion of religion—Islam, Buddhism or otherwise—from the public domain (schools especially).

Given the limited interest in Muslims amongst culturalist Chinese and the party-state's hard line on religion, it is hardly surprising that the study of Islam and Muslims in modern China has largely been confined to historical introduction or interpretation rather than to intellectual inquiry into the faith and the people. This limitation not only hindered the development of a Chinese 'Orientalist' study of Muslims in China, but also politically conditioned Chinese scholars in the adoption and application of Western Orientalism to their study of Muslims. Furthermore, what little study of Islam and Muslims has been conducted in Chinese in modern China has been largely confined to the Hui, while the Muslim Uygur has largely been ignored. This is due in part to the language barrier, and also to the geographic segregation of the Uygur who are predominantly concentrated in the far West. The geopolitical importance of Xinjiang as a frontier province has also long persuaded the Chinese regime of the necessity of integrating it with Inland China. All of this has made the Uygur a culturally exotic ethnic group to Chinese society, and a politically unstable community to the state. This has created cultural distance between the Uygur and the wider Chinese society, making the Uygur the less familiar or even unfamiliar strangers to the majority of Chinese.

Mainstream Discursive Repertoires About Muslims

The estrangement of Muslim communities, then, is both a consequence of a historical discourse of Chinese culturalism and is shaped by Muslim relations with the different political regimes. At the same time, this estrangement is all along substantiated and realised through the everyday discursive practices of the dominant Chinese Han. Whilst both academia and the public do not regard religion-centered minority cultures as negatively as government policy implies (Yi, 2007), they primarily treat minority cultures as a source of entertainment: with Chinese culture as the mundane taken for granted, and thus invisible, minority cultures stand out as visibly exotic (Wetherell and Potter, 1992; Harrell, 1995; Gladney, 2004). Meanwhile, educated within and echoing the evolutionary ideology of the Communist Party, Chinese Han usually tend to view religion as superstition or anti-secularism (and therefore anti-modern) (Yi, 2008). Holding these kinds of views of minority cultures, the majority of the Chinese Han is far from enthusiastic to learn about them. As a consequence, minority cultures remain on the periphery of the public and private life of the cultural-political mainstream.

More specifically, in comparisons of Islam and other religions in China, as case studies have shown (Yi, 2007), individual Chinese respondents perceive Islamic doctrines as too strict, making Muslims very pious and so 'natural' disciples. As evidence, respondents cite their impressions that Muslim live in closed communities separate from other groups. According to many Chinese, this self-segregation also means that perceived 'feudal customs' (such as patriarchy) are sustained and reproduced. At the same time, Muslims are labeled as 'innate merchants', a factor which is thought to determine Muslims' reluctance towards school education in favor of material profit. All this is claimed to be ingrained in the low quality (*suzhi*) of the Muslim community, in particular in their low levels of education.[2] These negative views of Muslims, allied to a traditional Chinese view of trade that belittles 'unscrupulous' merchants, results in a general impression that Muslims are untrustworthy.[3] Such percep-

---

[2] On the Chinese discourse of *suzhi*, see Anagnost (2004), Murphy (2004) and Kipnis (2006).

[3] In the era of the global knowledge economy, Chinese society no longer belittles commerce; yet, depreciative perceptions of the mainly self-employed Muslims are still governed by traditional frames of reference (Yi, 2005). Contradictions abound here, since all over South-East Asia, the Chinese (Han) are thought of as 'innate merchants', whose mode of organisation is described by Hill Gates (1996) as petty capitalist. A

tions lead the Chinese to try to prove that according to Chinese cultural traditions Muslims are culturally foreign and morally evil. The professed inherent nature of these alleged negative Muslim traits lead the Han Chinese and many other ethnic communities to deduce that Muslims are uneducable and incapable of change as well as being unapproachable and untrustworthy.

These Chinese discursive repertoires in relation to Muslims are typically reflected in the discourse of 'cultivation'—which is embedded in China's civilising projects (Harrell, 1995)—applied in evaluating and judging minorities by the degree to which different groups have sought to adapt themselves to Han Chinese culture in general, and state education in particular (Yi, 2007). Cultivation is thought to be a good thing when it works along the lines of assimilation to Chinese culture. Thus, those ethnic minority communities who are seen to be making an effort in this direction, for example, by sending their children to mainstream schools or removing their ethno-religious markers such as, Muslim headscarves, in public life, are praised (see Yi, 2006). Conversely, cultivation that reinforces ethno-religious tradition (Yi, 2008) is seen as retrogressive. Thus, in Chinese eyes, Muslims are deemed over nationalistic because of the way they cultivate their own ethno-religious tradition in sending their children to Mosques, withholding them from state schools, or 'stubbornly' wearing their ethno-religious markers. Such adherence to their own tradition is blamed for their 'resistance' to Chinese culture. Thus they are uneducable within the framework of supposedly advanced Chinese culture. Furthermore, as 'uneducable', Muslims are in fact seen as being more in need of education, or, 'modernisation'.

Islamophobia—Global and Local Discourses

Returning to the questions posed at the start of this chapter, two of the answers should now be clear. While more academic research into the extent to which Muslims are or are not excluded from economic, social and public life in China is urgently needed, it can justifiably be said that prejudice and discrimination against ethnic minorities, including Muslims, in China is embedded in Chinese culturalism against non-Chinese who are seen as comparatively uncivilised. Moreover, and in respect of Muslims, there is a specific 'phobia' at work,

---

comparable phenomenon is that of the so-called Chinese Han from South-Eastern China, who make up the majority of the overseas Chinese in South-East Asia, who are widely viewed by the rest of China as innate merchants.

which emerges from Chinese culturalism against Islam or Muslims that is to some extent distinct from that general xenophobia in regard of ethnic minorities in China. That said, in regard of the third question, I would argue that China's War on Terror against what is known as East Turkestan or Uyghuristan after 9/11, the crackdown on the Uygur riots in Xinjiang from July 2009 onward included, is not inherently related to prejudice against Islam. Rather, China's War on Terror is better seen as part of the stock response to challenges to the ruling power of the state from upheavals connected to any of its cultural or social minority communities. As a political and military action by the rulers against purportedly disloyal social or cultural communities and indiscriminately directed at any 'disloyal' groups. The Uygur, in the case in point (which in any case is only one of the ten Muslim communities in China), but just as easily Buddhist Tibetans (as in the crackdown on the Lasa riots in the Spring of 2008), the largely Chinese Han practitioners of Falun Gong (Ownby, 2008), or any other mobilised masses perceived as a threat to the stability of the power of the party-state.

China's War on Terror imports the legitimising discourse and cover of the global War on Terror, but is not best seen or understood from the same perspective or in the same context. The US-led War on Terror is an extension of the ethnic penalty suffered by settler and citizen Muslim communities in the West (such as in France and the Netherlands), at the hands of Western forces in Muslimistan, epitomised by the torture of Iraqi prisioners at the hands of American forces at Abu Ghraib. This and other forms of the War on Terror are underwritten by the Islamophobic discourse of the 'Arab Mind' (Butler, 2008). Such articulations of the War on Terror between global, externalising, Muslimistan centered discourses, and local, internal, nation-state framed expressions do not transpose along with the label to the Chinese case. If prejudice and discrimination against Muslims by the wider society in China is a form of Islamophobia, it is fundamentally embedded within Chinese culturalism.

18

ISLAMOPHOBIA IN TURKEY

Yasin Aktay

The very notion of Islamophobia in Turkey will strike some as an odd proposition. While it is the identification of Turkey with its overwhelmingly, at least nominally, Muslim population that accounts for what is seemingly disconcerting in the coupling of Islamophobia and Turkey, the intuitively greater obstacle concerns perhaps the very notion of Muslim Islamophobes. Yet Muslim Islamophobes there are, and Turkey is pivotal to their discussion.

Islamophobia in Turkey needs to be understood with reference to the context in which Kemalism as a cultural-political project restructured post-Ottoman society. The significance of Kemalism, however, extends beyond the Turkish Republic and the policies of Mustafa Kemal and his successors. Arguably, Kemalism describes the dominant political discourse which has held sway over most of Muslimistan since the end of the caliphate in 1924, and most of Muslimistan in the post-colonial period is characterised by the application of the experience which Kemalism typifies (Sayyid, 2003, p. 70).

The Kemalist political body relied on the repression of the Islamicate body, which required an elaborate system of bodily regulations. Since repression invites the possibility of the return of the repressed, Kemalism continued to be haunted by the return of assertive Muslim identifications (Sayyid, 2003, p. 3). This fear of Muslim identity was expressed in the slogan '*irtica hortladi*'—a notion which, through the imagery of a spectre conjured back from the dead, conveys the dread and repulsion of a reactionary return of religion in social or political life. The revival of religious identity in Turkey has, ever since, been held back under the pressure of this accusation, and its deployment has been one of the main forms in which Islamophobia in the Kemalist register has been articulated. It was the justification called upon in the legitimation of the Turkish military interventions in the *coups d'état* of 1960, 1980, and 1997. And when, in 2007, the military once more sought to intervene in the Turkish political process against the ruling Justice and Development Party (AKP) and the election of its Presidential nominee, Abdullah Gul, it did so again in the name of saving Turkey from being dragged back to medieval religious obscurantism.

The identification of 'backwardness' with all that which the Kemalist modernising project sought to expunge from the Turkish Republic was framed against a simplistic antithesis of secularism and religion. Its ideological foundation was a second rate translation of Western modernism. Thus the route to modernisation was followed through a strategy of Westernisation. However, to be Western was to cast off the trappings of Eastern/Islamic baggage, which paradoxically required continuously and obsessively emphasising the eastern-Islamic identity while trying to suppress it (Sayyid, 2003, p. 69). What in Europe could be described as the sociological process of the 'death of God', was rendered into Turkish as burying God into the (private) conscience of the individual. Turkish secularism was formulated in terms of the dictate that 'religion is an individual matter that is limited to the relationship between man [sic] and God'; it should have no social manifestation or influence beyond the confines of private conscience. Considering the distinct historical and contemporary sociological place of Islam in Turkish society of the time, this was essentially akin to burying the religion alive. Yet precisely because the secularists were only too aware of that very prominence and the entrenchment of Islam, that, in other words, what they pronounced dead and sought to bury as a corpse was indeed very much alive, the funeral rites were riddled with anxieties. Unsurprisingly, secularisation policies are saturated with the language and fears of an atavistic return of Islam and the policing and repression of manifestations of relapse. Hence the targeting of marked religious habituses (headscarfs, Qur'an courses, and general life-styles) assumed to symbolise that backwardness. The symbolic antithesis of 'the headscarf' and 'wine-drinking' is perhaps the most prominent, dichotomous example of this. While the headscarf is seen as the symbol of withholding from if not holding back Turkish development and movement towards becoming Western, and is consequently repressed, drinking symbolically signifies, and is endorsed, as the embrace of the modern. It thus comes as no surprise that in recruitment into Turkish State bureaucracies, Human Resources evaluations take more than passing interest in whether individuals are in the habit of drinking or not. Or that female students wearing headscarves are not allowed into high schools or even onto University grounds. Indeed, so powerful is the charged symbolism of the veil that discriminatory practices at work extend to husbands of women who veil. Their exclusion from the military and some bureaucratic positions is accepted and legitimate State practice, but being supported by normative official ideology it is also spreading into the private sector.

Turkish state ideology has, then, since the foundation of the Republic, been based on an imagined war against the agents of backwardness—a permanent war wielded as an instrument of exclusion. A permanent threat legitimises a permanent vigil, thereby justifying intervention by the military as the Guardians of the Republic. After the most recent intervention, the so called postmodern *coup d'état* or e-memorandum of 22 April 2007, however, legal proceedings were launched which constitute the first attempt to bring military intervention to account under the law. Though the legal case is still ongoing, what the investigation has already uncovered about the background to the history of military interventions has brought to light the deeply embedded nature of an organisation behind the various recent *coup* attempts. This organisation appears to have branches in the military, bureaucratic, academic, legal, business, media and even underground mafia worlds working in collaboration to prepare the conditions for a military *coup* against the government. The investigation suggests that this so-called Ergenekon organisation was responsible for a number of assassinations, the orchestration of actions by agents-provocateurs, and media operations designed to create the impression that the country was being taken-over by reactionary religious forces intent on implementing the Shariah, suppressing modern life-styles, enforcing the veiling of women, and cutting off Turkey's relations with the modern, Western world.[1] The 'exposure' of insidious and concerted forces at work prepared the ground for justifying military intervention, while media coverage of a number of fabricated stories about Islamists laid the ground for its receptive acceptance. Ultra-conservative religious figures made to appear representative, stories from everyday life about Islamists intol-

---

[1] Iran is typically held as the frightening fate of the country if the revival of backwardness was to take hold; depending on the agenda, Algeria or Saudi Arabia play a similar role. In a more recent media operation against the AK Party Malaysia was used to symbolise religious-based Muslim oppression of religious minorities and non-religious and secularist groups.

erant of drink and of secularist life-styles were brought into the limelight to exemplify what the future held for Turkey under Islamist rule.

Against this background, in May 2006 the offices of the daily newspaper *Cumhuriyet*, a renowned citadel of secularist ideology and a vocal opponent of all religious ideologies, was three times the target of attack by hand grenades. Though none of the attacks caused any death or injury, the message was driven home that reactionary groups were at work, for whom the life of secularists was of no account. In response to the attacks the Media rallied its analysts who reinforced the seriousness of the threat posed by a political Islam emboldened by support from a friendly government. A mere few days after the series of attacks on *Cumhuriyet* came a more shocking assassination attempt on members of the Council of State which left one Judge dead and several wounded. The apprehension of the perpetrator of the 17 May attack, however, changed everything, as the connection was then established between this and the earlier attacks, and his links were revealed to be with ultra nationalist secularist, not Islamist, groups, with ties to a shadowy network known as Ergenekon.[2]

The attack on the members of the Council of State was sensationally intended to send the strongest possible signal of the gravity of the threat of 'Islamic terrorism'. The timing and target, following the Council's ruling on the headscarf ban, appeared by itself to suggest the purported perpetrators and motives. A complaint had been brought against a head teacher who, though she did not wear the headscarf in school, was known to do so outside of it, on account that as a role model her practice would unduly influence her students. The Council's decision following upon prolonged trials, to uphold the ban, which cost the teacher's job, in effect represented an extension of the ban beyond the public realm with predictable outcries from an incensed Muslim public opinion.

The attack on the Council of State empowered a counter-response focused on the pro-Islamist government under the slogan: 'Turkey is secularist, and will remain secularist forever!' Major newspapers and TV channels reported the event as 'the Turkish 9/11'. The funerals of those killed in the attack, attended by senior members of the military and the judiciary received full television coverage. Yet, even while coverage of the attack was being elaborated along such lines, the police investigation was beginning to reveal its oppositional, anti-government ideology. This revelation took Turkey by surprise. The idea of 'the Turkish 9/11' collapsed.

---

[2] For an alternative, sceptical take on the Ergenekon conspiracy see Jenkins (2009).

The investigation became a turning point in the process of deciphering the workings of the Kemalist 'deep state' in Turkey. Assassination cells linked with the military were brought to light, as were plots and plans including *coups d'état* (code-named 'Moonlight' and 'Yellow Girl') that involved former senior generals. In a series of police raids, weapons and bombs were recovered from numerous places related to the people arrested in connection with the investigation and arrests. The plan emerging was intended to foster instability to the point where the threat of a looming imposition of Shariah law by the elected Erdogan government would pave the way for a call to the saving hand of 'the secularist army of Mustafa Kemal'.

Islamophobia, then, plays out within an integrated logic of the reproduction of power; moral panics about Islam are deployed as part of the strategy of the deep state vying with the elected government for control. Islamophobia, in this context, is an instrument of power. The 'Islamist Conspiracy', which it conjures up, inverts and masks the conspiracy against Islamism.

The official Kemalist discourse that has been assimilated into popular culture has developed on the politico-theological notion that Turkey is surrounded by sea on three sides and by enemies on all four sides. A prevailing siege mentality ensues. The resulting paranoid style of securitarian politics has, however, focused more on internal enemies, and its own peoples, than on the foreign, though these 'internal enemies' are in turn construed as agents of external enemies. Three figures make up the historical repertoire of internal enemies of Turkish nationalist discourse: 'separatists', essentially the Kurdish nationalists seeking to break (away from) the state; 'communists', serving Soviet interests against the state; and Muslims, agents of Islamist religious reaction seeking to capture the state.

The rise of left-wing political movements and the violent activities which accompanied organised left political mobilisation, lent support to claims that talked-up its apparent threat. Only later was it to become clear that the street violence associated with the left was actually largely organised and manipulated in order to prepare the ground and public opinion for military intervention. There was no communist take over in the planning nor did communism pose a realistic threat, though making it appear so paved the way for the military *coup d'état* of 12 September 1980. The similar ratcheting up of an Islamic menace, of the return of religious backwardness and prospect of an imposition of Shariah, has constituted the more sustained and ingrained justification for maintaining permanent military tutelage over the government.

The various military *coups* in the history of the modern Turkish State have been legitimised with reference to the Army's mission to guard the secularist foundation of the Republic established by Atatürk, against reactionary attempts to destroy it. When the Welfare Party, led by Necmettin Erbakan, whose discourse and originary political affiliations were Islamist, obtained the majority of the votes in the 1995 elections, a new wave of Islamophobia was licensed. An obsessive media focus on the religious—rituals, events, figures, rhetoric—reinforced the impression already created of a colonisation by regressive religion. To ward off such a threat, a series of measures were introduced, such as forbidding the headscarf in schools, restricting the use of 'religious' garb in public, tighter control of religious activities, reducing the number of *Imam-Hatip* schools [the Turkish state-sponsored version of *madrassas* instituted as vocational training secondary schools for government employed imams] and obstructing their path to university education, hounding Islamist sympathisers out of the civil service and universities, etc. Since the signs of reactionarism were essentially those that signaled Muslim identification the result was a kind of Islamophobic McCarthyism. Lifestyles and opinions—the Army officer who prays at home; the civil servant whose wife wears the headscarf; being in good standing with certain religious communities or harbouring sympathies towards religious-based civil movements—all became signs which not merely brought suspicion but were tantamount to proof of insurgent intent.

In 1997 Istanbul University instituted the application of a headscarf ban on Campus. Massive protest took place against this but Istanbul University's decision was followed by the extension of the ban to all universities. Though the ban was arbitrarily imposed and had no clear basis in law, it found widespread support in the legal profession and judiciary.[3] When legal recourse was made against the practice as discriminatory, the courts ruled in favour of the practice. The result was that tens of thousands of female students had to either leave their studies or compromise against their sense of religious obligation. Many opted to pursue education abroad. Discrimination based on the wearing of headscarfs had by this time become so ingrained, that rough treatment of women who veiled became acceptable. Students caught by security staff wear-

[3] Attitudes in the Turkish judiciary were deeply influenced by Islamophobic discourses surrounding and informing discussions of the headscarf. Attempts to seek redress by taking headscarf cases to the European Court of Human Rights, such as in the case of Leyla Sahin, were frustrated when the ban was upheld, causing some rethinking of attitudes to the European Union. On the European Court treatment of the case see Gunn (2005) and Aktay (2008, pp. 99–108).

ing headscarfs were humiliated and banished. Those who preferred to leave studies for work had to accept lower wages and standards because of their lower educational qualifications and provided a cheap reserve of labour for capitalism.

When, in 1998, the *Refah* (Islamic Welfare Party) was outlawed by the Supreme Court and its leader, Erbakan, restricted from political activities, its deputies reconstituted under the newly formed *Fazilet* (Virtue) Party. In the subsequent election of 18 April 1999, Merve Kavakci, a headscarved female candidate, was elected to the National Assembly. At her very first attempt to attend a meeting, however, she was prevented and forced out of the Assembly by protesting members of the Social Democratic Party. Soon after, she was prosecuted and even her citizenship entitlement taken away on account of her dual citizenship (an otherwise normally favourably regarded status). Her party's support of her, moreover, was taken as an excuse for launching a challenge in the Supreme Court to have the party itself banned.[4]

Also in 1998 the National Assembly revised the National Educational system to make the compulsory educational period eight years 'without interruption'. The implied and intended consequence was the closure of middle schools catering to the first three years of education, the Imam-Hatip together with the professional middle schools. The further intended consequence was, as proved to be the case, the drastic decrease even in the high school period of Imam-Hatip schools. Leaving nothing to chance, yet another regulation, this time focusing on entry into universities, prevented students from professional high schools, including the Imam-Hatip schools, from enrolment into any but the Theology Faculties, whether or not their results were higher than those of students from regular high schools. Closing any gaps the rule was retrospectively applied to cover even students already in the system. Students' rights and expectations violated and frustrated, they were treated as enemies of the state. Otherwise successful students were excluded and once again while some opted to pursue studies abroad, others dropped out of education.

The so called postmodern *coup* of 28 February—though it neither formally overthrew the democratic process nor brought the Army into power—is nonetheless in continuity with previous Army interventions in the political process, not least in respect of broader effects in the struggle for control of economic resources. The coincidence between the timing of the *coup* and the financial

---

[4] For a more detailed and first-hand account of the story of the first veiled woman in the Turkish National Assembly see Kavakci (2004, pp. 66–67).

crisis felt in the Turkish banking system, as well as the involvement of certain high ranking figures in the *coup*, contributed to a public perception of the *coup* as primarily economically driven and riddled with corruption. Under the impact of the severe economic depression that hit Turkey in 2001, such public perceptions, combined with the reaction to the mounting, licensed Islamophobia, paved the way for a political reversal.

It is against this context of a mass popular reaction to the *coup* of 28 February that a mere fifteen months after its formation the AK Party, under the leadership of the current prime minister, Recep Tayyip Erdoğan, emerged from the elections of 3 November 2002 with a majority mandate. The party which came to power was already a second successive reconfiguration forced by the proscription of the Virtue Party in June 2001. Erdogan himself was, at the time of his party's victory, banned from political office following conviction and jail time in 1998 for the public reading of certain lines from a poem which, though by a nationalist writer, read as an Islamist challenge. If Erdogan and AKP's victory stands as a reaction to the military intervention of 28 February, their success in turn prompted a counter-reaction against the government. In 2003–04 high ranking military were involved in the preparation of a *coup* against the government only frustrated because of the non-adherence of the head of the army, Hilmi Ozkok.

Publication of excerpts from a diary, kept by a high-ranking officer, in the weekly magazine *Nokta* in 2007 are revealing of the nature and detail of the planned intervention.[5] It became clear, for one thing, that proposed moves against the Government had been mooted among the military ever since the Government came to power. For another, that *coup* plans envisaged a series of preparatory initiatives designed to legitimise intervention. Admiral Özden Örnek, the presumed author of the diary, appears to have withdrawn from the organisation to which he had originally been invited after coming to the conclusion that contrary to the motives which first drew him in, the planned *coup* was motivated more by personal ambition for power than the avowed salvation of the Republic and its secularist foundations. Safeguard of the secular Republic was, however, its cover, and its justification prepared through a psychological propaganda campaign centred on the demonisation of Islamism. Both information in the published diary and documents revealed by the Ergenekon

---

[5] *Nokta*, no. 22 (29 May–4 Apr. 2007). After publishing this diary the magazine came under prosecution from the Military Court and was consequently closed down by its owner a few months later.

investigation, expose the innumerable manipulations at work to foster the image of Islamists as terrorists. Thus, even while the motivations and links to secularist-nationalist groups was being established for the assassination of three Christian missionaries in Malatya in April 2006 and of Bishop Santoro in Trabzon in 2005, both were immediately attributed to Muslim organisations and cited in the major media channels and newspapers as representative examples of an Islamic terrorism nurtured by the policies of the AKP government. This Islamophobic moral panic centred on Islamic terrorism was ratcheted-up on the eve of the Presidential election.

From the moment the JDP secured its surprise majority vote and obtained some 360 seats in the parliament, secularist circles started mounting a concerted campaign centred on a looming threat. That threat was the very real possibility now created by the parliamentary majority that the Government would get its own candidate into the Presidency. The political system in Turkey has been conceived on the basis of a tacit separation of state and government. The AKP government represented a victory of the periphery against the centre, and the centre, which saw itself as the natural governing class was not happy at the prospect of also losing the state. Erdoğan Teziç, head of the Council of Higher Education, perfectly expressed this reaction when, in a speech in 2007, he stated that 'they seized the government, that is terrible enough but now they insist on taking the state, too. But they should know that the state will not be delivered to them so easily, it was won by blood and it will be lost again only with blood'. In this sense, Islamophobia is the discourse of the power elite struggling to secure the foundations of its own legitimacy and hold on power. This hold on power, closely linked with control of the presidency, trumps the functioning of democracy. Thus it is that the former Attorney General, who led the banning of the Welfare Party on the grounds that it was not a secular party stated that 'no matter how many votes they receive, even if they win ninety percent of the votes, a party which is suspected of being against secularism will not be allowed to come into government'.

On the eve of the Presidential election, with the AKP fielding Abdullah Gull's candidacy, this attitude was rife and urgent. Turkey's oldest newspaper, founded by Mustafa Kemal and mouthpiece of Kemalism launched a provocative campaign of televised and press advertisements under the slogan 'Are you aware of the danger?'. The danger being the election to Çankaya Köşkü [the presidential residence] of a candidate whose wife wore the headscarf—the superimposition of the veil and Çankaya Köşkü thus exacerbating the symbolic clash, and the Islamist takeover and violation of the ultimately sacrosanct secular space of Kemalism. The newspaper itself had a rather limited circulation, but combined with television and take up of the campaign by the various secularist circles it gathered momentum. More importantly, this was only one symbolic expression of a broader articulated and overlapping reaction which spanned from the mobilisation of military officers, paramilitaries and Kemalist youth associations at mass rallies, to moral panics around Islamisation through to counter-information pinning assassinations on Islamist terrorists. The fundamental implicit message was the warning of a military *coup* if the government sought to alter the secular/Kemalist nature of the Turkish republic. Its justification was laid by turning the Islamists into the violators, society into victims, and the Army into its Guardians. Thus it was in speeches and opinion pieces on television and the printed media that the dominant discourse emerged as the threat to both ethnic and religious minorities and to the secular lifestyle of ordinary citizens under an AKP Islamic Republic. Thus, despite the AKP's demonstrable record of initiatives to integrate Kurdish, Alevite and other minority identities into the system and to establish a new pluralist social and national contract with minorities; despite the absence of violations or intentions to violate secular life styles, and the—on the contrary—visible mass targeting of veiled women and Muslim lifestyles, the moral panic centred on a purported sinister plot to implement the Shariah. The paradoxical result, was mass demonstrations mobilised in defence of the Republic and against an entirely phantasmatic future encroachment on freedom of liberal life styles, calling for the arbitrary denial of the immediate and concrete democratic freedoms of a presidential candidate and of headscarf bearing fellow citizens. The Islamophobic discourse is not dispelled by the 'facts' of the AKP's actual policies or of the concrete contexts, agendas, agents and supporters of Islamist politics. It is the articulation of an assertive Muslim identity as such that is at stake. Islamophobia in Turkey is the product of a systemic and systematic process engendered at the service of the power elite of the Republic whose perpetuation in power is secured by the production of moral panics around Islam(ism). Mass conspiracy is an important element in the generation and maintenance of elite dominance. As Aktay, Oplinger and Talbot (2004, p. 105) state, conspiracies can certainly be based on fact but the factual kernel to the conspiracy is often dramatically exaggerated or even entirely fictitious. Such conspiracies are built on the, often ruthless, dramatisation of a moral boundary and the use of vague categories of deviance ('ideological mopery') to populate the fictitious underground with labeled conspirators of the most nefarious kind. These processes generate sufficient insecurity in the general population to justify the application of enhanced measures of social control claimed as commensurate to the nature of the menace at hand. Elite dominance of the state can come to depend, in part, on the successful manufacture of conspiracy. Turkish Islamophobia constructs an Islamist conspiracy that renders Islamophobia's truth. Turkish Islamophobia again demonstrates that being a Muslim does not, as essentialists accounts might maintain, make one immune from peddling Islamophobia, for Islamophobia is not about Islam per se, but rather its representation as a disruptive force in society, and in this regard, those who call themselves Muslims are just as capable of seeing Islam as a problem as those who are not Muslims. Muslim Islamophobia is often found among the political-cultural elites that hold sway over most of Muslimistan, where it functions as an adjunct to Kemalism. Muslim Islamophobia feeds into and feeds on more generalised forms of Islamophobia. Non-Muslim Islamophobes cite this Kemalist Islamophobia as a way of legitimating their Islamophobia, while many of the tropes of Kemalist Islamophobia are based upon a recycling of themes associated with Western globalised expressions of Islamophobia.

19

RECLAIMING THE TURK'S HEAD

Mohammed Siddique Seddon

The 'Turk's Head' is a familiar and fairly ubiquitous sign on the built environment of Britain. There is hardly a city or town in Britain that does not have a public house sporting one. Borrowed from the days of a greater sobriety, the origins of this 'demonic' caricature lie in the seventeenth-century fad with coffee, when the 'Turk's Head' was frequently used to advertise the location of a coffee-house. As tobacco was equated with the barbarous practices of the 'New World' natives, coffee was then the drink of the Muslim 'infidel'. Recognising the 'Turk' in the Turk's Head requires the same estrangement that it takes to see past the familiar blandness of the Starbucks coffee culture. Coffee, as Nabil Matar reminds us, was then perceived as a serious threat to Christian beliefs and English culture—'Coffee could be a Muslim agent to entice Englishmen away from their religion and turn them into renegades: coffee was as dangerous as "Alcoran" [al-Qur'an] because it threatened the fabric of England's Christian society' (Matar, 1998, p. 112). The introduction of Coffee presented yet another threatening variant of the religious, cultural and political expansion in central Europe by the Muslim other, perhaps an even more insidious one, because enslaving of the will, taking over from within, and hence a source of anxiety (Anidjar, cited in Shaikh, 2007, p. 242).

The link between the use of the iconic 'Turk's Head' and coffee is not a casual one. It is a relic from crusader times when European Christians returned from their holy wars against Muslims displaying a grotesque and menacing crest of the 'Saracen', a reminder of the medieval 'clash of civilisations' between Christendom and Islam (Matar, 1998, p. 115). Whilst the Saracen's head was replaced with that of the Turk's in the more congenial cultures of seventeenth century coffee consumption, the overall impact was (and, with the Turk now having given way to the more generic Muslim, arguably remains) the same: 'the Saracen/Turk/Muslim is coming!'

By employing anti-Muslim characterisations and representations, the English were trying to tame their fear of the Muslim other, not just in terms of the cultural imposition of Ottoman-style coffee-houses, but more importantly in the perceived religious, political and military Muslim hegemonic menace to European civilisation. Such representations drew on an older repertoire whose strands are multiple and shifting. Orientalism as a system of scholarship can be said to have began in the early fourteenth century with the establishment by the Church Council in Vienna, of a number of chairs to promote the understanding of the Orient (Turner, 1994, p. 37). It was a knowledge that took 'Christendom' as the frame of reference by which all else was measured. In post-Reformation Europe, Christianity continued to inform attitudes towards religious others, and though these now included Christian Catholic and Protestant others, they too could be configured and confounded through transpositions of the Turk. At the same time that the identity of Christendom and the authority of the Church were unraveling along the fault lines of the Reformation and Counter-Reformation, the convergence between the conquest of the last Muslim state in the Iberian peninsula and the 'discoveries' of the northern and southern Western hemisphere were fashioning Europe both internally and in relation to the rest of the world. In the transpositions brought on by both misrecognition and the triangular movement of peoples and representations, contamination and inter-changeability confused, tamed and unsettled European notions of American 'Indians' and Moors (Matar, 1999, pp. 100–106; see also Fuchs, 2001). If historical and civilisational links between Europeans and Islam made for evolving differentiations in respect of the primitiveness of the 'Indians', the vanquished condition of the latter in contrast to the ever-present military might of the Turk and threat of the Barbary pirate more importantly made for contradictory symbolic representations. While conflating them made for imaginary resolution of the threatening Muslim through the domesticated Indian, the real difference also reasserted itself symbolically. The 'Age of Reason' transfigured its political anxieties through its own fantasy structures of an Oriental Despotism which Romanticism and Liberalism inherited and developed in co-constituted inverted images. But the imperialist expansion, which reached its zenith in the nineteenth century, saw European colonial control of Muslimistan produce a domesticated Orientalist imaginary which survived de-politicised in the low brow caricatures of seductive oriental promise and exotic mystery, permeating the fantasies of twentieth-century advertising and eroticism until the shock of anti-colonialism, post-colonial settlement and the Iranian Revolution required their overtly re-politicised reinvention. The Turk's Head is traversed by this millennial historical repertoire. Through all these historically successive and concurrent shifting tropes and figurations, familiarities and estrangements, encounters and distancing, one thread arguably structures a determining continuity: the theologico-political formation rooted in the developed eschatology and mythological representation of medieval and reformation figurations and their secularised Enlightenment and post-Enlightenment versions. To this, Islamophobia bears a family resemblance.

The presence of Muslims, like that of other ethnically marked groups but with the particularity of its perceived religious essentialism, has challenged embedded and exclusive notions of 'Britishness' and the conceptions of religion, culture and identity which underpin its dominant institutionalised expression (Khan, S., 2006). Thus any discussion of Islamophobia in the context of British culture and national identity must be understood within the relationships of power between different groups informed by both colonial British history and contemporary identity politics. Arguably, embattled 'Anglo-centric Britishness' reaffirms its cohesiveness through aggressive Islamophobia.

While politically constructed Anglo-centric British identity is framed through debates about the primordiality or modernity of 'nations', it can be argued that such identity questions are the consequence of the territorialised and statist forms of national identity established by the Westphalian formation. Within such political structures, the boundaries of national identity are as politically constructed as the borders, laws and 'national traditions' by which the modern nation-state and its people are identified. If contemporary 'imagined' Englishness finds difficulty in reconciling the historical, religious and cultural tensions arising out of a politically constructed sense of English-Britishness, the problems of British identity are even more compounded in respect of multiculturalism. This is because traditional notions of 'Britishness' are overwhelmingly 'white and Christian' and as such foreclosed of the openness to truly embrace religious pluralism and cultural diversity. Even allowing that in the British context representation and provision for 'Asianness' has now been well facilitated in many social spheres, the assertion and affirmation of a distinct Muslim identity in this same context has not, and is deemed exceptionally problematic.

The assumptions that the integration of Muslims into a British national identity is not possible reproduces a discourse of difference that is located in Orientalism (Seddon, 2004, p. 131). Leela Gandhi (1998, p. 126) has described this divisive form of representation as 'procedures whereby the convenient Othering and exoticisation of ethnicity merely confirms and stabilises the hegemonic [and exclusive] notion of "Englishness"'. In this reading, Islamophobic 'othering' represents an inverted form of self-definition and identity reification because in the final analysis, the non-Muslim self is constituted as what the Muslim other is not. In the context of the politics of the migration and settlement of postcolonial communities it was used to ignite racist fears of being 'swamped', displaced and demoted, by the numbers, alien cultures and religions of the 'invading' other. The emergence and assertion of Muslims re-inscribed the terms of exclusion. The populist nativist conception of British as synonymous with being 'white and Christian' re-formed in the post-imperial mirror of the other, was re-signified through and as a racialised conception of a cultural exclusivism of national identity and the political culture of liberalism. Given that the largest minority groups amongst Britain's new communities are Muslims, it has not been difficult to exploit and fan anxieties that Islam in its essential theologico-political 'alienness' embodies the biggest threat to national identity and the 'British way of life'. The measure of the purchase and pervasiveness of this fear is the disturbing acceptability of pervasive expressions of Islamophobia.

In this the figure of the 'British Muslim' becomes the ground of especially charged political signification. For some, on both sides, it is an oxymoron. For others, the very means of domesticating Islam. For others still, the means to deconstruct the foreclosure of exclusivist British identity. Muslim communities in Britain and the West like all diasporic groups experience and engage in cultural transformation in the process of negotiating migration and settlement, and these experiences have found expression in the establishment of religious and cultural practices and institutions that both maintain traditional aspects of communal religious and cultural identity and facilitate new expressions of self-identity. Even though it can be argued that a Muslim identity cannot be confined to the nation-state, the emergence of a distinct British Muslim identity conforms to both the 'local' and 'global' paradigms. In this new hyphenated identity construction Muslims in Britain are able to tailor the cultural and religious facets of 'who they are' in order to accommodate their own social realities. In other words, the universalism of Islam as a religion with its own way of life and belief system, and its localised assemblages of organised social structures and institutions that are geo-culturally specific, accommodate a fusion of facets of British and Islamicate (religious) identities—a fusion that destabilises both traditional notions of what a Briton is and what a Muslim is (Ramadan, 2002, p. 208; Winter, 2003, pp. 8–9). But this is neither a matter of simply incorporating 'Islam', either in the institutional framework of religions or in their cultural mapping, nor of correcting misrepresentations. It is also a matter of addressing the embedded structures of exclusion in patterns of discrimination against Muslims.

Despite new legal extensions designed to cover loopholes in specific forms of religious discrimination, the problem, in respect of the protection and recognition afforded Muslims, remains constrained by the historically sedimentary and hegemonic constructions of 'race' and the theologico-political. The resultant effect of overlapping forms of colour and cultural discrimination within the existing juridical system means that Muslims in Britain suffer what Modood (2005, p. 16) defines as 'double racism'. Intrinsic to this nexus, is the imbrications of both the theologised, demonic Muslim other of Medieval Christendom and its early modern recompositions, the geo-cultural 'distancing' of Islam via the discourses of post-Enlightenment Orientalism (Said, 1995), and the modern manifestations of xenophobic Islamophobia in the developing multicultural and religiously pluralistic spaces of modern Britain and Europe. The fundamental question concerns the relations between the three historical formations and their differentially constituted regimes of truth. Whilst many stress the phenomenon of contemporary Islamophobia in discontinuity from all previous manifestations of anti-Muslimness, this chapter argues for a greater continuity; one threaded through the positioning of Islam in respect of the (albeit evolving) Western theologico-political formation. Its figurative continuity in difference is perfectly captured in the mundane ubiquity of the symbolically charged Saracen's Head turned Turk's Head turned whole Muslim.

20

ISLAMOPHOBIA AND HELLENOPHILIA

GREEK MYTHS OF POST-COLONIAL EUROPE

Rodanthi Tzanelli

If 'Islamophobia' is the *phovos* (fear) of Islam, then for a peripheral country such as Greece it harbours the paradox of a political *diplopia* that allowed the 'nation' to survive through times of hardship, often at the expense of minority cultures. Rather than trying to promote an all-embracing definition of the term, this essay examines its contextual emergence and diachronic develop-ment. In the Greek context, one conditioned by political pronouncements of the country as the origins of European civilisation (of the triumph of *Kultur* over *Zivilization* [Elias, 2000]), Islamophobia can be examined in three forms. The first refers to the concept as a historically situated encounter of a yet-to-become nation with an equally ill-defined predecessor of its Turkish counter-part, the Ottoman Empire. The second form of Islamophobia involved Greek statist responses to transmutations of Islam—notably, the Turkish nation of the Kemalist and post-Kemalist era. The Greek state's target would subse-quently diversify to embrace the newly born Albania of the following century, rendering it as an accessory to Turkey and the Slavic Balkan peoples, especially those who had espoused communism. The final form of Islamophobia com-prised a metanarrative of the first two. This originated in the dual institutional development of Greek identity as the product of Western civic traditions and the sacred child of a theological discourse upheld by the Orthodox Church.

Not only does this sum up the ideological complex of Greek nation building, it also uncovers the native horror for Islamicate culture as one of its preconditions. The marginality of Greece in the geopolitical arena would eventually translate into a redeeming narrative, according to which Greece stole the seeds of Western civic-democratic teachings to implant them in Europe's Eastern backyard, the southeastern Mediterranean region. The tree that grew out of this venture was supposed to bear the fruits of universal progress. The fact that, to this date, Greeks consider themselves a 'European' people with an Eastern *habitus* but Western *civilité* bears testimony to their split *mentalité*: Eastern by proximity but Western by necessity. By *habitus* I allude to the cultural *ethos*, the anthropological definition of habit as a ritual and a way of life, but also the moral sphere occupied by a People. I do not intend to reify Greekness in this essay, only to track the historic trajectories of habitual self-narrations, the ways in which the plurality of identity was and is performed and produced in everyday life. Inevitably, however, I find myself trapped in the selfsame allegorical imperative that gives shape to a distinctive cultural *habitus*: a way of life becomes a binding force when it is 'imagined' (Anderson, 1991), narrated and performed by individuals for the collective.

This essay may be placed amongst those debating the genealogical conundrums of Islamophobia, outlining the conditions of its emergence in a Greek context. But the very examination of context necessitates a discussion of its morphology—for, as a heuristic device, it exists only in relation to other, similar conditions, such as the fear of communism or more generally the fear of the *heterodox* (those of a different *doxa*, a different objectified social order). Hence, for the Greek 'nation' Islamophobia has always been a convoluted version of xenophobia. The term refers to the *phóvos* (fear) of the *xénos* (Delanty and O'Mahony, 2002, p. 163), the inseparable pair of the 'foreigner' who is excluded from, and the 'guest' who is invited into the intimate sphere of the home, the *patria* or masculinised homeland. *Father*land gives away the hierarchical structure of national identity by gendering its qualities: of course Muslim minorities, Greek diasporic groups and communist constituencies partook in Greek nation building, an intimate voice would admit; the denial of credit for their contribution in majoritarian political discourses only serves to prove their significance. In such discourses, Hellenic norms served to demonstrate how noble common causes were betrayed by friends or insiders—the Kavafian Efiáltes who knows your weaknesses from within. As Balibar has it, the fear of the stranger (a 'nightmare', as *efiáltes* denotes) enables the 'imagined' community' to define its internal limits, constructing 'a problematic of purity, or better, of purification' and 'indicat[ing] the uncertainty of identity, the way in which the "inside" can be penetrated or adulterated by its relation with the "outside", the foreign' (Balibar, 1994, p. 63). A nation institutes its People, its unifying signifier (Gourgouris, 1996, p. 18), 'not by suppressing all differences, but by relativising them and subordinating them to itself'. Simultaneously, however, discursive constructions of a unified People seek a place in a wider human whole, a polity that exceeds the boundaries of the nation. If, internally, the nation is dependant upon politicised cultural characterisations ('us' and 'them', natives and aliens, outsiders and insiders) (Hedetoft, 1993, pp. 281–300), externally it strives to assert its belonging in a transnational public sphere (Balibar and Wallerstein, 1991). Systemic political belonging thus mirrors subsystemic (national) integrative processes. All European nations were constructed through radical distinctions between members and non-members (Spohn, 2005, pp. 1–16).

In what follows I attempt to outline the various forms Greek Islamophobia assumed in the course of Modern Greek history, arguing that all of them took shape through intercultural encounters. This has implications. First, it suggests that I do not regard 'Greek identity' as unchanging but as a dialogical product of plural nature (e.g. 'identity' and Greekness are understood in relation to a series of identifications and negations). Second, I advocate geopolitics of identity, tracing Greece's political others through space: geographical proximity matters. This leads me to the third point, which relates to Islamophobia's role in Greek nation building: the plurality of Greek 'Islam', its mediations through Turkish, Balkan and Western discourses, presents it as a *problematique* of both academic and practical nature rather than the project of a singular political agency. Even my essay should be read not as an objective account but as an epistemological contribution that opens the floor to further academic and political dialogue.

Western Histories, Eastern Routes

The process of Greek nation-formation is representative of past and present geopolitical visions of Western European belonging (Gourgouris, 1992, pp. 43–71). Greece was institutionalised in the early nineteenth century with the help of three powerful patrons (Britain, France and Russia) who strived for control in the Southeastern Mediterranean region. This political interest partly originated in the Western philhellenic project—the desire of politicians, art connoisseurs, travellers and scholars from Western countries to retrieve from the nineteenth-century Greeks an imagined ancient civilisation on which the West had formed its self-image as 'European' and 'civilised' (Bernal, 1991). This crypto-colonial (Herzfeld, 2002a, pp. 899–926) project (the symbolic colonisation of regions that fell in the cracks of neat political classifications by powerful Western countries) was a perverted version of nationalism: a few centuries down the line, the modern Greeks had become a completely different amalgam of 'races', a fragmented *ethnos* with radically different experiences and cultural dispositions from those attributed to the fictional characters of the Hellenic *polis* by Western dreamers. These modern Greeks could not live up to Western demands, because of their many alleged shortfalls: they were disorderly, 'Oriental' in their habits (e.g. liars and unreliable just like their former Ottoman rulers), and with aspirations to become a great nation that controls the region—a rather inconvenient development for Western economic interests. As Said (1978) has explained, the denigration of the colonised assisted in the consolidation of Orientalist projects. In Greece's case this denigration was coupled with the internalisation of an excessive Western admiration for things Hellenic (what I term *Hellenophilia*), such as ancient Greek philosophy, democracy and order. At various points in the history of modern Greece this past played the role of both the other/ stranger, who lives outside Greek history, in the domain of Western Orientalism, and the same, who belongs to the process of Greek *ethnogenesis*. This Greece stood naked, 'without columns' to borrow Holden's (1972) apt metaphor, and therefore exposed to external criticism by powerful political others who multiplied with the passage of time. In the same way that Todorova (1997, p. 13) saw in Western conceptions of the Balkans Europe's 'incomplete other', modern Greece stood between the two geopolitical poles (East and West) as Western Europe's incomplete self-image.

I use this genealogy to suggest that *modern* Greek Islamophobia was the offshoot of Western Orientalism, and that it did not relate to the fear of Islam as such, but the fear of Western criticism for Islam's alleged adulterating properties. I stress the modern dimension here, because the Ottoman past and its religious-political dimensions point in a slightly different direction I explore later. Concealing the damaged, orientalised image behind the purified, Christian European 'face' became for Greeks a habitual move in political encounters and negotiations with Western countries from within—and later without— Europe. In the 1850s this tension conditioned a temporary occupation of Athens by the British fleet, and in 1870 it led to Greece's temporary falling from European grace due to widespread brigandage (Tzanelli, 2009). In 1919

Britain and France assisted in, but did not solely instigate, the revival of Greek-Turkish rivalries in Asia Minor (a region coveted by Greeks even before the First World War), which precipitated a catastrophic conflict (1919–1922) and inadvertently contributed to the rise of Turkish nationalism (Eddy, 1931; Smith, M.L., 1973; Kitromilides, 1992). Significantly, the expelled populations of Asia Minor, who regarded themselves as both pure Hellenic descendants and cosmopolitan subjects of high culture, were seen in the Greek metropolitan context as half-Oriental groups that were granted citizenship rights they did not deserve. Not only did poverty and explicit Greek policies of Hellenisation in the newly-acquired Macedonia push them to the North of the country in search for jobs and residence, they also gave them a social identity that some historians recognise as left-wing and working class. Ensuing internal and external conflicts (dictatorships, another World War and a civil war) promoted an identification of their working-class identity with the new global communist 'threat' that would haunt Greece in the decades to come. During the Second World War, the British and American governments were involved in the Greek civil conflict (1944–1949), thus globalising the Greek Question and its patrons. In the Cold War era Greece was caught between the Western and Soviet spheres of influence, which split the country into two equally ruthless factions (royalists and communists). Things turned 'right' for the worse when a dictatorship (1967–1974) marshalled the belief that Hellas is the cradle of European civilisation, bestowing it also with a conservative Christian Orthodox dimension (Herzfeld, 2002b, pp. 13–15). As a result, Greek foreign and domestic policies were overdetermined by what Diamantouros (1983) calls 'underdog culture': a combination of Christian and Hellenocentric exclusiveness, which renounces foreign interventions and attacks cultural and political difference. In order to be European the modern Greeks had to both exorcise Turkish habits and stay away from those political beliefs the Balkanised 'commies' (a label wrongly attached to many deviant identities at the time) introduced in a politically divided Greece. The internalised discourse of Greek exceptionalism, demonstrated in the fact that Greek culture, though European by historical association, is politically marginalised and constantly ignored in academic debates on European identity, has been the focus of critical scholarship (Gallant, 1997, pp. 209–216). The idea of Greek exceptionalism echoes Anderson's modular argument, according to which Hellenic Greekness is constantly and retroactively (*Ibid.*). narrated for internal and external consumption. Internally, this fulfils the needs of the Greek imagined community to see itself as a uniform entity progressing in linear, historical time (Anderson, 1991,

p. 193). Externally, it provides the nation's significant others with a familiar reference point that secures the unanimous recognition of Greek modernity (Tzanelli, 2008, p. 499).

Social to Cultural: Experience and Allegory

The fear of Western criticism was superimposed on a more intimate encounter with Islam nevertheless: another retroactive narration of Greek national identity placed Greek-ness centuries before the establishment of the state in the nineteenth century, during Ottoman rule. This produced another version of Islamophobia, which was hooked on pseudo-religious understandings of Greek nationhood that Orthodoxy allegedly protected from oblivion after the fall of Byzantium. It is in this conjunction of circumstances that Occidental versions of Islam were domesticated to produce a semi–theological narrative of *Greek* modernity: the myth of the 'secret school' (*kryfó scholió*) the progenitors of the Greek nation held in dark cellars during the four centuries of Ottoman occupation to educate young generations, highlighted both the 'oppressive' nature of Islam and the fusion of ethnic liberation with the Western pedagogical project of nationalism. I will explain what I mean through a story.

Ideological viewpoints are also experiential ones: take, for example, how official registers place the etymological origins of my hometown[1] at the very borders of 'Europe proper'. The name is associated with a controversial denial: the town is the *Mi* ('no')-*Chania* (of Crete). This etymology is the site of a local experience (Dilthey, 1976, pp. 209–210) accompanied by a mythical presentation of Michaniote history that has acquired the value of oral tradition. *Onomatopoieía* (name-making) reveals the dramaturgical nature of name-production in society, the ways the social is constructed through story telling. Insignificant though it may seem in the grand scheme of European politics, the core myth of Michaniote origins works as an allegory for the place of Greek identity in Europe. By allegory I refer to public announcements of narratives that take place elsewhere (*alloú*)—otherwise put, public speech (in the *agorá* or public market of the city state) with private meaning. Historically, the town of Michaniona belongs to a cluster of villages and towns (Angelochori, Kerasia, Baktse, Perea) founded by refugees who fled the coastal parts of the crumbling Ottoman Empire after or during the last Turkish-Greek war. 'Néa' (new)

[1] Nea Michaniona is a town situated on the western side of the Thermaikos Gulf, 75 km away from Thessaloniki, the largest city of northern Greece.

Michaniona claims direct descent from 'Palaiá' (old) Michaniona, a village close to the historic town of Peramos. The myth of Michaniote origins (Peramos Homepage, 1998; Bogas, 1964) maintains that the originary Michaniotes were Cretans from Chania who abandoned their native land because they could not accept the Ottoman 'yoke'. Another anti-Turkish version has it that these Cretans were warriors who fought for the last Byzantine emperor, Constantine Paleologos, during the Ottoman siege of Constantinople (Istanbul) in 1543. These warriors perceived the fall of the Byzantine capital as a sign of their own military incompetence. Ashamed, the survivors sailed in Propontis. Their trek ended when they approached the peninsula of Kyzikos, where they decided to stay and found thirteen villages, vowing to forget their origins and start anew. Their determination to obliterate this past convinced them to name one of the new villages *Mi–Chania*.

The passage from collective reconstructions of tradition to its official recording presents us with a rueful replacement of historical discourse, traditionally used by Greeks in self-presentation to powerful outsiders, with narratives of *custom* (Herzfeld, 2000; Sutton, 1998): the legend created analogies between the movement and settlement of Asia Minor and Propontis refugees in 1923 and the journey of Cretan warriors in 1453. As a result, this local tradition retained a close relationship with the national tradition (Tonkin, 1992, p. 87) of the collapse of Byzantium, still presented by Greeks as the Christian progenitor and guardian of Greekness. It may not be coincidental that this legend appeared in the local newspaper in the beginning of the 1990s, when Michaniote society was undergoing economic and ethnic-social changes that threatened established notions of local identity and national belonging (e.g. incoming labour migrants and a rapid cosmopolitanisation of rural Greece). As Collard has explained, Greeks have a tendency to describe things that they never experienced, such as the Ottoman occupation, but to avoid narration of more recent experiences in terms of misremembering. She argued that this historical regression might be the result of a change in the way identity is handled locally. A collapse in dichotomies (us versus the 'others') that kept this narrative alive is often symptomatic of such change (Collard, 1989, pp. 89-109). Pressures imposed on Greece in the aftermath of the 9/11 tragedy, alongside the transformation of the Mediterranean region into a *de facto* 'melting pot', a transit zone for immigrant populations that cross the 'Oriental borders' of Africa and Asia to join an enlarged Europe, may also account for the re-emergence of this local tale of origins. The symbolic merges with the physical/geographical into a socially meaningful allegory: the Cretans both embody the ultimate Greek values of heroic self-sacrifice and patriotism (ideals related to the Ottoman and Turkish rule as well as the Second World) and the stereotype *par excellence* of the uncivilised—they are, in other words, the Greek 'savage within' (Herzfeld, 1985, p. 9). The denial of Cretan identity by the alleged founding fathers of Michaniona symbolises both the departure of the Michaniote community from the margins of Greekness and the very practice of forgetting this marginality. The narrative process itself 'purifies' Michaniote Greekness from its Ottoman/Turkish legacy, reinstating its 'European' status.

CHANIOTES = MICHANIOTES = GREEK MARGINALITY	MEMORY
	↓
MI-CHANIOTES = REFUGEE INTEGRATION = GREEK	FORGETTING

The story proffers a version of Islamophobia that assisted in the construction of a distinctive nationalist façade. Its pronouncement became a habitual (as in *habitus*) strategy that both resolved internal cultural inconsistencies and externally imposed marginalisation (Beck, 2002, pp. 17–44).

Global Phenomena with Balkan Implications

I presented this story because it linked subjective histories to past global transformations. Before discrediting such homological thinking as peasant trivia, we may want to examine other potential ramifications it may have—especially those that linked the destinies of ethnic groups that occupied the same neighbourhood. I refer to Greece and Albania for reasons not immediately evident. Suffice it to repeat that from the outset I viewed Greek identity and Islam as plural, a move that allowed me to present them as hosts of many influences. Here I move on to explicitly regard Greece as a host of migrations—precisely the underlying point my compatriots inadvertently made through their legend. In contemporary politics cultural migrations allegedly re-enact civilisational clashes (Huntington, 1993, pp. 22–49)—yet another form the nationalist discourse of resurrection may assume. But, unlike Huntington's apocalyptic mantra, my argument serves to stress the functional role such clashes (fusions) may have in the production of identity. In a different theoretical jargon we might have discussed this as the cosmopolitan condition, but this would deviate me from my point here.

What I am trying to say, contrary to the rhetoric of 'anti-immigration' politicians and elements of the popular press, is that patterns of movement and mobility are not an 'unfortunate accident' or the result of any weakness of will in guarding borders as Huntington would have it. Rather, they are an integral element of the workings of the global economy, and have been since at least the late nineteenth century when the so-called 'great transformation' (Polanyi, 1944) created a market society in which the needs of the capitalist economy began to direct the policies of states. The needs of the economic system continue to drive the movement of human populations, but at the same time differentiate people according to their perceived usefulness. I will, nevertheless, move beyond a purely economic take to remind that human migrations do not facilitate capital mobility solely: ideas, customs and cultural perceptions are part of the luggage that slips customs control but never escapes prejudice upon arrival at the host country.

In the context of transcontinental labour mobilities Greek Islamophobia has manifested itself as Albanophobia. Ironically, such global scenarios take us back to the local scene: Michaniona was split into political camps for example, when an Albanian student was elected flag-carrier in a local parade in 2000 and in 2003. Given the peculiar place of Albanian identity in Modern Greek history (some times as a Slavophone, at other times as a Muslim and communist 'other'), the bewildered student found himself representing the Greek archenemy (Tzanelli, 2006, pp. 27–49; 2007, pp. 1–20). Today the fear of pollution informs certain Greek attitudes towards immigrants, conflating notions of race and culture. In 1996 anthropologist Nadia Seremetakis, then Advisor to the Greek Ministry of Public Health, discovered an association between Albanian (and other) immigration to Greece after the opening of EU borders, and stories about 'waves of infections crossing Greek frontiers' (Seremetakis, pp. 489–491). Research into migrant labour in Greece showed that Greek attitudes towards Albanian workers are biased, manifested in the use of pejoratives such as 'dirty', 'cunning', 'untrustworthy' and 'primitive' (Lazaridis and Wickens, 1999, p. 648). The idea of dirt gestures towards a form of symbolic racialisation of cultural difference, supporting Greek self-perceptions not simply as European, but as European *par excellence* (Greeks as the purest descendants of European civilisation). Needless to add that this mode of cultural engagement does not apply to all foreigners: qualifications are introduced for the same ethnic categories when individuals, including immigrants, manage to join the community—to become ('be christened') 'natives'. Naming, acquiring a Christian name, translates into claiming and demarcating one's own territory to safeguard it from foreign invasions. The informal vocabulary is accurate: the personal and the political may continue to occupy different domains in Greek culture but they communicate when Greeks engage in the politics of property. In any case, through this remark we arrive at the same destination: associations of crime, pollution and political disorder are as old as the Hellenocentric project of European modernity. The 'criminal' label serves an important role here as a reassertion of basic Enlightenment assumptions about one's humanity—the criminal is after all the law-breaker who forgoes the right to be treated as a full and free human being. Here we gain valuable insight into the ways the first two versions of Islamophobia communicate with the third variation, which relocates Western discourses of human progress in the Balkan space.

But I rush: first I want to argue that contemporary Greek Albanophobia is not just homologous but also a historically evolved variation of a nineteenth-century scholarly controversy that presented the Illyrian-Slav 'races' (the alleged Albanian progenitors), as the main polluting source of Hellenic civilisation—or, at least, what survived of it in the modern Greeks (Skopetea, 1999, p. 155). The controversy mirrored geopolitical conflicts in Europe, translating them into the Aryan project that resurfaced in a Nazi context but also in other post-colonial environments around the world. We find this fear of racial-as-cultural contamination in the debate on the nature of nineteenth-century Greek banditry, a phenomenon that continued living in double representational regimes until its extinction: in national politics it remained a form of resistance against Ottoman rule, whereas in the international political arena it figured as a form of 'crime' perpetrated by Albanians, Vlachs and 'Turks' (Tzanelli, 2002, pp. 47–74). The Albanian-Vlachs of this discourse were Turkish conspirators, and therefore a source of contamination too. It is not coincidental that the same separation of good from bad brigands was applied by political 'dissidents' during the Greek Civil War to communists who engaged in guerrilla warfare with Western and Greek military: in this case, one side's hero was another's villain, but the practice itself defined who is one of our own and who is a criminal. Again, then, we see how a separation of the private from the public served to protect national boundaries.

Hence, adopting a diachronic perspective is necessary to appreciate the significance of this separation, especially since subsequent changes in political conditions of the Balkan *Raum* would pave the path for long-term quarrels among emerging nation-states. With the foundation of a separate Albanian state (1911), the Albanian populations of southern Greece (the so-called

Arvanites) were deemed by the Greek state to be assimilated, Hellenised, ex-Slavs; the Albanian groups of the North, however (Muslims by religion and Albanian citizens after 1913) were regarded as enemies of Greek unity and purity. The 'Northern Epirus' Question, that part of Albania that the Greek state tried to incorporate before the foundation of the Albanian state in 1911 on the grounds that a substantial Greek minority existed in the region, fuelled hatred against the Muslim Albanian groups in the region, which became the main target of Greek nationalist propaganda. The ensuing controversy over the name of the FYROM in the aftermath of the collapse of Yugoslavia further complicated the picture, casting Albanian Muslims as potential usurpers of Greek territories. A process of minoritisation poisoned interethnic relations in the Balkans, sowing cross-national discord and suspicion. In this conjunction, the Albanian and the Muslim (and in the context of the 1940s Greek civil conflict the Yugoslav communist), merged into a single nightmare to sustain a phobia that was neither solely directed against Islam nor intended specifically for Albanians; the target was also communism, which by the 1950s had been ostracised from the Western sphere of modernity. Communism, Islam and Albanian identity were consigned in the same pit of backwardness, in turn coloured black, accused of disorder and excluded from the Greek nation that was still fighting for a place in global politics as the unrecognised descendant of Europe.

Islam in Modern Greece

Islam as a culture and a polity is part of Greek modernity. The Muslim presence in Greece is not new—if anything, it dates back to the selfsame history that re-invented the Michaniote community. The Lausanne Convention (1923) that ended the Greek-Turkish war and regulated the exchange of populations between Greece and Turkey did not include the Muslim communities of Western Thrace. This minority, the only officially recognised one in Greece, consists of Turks, Pomaks and 'Gypsies',[2] numbers about 112,000 people and

---

[2] The term retains a moral ambiguity. Scholars tend instead to refer to 'Roma' populations whose entry in the Byzantine Empire is described in equally ambivalent terms (as an 'invasion'). This is significant, as some Greek historians tend to examine these movements in the same way they view the Illyrian movements of medieval times—through the prism of Fallmerayer's theory. Thus, language is the primary criterion to designate such ethnic groups. The Roma's linguistic identity is probably prioritised

is governed by its own internal hierarchies based on language and religion. A number of problems regarding incomplete (educational and administrative) integration and bilateral political pressures (from Turkey and Greece) suggests that the projection of a coherent 'community' image outwards provides security for these populations (Antoniou, 2003, p. 162). Raising claims to Turkishness functions as a form of 'symbolic capital': often, 'Islamisation' becomes a resentful reaction to external pressures originating in extreme nationalist reactions, racism and covert social exclusion. Navigating through the structures of a nation-state that was born to be the core of Europe 'proper' but was eventually interpellated as its political pariah turned these ethno-religious groups into a psychological miniature of Greek nationalism. I do not equate Islamophobia against these groups with racism, however: Greece's centrality in Europe's self-image as white and civilised, may suggest Islamophobia's communication with Western racism in this context, but the history of Greek diasporas—including that of Asia Minor—flags the difficulty to support any neat racial demarcations in a Greek cultural context. A more important mythical overlaying (Hutchinson, 2005), which flattens Greek history under the burden of a globalised War on Terror, prioritises recent configurations of modernity in relation to transatlantic developments, drawing local versions of Islam into this vortex. For the Greek state the new 'Islam' must be treated as a shared enemy—or, as George W. Bush bluntly put it in 2005, you are either with us or against us.

---

to match a specific reading of Roma history through official Byzantine records that 'bear testimony' to their 'hellenisation' in the middle ages by the fictitious Byzantine 'Greeks'. Some also suggest that 'Roma' ('free man') is the preferred self-designation of these ethnic groups, a claim that does not take into account social context. In Greece, for example, the 'Gypsy' (*gýftos*) retains negative connotations, as it is habitually used to describe low-life individuals. To be a *gýftos* is to be homeless, stingy, petty, dirty and therefore coloured black—another clear link between ideas of 'dirt' as matter out of place and racial belonging. Gypsies are historically linked to India (the Sind region that now belongs to Pakistan) from which they moved to Persia and then to Byzantium fleeing Ottoman persecution. Interestingly, the Greek word *athínganos* (from which modern 'gypsy' comes) is literally the 'untouchable'—a clear connection between race and civilisation that may even date back to the Hindu caste system. The term 'gypsy', however, has also been used by the Roma to generate plausible links with Egyptian civilisation. All these designations suggest implicit (classificatory) uses of Roma identity in Orientalist discourse.

The *Athens 2004* backstage is indicative of this development: coerced into 'inviting' NATO troops to 'guard' the Olympic athletes from potential terrorist attacks, and in order to reciprocate for the favourable comments on Greece's progress on the Olympics by New York Mayor Michael Bloomberg who presented Athens as the birthplace of the Olympic phenomenon, the Athens Organising Committee (ATHOC) acted as the nation's spokesperson (Tzanelli, 2004, p. 432). Little room was left for the expression of resentment against a West whose gratitude for the gift of Hellenic civilisation is eternally deferred (this is a gift that British colonisers 'stole', after all, if we count the Elgian theft in the equation). These perverted feelings could only find an outlet in ceremonial aspects of Olympism that narrated the nation's dramatic comeback in the cosmopolitan arena. Ceremony and politics complemented each other nevertheless: four years before the Games, the Greek socialist government had approved the construction of the first large-scale mosque and Islamic cultural centre for the needs of the Muslims in Athens, but the project was met with criticism by the Democratic Party because it was incorporated into legislation involving the 2004 Olympiad—essential for the rectification of the Greek political and cultural image abroad. The politicisation of the controversy was not clear-cut (see also Hellenic Republic, Embassy of Greece) but subject to the needs of the moment: a former minister and member of the then ruling party had also argued that for such a gesture to be realised there should be some form of reciprocity from Turkey, whereas a socialist deputy had expressed fears that the Islamic cultural centre would turn into an international terrorist hub (Antoniou, 2003, p. 170). The internalisation of an American Islamophobic discourse threatens to tear away the solidary fabric of the nation-state in the same way that it divides otherwise peaceful localities.

Extremist political organisations do the greatest damage with their adherence to the binary logic of Christian Hellenocentrism. Take, for example, the socialists' preference to nominate a Greek Muslim in the 2006 elections—a grand political statement in light of Ankara's attempts to create a climate of 'controlled tension' in Western Thrace.[3] Right-wing nationalist groups such as La.O.S. (*Laikos Orthodoxos Synagermos*) were quick to interpret this as an irresponsible attack on 'national values' (Kouriannidis, 2006) when it could also be considered as a gesture of inclusivity. An identical attitude was adopted on other occasions, when political parties tried to diffuse tensions by extending the hand of friendship to 'strangers' (such was the case of former conservative

[3] See *E Kathimerini* (2006) www.ekathimerini.com (12 May).

leader, Evert, who supported the naturalisation of the Albanian flag-carrier in 2000, even though certain clauses applied to this gesture). Such statements, replete with covert hostility against a nebulous 'Marxist threat' that is unleashed on Greek Orthodoxy, affects economy and de-Hellenises education,[4] repeat the post-Second World War Albanophobic *leitmotif* in which the 'enemy' is both communist (often conflated with 'socialist') and Muslim.

No institution holds faster to Eurocentric Hellenophilia than the Greek Church, which operates as a state within the state. The Orthodox faith is inextricably intertwined with Greek identity: for many centuries and in the absence of an administrative core, it operated as a cohesive force for the Greek *ethnie* (Roudometof, 1999, p. 255). Because during Ottoman rule the colonised ethnic groups were placed under the *millet* system, administrative units based on religious belief, religion developed into the most immediate form of ethnic identification (Just, 1989, pp. 71–78; Karakasidou, 1997; Kitromilides, 1989, pp. 166–176). It has been noted that an emerging secular conception of identity-as-citizenship clashed with religious understandings of identity in the nineteenth century during the formation of Balkan imagined communities. But Christian religion remained the definitional element of the *Rum*-millet that included other *ethnies* except for the Greek. In fact, despite its secularisation, Greek nationalism always drew upon the religious vocabulary to articulate itself (see Tzanelli, 2008a, Chapter 6). The tradition of Byzantium, which is claimed as Modern Greek heritage and presented as yet another version of the 'Fortress Europe' discourse, fuses with the apparently contradictory history of ancient Hellas, also retroactively presented as Modern Greek heritage. Byzantium corresponds to the intimate face of Greekness (that of a feminised *Romiosini*, the Greekness of the *Rum-millet*), whereas ancient Greece is the public façade of the nation. In between these two traditions stand the 'dark ages' of Ottoman rule, the so-called *Tourkokratía* that seals modern Greece's fate as the fallen angel of Western modernity. The secular language of nationalism meets the religious language of sin to paint a discourse of political theodicy from which modern Greece cannot find absolution. The predicament of Greek modernity, the Orthodox Church suggests, presents Islam as Satan's reincarnation from which we can be redeemed only if we turn our back on some 400 years of shared history—if we forget who we are and how we arrived here. But stoning Greek Islam (the 'Eve of

[4] See opening statement of *Hellenic Lines*, 17 April 1996 at http://www.e-grammes. gr [Last accessed on 31 Jan. 2009].

Europe') is a rational choice that provides little consolation, as in Greek folk wisdom the Antichrist is also embodied by the treacherous 'Frank' (Stewart, 1991, p. 141), the Westerner who stole the riches of Hellenic wisdom without reciprocation. Orthodoxy's predicament of Greek modernity is a hoax: Greek Christians are invited to choose between a rock and a hard place.

One only need mention the indecorous outburst of the Metropolite of Kala-vryta, Ambrosios, in 2000 during the episodes in Michaniona, who presented the Greek flag as an inalienable Greek property (just like one's 'wife and car') that cannot be 'appropriated' or 'borrowed' by an Albanian immigrant (Tza-nelli, 2006, p. 39). The subtext of this comment, sexist and nationalist at the same time, erected symbolic boundaries to protect Greekness from an imagi-nary Islamic invader. The statement, which caused immense embarrassment to the Greek government, the Archbishop and other high-ranking members of the Greek Church, did not differ that much from others made by the extreme right. Likewise, a local bishop publicly renounced the creation of a mosque in the centre of Athens as objectionable by the 'average Greek' (Antoniou, 2003, p. 170)—a discourse embellished with the idea of an oncoming danger. The constitutional recognition of Orthodox religion as the Greek state religion comprised a violation of the European Convention on the Defence of the Fun-damental Human Rights, which Greece has signed (Pollis, 1992, p. 189). Such 'cultural intimacy' (Herzfeld, 2005) came at a heavy price: for a long time, the clash of the spirit and the letter of the European Convention with the spirit and the letter of the Greek Constitution posed serious obstacles to Greece's European integration.

An explicitly theological discourse eventually met a legal one, when the Greek constitution recognised the Muslim community's religious life. This comes in the form of the appointment of *muftis*, respect for Islamic family law, the administering of *vakif* (endowments), the training of minority teachers at the Academy in Thessaloniki and the management of Islamic religious schools (*medrese*). These legal privileges do not always resolve racial tensions on the ground, and there have been reports of administrative discrimination (Anto-niou, 2003, p. 164). It is telling that the construction of the mosque in Paiania for *Athens 2004* was supported by the embassies of Arab countries: following a pattern pursued by other European governments, the Greek Ministry of For-eign Affairs sanctioned a form of diplomatic subcontracting (a reversal of the pattern of Ottoman capitulations involving the surrender of extra-territorial privileges to a Muslim power by a non-Muslim one [Michot, 1997]), which inadvertently excluded the alleged beneficiaries of this venture from the negotiations (the Thracian *muftis* and any Greek bodies representing the Muslim minority [Greek Helsinki Monitor, 2003]), It also nevertheless took a problem out of a dead end, a context plagued by ethno-religious conservatism before which even state power cowers.

The Unbearable 'Thin-ness' of Cosmopolitanism

This reactive attitude stands in striking contrast to the situational recognition of Islam as a cultural component of Greek culture. This is a strange game that calls for the recognition of cultural fusions as valuable while seeking ways to efface difference in the name of purity and monism. The official face of Greekness is generously supported by the surviving archaeological interest in Greek heritage (both Byzantine and Hellenic) whereas its Ottoman survivals stand apart as its poor relatives, exotic displays for both internal consumption and the global 'tourist gaze' (Urry, 1990). These tendencies relocate the Orientalist movement within the Greek continental margins, revealing the ambivalence the self-christened 'children' of Hellas feel towards Europe's 'true lineage' to follow Sardar's comment (cited in Brooks, 2007). Occasionally, this Ottoman past dissolves into a post-national landscape, and at other times it re-emerges with a vengeance: consider the initiative of the Benaki Museum of Islamic Art in Athens, currently hosting an exhibition of 'snapshots' of Islam (photo project 'The Modern Arab World') to dispel enduring stereotyping of Islamic cultures, and juxtapose it to the resentment displayed against Muslim immigrants in Greece by Greek workers and other natives (Athanasiadis, 2008). In practice, Greek society is evolving into a 'multicultural melting pot', but Hellenocentric resistances to change are as strong as ever. Aesthetics re-negotiate political mentality primarily for the middle classes: take for example the cafes of Thessaloniki that are hosted in buildings surviving the Ottoman era, or the tavernas that serve Turkish-Greek delicacies to *bon viveurs* and foreign visitors alike. *Myrovolos*, an eaterie at the centre of the city's market, remained a *katagógion* (underground facility) that gathered questionable characters for decades, as I found out in my student years. In more recent years, however, it was smartened up to attract both a neo-Orientalist *clientele* and local folk musing over 'the old days' of Anatolian culture. Greco-Roman and Byzantine architecture is maintained intact; its adulteration by consumerist needs is not welcome. But *rebétiko*, a music culture that migrated to the mainland together with Asia Minor refugees at the start of the twentieth century to revamp Greek cultural taste, operates as a welcome

cosmopolitan statement, despite its historical specificity. So does the infamous *tsiftetéli*, a Turkish-Greek version of belly dancing transmogrified in the era of global ethnic music into a bodily expression of individualism (see Herzfeld, 2000, p. 160; Cowan, 1990), a feminised art of self-presentation that draws upon Orientalist stereotyping of sensuality to complement the virulent face of Greekness preserved in *eghoismós*.[5]

Η Πρίγκηπος, a café-bar in the centre of Thessaloniki, is very popular with students and visitors alike. It was named after an island (*Büyükada*) of the Propontis (the Straits that link Europe with Asia). The building, part of the pre-

---

[5] Drawing on the idea of egoism as self-centredness, the term refers to masculinised self-presentation (the public display of social identity). See Herzfeld (1985, p. 11).

liberation period architecture of the city, is situated opposite the house of Kemal Atatürk, the 'founding father' of modern Turkey, which is now hosting the Turkish consulate. The upper photo (overleaf) is a snapshot of the façade: the style is reminiscent of the old Greek coffee shops (*kafeneíon*); the lower photo shows a corner of the interior, replete with a water-pipe (*nargilés*) and an image of the Byzantine *Aghia Sofia*, a former Christian temple in Istanbul that figures in Greek nationalist discourse as part of the Greek-European heritage (Image courtesy of Paraskevi and Evelyn Tzanelli, 2009).

In a country whose global image was shaped by a Mexican Zorbas and a salad that is Greek only in name, cosmopolitan Orientalisms deal a blow to Islamophobic intransigence and its Hellenocentric origins. A question remains, however: how much of this translates into social change of universal significance and applicability and how much is simply mobilised for the 'conservation' of a public façade that safely stirs away from European criticism?

21

TROUBLED BY MUSLIMS

THAILAND'S DECLINING TOLERANCE?

Duncan McCargo

Thailand has a Muslim population estimated at around 5 per cent—though the exact figure is disputed—in a country with an overwhelming Buddhist majority. While the country has little tradition of overt religious bigotry, and Buddhism remains an informal national religion rather than an official one, the idea that Thai Buddhism is deeply tolerant of religious diversity is rather problematic. Buddhism is tightly regulated by an ageing gerontocracy of senior monks—the Supreme Sangha Council—who seek to maintain both orthodoxy and orthopraxy through various forms of internal repression. Other religions are similarly monitored by agencies or proxies of the Thai state. Since 2002, Islamic, Christian, and other religious groups have been overseen by the Department of Religion (part of the Ministry of Culture), while a National Office of Buddhism is located in the office of the prime minister. Registering a new Christian church in Thailand is virtually impossible, since the Department of Religion asks the existing registered churches whether new applicants should be regarded as genuine Christians, with predictable results. As a consequence, many Christian and other religious organisations operate without formal registration.

In relation to Islam, the Thai state has created the position of Chularaja-montry, and treats the office-holder as the 'spiritual leader' of the Muslim population of Thailand. The current Chularajamontri is a nonagenarian ex–MP. The Chularajamontri presides over the Islamic Council of Thailand, a national committee. Each Thai province with a significant Muslim population has its own provincial Islamic committee, members of which are elected by the imams of all officially registered mosques. The 2005 provincial Islamic Council elections were characterised by accusations of vote-buying and other dirty tricks, allegedly orchestrated by the military and figures associated with political parties. In 2006, a former minister assumed the supposedly independent role of Secretary-General of the Islamic Council of Thailand, allegedly claiming in a television interview that Prime Minister Thaksin Shinawatra had assigned him to this position.

The politicisation of the Islamic Councils at all levels reflects both official and public nervousness concerning the loyalty and trustworthiness of Thailand's Muslim minority. This anxiety has a couple of major causes. One is the greater visibility and more overt piety of Thai Muslims: mosques are proliferating, and headscarf wearing, rare only a decade ago, has become common even among Muslims living in Buddhist-majority areas. But the primary cause of Buddhist unease is the ongoing political violence in Thailand's southern border provinces of Pattani, Yala and Narathiwat, along with four districts of neighbouring Songkhla. These Malay-speaking areas, where Muslims amount to around 80 per cent of the population, were only formally incorporated into Siam (later Thailand) in 1909, and have long been a site of 'separatist' resistance to the Thai state. A full-blown insurgency that began in the 1960s declined in the early 1980s, as a result of a social compact between the Thai state and Malay Muslim elites. However, the deal began unravelling in the new millennium, and in 2004 a series of dramatic militant actions—matched by draconian state responses—signalled a full resumption in hostilities.

Since then, more than three and a half thousand people have been killed in a conflict that has attracted little international media attention—despite the fact that the level of violence makes Southern Thailand one of the world's most intensive insurgencies, second only to Iraq and Afghanistan during the same period. The militant movement in the South has not claimed responsibility for its actions, or even identified itself by name. All the evidence suggests that this is a network-based movement organised in small cells; most attacks are carried out by teams of disenchanted young men, some of whom have been indoctrinated by their teachers at *pondok* (traditional Islamic boarding schools) and private Islamic schools (which teach the regular Thai curriculum in parallel with a religious education). The movement has targeted Thai security forces and government officials, as well as ordinary Buddhist traders and rubber tappers. Yet despite public perceptions—among Thais from outside the region—that the major victims of the violence are Buddhists, in fact more Muslims than Buddhists have been killed and injured. Some are targeted on the grounds that they have betrayed the Malay cause or are *munafik*—traitors to the religion. Others fell victim to extra judicial killings by the authorities. Human rights organisations have documented patterns of disappearances and the use of torture by the Thai army and police. Such methods provide propaganda victories to the militants and fuel resentment against the Thai state.

While the ongoing conflict has made life in the 'Deep South' of Thailand extremely difficult for both Buddhists and Muslims, especially in the so-called 'red zones', generally rural areas, where militant activity and state responses are most concentrated, the violence also has considerable ramifications for the rest of the country. During 2005–06, the Thai government established a fifty member National Reconciliation Commission (NRC), chaired by the distinguished former Prime Minister Anand Panyarachun. While the NRC was welcomed by Malay Muslims in the South, it produced a hostile reaction from many Buddhists in the region; in late 2005, senior monks in the affected provinces petitioned the government to disband the Commission, arguing that it was taking sides with terrorists and promoting religious division. The petition reflected a growing mood of Buddhist chauvinism in Thailand, prompted partly by a number of attacks on monks and temples in the South. Three monks were killed in 2004, and one in 2005. The October 2005 attack at Wat Phromprasit in Pattani was particularly horrific, involving the killing of an elderly monk and two temple boys, as well as the destruction of Buddhist images.

At the same time, Buddhist temples were not always sites of neutrality in the ongoing conflict. After January 2004, many temples were turned into improvised military and police bases for the forces deployed to secure the region. Soldiers were ordained into the monkhood to help sustain temples and preserve them as sites of Thai national identity. Some of these soldier-monks still carried weapons, in violation of monastic rules. In October 2004, the Queen of Thailand had fuelled tensions in the region by calling upon all 300,000 'Thais' (in other words, non-Muslims) living there to learn how to shoot. As a result, Buddhist villagers had received weapons training and most had armed themselves. The military, under the guidance of royal aides-de-camp, had organised teams of Buddhist defence volunteers to protect temples and associated communities from attack. In some places, unofficial Buddhist militias had been formed; one such group known as Ruam Thai, with an estimated 6000 members, was trained and organised by a staunchly royalist Yala police colonel, Phitak Iadkaew, supposedly in his spare time.

The rise of anti-Muslim sentiment in Bangkok and other parts of Thailand was palpable in the wake of the resurgent southern violence after 2004. Such sentiment could be clearly seen on popular web-boards and blog sites. Every time attacks on Buddhists made the headlines in Bangkok, hostile and derogatory web postings would appear on these sites. A thread on one such site headed 'Speak up if you hate Southern assailants' received 309 comments in one year from May 2004, many containing foul language and insulting remarks about Islam and ethnicity. Most postings on this and similar themes expressed feelings of hatred and violence, and challenged other Buddhists to resist Muslims aggressively. When suspects were arrested, most posters expressed satisfaction with and support for the security forces. Feelings of intense hostility were commonly expressed, including suggestions that Buddhists blockade Muslim villages and start fighting back. Some posters expressed support for extra-judicial killings in highly emotive language.

Such sentiments were echoed in milder ways by some popular and prominent Thai Buddhist monks, who invoked highly nationalistic arguments concerning the inter-connectedness of 'Nation, Religion, King' (a standard shibboleth coined by a former Thai monarch) in support of resisting Muslim aspirations and supposed encroachment. Some monks painted apocalyptic images of a future in which Thailand might become a Muslim-majority nation.

By the standards of many other Asian countries, Thailand—beyond the Deep South—has relatively harmonious communal relations. Nevertheless, the Southern conflict is helping to strip away the illusion of tolerance in Thailand, exposing the emergence of an Islamophobia that contains the seeds of further potential social division. Both secular and religious leaders have so far appeared reluctant directly to address or tackle these growing feelings of resentment, blame and even hatred.

22

'BREAKING THE TABOO
OF MULTICULTURALISM'

THE BELGIAN LEFT AND ISLAM

Nadia Fadil

The beginning of the twenty-first century is marked by a new conjuncture in the multicultural debate in Flanders, Belgium's Dutch-speaking, wealthiest, and most densely populated region of Belgium.[1] The call to ditch the seal of 'political correctness' purportedly sheltering multiculturalism from overdue critique turned into one of the leitmotivs of debates on the political left. Inspired by interventions such as those of the Dutch intellectual Paul Scheffer (2000), consensus gathered on the need for honesty in facing up to the realities of multicultural society in all its ugliness, without taboos or complexes. This 'new realism', to borrow Baukje Prins' (2004 [2000]; 2002) formulation, is contrasted to the complacencies of apologia and self-censorship. The latter supposedly characterised a period when the left is said to have remained silent about the problems posed by minorities, such as the high levels of criminality and criminal behaviour among migrant youth in the larger cities, high levels of unemployment, welfare dependence, and the cultural maladjustment and

[1] This paper was written during my stay at the RSCAS of the European University Institute as a Jean Monnet Postdoctoral Fellow during the academic year 2008–2009.

problematic integration of migrant communities. The alleged self-censorship within the left is, moreover, viewed by some as one of the main reasons for its failure to meet the challenge of the rise of the right wing Vlaams Blok/Belang party which, since its electoral breakthrough in 1991, has set the terms of the multicultural debate in Flanders (Jacobs and Swyngedouw, 2002).[2] Thus, for instance, in 2002 Yves Desmet, chief editor of the leftist newspaper *De Morgen*, denounced the left's incapacity to adopt a stronger, repressive discourse towards the criminal behaviour of Moroccan youngsters—whom he described as 'cunt-Moroccans' [*kutmarokkanen*] (Desmet, 2002). In an interview on the social problems of the notorious Antwerp neighborhood of Borgerhout, the left wing journalists Rudi Rotthier and Filip Rogiers argued in 2001 that 'the problems caused by multicultural society' combined with the left's incapacity to address them was one of the main reasons for the Vlaams Blok's success in that neighborhood.

This chapter examines the contours of this 'end to political correctness' discourse in public debates among the progressive left in the Flemish context since 2000, and how its distinctive focus came to centre on Islam. The category 'left' is here used descriptively rather than normatively to refer to politicians, intellectuals and journalists who describe themselves as on the left and/or 'progressive'.[3] While the category spans a range of opinions, the focus here is specifically on those who have argued for the need to adopt a 'new' and 'less politically correct' discourse on multiculturalism. An important characteristic of these new critiques is their explicit targeting of Muslim minorities on the basis of a 'culturalist framework', which posits an ontological difference between Islam and dominant society, and grasps Muslims and their conduct through (a specific understanding of) Islam. Social behaviour and attitudes of Muslims is thus primarily accounted for through their 'cultural' and/or

---

[2] Following its condemnation in 2004 for disseminating hate speech and racist discourses Vlaams Blok changed its name to Vlaams Belang. For an account of its development see Delwit and De Waele (1998), De Lange (2008) and Jacobs and Swyngedouw (2002).

[3] The increase in popularity of the term 'progressive' over that of 'left' over the past few years is reflected in the change of name of the 'Socialist Party' [*Socialistische Partij, SP*] in 2002 to 'Social-Progressive Alternative' [*Sociaal-Progressief alternatief, SP.a*]. The term 'Progressive' is considered to be more inclusive than 'left' in its concern with not only redistributive questions but also ethical questions (and thus encompassing also of people from the liberal party). For an account of this semantic expansion of the socialist party, which is also seen as an ideological slide, see Verscheuren (2003).

'religious' background. The popularity of this culturalist register is by no means new. Several scholars have documented the emergence and development of what some have coined a 'new racism'. The latter is characterised by a process of 'othering' that hangs on the perceived 'cultural differences' rather than differences in skin colour.[4] The racialised 'others' are then seen as essentially governed by 'culture', which is understood in static and essentialist terms and subordinated to the 'dominant' culture (see Modood, 1997; Gilroy, 2002 [1987]). The popularity of this culturalist register increased in the post-cold war era, especially towards Islam, as the roots of the conflicts between states or entities were increasingly situated at a 'civilisational' or 'cultural' level. It also draws on a centuries old Orientalist tradition, which posits Islam as a radically different entity from 'the West' (Said, 1995; 1997). The result has been the construction of Islam into a geo-political and cultural and religious entity, which is deemed to pose a particular challenge to 'Western civilisation' (Huntington, 1992). Hence, rather than announcing a new development, the dissemination of this 'culture talk' (Mamdani, 2004) vis-à-vis Muslims in a post 9/11 context is a continuation of a discursive framework which has been gaining popularity over the past twenty years.

Since 2000, this call to challenge the public recognition of minority culture in general, and Muslim culture in particular, emerged as an important theme among certain segments of the Flemish political and intellectual left, framed as one of the ultimate taboos that had only rarely been addressed. That very year Antwerp alderman of education, Robert Voorhamme, stated that 'the migrant culture impedes upon every form of integration' and urged the need to address non-liberal cultural practices, such as female subordination and homophobia, among minorities (Brinckman, 2002). It is with the dissemination and spread of this culturalist register among self-declared Flemish progressive voices, and how the latter attained a particular expression in this specific intellectual/political field, that this chapter is concerned. The first part examines how culturalist and Orientalistic schemes, which reproduce the idea of an ontological difference between Islam and the West, emerged as the dominant analytical grid by problematising and discrediting other perspectives. The second part focuses on how the advocates of this discourse have in recent years positioned themselves as the 'true heralds' of a left and progressive front. I sug-

---

[4] It remains a point of discussion whether 'older' forms of racialisation which draw on a differentiation on the basis skin colour have disappeared. Modood (1997, p. 164) has argued that cultural racism is characterised by a conjunction of racialisation (differentiation on the basis of skin colour) and cultural difference.

THINKING THROUGH ISLAMOPHOBIA

gest that their calls for an end to political correctness among the left signal not only the consensualising dissemination of a culturalist register, but articulate a conjunction between liberal and nationalist governance.

Flemish Nationalism, Multiculturalism and the Left

What once figured as a predominantly rural and impoverished region has over the past century developed into one of the wealthiest regions of Europe, steeped in a regional nationalism that has propelled the country towards increasing federalisation. In the process, Flanders has developed into an autonomous cultural and regional entity distinct not only from its French speaking southern counterpart, Wallonia, but also from its northern neighbour, the Netherlands. Previously an area of emigration (by the end of the nineteenth century, mostly to Wallonia and France, but also to the US), Flanders gradually turned into one of 'immigration', attracting a large part of Belgium's current documented and undocumented migrants.[5] Immigration flows to Belgium before 1974 were mainly the result of a national immigration policy targeting low-skilled workers to fill in for the post-WWII labour shortage. Workers were initially recruited from Italy, Spain and Greece, and in the early sixties also from Morocco and Turkey. Since 1974, however, such inflows from non-European countries are restricted to marriage, asylum, or education.

The presence of immigrants turned into an important, yet sensitive, political issue in Flanders in the early nineties with the electoral ascendance of the *Vlaams Blok*. In 1978, a number of dissidents split from the Flemish nationalist party, *Vlaamse Unie* [Flemish Union], in protest at the signing of the Egmont pact, an agreement that laid the basis for the reorganisation of the country into communities and regions. The *Vlaams Blok* [Flemish Blok] was established, and distinguished itself by its explicit separatist agenda and anti-immigration stance.[6] Several scholars have indicated that the problematisation of the 'multicultural question' in Flanders has been closely intertwined with the emergence and electoral successes of this right wing party (Jacobs, 1998; Blommaert and

[5] Flanders has numerically the largest number of immigrants; Brussels-Capital Region the largest number of immigrants as a proportion of the population. See http://www.npdata.be/Data/Vreemdelingen/NIS/Loop/inhoud.htm.

[6] Arnaut, K. and Ceuppens, B. (2004), see in the emergence and popularity of the Vlaams Blok the radical expression of a conception of Flanders as a culturally homogeneous and territorially anchored entity.

Verscheuren, 1992).[7] Whereas immigration flows marked the country since at least the second half of the twentieth century, the establishment of a policy geared towards the successful 'integration' of immigrants would only emerge at the end of the eighties, two years after the first electoral breakthrough of the party (Jacobs, 1998; Blommaert and Verscheuren, 1992). [8] The result has been a systematic coupling of the two issues. Thus, the electoral success of the *Vlaams Blok* has often been treated as a *symptom* of social problems (related to multiculturalism). Correspondingly, it was believed that a successful integration of minorities would lead to a decrease of support for the party and its eventual demise.[9]

Large segments of what can be described as the 'progressive-left' in Flanders were mobilised in the late eighties and nineties against the electoral success of the *Vlaams Blok* and for the voting rights of migrants. Dirk Jacobs' (1998) study has shown that the question of voting rights of migrants had already become a political theme in the early seventies thanks to the mobilisation of the syndicalist movement. Yet, with the electoral success of the Vlaams Blok, it quickly turned into a highly sensitive theme which most centre-left political parties shied away from leaving mobilisation around this question to civil society (until, in the post-Maastricht conjuncture, Belgium was forced to bring its legislation in line with European directives in 2003). Different organisations were created to meet this challenge (e.g. Vaka-Hand in Hand; Charta 91, Blockwatch, Liga voor Mensenrechten). None, however, led to an interrogation of the ethno-nationalist imaginary upon which right-wing nationalist parties thrive. Some anti-racist agencies even shared the same ethno-nationalist postulate, which stresses the need for migrants to 'integrate' and links multiculturalism with social problems. Thus, for example, the Royal agency for migration policy [Koninklijk Commissariaat voor het Migrantenbeleid], charged with implementing the integration policy, also drew on a homogeneous representation of Flanders in its approach to the question of migrants and their 'integration' (Blommaert and Verscheuren, 1992). The political

---

[7] I use the notion of problematisation as defined by Foucault (1984), i.e. the constitution of a particular domain of social life into the object of regulation.

[8] The Royal Commission for migration policy [Koninklijk Commissariaat voor Migrantenbeleid] was established in 1989, one year after the electoral breakthrough of the Vlaams Blok in the federal parliament.

[9] This is also explicitly posited as such in the KCM note on integration, which holds a mid-way position between an assimilationist and a pluralistic perspective (for further discussion see Blommaert and Verscheuren, 1992).

ascent of the Vlaams Blok was mostly analyzed as a symptom of a deeper social malaise, caused by neo-liberal politics or a democratic deficit.[10] The idea that the left was silent on the problems of multicultural society and that it maintained a 'cuddle policy' [*knuffelbeleid*] towards migrants became a popular narrative in right wing and conservative circles. Since the turn of the century, however, self-declared leftist intellectuals have also taken it up.

The Problem With Islam

The 'breaking the political correctness' narrative has, since 2000, found a distinctive articulation around the idea that Islam and Muslims pose a particular challenge central to the contemporary 'malaise' of multiculturalism. Whereas some issues of cultural diversity and heterogeneity have posed particular problems to the quest for a collective commonality, Islam, so the narrative goes, poses a fundamental challenge. Its advocates construct Muslims as a distinct category, with a peculiar set of (cultural, religious and social) characteristics that sets them apart from the 'majority' society and ratifies their status as 'outsiders'. An example is provided by Bob van den Broek (2000), a self-declared left commentator on multicultural issues, in a response to Paul Scheffer's essay:

Before applying Scheffer's article in a Flemish context, we must first clarify our concepts. In what follows, migrants—whether they have acquired Belgian nationality or not—will be called 'allochthons'. *A contrario*, all other inhabitants will be designated as 'autochthons', hence as original inhabitants of this country. It's clear that the notion of 'allochthons' covers many layers. The Americans who work in the Flemish language valley, or a Dutch person who lives here due to the (for him) attractive tax regime are *sensu strictu* also allochtons. Yet in this article, this category will primarily be used to designate the allochthons from the Muslim community. The societal problems many, justifiably or unjustifiably, note are indeed often linked with members of this community.

The dichotomy '*autochton*' and '*allochton*' is very commonly used in Flanders, and serves to differentiate 'natives' from people of 'foreign origin'. In practice, however, as in van der Broek's piece, *allochton* is rarely understood to encompass Western-Europeans or Americans, and essentially denotes 'non-Western' ethnic and cultural minorities. It is, in other words, a racialising device, and marker of radical alterity.[11] The category Muslim is a further homogenising

[10] See for instance the manifesto of Charta 91, http://www.charta91.be/.
[11] For a critical analysis of the usage of this dichotomy and its racialising effects see Bommaert and Verscheuren (1992), Rath (1991), Arnaut and Ceuppens (2009).

one, undifferentiated along ethnic, generational, sexual or social lines. Thus, whereas the primary category *allochton* is seemingly primarily justified on economic grounds, by reducing social differences to differences of origin, and Muslim as an undifferentiated category to *allochton*, van den Broek reproduces a culturalist schema.

The constitution of Muslims into a distinct (and alien) group finds further explicit justification in the many contributions which problematise the 'intrinsic cultural characteristics' of Islam. In his seminal essay 'The Multicultural Drama', the Dutch essayist Paul Scheffer (2000) called into question the general applicability of the Dutch pillarisation model, introduced as a means to secure peaceful coexistence between the different Christian (Protestant and Catholic) streams, and its continuing usefulness as a model of integration in the 1990s. Crucial to his argument, is the lack of 'common ground' between Christianity and Islam, and the claim that 'the role of Islam simply cannot be compared with that of Christian confessions'. Similarly, Scheffer points to the rejection of separation between Church and State in Islamic milieus, and the impossibility of apostasy. In his most recent work, *Het Land van Aankomst* (Scheffer, 2007), he further notes the new and unprecedented minority position in which Islam finds itself in Europe, incompatible with its centuries old position of dominance in the Muslim world (Scheffer, 2007, p. 360).

The 'specificity' of Islam, justified through the postulate of an ontological and epistemological incommensurability between 'Islam' and 'Christianity', is based on essentialist and Orientalist representations (Said, 1978; Geisser, 2004). Whereas such Orientalist culturalist accounts had hitherto prevailed in right wing and conservative circles, the displacement of socio-economics by culturalist frameworks as the primary grid of analysis on the left is one of the main 'novelties' of the post-9/11 debate. A once marginal analysis, gradually pushed throughout the nineties by conservative political analysts into the paradigm for the new post-89 geo-political conjuncture (Huntington, 1993; Bolkstein, 1991), expanded after 9/11 into the hegemonic paradigm across the left-right political divide (see also Arnaut et al., 2009).

Benno Banard and Geert van Istendael's (2008) seminal and widely commented essay 'Message to the right-minded left: why we defend the headscarf ban' is a representative example. Published as an open letter in support of the ban of religious symbols (i.e. the headscarf) from public offices in the small Flemish town of Lier in January 2008, it primarily addresses progressive intellectuals who opposed the ban. Condemning manifestations of support for the right to veil on the left, as incompatible with a progressive and anti-clerical

agenda, the authors argue that such a misguided stance stems from the ignorance, on the part of its supporters, of 'the essence of Islam':

What we, and many other decent and not totally irrational intellectuals mean, is that
the discussion should be about the essence of Islam. Yet many leftist friends prefer [to
maintain] a glowing ignorance about this religion. But it is absolutely important to
understand that our criteria—all our dear civil freedoms, of which neutrality is a structuring principle—are meaningless in the theological space of the Prophet. Islam professes a totally different vision about religious and political reality than Judaism and
Christianity, the religions on which the Prophet [Muhammad] drew inspiration and
which he fought in his Qur'an with fire and sword.

Interventions such as this pit Islam as a static religious formation with little
affinity to the Western trajectory of Christianity and Judaism. An opposition
is posited between a distinct set of positive values (civil liberty, tolerance, neutrality) attributed to 'the West' and its religious formations (Christianity and
Judaism), and their negative opposites (such as violence and intolerance) essentially linked with 'Islam'. The avowed ignorance of supporters sympathetic to
the right to veil is contrasted to, and reinforces, the authors' self-declared
expertise and grasp of the 'essence' of Islam. Such claim to expert knowledge
is part of what French sociologist Vincent Geisser (2003) describes in *La nouvelle Islamophobie* as the emergence of a new 'expertise of fear'. Geisser shows
how self-declared experts—mostly journalists and security experts, occasionally academics—have turned into the main carriers of a 'new' Islamophobic
discourse in France in the post 9/11 context. An important characteristic of
this discourse is the persistent discredit thrown over the knowledge produced
by scholars specialised in Muslim societies or the presence of Muslims in
Europe (Geisser, 2003, pp. 57–58). Whereas in the French context these claims
of expertise serve mostly to attack the validity of academic knowledge of Islam,
in the context of interventions such as Banard and van Istendael's it serves to
discredit any account which refuses essentialist representations of Islam and/
or adopts a different understanding of secularism.

Presenting oneself as an 'expert', and accusing other left intellectuals of
naiveté, has developed into the preferred tactic to legitimise the dissemination
and consolidation of similar Orientalist clichés within left progressive milieus.
In this it bears great similarity to the 'new realism' inflexion Prins identifies in
the critical discourse on the 'ugly reality' of multiculturalism. Also similarly,
dissenting views are cast and dismissed as 'apologists', now of Islam. What distinguishes them, then, is a claim to truth that lifts their interventions above
and beyond merely different political positions: a claim to truth grounded on

knowledge of the essence of Islam. Such claims, mutually reinforcing, abound. The numerous problems encountered with 'Muslims', argues Johan Sanctorum, should make us realise that 'things with Islam will never settle—it is just not a religion like another'. Sounding the alarm he asks: 'Is right-minded Flanders finally ready to wake up from its 'unity-in-diversity' idyll, wherein Islam would be only one composite of the multicultural cake?' (Sanctorum, 2008, p. 63). Jan Leyers, a popular journalist and the maker of the widely viewed documentary *The Road to Mecca*, claims a similar epistemological privilege in his views on Islam on the basis of his road trip through North Africa and the Middle East. In a number of interviews, he describes the fundamental differences he encountered while making his documentary—such as the fact that Muslims are still guided by 'Qur'anic certainties', which prevent them from questioning their beliefs and worldviews, or their radically different understanding of sexuality and gender relations. On one particularly telling occasion we see how this is used to challenge 'academic' readings:

A statement I found fascinating was that of the [political] scientist from [the University of] Ghent, Sami Zemni. He was invited as a guest at *Terzake* [a popular political television show] on the day of the elections in Morocco. It still seemed like the conservative party PJD would win the elections, which eventually didn't happen. Kathleen Cools [the anchorwoman] asked Zemni whether Morocco wasn't facing a choice between modernity and tradition. And Zemni answered: 'No, its two forms of modernity'. That's when I thought: 'what the hell?'. Look, if I was ever to paint a banner and go demonstrate on my own, it's against such hypocrisy. Nobody can convince me that a party that calls itself Islamic, even if moderate, can be linked with what we understand as modernity. PJD women are so modern that they distribute pamphlets wearing face-veils. Well, that's where it stops for me. Another modernity? Modernity starts with showing your face. Call the PJD approach practical or desirable for Morocco. But don't call it 'modern'. Or we would have to start seriously discussing our conceptual apparatus (Leyers, 2007).

By presupposing an incommensurability between political Islam and modernity, Leyers not only places these movements—and the distinctive characteristics he links with them such as face-veiling—outside of modernity, but he also redefines and narrows the signification of 'modernity' down in a very particular way. But Leyer does not merely contest Sami Zemni, a scholar of the Middle East and North Africa, and his claim that the PJD could be grasped through the rubric of 'alternative modernity'. Leyers posits his critique with a self-evidence and self-righteousness which not merely contests but ridicules and disqualifies in advance the very possibility of Zemni's alternative reading.

The 'new political correctness', as these examples suggest, is substantiated both in a particular analysis of 'the problems' of multicultural society and in a distinctive reading and understanding of Islam whose claims to truth are founded on the symbolic violence of a real world expert authority unmasking political and academic naivite.

Redefining the Left, Defending 'Our' Values

This problematisation of Islam is produced not only through the cumulative critique of certain 'characteristics' ascribed to the religion and its adherents, as described above, but also and simultaneously by an equally sustained enunciation of what is described as the 'impossibility' of criticising Islam and Muslims within the left. This was, of course, a familiar claim in conservative and right-wing critiques of multiculturalism. Thus the legitimacy and validity of the term 'Islamophobia', for example, was disqualified as a tactic deployed to silence any criticism of Islam (Doornaert, 2004, is an example). More recently, however, the same claim has also been taken up by progressive voices. The Dutch polemicist and journalist Joost Zwagerman, whose work also receives considerable attention in Flanders, in his latest polemic dwells at length on the impossibility of criticising Islam or Muslims. Commenting on the Dutch public debate, he argues that terms such as 'fascist', 'Nazi' or 'racist' are often used to intimidate intellectuals who dare to criticise Islam or Muslims (Zwagerman, 2009). Having 'dared' to publish his critique and publicly denounce Islam, Zwagerman, in a rhetorical move that Prins identifies as a characteristic feature of the new-realist genre (Prins, 2004 [2000], pp. 35–36), thus establishes his own claim as an uncompromising and bold voice prepared to speak out against the taboo on Islam and multiculturalism. Proponents of the new realism, as Prins argues, present themselves as people with 'guts', who dare to challenge the moral and intellectual consensus around multiculturalism. What Zwagerman contends, however, is not only the impossibility of criticising Islam, in general, but also the way progressive ideals have been 'abused' for the defence of Muslims and Islam. Those who are targeted in this specific context are not political or intellectual adversaries, but rather allies, fellow travelers on the left. The call for an 'end to political correctness' is hence as much characterised by the deployment of a culturalist register, as by a concerted attempt to establish a 'new consensus' in the left-progressive camp. Differently put, by laying claim to a left-progressive intellectual stance, and challenging the way the latter has addressed issues on multiculturalism and Islam, such proponents portray themselves as the genuine guardians of a left and progressive 'orthodoxy'.

I draw here on the work of the French sociologist Pierre Bourdieu. In *Outline of a Theory of Practice*, Bourdieu (2006 [1977], p. 164) distinguishes orthodoxy and heterodoxy from a 'doxic mode', which is fundamentally grounded on 'misrecognition' of the limits of a particular order, and which leads to the sense of obviousness, self-evidence, and naturalness of a particular 'reality'.[12] Orthodox and heterodox positions, on the other hand, belong to a field of opinions where the doxic mode has lost its natural status, and where different discourses compete. While the orthodox mode seeks to restore the field of the doxa, heterodox approaches tend to broaden this field of opinion by 'pushing back the limit of doxa and exposing the arbitrariness of the taken for granted'. Orthodoxy is in this sense defined as the 'imperfect substitute' of a doxic mode (Bourdieu, 2006 [1977], p. 169), whereas heterodoxy is that which tries to expose the particularities of this doxic mode. Applying this Bourdieusian model, and more particularly his definition of orthodoxy, allows us to grasp the 'progressive left' as a field, which consists of a heterogeneous set of players with distinctive viewpoints who are in a continuous struggle over its 'consensus'. I contend that the recent surge of self-declared leftist critical voices on issues of multiculturalism can thus be read as attempt to carve a 'new orthodoxy', i.e. to establish a set of 'truth claims', as 'core values' for a left and/or progressive intellectual standpoint.

These attempts to carve out a 'new orthodoxy' appear first in the *mea culpa* offered by several of its proponents, who admit their own slowness and failure to acknowledge and address the problems with multiculturalism. Thus the philosopher Johan Sanctorum, for instance, finds satisfaction in the fact that left-progressive intellectuals have finally discarded the strategy of denial and adopted a 'new *parler vrai* that also acknowledges its own divagation' (Sanctorum, pp. 162–163). The latter is, for instance, well exemplified in a comment by socialist alderman Robert Voorhamme, in the course of a seminal interview, on Ayaan Hirsi Ali's claim that the left had failed to acknowledge the problems with Muslim culture:

Being an emancipatory movement, socialists have traditionally always been tolerant towards other cultures and religions. But they forgot that respect for universal values transcends this tolerance. This resulted in a complete abdication. We wanted to be nice

---

[12] Bourdieu also links the stability of a doxic mode of representation with the stability of social structures: 'the more stable the objective structures and the more fully they reproduce themselves in the agents' disposition, the greater the extent of the field of doxa, of that which is taken for granted' (2006 [1977], p. 166).

to immigrants, we wanted to protect them. All well and good. But our blindness prevented us form seeing that fundamental issues had been overlooked [...]. For years socialists have expected respect for universal values from their militants. But they [the militants] don't see why they should be living with people who don't care about these values. They don't understand why we accept things like that. We even blamed them for signaling those problems. That is totally incomprehensible (Brinckman, 2002).

Voorhamme not only acknowledges having erred, but expresses it in the mode of repentance. Repentance is firstly shown for neglecting 'universal values' in the name of 'tolerance'. The two thus set as conflicting values through an opposition between 'tolerance'—the category through which 'cultural difference' is addressed—and 'universal values'. Secondly, Voorhamme also demonstrates repentance for the way socialists behaved towards their own 'militants', depicted here almost as victims of the elite's arrogance. This opposition between the 'elite' who failed to listen and 'the militants' who 'signaled' the problems, not only delegitimises the elite as estranged and alienated, but also reinstates the militants as ultimate 'truth holders', who have primary access not only to the realities on the ground but also to the very 'universal values' the elite professes yet fails to follow. Voorhamme's repentance seems thus to fulfill a double function. It not only serves to delegitimise his earlier standpoints and cast them off as 'morally wrong', but also as a catharsis which 'purifies' his voice and grants his actual position a newly reclaimed orthodoxy.

This articulation of a new orthodoxy furthermore also appears in the way certain positions are attacked for reflecting a 'double standard'. The acceptance by progressive minded people of Muslim practices such as the veil in the public sphere, for instance, is dismissed as in contradiction with the left's anti-clerical legacy. The Flemish publicist Bob van den Broek (2000), for one, has expressed his 'surprise' that left-progressive voices in Flanders 'oppose the tutelage of the Catholic Church, yet at the same time accept the cultural-religious segregation of the allochthonous community'. The leftwing journalist Rudi Rotthier also declared in an interview feeling disturbed by the left's efforts to present Islam as a peaceful religion, something he not only disagrees with, but sees as contradicting the anti-clerical premises endorsed by the left (Rotthier and Rogiers, 2001). Moreover the Dutch journalist Joost Zwagerman (2009, p. 39) discerns a 'double standard' in the way the left has always exalted at criticism of the catholic establishment, yet condemned similar critiques against Islam. By challenging the alleged 'inconsequentialism' of the left, the authors position themselves as the 'real' defenders of leftist values and as the 'pure' voice of the leftist project.

The delineation of a new orthodoxy is, lastly, expressed through an explicit restatement of a set of values and ideals that are substantiated in a distinctive way. One of them, as illustrated by the well-known journalist and writer Geert van Istendael (2008), is secularism:

Today, strangely enough, the veil is harshly defended by people who have not the least bit of Islam in their body (...). They are young people who never knew the pre-Conciliar period, and they should thank the Lord for it, but instead Catholicism has become something vague to them. These young people of Belgian background who defend the headscarf from progressive, say leftist, convictions are mostly naïve about religion. Or no, even foolish, that is the term (...). Indeed, those young people have no idea about the huge, suffocating power a century old world religion develops once it encounters limits that are imposed upon it. (...) When they defend the headscarf in newspapers, they often talk about the cold neutrality such a prohibition on headscarf at public offices could lead to. (...) This is dazzling. Almost unbelievable. Sad. People who had the privilege to study should know better. There's no excuse for them.

In this passage, van Istendael critises the *naïveté* he discerns among a younger generation that considers itself left and progressive yet which, according to him, fails to identify the dangers of religion and therefore abdicates in a quite inconsequential manner to its contemporary manifestations. Van Istendael poses himself here as not only as expert, but also as guardian of an anti-clerical tradition. Secular values are thus re-stated, yet in a very distinctive manner— one that precludes the possibility of a pro-*hijab* standpoint—in the name of a return to those same secular values.

The 'New Left' as Herald of Liberal Nationalism

It seems like Europe is finally and painfully waking up. Historians will one day wonder why it took so long before Western intellectuals realised that their permissiveness would end up destructively. The whole period between 1970 and today has been lost to political correct idle talk, which applied enlightenment philosophy to an utterly obscurantist oil stain (Sanctorum, 2008, p. 74).

Sin, repentance, salvation. These are the themes which modulate the 'breaking the political correctness' narrative which over the past few years has been mobilised by self-declared 'left' and 'progressive' intellectuals in their attempts to establish culturalist and Orientalistic schema as the primary analytical grid through which multiculturalism in general, and the presence of Muslim minorities in Western-Europe in particular are apprehended. The sin is that of the left's shared responsibility in 'the multicultural drama' and its 'permissiveness', which is linked to the blindness to Islam's 'obscurantism' and the neglect of the left's own avowed values. Repentance takes the form of an acknowledgement of this 'wrongdoing' and the commitment to remedy it. The promise of salvation is held by the fact that the repentant turn into the holders and guardians of 'left-progressive' values in their 'purest' forms, and commit themselves to its defence. This last theme, the idea that Europe needs to be 'defended', has gained particular prominence over the past few years. We have already seen it in the quote from Sanctorum cited above. We find it also in the work of Dutch journalist Arthur van Amerongen who, in his book *Brussel/Eurabia*, warns against this ever-expanding 'Muslim threat': 'I had been completely wrong [...]. At the end of my stay in Brussels my other perspective was muted. I had become convinced that Islam is a divisive element. [...] in Brussels I only saw ghettos filled with Muslims with Middle-Aged viewpoints who do not seek contact with Belgian society in any way. Even more, they despise this society' (van Amerongen, 2008). Banard and van Istendael (2008, pp. 170–171) also note that: 'Quite a few leftist intellectuals defend in the name of emancipation the Islamic right to its mildest form of terrorism: female subordination [i.e. the headscarf]. 'Freedom of choice' is what the left cries out with an acute voice. Europe would dismantle itself out of respect for its own principles'.

Such accounts do not stand alone, but resonate with broader and more global discourses which insist upon the incommensurability between Islam and the West, and the need for Europeans to stand up for their values and against the threat of the slow but steady 'Islamisation' of Europe.[13] Such theses as *Eurabia* (Ye'or, 2005) are not new and gained increasing popularity in right wing circles in the post 9/11 conjuncture. But in the last few years their hold has expanded also among self-declared progressives producing a new chauvinism (see Bawer, 2006; 2009). Within it, a new relation of equivalence has been established between 'progressive-left' and 'Europeanness' in the form of an identity which is not predicated on the nationalism of distinctive national cultures and territories but, no less exclusively, on a set of 'universal' values, with the left as its guardians.

In *Regulating Aversion*, Wendy Brown outlines how liberalism has turned into a privileged civilisational discourse and practice in the age of Empire. She defines liberalism as 'a contingent, malleable, and protean set of beliefs and

---

[13] See in this regard the right-wing international network '*Stop the Islamisation of Europe*' that emerged in Denmark but works in close collaboration with other right-wing activist in different European countries http://sioe.wordpress.com

practices about being human and being together; about relating to self, others and world; about doing and not doing; about valuing and not valuing select things. Liberalism is also always institutionalized, constitutionalized, and governmentalized in articulation with other cultural norms—those of kinship, race, gender, sexuality, work, politics, leisure, and more' (Brown, W., 2006, p. 23). Liberalism, Brown contends, operates as governmentality through the selective ascription of a 'civilisational' and 'free' status to certain forms of life. Other forms of life, on the other hand, which fall outside the liberal spectrum, are seen as 'barbaric', incapable of similar liberal values, and even potentially 'threatening' to one's own liberal lifestyle (Brown, 2006, p. 179). Brown's work adds to the critical literature that examines the way liberal modes of governmentality are at the heart of contemporary nationalist aspirations (Asad, 2003 and 2007; Butler, 2004). The point made is not that new forms of dominance are falsely legitimised by liberal values and norms, but rather that these exclusionary mechanisms are a modality through which liberalism operates.

Building on this argument, I suggest that the recent call for an 'end to political correctness' *vis-à-vis* Muslims by the proponents of a left-progressive discourse articulates the dissemination and triumph of a particular form of nationalism which has liberalism—as a mode of governmentality—at its heart. 'Otherness' is here not only problematised but also regulated according to liberal scripts. Those who are seen to fall outside this realm of 'humanity', the ungovernable others (i.e. the 'terrorists', the 'fundamentalists') become the object of repression. Approaching the 'end of political correctness' as a new form of nationalism allows us to understand the kind of above-cited interventions, which present liberal values as under threat from a creeping Islamisation, as one of its aspects. This liberal nationalism is accompanied also by a new Malthusianism, yet one which substitutes a preoccupation with 'life forms' for 'birth rate' and 'high demographic presence'. Muslims are depicted as a threat to the national imaginary to the extent that they remain ingrained in an 'uncontrollable' religious orthodoxy. The latter brings us to what Ghassan Hage has described as the 'Anglo-decline discourse'. In *White Nation*, Hage (2000) analyses discourses which present Australia as 'under siege' from an uncontrollable influx of Asian immigrants. Rather than casting it as an epiphenomenon of the 'new racism', Hage takes them as a reflection of the governmental aspirations of nationalism.[14] He views them as a specific modality

---

[14] Hage (2000) problematises the reading which assimilates this discourse to new forms of racism, arguing that such a description not only fails to offer an understanding of

of the operation of the 'White fantasy', which works towards maintaining a sense of control over the 'national space' and the 'national imaginary'. Sanctorum's above quoted narrative of 'decline' becomes an expression of the sense of failure in containing and governing 'otherness'.

In contrast to more traditional chauvinistic forms of nationalism this liberal nationalism is not only more difficult to grasp but also to challenge, because it appeals to 'values' and 'norms' widely perceived as universally claimed and shared. Thus the liberal regulation of 'otherness' can not only count on much greater approval, but is in many cases enacted by the 'subjects' of discipline themselves.[15] Because other cultures are no longer challenged for their cultural difference, but for their failure to deliver 'free' and 'emancipated' subjects, the space for diversity has become even smaller than ever before.

---

the functionality of this narrative, but also fails to address the fact that many advocates of this discourse do not consider themselves 'racists' and do not wish to associate themselves with this 'ugly and bad' term (Hage, 2000, p. 184).

[15] See in this context the case of Ayaan Hirsi Ali whose discourse has been critically analyzed by Sonja van Wichelen and Marc de Leeuw (2005) De Leeuw and van Wichelen (2005).

23

'DON'T FREAK I'M A SIKH!'

Katy Pal Sian

The Sikh Diaspora in Britain seems to be haunted by stories of young Sikh women being duped by young Muslim men into converting to Islam. This is the story of 'forced' conversions; it is a cautionary tale that has, through successive retellings become deeply ingrained within the Sikh BrAsian imaginary. It is the story of the 'brave and courageous' Sikhs trying to save 'their girls' from the 'Muslim predator' whose only aim is to 'coercively' convert by means of trickery, lies, deceit and manipulation. The drama of these forced conversions forms the theatre where seemingly intractable hostility between two BrAsian communities—Sikh and Muslim—is played out. Sikh-Muslim conflict finds its most consistent, most sensationalist and most lurid expressions in these tales of forced conversions. There is, however, little if any evidence to support them outside the Sikh community. Furthermore, the centrality of these forced conversion narratives within Sikh circles is not mirrored among Muslims. This makes for an oddly one-sided conflict, yet one that shows little sign of abating.

In the wake of the War on Terror many in the Sikh diaspora have made a conscious effort to distinguish themselves from the Muslim *ummah*. Although historically this distinction is not novel, the effort to demarcate this difference has, in the context of postcolonial settlement in Britain, been enforced to a much greater extent and become more prominent as the risks incurred in being mistaken for Muslims became correlatively, and occasionally tragically, higher.

In the attempt to avoid being confused for Muslims, many Sikhs seem to have accepted some of the Islamophobic themes that circulate widely within contemporary Western societies. The idea of a Muslim threat common to most variants of Islamophobia can be found within the current hegemonic constructions of Sikh (BrAsian) identity. This articulation of an antagonistic Muslim other against which a Sikh identity can be formulated, however, also has two major historical antecedents within Sikh discursive horizons: Mughal repression of the nascent Sikh community in the seventeenth century and the trauma of ethnic cleansing that accompanied the partition of British India in 1947.

It could be argued that one of the key motifs within Sikhism is unfettered persecution of the emergent Sikh community by the Mughal *padishah*. Narratives of the martyrdom of Sikhs at the hands of Muslim authorities are part and parcel of Sikh upbringing, whether through religious institutions or family life. In these narratives the Mughal aim was not merely to discipline a restive population, but to destroy the identity of the Khalsa. In them, the Mughals personify Muslim tyranny rather than political rulers seeking to uphold their position in the face of centrifugal challenges, and the persecutions are seen as nothing short of an ideological campaign to destroy the very way in which Sikhs imagine themselves, their land and their destiny. Different existential anxieties surrounding the identity of the newly formed community concern prospective fears that Sikhism might be reduced to being a spiritual conveyor belt for the transformation of Hindu polytheism into Islamic absolute monotheism via Sikh notions of one God; that Sikhism, in other words, might become a stage in the conversion of Hindus into Muslims, rather than an intrinsic faith with its own authentic way of life. The idea of a Muslim campaign of forced conversion powerfully amalgamates these two existential challenges to the emergent Sikh community; on the one hand, the challenge posed by a powerful overarching imperial structure in the form of the Mughal Empire; on the other hand, the challenge from below, that Sikhs might for a variety of reasons decide to embrace the institutionally privileged monotheism of Islam.

Clearly the image of Islam as a religion spread by the sword and forced conversion is one with both long antecedents and wide resonances in the Western tradition, and this is where some may locate the question of Islamophobia and its Sikh and Western articulations. For others the onus of the question lies in whether or not it is the Muslimness of the Mughals that is the mark of their 'othering' within the Sikh narrative. While neither is irrelevant, a more nuanced approach is required. The historical Sikh representation of Mughal persecution takes place within a distinct structural ensemble in which Mughals were the rulers of India and the Sikhs a subaltern community within that imperial structure. In Mughal India Muslims constituted a powerful ruling elite able to institutionalise their privilege and authority. However, in Britain Muslims are but one of the contending ethicised communities whose capacity to exercise autonomy is extremely limited. It is not whether Mughal persecutions are or are not an example of Islamophobia that is meaningful, but how tropes of Mughal persecution have been mobilised at the expense of other narrative traditions available to Sikhs. The anti-Muslim narratives circulating within the Sikh Diaspora in the UK feeds on and replays foundational fears that Sikhs would/will be subjugated by Muslims, but are not caused by them.

These foundational fears also find more recent confirmation of the Muslim threat in narratives of the suffering of Sikhs at the hands of Muslims during partition. Partition narratives within the Sikh Diaspora present a similar relation with Islamophobic discourse. The rape of women in front of male relatives, and forced conversions, both of which were generalised within the brutal and extreme forms of organised communal violence and persecution waged in the context of the partition of Punjab, doubled the violation of sisters/wives/daughters at the collective level as the violation of community and nation (Purwar and Rughuram, 2003, pp. 160–164). With the honour of the community vested in women many men in Sikh families urged and often forced the women to sacrifice their lives. Hundreds of women in many villages were often made to jump into wells because of fear of abduction, rape and forced religious conversion. Both the atrocities and the sacrifices cut across and were replicated among Hindus, Muslims and Sikhs. Partition, like the Mughals, is not the cause of reoccurring tensions between Sikhs and Muslims, it is rather a language adopted by Sikhs to construct a 'threat' and in so doing weave a Sikh identity in the UK.

Today, we see the two narratives of Mughal repression and Partition persecutions being mobilised to add veracity to stories of forced conversions of Sikh girls by Muslim (male) predators. Within this context Sikhness and Sikh identity is doubly structured both on inclusion/racialised exclusion from British society and in antagonism to and demarcation from Muslims: Sikhs represent modernity, 'Westerness', independence and equality, Muslims represent backwardness, 'non-Westerness', oppression and patriarchy. At the heart of this forced conversion narrative around which anxieties and warnings are articulated, is the figure of the Sikh girl. This too, encodes the same double structuring. Sikh girls are the focus of this particular narrative because of the anxieties their growing agency evokes within the Diaspora. In the UK, Sikh women are perceived as possessing too much autonomy, destabilising traditional Sikh male identities and roles, and exposing girls to predatory Muslims whose fiendish figure in turn helps rein in the women and shore up patriarchal power. Through the figure of the Muslim antagonist old fantasies are re-played, and against the backdrop of Britain's postcolonial ethnoscapes the forced conversion trope re-engages, stabilises and regulates the community. Against the unsettlement of diasporic experience, the Muslim folk devil writ large and Sikh girl conversion stories run rampant reinforce community boundaries and Sikh identities.

The forced conversion narratives display a resemblance to other forms of Islamophobia: the fantasy figure of Muslim puppet-masters secretly financing young Muslim men to seduce Sikh women; confirmatory exposure of coded messages in the Qur'an which all Muslims are programmed to obey; uncovered conspiracies revealing how non-Muslim societies are subverted or threatened by Muslim powers to ease the predatory practices of Muslim men. The figure of the Sikh female body and the predatory Muslim male helps construct a homogeneous Sikh community despite migratory displacements. The antagonistic discourse subscribed to by the Sikh Diaspora re-scripts existential fears in BrAsian contexts through the available and deeply embedded narratives of Mughal persecution and Partition turmoil. These Sikh narratives, in other words, represent both the possibility of a Sikh identity and the failure of that possibility to be fully realised. The failure of Sikhism to fully constitute Sikh subjects in the conditions of the Diaspora is projected onto the figure of the Muslim.

Recent years have seen the development of a Sikh variant of Islamphobia: it shares some of the themes associated with generalised Islamophobic discourse but it also has unique inflections, reflecting the particularities of Sikh history and contemporary postcolonial diasporic circumstances, which make for a 'Sikh Islamophobia'. That is, an Islamophobia that is thoroughly contemporary but retrospectively projects itself into the Sikh past to erase the traces of its contingent construction and present the Muslim threat as intrinsic and essential. The appearance of t-shirts bearing the legend: 'Don't freak I'm a Sikh!' points to the complexity of Sikh-Muslim relations. This is the case even allowing for the opportunism of the market, for behind the fetishism of small differences by which ethnicised minorities can comfort the great ethnically unmarked, there is a deeper anxiety which points to the fears that if Sikhs can be mistaken for Muslims the claim that Sikhs have transcended their racialised framing may perhaps be more precarious than many hoped.

24

'ISLAMOPHOBIA'

A NEW RACISM IN FOOTBALL?

Peter Millward

On 26 August 2007, Middlesbrough Football Club (FC) hosted a football match against local rivals Newcastle United FC. The game finished in an entertaining draw, however the event was particularly noteworthy because a large number of Newcastle United fans had repeatedly chanted that Middlesbrough's new star signing, the Egyptian forward, Ahmed Hossam Hussein Abdelhamid (known as Mido) was a terrorist bomber. Two days later, on 28 August 2007, a *Guardian* newspaper front-page headline, 'Islamophobia: a new racism in football?', posed an important question. Answering it opens up the discussion of Islamophobia to wider conceptual and policy issues which transcend the Mido affair.

Spectator racism has long been conceived as a problem within football in both the UK and abroad but very little has been said about the issue of Islamophobia in sport (Burdsey, 2007, p. 57). It is well established that football grounds have—at least in the past—provided an arena in which prejudiced values have prospered (see for instance, Back et al., 2001; Garland and Rowe, 2001; Robson 2004; Jarvie, 1991). However, it is uncertain whether such problems emerge in society and are brought into the football stadium or are developed in the highly passionate—though often prejudiced—football environment (Williams, Dunning and Murphy, 1992 [1984]).

It is highly unlikely that clubs deliberately set out to exclude Muslims and other BrAsian football players but their policies and procedures do deliver this result. Thus Burdsey (2006) suggests that football clubs draw upon a range of 'commonsensical' popular discourses to account for the lack of BrAsian professionals. This claim could be evidenced by the football 'pop-writer' Dougie Brimson's (2006, p. 180) question:

[D]oes anyone believe that they [football clubs], along with every other club in the land, haven't considered the impact a twenty-goal-a-season, British-born Asian striker would have on their balance sheets? Are the anti-racists so arrogant that they continue to believe that clubs located in the middle of predominantly Asian communities, such as Bradford, Leicester and L*t*n [Luton], haven't even thought about the commercial possibilities a locally born player would provide?

Instead of looking for the underlying and structural reasons, Bains and Johal (1998) similarly argue that 'common sense' reasons prevail, such as the idea that BrAsians cannot play football, consume the wrong foods or have a lack of 'natural' enthusiasm for the game. Brimson (2006, pp. 180–182), who offers all of these suggestions when answering his question, is a case in point. Viewed in this way, an 'everyday' level of racism can be found in the way sport-related groups do not question the reasons why there are apparent progression problems for BrAsian athletes. At an amateur level, for example, Burdsey states that BrAsian football players are forced to assimilate into white hegemonic 'lad' culture in order to fit in with their teammates (Burdsey, 2004). Back et al. (2001, pp. 139–140) substantiate this claim with a vignette which recalls how a British-Pakistani amateur football player in Manchester was made to feel uncomfortable by teammates after he took them to his family's 'dry' curry house in the Rusholme district of the city. Thus they too appear to infer that the only way Muslim players are accepted into British, non-Muslim sports' teams is if they are to be subsumed by white, masculine values.

Yet, the issue of Islamophobic prejudice in football needs to be carefully addressed. There are at least two serious potential social repercussions that could emerge as a result of the continued existence of such dispositions. First, although Islamophobic chants might not immediately create widespread societal prejudice, unless they are stamped out there is a risk that they may begin to seep into mainstream culture. (Certainly, the recruitment of football hooligans prominent in the ranks of various recent anti-Muslim street campaigns shows how casual Islamophobia can be transformed into something more concrete and concentrated.) Second, the unpleasantness of such chants for Muslims (and others who share in the sense of offense) at football games—whether such individuals are participants or fans—may be considerable, and the continued existence of such behaviours could further pronounce football grounds and training pitches as non-Muslim spaces.

However, the answer to such problems is unlikely to come in the coercive measures of point deductions or widespread fan lockouts as suggested at football's first Faith Summit, held in April 2008 (Butt, 2008b). It must be remembered that many contemporary racisms grow from the perception that non-white British citizens receive preferential treatment from authoritative organisations (see Copsey, 2004; Richardson, 2005; Rydgren 2003; 2004) and it is likely that punishing an entire set of supporters for the actions of a sizable minority would only reinforce such attitudes. This is especially the case as the results back up King's (2000) argument that many fans do not want football ground atmospheres to be further 'sanitised'. So, it is possible that such punishments, while appearing to treat the dispositional symptoms (i.e. Islamophobic chants), will not address the underlying wider social prejudices that are used to berate football opponents and may even accidentally deepen such prejudices. Instead, the FA and football clubs should work with, rather than potentially punish, fan groups to genuinely change public stereotypes of Muslims. This may be a slow process but is far more likely to be enduringly successful than draconian methods. Without wishing to downplay the damage that Islamophobic abuse may have upon English football culture, the development of such values should be part of a wider framework to combat social prejudices. The influence of the FA, its member clubs and the relatively small band of Muslim players could play a modest role in the success of meaningful anti-racist strategies.

25

FUNDAMENTAL FICTIONS

GENDER, POWER AND ISLAM
IN BRASIAN DIASPORIC FORMATIONS

Ruvani Ranasinha

The last two decades mark the increasing global profile of Islam and Muslims, the reconfiguration of Britain's race-relations landscape around issues of religion, and the shift from racism to Islamophobia. How does this inform the reading of several contemporary BrAsian novels and screenplays that explore Britain as a crucible for the multiple local and global tensions negotiated in an emergent generation of British Muslims? Moreover, do these fictional texts subvert the dominant British public discourse that equates Islam with the repression of women, and as therefore incompatible with British society? Or to what extent, do these diasporic fictional representations, particularly of Muslim women within British Muslim communities repeat hegemonic constructions of Islam as antithetical to women's rights? Furthermore, how have these different mappings shifted in the intervening decades between the publication of Salman Rushdie's (1983) *Shame*, and Hanif Kureishi's prescient exploration of the intersection of gender, sexuality, race and Islam in his novel *The Black Album* (1995) and screenplay *My Son the Fanatic* (1997), and the more recent explorations of gender, class and violence in the context of working-class British Muslim communities in the very different contexts of the twenty-first century in Nadeem Aslam's (2004) *Maps for Lost Lovers*. Concerns over the status and identity (and therefore representation) of Muslims in the West are more specifically politically charged in the wake of 9/11, 7/7 and the global War on Terror that inflame and conflate questions of Islam, immigration, security and citizenship, and inform hegemonic constructions of fundamentalism and British Muslim gendered identities. These normative identities feature prominently in debates on British multiculturalism, and have become an acceptable vent for Islamophobia. In this context, what role do these filmic and literary, male-authored diasporic texts play in the continued projection of a 'clash of civilisations' between a 'secular' West and 'Islamic fundamentalism' with conceptions of female Muslim identity polarised between liberated non-believers and the oppressed faithful? While Rushdie's novel *Shame* primarily engages with the rising tide of Islamisation in Pakistan under Zia in the 1980s, it touches on the gendered violence of 'honour killings' among Pakistani communities in Britain (Rushdie, 1983). The novel invokes the spectre of Anahita Muhammad murdered by her own father for her relationship with a white boy in London's East End. Significantly the novel traces and 'repatriates' this patriarchal violence 'back East [to Pakistan] to let the idea breathe its favourite air' (Rushdie, 1983, pp. 86 and 118). This account of the diasporic elaboration of 'honour-killing' thus evades the role of British racism in shaping the male oppressor's behaviour. In contrast to Rushdie's novel, both Kureishi and Aslam's work, albeit to differing degrees and in different ways, contextualise the oppressive practices and persistence of gendered violence within (and outside) British Muslim communities by foregrounding the community's structural subordination in Britain. Underscoring the reification of traditional gender identities as a result of migration, and the role of race-relations in shaping 'ghettoism' complicates representations of Islam as inherently oppressive to women. At the same time, the troubling marginalisation of female Muslim subjectivities in the work of both authors, particularly the absence of those who wish to synthesise their Muslim background with notions of gender equality, ultimately reinforces hegemonic constructions of Islam as antithetical to women's rights.

Hanif Kureishi has long been interested in the rise of diasporic forms of radical Islam amongst young men. He deals with this theme most explicitly in his novel *The Black Album* and in his screenplay *My Son the Fanatic* written in the aftermath of the Rushdie Affair and the First Gulf War. In *The Black Album* the resurgence of radical Islam and militancy amongst a group of Muslim students at a derelict North London college is a concrete response to racial aggression. One of the most powerful scenes of the novel depicts the Muslim students' all-night vigilante patrol to protect an Asian family living in fear of further racial attacks in a run-down, racist housing estate in London's East End. The text also emphasises the way, as Kureishi puts it, '[f]undamentalism provides security' (1997, p. xii) and the assertion of an Islamicate identity as a positive identity for Asian youth. As former druggie Chad insists 'No more Paki. Me a Muslim' (Kureishi, 1995, p. 128). In Kureishi's screenplay, *My Son the Fanatic* set in the northern industrial mill town, young Farid confronts the insidious forms of racism that his father Parvez is prepared to overlook, and this exclusion in part encourages him to reinvent himself and adopt radical Islam. To the horror of his father who loves Scotch, Jazz and bacon-butties, Farid abandons his white fiancée, accountancy career, guitar and cricket playing to embrace a radical sect of Islam.

In *My Son the Fanatic*, the young Muslim boys' militant response to racial exclusion is to both reject and demonise the West. Inspired by a *maulvi* visiting from Lahore the young acolytes launch a demonstration against local sex–workers that erupts into misogynist violence against 'Other' women perceived as depraved. The Muslim men harass, assault and spit on the sex–workers and firebomb their base (Kureishi, 1997, p. 114). In this way, the rise of radical Islam amongst these young British Muslim men is portrayed in terms of an assertion of masculinity and masculine violence. Such representations in a text where the only *devout* Muslim characters featured are 'fundamentalist' (Kureishi unproblematically reproduces and trades on the term and category 'fundamentalist' as I have argued more fully elsewhere [Ranasinha, 2002]) and oppressive to women both outside and within their own community (Farid favours gender segregation within the home, claiming 'many women lack belief and therefore reason' [Kureishi, 1997, p. 69]) serve to reinforce notions of Islam as inherently oppressive to women). At the same time, the suggestion that the adoption of a compensatory hyper-masculine identity stems from their subordination in majority British culture complicates this representation, a connection that is more explicitly dealt with in Aslam's novel, as we will see.

Kureishi's texts narrate the phenomena of the rise of militant Islam in diasporic contexts in terms of an oedipal drama on the part of adolescent British Pakistani males who challenge their fathers' authority. These 'second-generation' Muslim sons seek to reassert religious traditions and prohibitions their quasi–liberal 'renegade Muslim' fathers have abandoned. While Kureishi's first generation secular male protagonist fathers—Nasser in *My Beautiful Laundrette*, Shahid's father in *The Black Album* and Farid's father Parvez, in *My Son the Fanatic*—all poke fun at 'self-righteous hypocritical mullahs' (Kureishi,

1995, p. 156), their wives' relationship to Islam is barely explored. Nasser's wife is a superstitious, shadowy figure and Parvez's wife, Minoo, is a stereotype of the traditional and disempowered Muslim woman, who ultimately leaves for Lahore. Nasser and Parvez turn to white lovers (the transgressive white lover being a familiar and habitual presence in Kureishi's work). Shahid's mother 'kept to herself' along with her friends, sisters and their children, 'as if they were living in Karachi' (Kureishi, 1995, p. 52). In this way these first-generation female characters from Muslim backgrounds are presented as not having 'benefited' from gender equality in Britain.

While Kureishi's younger BrAsian female characters defy patriarchal authority and deconstruct tropes of the submissive, asexual, uneducated Asian woman, his 'liberated' female characters come from privileged Pakistani backgrounds who spurn Islam, notably Zulma, Chili's patrician wife in *The Black Album*. Alternatively, and more usually, his British-born feminist Asian characters from Muslim backgrounds (Yasmin in his early play *Borderline*, Tania in *My Beautiful Laundrette* and outspoken, self-educated feminist Jamila in *The Buddha of Suburbia*) can only achieve autonomy and self-liberation by withdrawal and rejection of community, culture and religion. In this way his work repeats hegemonic constructions of British Muslim women by continuing to represent assimilation into a *secular* British culture/Western global modernity as a progressive narrative for South Asian Muslim women.

The only snapshot Kureishi offers of a British Muslim feminist subjectivity is the character of Tahira, part of the Islamic posse in *The Black Album*. 'Devoted to the cause' she 'insisted' on accompanying (Kureishi, 1995, p. 126) the 'brothers' on their vigils against their will. Proud to wear her *hijab*, she is quick to point out her Muslim 'brothers' double standards: 'you urge us to cover ourselves but become strangely evasive when it comes to your own clothes' (Kureishi, 1995, p. 105). She is sympathetic towards Shahid because she finds him 'broader than the others' (Kureishi, 1995, p. 219). Her comments suggest an incipient desire to interpret Islam in ways that give her greater agency, whilst suggesting a feminist identity grounded in cultural and religious traditions that complicate liberal, feminist conceptions of gender. Yet none of this is explored; only hinted at. Like many of Kureishi's female characters she exists only on the periphery, endowed with catchy one-liners, but little substance. Feminist resistance to patriarchal structures within diasporic South Asian Muslim communities in Britain remain similarly elusive in Nadeem Aslam's fictional exploration of the gendered violence of 'honour killings' in his novel *Maps for Lost Lovers*. The narrative is set (like *My Son the Fanatic*) within a working-class, self-enclosed, ghettoised Pakistani immigrant community in a bleak English town, which its Muslim residents rename 'the desert of loneliness' or 'the wilderness of solitude'. The novel is constructed around the double murder of Chanda and her lover Jugnu by Chanda's brothers, Chotta and Barra. They avenge the lovers' open, 'sinful' cohabitation, which caused a scandal in their claustrophobic neighbourhood. Chanda and Jugnu's relationship was widely 'condemned as sinful' even though Chotta's own sexual affair with Kieran was not entirely a secret. The brothers' boastful confession in Pakistan, to general agreement, that 'It was a matter of honour', for men 'brought up to defend their women's honour above all else', contrasted with its denial in Britain for fear of jail is depicted as the senseless action of bruised, hypocritical masculine ego (Aslam, 2004, p. 347). The brothers claim to have been driven by 'shame' over the conduct of their 'twice-divorced' sister Chanda, a 'shameless whore' and her lover Jugnu (Aslam, 2004, p. 354). Chanda refused to 'erase' herself and comply with her male family members' demand that she wears the 'all–enveloping *burka*' so she would not be recognised as related to them (Aslam, 2004, p. 342). Fired by the 'gossip', 'pity' and the 'crude-talk' of 'male strangers uttering their sister's name with such familiarity' (Aslam, 2004, p. 350) the brothers defend their murderous actions in sexualised, masculine terms conveying their perception of emasculation: 'We are men but she [Chanda] reduced us to *eunuch bystanders* by not paying attention to our wishes' (Aslam, 2004, p. 342).

This dramatic and moving portrayal of Muslim life in this specific community shifts somewhat uneasily between suggesting that laws and the name of Islam are invoked as a pretext for asserting patriarchy, as well as simultaneously locating the injustices that arise in the story as endemic to Islam. At certain points, the narrative explicitly contextualises and connects (rather than condones) the working class Pakistani male tendency for domestic violence within their own disempowerment in Britain. A South Asian bus driver is subject to degrading racial abuse when he intervenes with a gang of white male youths who refuse to pay the full fare for their journey. A white male passenger calls him 'Oi, Gupta, or whatever it is you call yourself, Abdul-Patel. Mr Illegal Immigrant-Asylum Seeker!' and orders him back to his driver's seat as 'when an adult orders a child' instructing him to 'Show us some respect. This is our country, not yours.' Powerless, without adequate English and fearful of his job he leaves the bus and 'sits on the side of the road ... with his head in his hands'. The narrative then switches to a Pakistani woman passenger, Chanda's mother. While she shares his humiliation 'her body is burning, her blood flooded with heat', she reflects 'I hope the driver won't take his humiliation out at home later today ... lashing out at his *own* children, and the wife' (Aslam, 2004, p. 178). In this instance the novel suggests violence against women is not simply a function of patriarchal religious, cultural traditions.

At the same time, as in Kureishi's work, Aslam's novel offers limited positions for the community's women. The majority of women in the community are either victims, or perpetrators of violence enacted against women. The latter are represented as the most doctrinaire preservers of the religious morality and Islamic notions of gendered propriety that dominates this community. As in Kureishi, the only female Muslim character to achieve some autonomy, Mah-Jabin (the adult daughter of Kaukab and Shamas), does so by individual withdrawal and self-distancing from her community. (Chanda, the most transgressive woman in the novel, is murdered. She remains a shadow, while her murdered partner Jugnu is recalled in rich detail.) Mah-Jabin's mother Kaukab sees notions of gender equality as the imposition of 'Western' gender norms on Muslim culture. However, Aslam counters this idea—and the version of Islam Chotta and Barra advance—by celebrating the representations of women in poetry of Wamaq Saleem and lyrics of Nusrat Fateh Ali Khan. The novel identifies the Sufi tradition of Islam (to which Khan belongs) as evidence of gender equality as part of a much older aspect of Islamic culture: 'in the poet-saints' verses the women rebel and try bravely to face all opposition' (Aslam, 2004, p. 192). In stark contrast to Kureishi's and Aslam's, Meera Syal's feminist characters in her screenplay, *Bhaji on the Beach* (1992), and novel, *Life Isn't All Ha Ha Hee Hee* (2000), subvert patriarchal structures from within notably *non*-Muslim South Asian communities, and thus marks the emerging split between BrAsian female and Muslim female subjectivity.

Overall these texts engage with the conflicting yet overlapping parameters of gender, piety and secularism in limited ways, and the absence of representations of faith-based resistance within diasporic South Asian Muslim communities in Britain ultimately feeds into notions of the repression of women as endemic to Islam.

26

GENERATING ISLAMOPHOBIA IN INDIA

Dibyesh Anand

Islam has a long history in India. Islamophobia—a coherent and identifiable set of prejudices and stereotypes that generates fear of Islam and fuels a reaction to counter it—however, is more recent.[1] Until the nineteenth century, identities in South Asia were more fluid, narrow and marked by extreme plurality. The distinct categories of Hindu or Muslim emerged with modernity, consolidated by the British practices of identifying and enumerating on the basis of religion (see Jones, 1981), elite competition over limited largesse offered under the colonial setup, revivalist movements to reclaim authentic traditions, and the rise of nationalism. The Nationalist movement was successful in ending colonial rule in 1947, but with the partition of British India and the violence that accompanied it, the position of Muslim minorities in independent India became more precarious. Many decades on—with occasional communal riots, three Muslim Heads of State, visible presence of Muslims in the cultural sphere including the Mumbai film industry, and the overwhelming socio-economic backwardness of the majority of Muslims (as attested most recently by the Sachar Committee Report of 2006)—Muslims remain very much a part of India.

Reference to the divergent paths of Pakistan and Bangladesh, where demographic and constitutional shifts helped put the stamp of the majority religion

[1] See Anand (2009) for more developed discussions of sections of this chapter.

on the body politic, helps draw out India's difference. The Indian political system, with all its flaws, contradictions, and hypocrisies, remains committed to secularism (defined more in terms of multi–religiosity rather than a separation of state and religion). This has been possible because Islamophobia, as a coherent ideology, has not taken root amongst the majority of Hindus. If we look at electoral politics, most Hindus do not vote as Hindus (the same is the case for Muslims, though commentators often talk of a Muslim vote bank), but on the basis of their interests and identities based on a complex mix of caste, gender, and locality. Absence of Islamophobia does not mean an absence of prejudices and discriminatory behaviour based on them. While the secular state remains fixated on the symbolic celebration of religious diversity and a political appropriation of the conservative elite, the socio-economic backwardness of Muslims remains ignored. There is, however, no widespread conceit of Islamophobia as such in public life and state institutions.

The only actors who invest heavily in the creation of an Islamophobic common sense are the Hindu nationalists. Scavenging upon existing prejudices against Muslims (while correspondingly underemphasising prejudices based on caste), through their writings, speeches, public action and social work they foster, generate and produce knowledge of the 'Muslim Other'. That Hindu nationalists have failed to convert the majority of Hindus into their constituency in electoral terms does not change the fact that they have become a visible part of the political landscape. As such, therefore, their Islamophobia merits attention.

The discourse of Hindu nationalism—'Hindutva'—is best understood as a collection of eclectic ideas, images, and practices. Hindutva is akin to 'majoritarian nationalism' that combines cultural hubris with political anxiety about the presence of minorities in the body politic. There are many consistently identifiable patterns in the discourse of Hindu nationalism, yet beneath the illusion of consistency there is a selective amnesia of several contradictions that populate the Hindutva worldview. Here, I highlight a few of those contradictions and fantasies that lend meaning to the majoritarian nationalism of Hindutva. The contradictions are as much a source of weakness as of strength. They militate against a coherent large-scale political movement, but they also provide a flexibility, 'fungibility' and ambiguity that enables the extremist, parochial and illiberal ethos of Hindutva to pass itself off as moderate, universalist and enlightened.

Hindu nationalism is a celebration and affirmation of the Hindu Self, but it derives its meaning only from a negation of the minority 'Others' (primarily

Muslims but also Christians) and their allies (Communists, Secularists, and the Westernised elite). The Hindu Self is represented as a self-evident category of identity that has existed for millennia. Going against the mainstream Indian nationalist movement, Hindu nationalism in the twentieth century sought to present the Hindu Self as the Indian Self, rendering non-Hindu Indians as untrustworthy Others, anti-Hindu and invariably anti-Indian. Hindutva, it should be stressed, seeks to create a unified Hindu *samaj* not by removing hierarchies, nor by redressing the historical and contemporary injustices suffered by many Hindus, but by shifting the blame for all ills onto the 'foreign Other'. Promotion of Islamophobia allows for an ignoring of contradictions and oppressions amongst Hindus. Everything that is wrong within Hinduism is a product of a society perverted through a series of foreign invasions mostly by Muslim rulers. Reform of Hinduism is touted only as a tool to counter the possible appeal of Islam or Christianity for the hitherto unprivileged and oppressed Hindus. There is no evidence of a genuine desire to make Hindu religion and practices progressive. By creating the spectre of the dangerous 'Other', inimical foreigners within the rightful homeland of an indigenous Hindu body politic, Hindutva seeks (not very successfully) to brush under the carpet the tensions existing within the category 'Hindu'.

The Hindutva story of Hindu Self is thus a story of non-Hindu/anti-Hindu Other. Despite the half-hearted claims made by some Hindu nationalists in the BJP that Hindutva is neither anti-Muslim or anti-Christian but universalist, and accepting of Muslims and Christians who accept living on the terms set by Hindutva, even a cursory examination of the philosophy and ideology of all strands of Hindu nationalism shows that the representation of religious minorities (Muslims and Christians) as inimical, foreign, anti-Hindu and therefore anti-India is an obsession for many.[2] It depicts a Hindu *samaj*, *sanskriti*, and *sabhyata* (society, culture and civilisation) under siege from Islam and Christianity. This, according to Hindutva, is not a nightmarish prospect but a present reality. Deploying various stereotypes, the minorities, Muslims especially, are presented as waging a war against Hindu India. The extremely diverse Indian Muslims are reduced to a singular stereotyped identity—'Muslim'—invested with a belligerence and fanaticism that individual Muslims cannot escape.

Hindu nationalists may differ amongst themselves over the root of this supposed Muslim fanaticism—moderates in the BJP, for example, may blame some

---

[2] See for instance, speeches and writings of VHP leader Ashok Singhal (2005 and n.d.).

Muslims for disloyalty and terrorism without mentioning Islam as a religion or the Prophet Muhammad. But most Hindu nationalists from the Sangh Parivar, especially VHP, Bajrang Dal and even the RSS, do not shy away from rejecting Islam in its entirety as the enemy. Painting all Muslims with the same Islamophobic brush, Hindutva plays a game of fear which trades on a prevalent Islamophobic repertoire: Islam by its very nature is fundamentalist (the idea of moderate Muslims is an oxymoron); the history of Muslim rule in India is nothing but a catalogue of violence, plunder and rape of Hindus; Muslims are solely responsible for the partition of *Akhanda* India and those Muslims who stayed back in India did so because they were not satisfied with a separate Pakistan but desired the Islamisation of entire India; Muslims, with the active backing of Pakistan and Gulf money, are waging a continuous war against Hindu India. A complementary strategy is to portray problems faced by Hindus as a local manifestation of a global phenomenon, thus a contextualised understanding of political Islam in different parts of the world, India included, is eschewed in favour of the simplistic picture of a Global Jihad waged against non-Muslims. Terrorism, violence, genocide of Kashmiri Hindus, conversion, illegal infiltration by Bangladeshi Muslims, seduction and rape of innocent Hindu girls (see also Sian, this volume), and over-population are all conjured up as weapons deployed by the traitorous Muslims to overwhelm Hindus in India.[3] Christians, too, are said to collude in this war by seducing poor Hindus into conversion and by encouraging separatism in the North East. By thus stereotyping Muslim and Christian minorities as the irredeemable anti-Hindu, anti-India Other, Hindu nationalism generates a politics of fear.

Such poetics and politics of fear (Anand, 2011 forthcoming) are also instrumental to explaining away the use of violence by Hindu nationalism. Violence is central to an understanding of Hindutva and directly connected to Islamophobia; it provides the rationale for as well as becoming the product of, Hindu nationalism. While Hindu nationalists frequently indulge in violence, the originary violence is projected onto Muslims. Anti-minority violence is then legitimised by describing it as either a justified reaction, or the product of long suppressed hurts patiently suffered by the Hindu *samaj* (Brass, 2003; Hansen, 1996). In this way, the sufferings of Muslims in Gujarat in 2002 and of Christians in Orissa in 2008 are seen not as the conscious pogroms or well-planned campaigns of violence that they were, but as the regrettable yet justifiable and

---

[3] For a sample of Hindutva writings on this, see Goel (n.d. [originally published 1981, revised 1992]), Krishnaswami (n.d.), Swarup (n.d.), and Chaturdashi and Varsha, (2010).

understandable reactions of an awakened Hindu community. By the same token, the state too is absolved of all responsibility—what, after all, can it do when it is the entire Hindu *samaj* that lashes out in hurt caused by arrogant expansionary minorities? Thus, in the Hindu nationalist view, is the complicity of politicians, the police, activists and the general populace bracketed under the rubric of the aroused Hindu nation. And with it, individual responsibilities and state complicity explained away. If it is the abstract Hindu nation that has reacted to the originary violence of expansionary minorities, how does one begin pinpointing responsibility for the violence? Numerous, well-documented, acts of anti-minority violence committed in the name of Hindutva do not disrupt this self-understanding of Hindu nationalists who see themselves as the wronged party.

Hindu nationalism can be conceptualised as a discourse of security, yet it feeds insecurity into society. Minority Others, in alliance with secularists and communists, are waging a war against the Hindus. Chief among them, the stereotyped Muslim figure is represented as a danger to Hindu security at different levels: individual Hindu—especially female—bodies, Hindu neighbourhoods, Hindu India, as well as the entire world. In the face of such hostile foreign religionists, Hindutva prescribes a multi–pronged response to secure the potent Hindu nation to which it aspires: a propaganda warfare to 'reveal' (in practice, manufacture) the conspiracy of minorities and their secular allies to fool Hindus into believing that there is no danger; socio-cultural mobilisation of Hindus so that they are proud of their unified Hindutva identity; political organisation of Hindus to ensure that they form a vote bank; capturing the state to reflect Hindutva interests; and using violence against minorities in the name of securing the Hindu body politic.

Hindu nationalism fantasises potency (of a Hindu collective), yet it fears impotency. Nationalism, for Hindutva, is a politico-cultural project to create, awaken, and strengthen a masculinist-nationalist body.[4] I have elsewhere (Anand, 2008), conceptualised the extremist beliefs of Hindutva (as held especially by Bajrang Dal and less overtly by VHP) activists as a 'porno-nationalism' (see also Sarkar, 2002). A porno-nationalist imagination of the hyper-sexualised Muslim Other performs two concurrent moves: it assures the Hindu nationalist self of its moral superiority and yet instils an anxiety about the threatening masculine Other. Hindu nationalism, despite claiming to represent

---

[4] For an incisive treatment of sexuality, gender and Hindutva, see, for example, Bachetta (2004); Gupta (2001); Jayawardena and De Alwis (1998) and Anand (2007).

the majority Hindu community, has at its core a deep masculinist anxiety which, it claims, will be solved through a masculinist, often bordering on militarised, awakening. The disjuncture between the imagined militarised Hindu nation and the actual fact of a rich plurality of Hindu society turns the rage of Hindutva against the Hindus themselves. The Hindu nation becomes a rarefied ideal, which only the Sangh Parivar and its sympathisers are capable of appreciating. Other Hindus, under the spell of anti-Hindu ideas of Secularism, Communism, 'Macaulayism', Westernisation, Women's emancipation, and even Democracy, remain ignorant.

Hindu nationalists speak of Secularism and Democratic Rights with a 'forked tongue' (see Hansen, 1999; Ludden, 1996), They reject the mainstream version of secularism as appeasement of minorities and as pseudo-secularism; argue that a genuine democracy should recognise the primacy of Hindu majority, and argue for the Uniform Civil Code and against Article 370 in the name of equality. But the same Hindu nationalists also reject secularism as alien (since only Hindu *sanatana dharma* is 'true secularism'), claim that the celebration of the diversity of Indian culture is a conspiracy to erase the essential oneness of India as expressed in *sanatana dharma*, promote the Hinduisation of public life, appeal to Islamophobic Western ideologues to support their case, criticise state measures to promote equality (such as the right of daughters to have a share in paternal property) and progressive social and environmental movements as anti-family, and express intolerance of dissident views by beating up artists, writers and activists.

Hindutva has a bigger goal of socio-politico-cultural transformation. Setbacks in elections are seen as peripheral to the long-term vision of a *Hindu Rashtra*—after all, against a narrative of continuous war between hostile religious groups spanning more than a millennium, a decade of setbacks is not a big deal. Democracy in India has less to fear from existing Islamophobic majoritarian nationalist actors and more from the campaign of Hindu extremists to generate Islamophobia in the wider society.

27

WHO'S AFRAID OF ISLAMOPHOBIA?

AbdoolKarim Vakil

One of the themes that define this volume is the move away from both uncritical transhistorical uses of the term Islamophobia and no less uncritical dismissals of the term. The volume navigates a course betwixt and between these two
extremes, pioneering a path to a series of investigations of Islamophobia that
are predicated on the articulation of Muslim agency as its necessary ground.
In other words, it is Muslim autonomy in the context of the postcolonial condition that discloses the politics of Islamophobia.

Clearly, none of the contributors to this volume could be said to consider the
term Islamophobia unproblematic; several indeed have featured prominently in
the critical debate on its limitations and potential. All, moreover, would understand their essays here, if anything, as furthering, rather than suspending, the
work of critique, yet doing so *with* the term rather than abandoning it. A commitment to Islamophobia as a term and concept, then, is one possible reading of
the answers advanced in the various contributions to this collection. Such a commitment is not made in ignorance of criticism of the term or of its conceptual
limitations, nor does it reflect a failure to acknowledge this criticism. On the
contrary, it is made in full engagement with them. Three moves are involved here
in what we can perhaps describe as a grounded conceptual thinking through of
the term, which is simultaneously a leap forward in its usage.

First, understanding that 'Islamophobia', like other conceptual terms, is not
reducible to the etymology of the word, nor fixed in its usage by 'originary'

formulations such as that of the Runnymede Trust Report. Moreover, that usage, and especially effectiveness, is not only not hampered by lack of accepted definition but rather enabled by it, as indeed by proliferating narratives of its many histories. Second, that (apparently paradoxically) precisely both such contestation and such histories make a case for sticking with the term rather than abandoning it. Third, such a leap forward in the term's usage, which is thus contingent rather than arbitrary, must, following Foucault (2000, pp. 114–115), arguably precede and advance its more robust conceptualisation and vindication, rather than the other way around.

To ask whether Islamophobia is a valid term or not is to miscast the issue. Islamophobia is essentially contested as both phenomenon and term, both in what it names and as a name. Lack of an accepted definition, inconsistency of use, or multiple and proliferating narratives surround every contested concept. In practice, beyond the concerns of lawyers and academics much of the work done by the term Islamophobia is effectively done in the absence of any definition, and not infrequently in articulation with, rather than exclusive of, alternative concepts and terms, sometimes even privileged over it.

Arguably its validity for those who commit to it is in the naming. It is part of the struggle for the 're-description' of social reality, including of the language and categories of the social sciences, and of the Law as the legitimation and institutionalisation of struggles over that social reality. Borrowing from Terence Hawkes, it matters more what we mean by Islamophobia, than what Islamophobia means in any essential sense (Hawkes, 1992). That does not make our commitment to Islamophobia as a name arbitrary. It is contingent. We do not, after more than ten years of polemics over the term, start from a blank slate. However much we may find the term 'unfortunate' or 'less than ideal' the choice is in part determined by the battle lines already drawn over the term.

There is, in other words, already too much invested in the term, and this on both sides. Both where it has gained currency and institutional traction—through its use by local and international organisations, by ordinary Muslims, community media, and academics for monitoring and advocacy, or merely as an indexing term, which in turn configures the ways information and history is retrievable—and where it has been specifically rejected in favour of other terms, particularly by state bodies, and its use therefore acquires an oppositional dimension. As in the latter case, and more generally, the term has been invested by all sides with political and polemical capital. It is the term plus its social histories, including contestations, in materially embedded forms.

As a consequence of its name, moreover, the term and concept Islamophobia has lent itself to a series of contestations which have come to hinge on the
constituent elements of the neologism—'Islam' and 'phobia'—which, regardless of whether or not they miss the target, productively unpack the substantive
issues at stake in particular ways. Thus, and to recall familiar ground, the 'Islam'
(all the more so for its capitalised form) in the term has drawn the fire of both
sympathetic critics, who see it as at best a confusing misnomer more correctly
identified and redressed as anti-Muslimism or anti-Muslim racism, and of
hostile critics, who round on the exceptional protection invoked for Islam
which, as they argue, as a faith or religion, as an idea, doctrine or dogma, must
not be shielded from critique, and correspondingly, confers on Muslim a religious and hence a 'voluntary' identity, unlike the 'involuntary' identities of
'race' which anti-racist legislation already protects. Similarly, 'phobia', on which
the critical charge of the term therefore entirely comes to lie, is decried as a
vague and psychological fear or hatred,[1] irrational, and therefore hinging on
the separation of 'reasoned' vs. 'unreasoned', 'justified' vs. 'unjustified' criticism
of Islam.

The point, then, is not that these are red herrings (though in reducing concept to etymology they are that), but that they only configure the problem
along particular lines. In as much as the concept of Islamophobia speaks to a
social phenomenon, any term or conceptualisation advanced to combat it
would have given rise to contestation. Given that it took this name, it configured the lines of battle in the particular ways noted: one that exposes the blind
spots of the grammar of race and the category of religion in affording protection to Muslims. At the same time, and for this very reason, post-Runnymede
efforts, particularly by Muslims, to develop a concept to extend such protection, were drawn to this name.

The international currency of the term 'Islamophobia' undeniably established itself under the impact of the Runnymede Trust Commission and
Report (1996–1997) and its reception. That this was so is in part owing to the
rather obvious fact that this was the first comprehensive combined survey and
policy intervention on an increasingly prominent phenomenon and against a
context of heightened global problematisation of Muslims as Muslims. That

---

[1] For Rattansi, for example, the 'phobia' in the term is 'unhelpful, because of its implications of mental illness and pathology' (2007, p. 108; also 2005, p. 295, where this is
curiously signalled as 'a hitherto neglected aspect of the concept') presumably in a sense
exceptionally different from, for example, its presence in the term 'homophobia'.

it emerged in the context of the United Kingdom raises interesting and important questions about its conditions of possibility (see, for example, Vertovec, 2002). But while a focus on the UK context is indeed significant it may also obscure the fact, which has perhaps not been sufficiently emphasised, that the most significant factor in its critical purchase has been the interplay of local and global contexts. The very similitude of the word Islamophobia in its various vernacular transliterations connects and informs the struggles in its name in ways which both subvert localising histories and contexts and articulates them globally.

Drawing on Pierre Bourdieu's discussion of 'the social conditions of the international circulation of ideas', we can say that texts travel without their contexts, without their field of production, and are inserted into differently configured fields of reception which will to a large extent re-frame sense and function (Bourdieu, 1999; see also, Said, 1994). To some extent, therefore, where the term is taken up it is less a straight forward matter of re-clustering anti-racist struggles in each context through and around the 'importation' of the Runnymede concept and agenda, and more a question of how the Runnymede concept and agenda and the term Islamophobia itself, cut loose from Runnymede definitions, is redeployed and re-signified in new local contexts. The meaning of Islamophobia is relationally configured in tension with the terms, and conceptions, it is privileged over and against, each of which, in turn, has its own local histories of reception, contestation and institutionalisation. With Bourdieu, we should also note the role of sponsors and gatekeepers in the take up and contestation of the term. In this respect who first introduces the concept, for what purposes, with what capacity to impose and shape the reception and terms of discussion is not irrelevant. A similar point about operationalisation and reframing applies to the circulation, translation and reception of key documents, and reports, underscoring both how the monitoring and statistics is concept dependent, and how the interpretation, conclusion and recommendations are refracted by transnational, national and local juridical but especially political and ideological frames and grammars of race.

It is only too common to come across references in the literature, whether academic, media, or public policy, which, while fully recognising a troubling phenomenon which needs addressing, find Islamophobia conceptually lacking. For some critics this is a matter of insufficiency. The abstract of one article on 'Anti-Muslim racism' in the context of the securitisation of the state in Europe, for example, concludes with the assertion that 'this is not *just* "Islamophobia" but structured anti-Muslim racism' (Fekete, 2004, p. 3, emphasis added);

exactly how the latter goes beyond the former is not spelt out. Another article, discussing the negative portrayal of Arabs in the context of the parallel histori- cal interplay of security, geopolitical and immigration agendas in the US, simi- larly makes an argument for the concept of 'anti-Arab racism' over both 'Orientalism' and 'Islamophobia'. On the grounds that 'the media treatment of Arabs in the United States has gone *beyond* Orientalism and Islamophobia', it argues for their 'subsumption' under rather than replacement by his pro- posed term (Salaita, 2006, p. 247) suggesting that the supplementary work required, which these terms lack, is that done by the introduction of the word racism. For other critics, the problem is more fundamental. Of these, some preserve the term while entirely redefining it (for example, Sander, quoted in Otterbeck and Bevelander, 2006); others reject it in favour of variants of 'Mus- lim' centred namings. Maussen provides a good example. He rejects Islamo- phobia for, firstly, conflating different kinds of discourse on Islam and failing to differentiate between 'speech and discourse on the one hand, from acts on the other hand'; secondly, because Islamophobia based approaches to anti- Muslim discourse are embedded in the ideology critique tradition and hence in the neo-Marxist trappings of ideology as illusion; thirdly, because both on this account and in the charge of 'mental illness' imputed in the term there is a delegitimation of opponents which is incompatible with democratic concep- tions of public debate (Maussen, 2006, pp. 101–102). Aix, too, rejects the concept of Islamophobia as lacking; this time, because Islamophobia is based on a culturalist approach which, he argues, is both too narrow and inadequate for the analysis of the complex layering of historical, socio-economic and political contexts of the Spanish case, and necessarily entails the terms of a clash of civilisations thesis. Quite why the Spanish case is in respect of this multiple layering of factors exceptional, as opposed to merely particular in its specific historical form, is neither clear nor convincing; as indeed is the reduc- tion of Islamophobia to culturalist terms, and indeed to Huntingtonian prem- ises (Aix, 2006, pp. 227–300). All these examples are representative of the way criticism of the concept essentially either draws on etymological readings of the term or simply projects arbitrarily imputed meanings, deduced from the name or generalising from particular applications of the term, and define the concept by them.

In particular, given the prominence accorded to the issue, why should Islam- ophobia be understood to either terminologically or conceptually preclude racism, and to not be itself a form of racism? Numerous contributions spurred in response to post 9/11 developments in the US context have detailed the historically shifting regimes of racialisation of Arab and Muslim presence, and the contemporary 'racing of religion' and of Muslims legislated through regimes of exception and special registration.[2] While particular national territorialised regimes across Europe focus on 'their' predominant ethnically marked Muslims, such as 'Asians' in the UK context, Turks in Germany, Moroccans in Spain, Algerians and Moroccans in France, Lebanese in Australia, etc, similar processes of racialisation and criminalisation of Muslims are at work, here and globally, in the Balkans, the Caucasus, Russia, China, Southeast Asia, Australia and Africa.[3]

In respect of the conceptualisation of Islamophobia and particularly of criticism raised against it, the import of the kinds of analyses advanced in this literature and developed in the chapters here published is fundamental. It means, first of all, that neither Muslims nor Muslim subjectivity is essentially or reducible to a 'religious' or 'faith' matter. Moreover, that the involvement of 'Islam' too does not relegate discussion to a theological register or matters of belief or doctrine. Religion is 'raced' and Muslims are racialised. It means also, secondly, that hostility to Islam cannot be separated from discrimination against Muslims in the neat and unproblematic ways many critics (following Halliday, 1999) purport. Where Islam is integral to Muslim identities, the denigration of Islam impacts on Muslim respect and self-worth, but what is primarily and fundamentally at stake in this is not a matter of the protection of belief per se, but rather of unequal relations of power, legal protection and institutional clout, in the context of entrenched social inequalities and capabilities. Finally, and crucially, the most pernicious resistance to Islamophobia, then, resides in the tenacious residuality of race in anti-racist discourse. The resistance to recognising Islamophobia as racism is rooted in the contention that for discrimination against Muslims to count as a form of racism Muslims would have to be a race. Paradoxically this applies even alongside full acceptance of the inexistence of races while all the same reserving racism to the targeting of 'races',

---

[2] See, for example: Akram and Johnson (2002); Ahmad , M. I. (2002; 2004); Cainkar (2002); Hasan (2002); Ho (2004); Chon and Arzt (2004–05); Bonikowski (2005); Mobasher (2005); Bayoumi (2006); Mignolo (2006); Behdad (2008); Sheth (2009, Chapters 4 and 5).

[3] Among others: MacMaster (2003); Modood (2005); Bhattacharyya (2006; 2008a; 2008b); Poynting and Mason (2007); Kundnani (2007); Sivanadan et al. (2007); Sayyid (2008); Razak (2008); Meer (2008); Silverstein (2008); Fekete (2009); Tyler (forthcoming).

properly demarcated in scare quotes, yet ultimately still predicated on something recognisably 'racial', which in the last instance means 'biological' or phenotypical. But neither 'biological' nor 'cultural' racisms have ever operated in exclusion of the other, but rather, as a continuum, historically shifting in relation to formations of power. Even critics who recognise that Muslims can be racialised even while noting the very difficulty in disentangling 'hostility towards Islam' from 'hostility towards Muslims', maintain the helpfulness of differentiating 'Islamophobia' to denote the first, from the use of 'Muslim-phobia' for the latter (Brown, M.D., 2000). Yet even then, the continued use of 'Islamophobia' performs the function of articulating different invocations of the problematisation of Muslims under its name.

In this sense definition is secondary. It is in this respect too, that the contributions to this volume can perhaps be said to conceptually deepen and expand the term. It is not that the diverse chapters, whether conceptual or thematic, do not explicitly or implicitly work with or advance various definitions and notions of Islamophobia. But they do so while deconstructing and exposing the Islamophobic formations that construe Islam and Muslims as a problem. The coherence of the volume does not, therefore, lie either in ambition to comprehensiveness or range, in respect of ontic expressions of Islamophobia, but rather in the articulations it weaves between the chapters, in much the same way as does the name Islamophobia between the diverse forms of contestation it wages ontologically.[4] Islamophobia in this sense is about contestation and the power to set the political vocabulary and legal ground of recognition and redress, naming and claiming Islamophobia as a social category with legal purchase. Contrary to what sympathetic critics have argued, that need not

---

[4] Crampton, drawing on Olsson, suggestively conveys the point with reference to what he calls 'the fisherman's' problem: 'The fisherman's catch furnishes more information about the meshes of his net than about the swarming reality that dwells beneath the surface' [Olsson]. The fisherman certainly catches real fish that were in the ocean (that is, ontical enquiry certainly can say truthful things about the real world). But if he tried to say something about the reality of the denizens of the ocean, his explanation would be related to the size of his fishing net. He wouldn't have much to say about whales or sharks, nor about sea anemones. The net therefore plays a double function of both revealing things about the sea and hiding or concealing them (Crampton, 2002, pp. 15–16). In brief, 'the ontic', is 'knowledge of specific things', the 'Ontological' 'the historical conditions of possibility of ontic knowledge', and a 'problematisation', an 'historically contingent disturbances of the ontological' (Crampton, 2002, p. 27).

necessarily directly require that Islamophobia be sharpened as a juridical instrument or legal category. What it does require, is that the circulation of the concept challenges, delegitimises, and shifts the ground to reveal the Islamophobic structures and strictures that prevent the racialisation of Muslims, the criminalisation of Muslim youth, or the delegitimisation of Muslim women's agency, for example, from being recognised. Islamophobia and the battle waged over its 'truth' is neither ultimately nor primarily a matter of marshalling empirical facts, rather it is one of the sites that constitutes the contemporary politics of becoming Muslim, and it needs thinking through conceptually.

BIBLIOGRAPHY

Aaronovitch, D. (2004), 'All Muslims are not the same', (16 Nov.), *The Guardian*.

Aaronovitch, D. (2008), 'Why the Left turned on Amis', (12 Jan.), *The Times*.

Abbas, T. (2007), 'Ethno-Religious Identities and Islamic Political Radicalism in the UK: A Case Study', *Journal of Muslim Minority Affairs*, 27:3, pp. 429–442.

Abrahms et al. (2000), 'A Symposium: American Power—For What?', *Commentary*, vol. 109, no. 1 (Jan.), pp. 21–48.

Abu-Lughod, L. (2002), 'Do Muslim Women Really Need Saving? Anthropological Reflections on Cultural Relativism and its Others', *American Anthropologist*, 104:3, pp. 783–790.

Afshar, H. (2004), 'Behind the Veil: The Public and Private Faces of Khomeini's Policies on Iranian Women', in Moghissi, H. (ed.), *Women and Islam: Critical Concepts in Sociology*, vol. 3, London: Routledge.

Afshar, H. (2007), 'Muslim Women and Feminisms: Illustrations from Iran', *Social Compass*, 54:3, pp. 419–434.

Afshar, H., Aitken, R., and Myfanwy, F. (2005), 'Feminisms, Islamophobia and Identities', *Political Studies*, 53:2, pp. 262–283.

Agamben, G. (1998), *Homo Sacer: Sovereign Power and Bare Life*, Stanford: Stanford University Press.

Agamben, G. (1999), *Remnants of Auschwitz: The Witness and the Archive*, New York: Zone Books.

Agamben, G. (2005), *State of Exception*, Chicago: University of Chicago Press.

Ahearn, L. (2001), 'Language and Agency', *Annual Review of Anthropology*, 30:1, pp. 109–137.

Ahmad, F. (2006), 'The scandal of "Arranged Marriages" and the Pathologisation of BrAsian Families' in Ali, N., Kalra, V.S. and Sayyid, S. (eds), *A Postcolonial People: South Asians in Britain*, London: C. Hurst & Co., pp. 272–288.

Ahmad, M. I. (2002), 'Homeland Insecurities: Racial Violence the day after September 11', *Social Text*, 20:3, pp. 101–115.

BIBLIOGRAPHY

Ahmad, M. I. (2004), 'A Rage Shared by Law: Post-September 11 Racial Violence as Crimes of Passion', *California Law Review*, 92:5, , pp. 1259–1330.

Ahmed, S. (2004), *The Cultural Politics of Emotion*, New York: Routledge.

Aix, J. M. O. (2006), 'Report on Islamophobia in Spain', in Jocelyne Cesari (ed.), *Securitisation and Religious Divides in Europe. Muslims in Europe After 9/11: Why the term Islamophobia is more a predicament than an explanation*, Brussels: European Commission, pp. 227–300, http://www.libertysecurity.org/IMG/pdf_Challenge_Project_report.pdf

Akram, S. M. and Johnson, K. R. (2002), 'Race, Civil Rights and Immigration Law after September 11, 2001: The targeting of Arabs and Muslims', *NYU Annual Survey of American Law*, 58:3, pp. 295–355.

Aktay, Y. (2008), 'European Values and the Muslim world: Turkish Cases at the European Court of Human Rights', *Global Change, Peace & Security*, 20:1, pp. 99–108.

Aktay, Y., Oplinger, J. T. and Talbot, R. P. (2004), *Barbed Wire and Body Snatchers: The Manufacture of Conspiracy and Elite Dominance*, unpublished ms; Turkish version published as 'Dikenli tel ve Vucut Avcilari: Komplonun Urietimi ve elit tahakkumu', in *İnsan Hakları Araştırmaları (Human Rights Review)*, 3.

Alam, M. S. (2006), 'The Latest Falsehood from the Advocates of Civilizational War: Not All Terrorists are Muslim', (posted 24 Oct.), http://www.counterpunch.org/shahid10242006.html

Ali, S. (2000), *Gender and Human Rights in Islam and International Law: Equal Before Allah, Unequal Before Man?*, The Hague: Kluwer Law International.

Alibhai–Brown, Y. (2007), 'It's time for civilised and honest engagement', (8 Oct.), *The Independent*.

Allen, C. (2002), 'A critical appraisal of the comparability of data collection processes and methodologies implemented by the National Focal Points of the European Monitoring Centre on Racism and Xenophobia', *European Monitoring Centre on Racism and Xenophobia Colloque*, (25 Jun.), Vienna: EUMC.

Allen, C. (2004), 'Justifying Islamophobia: A Post-9/11 Consideration of the European Union and British contexts', *American Journal of Islamic Social Sciences*, 21:3, pp. 1–25.

Allen, C., The First Decade of Islamophobia: 10 Years of the Runnymede Trust Report 'Islamophobia: A challenge for us all', http://mywf.org.uk/uploads/projects/borderlines/Archive/2007/Decade_of_Islamophobia.pdf

Allen, C. (2008), *Challenging Islamophobia—Ten Years On*, Postgraduate Seminar Series 2008, Theology Department, University of Birmingham.

Allen, C. and Nielsen, J. (2002), *Summary report on Islamophobia in the EU after 11 September 2001*, Vienna: European Monitoring Centre on Racism and Xenophobia.

Allen, W. (1966), 'The Gossage—Vardebedian Papers', (22 Jan.), *The New Yorker*.

Almond, I. (2006), 'Leibniz, Historicism, and the "Plague of Islam"', *Eighteenth-Century Studies*, 19:4, pp. 463–483.

BIBLIOGRAPHY

Almond, I. (2008), 'Terrible Turks, Bedouin Poets, and Prussian Prophets: The Shifting Place of Islam in Herder's Thought', *PMLA*, 123:1, pp. 57–75.

Amiraux, V. (2008), 'Religious Discrimination: Muslims Claiming Equality in Europe', in Bertossi, C. (ed.), European Anti-discrimination and the Politics of Citizenship, Basingstoke: Palgrave Macmillan, pp. 143–167.

Amis, M. (2008), *The Second Plane: September 11: 2001–2007*, London: Jonathan Cape.

Anagnost, A. (2004), 'The Corporeal Politics of Quality (*Suzhi*)', *Public Culture*, 16:2, pp. 189–208.

Anand, D. (2007), 'Gendered anxieties: Representing Muslim masculinity as a danger', *British Journal of Politics and International Relations*, 9:2, pp. 257–269.

Anand, D. (2008), 'Porno-Nationalism and the Male Subject: An Ethnography of Hindu Nationalist Imagination in India', in Parpart, J. and Zalewski, M. (eds) *Rethinking the 'Man' Question in International Politics*, London: Zed, pp. 163–180.

Anand, D. (2009), 'Hindutva: A Schizophrenic Nationalism', September *Seminar* 601: The Republic of Ideas, http://www.india-seminar.com/semframe.html [Last accessed on 13 Oct. 2009].

Anand, D. (2011, forthcoming), *Hindu Nationalism in India and the Politics of Fear*, New York: Palgrave Macmillan.

Anawati, C.G. (1976), 'Dialogue with Gustave E. von Grunebaum', *International Journal of Middle East Studies*, 7:1, pp. 123–128.

Anderson, B. (1991), *Imagined Communities: Reflections on the Origin and Spread of Nationalism*, London: Verso.

Anidjar, G. (2003), *The Jew, The Arab: A History of the Enemy*, Stanford: Stanford University Press.

Anidjar, G. (2008), *Semites: Race, Religion, Literature*, Stanford: Stanford University Press.

Anitha, S. and Gill, A. (2009), 'Coercion, Consent and the Forced Marriage Debate in the UK', *Feminist Legal Studies*, 17:2, pp. 165–184.

An-Naim, A. A. (1990), *Toward an Islamic Reformation: Civil Liberties, Human Rights and International Law*, New York: Syracuse University Press.

Anthias, F. (2002), 'Beyond Feminism and Mutliculturalism: Locating difference and the politics of location', *Women's Studies International Forum*, 25:3, pp. 275–286.

Anthony, A. (2007), *The Fallout: How a Guilty Liberal Lost His Innocence*, London: Jonathan Cape.

Antoniou, D. (2003), 'Muslim Immigrants in Greece', *Immigrants and Minorities*, 22:2, pp. 155–174.

Appadurai, A. (1981), 'The Past as a Scarce Resource', *Man (N.S.)*, 16:2, pp. 201–219.

Appadurai, A. (2006), *Fear of Small Numbers: An essay on the geography of anger*, London: Duke University Press.

Appleton, J. (2002) 'Who's afraid of Islamophobia?', (2 Jul.), *Spiked*, http://www.spiked-online.com/Articles/00000006D95B.htm [Last accessed on 12 Nov. 2002].

Appleton, J. (2004), 'Islam on the brain', (11 Aug.), *Spiked*, http://www.spiked-online. co.uk/Articles/0000000CA662.htm [Last accessed on 10 Sept. 2004].

Arnaut, K. and Ceuppens, B. (2004), 'Het Vlaams Blok als mysterie. Wetenschappelijke en politieke uitwegen', *Samenleving en Politiek*, 11, pp. 38–45.

Arnaut, K. and Ceuppens, B. (2009), 'De vage grenzen en ondiepe gronden van de raciale verbeelding in Vlaanderen' in Arnaut, K., Bracke, S., Ceuppens, B., De Mul, S., Fadil, N., Kanmaz, M. (eds) *Een Leeuw in een Kooi. De Grenzen van het Multiculutrele Vlaanderen*, Antwerp: Meulenhoff-Manteau, pp. 28–47.

Arnaut, K. et al. (2009), 'Het gekooide Vlaanderen. Twintig jaar gemist Multicultureel debat' in Arnaut, K., Bracke, S., Ceuppens, B., De Mul, S., Fadil, N., Kanmaz, M. (eds), *Een Leeuw in een Kooi. De Grenzen van het Multiculutrele Vlaanderen*, Antwerpen: Meulenhoff-Manteau, pp. 7–27.

Asad, T. (1980), [on Edward Said's Orientalism], *The English Historical Review*, 95:376, pp. 648–649.

Asad, T. (1993), *Genealogies of Religion: Discipline and Reasons of Power in Christianity and Islam*, Baltimore: John Hopkins University.

Asad, T. (2003), *Formation of the Secular: Christianity, Islam and Modernity*, Stanford: Stanford University Press.

Asad, T. (2007), *On Suicide Bombing*, New York: Columbia University Press.

Aslam, N. (2004), *Maps for Lost Lovers*, London: Faber & Faber.

Athanasiadis, I. (2008) 'Snapshots of Islam: An Athens Museum Seeks to Promote Understanding of the Modern Arab World', (8 Sept.), *Newsweek*, http://www.newsweek.com/id/156321 [Last accessed on 31 Jan. 2009].

Austin, J. (1995 [1832]), *The Province of Jurisprudence Determined*, ed. by Rumble, W., Cambridge: Cambridge University Press.

Bacchetta, P. (2004), *Gender in the Hindu Nation: RSS Women as Ideologues*, New Delhi: Women Unlimited.

Bacevich, A. J. (2005), *The New American Militarism: How Americans are Seduced by War*, Oxford: Oxford University Press.

Back, L., Crabbe, T. and Solomos, J. (2001), *The Changing Face of Football: Racism, Identity and Multiculture in the English Game*, Oxford: Berg.

Baily, J. (2001), '"Can you stop the birds singing?"—The censorship of music in Afghanistan', Copenhagen: Freemuse.

Bains, J. and Johal, S. (1998), *Corner Shops and Corner Flags: The Asian Football Experience*, London: Orien.

Bakhtin, M. (1986), *Speech Genres and Other Late Essays*, Austin: University of Texas Press.

Balibar, E. (1990), 'The Nation Form: History and Ideology', *Review*, 13:3, pp. 329–361.

Balibar, E. (1991), 'Is there a "Neo-Racism"?', in Balibar, E. and Wallerstein, I., *Race, Nation, Class: Ambiguous Identities*, London: Verso, pp. 17–28.

Balibar, E. (1994), *Masses, Classes, Ideas*, London: Routledge.

BIBLIOGRAPHY

Balibar, E. and Wallerstein, I. (1991), *Race, Nation, Class: Ambiguous Identities*, London: Verso.

Banakar, R. (2008a), 'Poetic Injustice: A Case Study of the UK's Anti-Terrorism Legislation', *Retfærd: The Nordic Journal of Law and Justice*, 3:122, pp. 69–90.

Banakar, R. (2008b), 'The Politics of Legal Cultures', *Retfærd: The Nordic Journal of Law and Justice*, 4:123, pp. 37–60.

Banard, B. and van Istendael, G. (2008), 'Bericht aan weldenkend links. Waarom wij het hoofddoekenverbod steunen', (8 Feb.), *De Standaard*.

Banks, S. (1999), *Ethical Issues in Youth Work*, London: Routledge.

Banton, M. (1967), *Race Relations*, London: Tavistock.

Barker, M. (1981), *The New Racism: Conservatives and the Ideology of the Tribe*, London: Junction Books.

Barlas, A. (2002), *'Believing Women' in Islam: Unreading Patriarchal Interpretations of the Qur'an*, Austin: University of Texas Press.

Bawer, B. (2006), *While Europe Slept: How Radical Islam is destroying the West from within*, New York: Broadway Books.

Bawer, B. (2009), *Surrender: Appeasing Islam, Sacrificing Freedom*, New York: Doubleday Books.

Bayoumi, M. (2006), 'Racing Religion', *CR: The New Centennial Review*, 6:2, pp. 267–293.

BBC News (online), (2009), 'MI5 Document on Binyam revealed', (30 Jul.), *BBC*, http://news.bbc.co.uk/1/hi/uk/8175684.stm

Beck, U. (2002), 'The Cosmopolitan Society and its Enemies', *Theory, Culture and Society*, 19:1, pp. 17–44.

Behdad, A. (2008), 'Critical Historicism' *American Literary History*, 20:1–2, pp. 286–299.

Ben, T. and Jawad, H. (2003), *Muslim Women in the United Kingdom and Beyond: Experiences and Images*, Leiden Boston: Brill.

Bennett, R. (2007), 'Martin Amis's threatening remarks about Muslims have gone largely unchallenged', (19 Nov.), *The Guardian*.

Bentham, J. (1996), *The Principles of Morals and Legislation, The collected works of Jeremy Bentham*, ed. by Burns, J.H. and Hart, H.L.A., Oxford: Oxford University Press.

Bernal, M. (1991), *Black Athena: The Afroasiatic Roots of Classical Civilisation, I: The Fabrication of Ancient Greece*, London: Vintage.

Bernard, A. (1927), 'L'Islam et l'Afrique du Nord', in *L'Islam et la Politique Contemporaine*, Paris: Felix Alcan, pp. 105–122.

Bernasconi, R. (2001), 'Who Invented the Concept of Race? Kant's Role in the Enlightenment Construction of Race', in Bernasconi, R. (ed.), *Race*, Oxford: Blackwell, pp. 11–36.

Bernasconi, R. (2003a), 'Hegel's Racism. A Reply to McCarney', *Radical Philosophy*, 119, pp. 35–37.

Bernasconi, R. (2003b), 'Will the Real Kant please Stand Up: The challenge of Enlightenment racism to the study of the history of philosophy', *Radical Philosophy*, 117, pp. 13–22.

Bernasconi, R. and Lott, T. L. (2000) (eds), *The Idea of Race*, Indianapolis, USA: Hackett Publishing Company.

Bhandar, B. (2009), 'The Ties that Bind: Multiculturalism and Secularism Reconsidered', *Journal of Law and Society*, 36:3, pp. 301–336.

Bhatt, C. (1998), *Liberation and Purity*, London: University College London Press.

Bhattacharryya, G. (2006), 'Wars on our doorstep—Islamicising "race" and militarising everyday life', in Lentin, A. and Lentin, R. (eds), *Race and State*, Newcastle: Cambridge Scholars Press, pp. 131–151.

Bhattacharyya, G. (2008a), 'Globalizing Racism and the Myths of the Other in the "War on Terror"', in Lentin, R. (ed.), *Thinking Palestine*, London: Zed Books, pp. 46–61.

Bhattacharyya, G. (2008b), *Dangerous Brown Men: Exploiting Sex, Violence and Feminism in the 'War on Terror'*, London: Zed Books.

Bhattacharyya, G. (2009), 'Trial by Media for Pakistani Students facing Deportation', [Letter to the editor] (25 Apr.), *The Guardian*.

Bhimji, F. (2009), 'Identities and Agencies in Religious Spheres: A study of British Muslim women's experience', *Gender, Place and Culture*, 16:4, pp. 365–380.

Bhopal, K. (1999), 'South Asian women and arranged marriages in East London', in Baror, R., Bradley, H., and Fenton, S., (eds) *Ethnicity, Gender, and Social Change*, Basingstoke: Macmillan, pp. 117–134.

Birt, J. (2005), 'Lobbying and Marching: British Muslims and the State', in Abbas, T. (ed.) *Muslim Britain: Communities Under Pressure*, London: Zed, pp. 92–106.

Birt, J. (2006a), 'Notes on Islamophobia', http://www.yahyabirt.com/?p=48 [Last accessed on 9 Mar. 2009].

Birt, J. (2006b), 'Good Imam, Bad Imam: Civic Religion and National Integration in Britain post-9/11', *Muslim World*, 96:4, pp. 687–705.

Birt, J. (2009), 'Islamophobia in the construction of British Muslim identity politics' in Hopkins, P. and Gale, R. (eds), *Muslims in Britain: Race, Place and Identities*, Edinburgh: Edinburgh University Press, pp. 210–227.

Birt, Y. and Lewis, P. (2010), 'The Pattern of Islamic Reform in Britain: The Deobandis between intra-Muslim sectarianism and engagement with wider society', in van Bruinessen, M. (ed.), *Producing Islamic Knowledge: Transmission and Dissemination in Western Europe*, London: Routledge, in press.

Blacking, J. (1973), *How musical is man?*, Seattle: University of Washington Press.

Blick, A., Choudhury, T. and Weir, S. (2007), *The Rules of the Game: Terrorism, Community and Human Rights*, York: Joseph Rowntree Reform Trust.

Blommaert, J. and Verscheuren, J. (1992), *Het Belgische Migrantendebat. De pragmatiek van de abnormalisering*, Antwerp: International Pragmatics Association.

Blum, L. (2002), *I'm Not a Racist But...*, Ithaca: Cornell University Press.

BIBLIOGRAPHY

Boellstorff, T. (2008), *Coming of Age in Second Life: An Anthropologist Explores The Virtually Human*, Princeton: Princeton University Press.

Bogas, E. A. (1964), *I Michaniona tis Kyzikou*, Athens.

Bolkestein, F. (1991), 'On the Collapse of the Soviet Union', Address to the Liberal International Conference at Luzern, http://www.liberal-international.org/content-Files/files/Bolkestein%201991.pdf

Bonikowski, B. (2005), 'Flying while Arab (Or was it Muslim? Or Middle Eastern?): A Theoretical Analysis of Racial Profiling After September 11th', *The Discourse of Sociological Practice*, 7:1–2, http://omega.cc.umb.edu/~sociology/journal/volume7%201&2.htm and http://omega.cc.umb.edu/~sociology/journal/Vol71& 2PDFS/Bonikowski%20-%20Fa%20%2705.pdf

Bourdieu, P. (1999), 'The Social Conditions of the International Circulation of Ideas', in Shusterman, R. (ed.), *Bourdieu: A Critical Reader*, Oxford: Blackwell, pp. 220–227.

Bourdieu, P. (2006 [1977]), *Outline of a Theory of Practice*, Cambridge: Cambridge University Press.

Bragg, B. (2006), *The Progressive Patriot: The search for belonging*, London: Bantam.

Brahimi, D. (1984), *La Vie et l'oeuvre de Etienne Dinet*, Paris: ACR.

Brass, P. (2003), *The Production of Hindu-Muslim Violence in Contemporary India*, New Delhi: Oxford University Press.

Bredal, A. (2005), 'Arranged marriages as a multicultural battlefield', in Andersson, M., Lithman, Y. and Sernhede, O. (eds), *Youth, Otherness, and the Plural City: Modes of belonging and social life*, Gothenburg: Daidalos, pp. 75–105.

Brewin, C. (2005), 'Turkey: Democratic Legitimacy', in Danchev, A. and MacMillan, J. (eds), *The Iraq War and Democratic Politics*, London: Routledge, pp. 93–110.

Brimson, D. (2006), *Kicking Off: Why hooliganism and racism are killing football*, London: Headline.

Brinckman, B. (2002), 'Volgens Robert Voorhamme (SP.A) staat de migrantencultuur echte integratie in de weg', (28 Sept.), *De Standaard*.

British Muslims Monthly Survey (1992–2002), Birmingham: Centre for the Study of Islam and Christian Muslim Understanding, vols. IV (1996) and V (1997).

Brittain, V. (2008), 'Besieged in Britain', *Race & Class*, 50:3, pp. 1–29.

Brooks, J. (2007), 'Deep Roots of Islamophobia', (13 Feb.), *Reading Islam*, http://www. readingislam.com [Last accessed on 30 Jan. 2009].

Brown, K. (2008), 'The Promise and Perils of Women's Participation in UK Mosques: The Impact of Securitisation Agendas on Identity, Gender and Community', *British Journal of Politics and International Relations*, 10:3, pp. 472–491.

Brown, K. B. (2007), 'Did Aurangzeb ban music? Questions for the historiography of his reign', *Modern Asian Studies*, 41:1, pp. 77–120.

Brown, M. D. (2000), 'Conceptualising Racism and Islamophobia', in Ter Wal, J. and Verkuyten, M. (eds), *Comparative Perspectives on Racism*, Aldershot: Ashgate, pp. 73–90.

Brown, W. (2006), *Regulating Aversion: Tolerance in the Age of Identity and Empire*, Princeton and Oxford: Princeton University Press.

Bunzl, M. (2005), 'Between anti-Semitism and Islamophobia: Some thoughts on the new Europe', *American Ethnologist*, 32:4, pp. 499–508.

Bunzl, M. (2007), *Anti-Semitism and Islamophobia: Hatreds Old and New in Europe*, Chicago: Prickly Paradigm Press.

Burchill, J. (2001), 'Some People will Believe Anything', (18 Aug.), *The Guardian*.

Burdsey, D. (2004), '"One of the lads"? Dual ethnicity and assimilated ethnicities in the careers of British-Asian professional footballers', *Ethnic and Racial Studies*, 27:5, pp. 757–779.

Burdsey, D. (2006), 'No Ball Games Allowed? A Socio-Historical Examination of the Development and Social Significance of British-Asian Football Clubs', *Journal of Ethnic and Migration Studies*, 32:3, pp. 477–496.

Burdsey, D. (2007), *British-Asians and Football: Culture, Identity, Exclusion*, London: Routledge.

Burleigh, M. (2004), 'Religious hatred bill is being used to buy Muslim votes', (9 Dec.), *Daily Telegraph*.

Butler, J. (2004), *Precarious Life: The Powers of Mourning and Violence*, London: Verso.

Butler, J. (2008), 'Sexual politics, torture, and secular time', *British Journal of Sociology*, 59:1, pp. 1–23.

Butt, R. (2008a), 'Muslim leaders back Livingstone as mayor', (3 Jan.), *The Guardian*.

Butt, R. (2008b), 'FA seeks power to dock points from clubs for religious abuse', (4 Apr.), *The Guardian*.

Caeiro, A. (2006), 'France', in Cesari, J. (ed.), *Securitisation and Religious Divides in Europe: Muslims in Europe After 9/11—Why the term Islamophobia is more a predicament than an explanation*, Brussels: European Commission, pp. 195–226, http://www.libertysecurity.org/IMG/pdf_Challenge_Project_report.pdf

Cainkar, L. (2002), 'No Longer Invisible: Arab and Muslim Exclusion After September 11', *Middle East Report*, 224, pp. 22–29.

Cantle, T. (2001), *Community Cohesion: A Report of The Independent Review Team*, London: Home Office.

Carby, V.H. (1982), 'Schooling in Babylon', in *The Empire Strikes Back*, Birmingham: Center for Contemporary Studies (London: Hutchinson), pp. 187–208.

Cashmore, E. (ed.) (2003), *Encyclopedia of Race and Ethnic Studies*, London: Routledge.

Cesaire, A. (2001), *Discourse on Colonialism*, New York: Monthly Review Press.

Cesari, J. (2006), *Securitization and Religious Divides in Europe: Muslims in Western Europe after 9/11—Why the term Islamophobia is more a predicament than an explanation*, Paris: Challenge.

Chaturdashi, M.K. and Varsha, K. (2010), '"Love Jihad"—A Jihadi Organisation to trap Hindu girls', (27 Feb.), *Hindu Janajagruti Samiti*, http://www.hindujagruti. org/news/6389.html

Chen, L. (1989), 'Zhongguo, Huayi, Fanhan, Zhonghua, Zhonghua Minzu—A Process of Realization of an Inherent Link and Development', in Fei X., Chen L., Jia J. and Gu B. (1989), (eds) *Zhongghua Minzu Duoyuan Yiti Geju*, Beijing: Central Institute for Ethnic Minorities Press, pp. 72–113.

Chetkovich, C. (2004), 'Women's agency in a context of oppression: Assessing strategies for personal action and public policy', *Hypatia*,19:4, pp. 120–141.

Chon, M. and Arzt, D. E. (2004–2005), 'Walking While Muslim', *Law and Contemporary Problems*, 68:2, pp. 215–254.

Christian, L., Groombridge, J. and Peirce, G. (2006), *Submission to the International Commission of Jurists Eminent Jurist Panel UCC Hearing*, (24 Apr.).

Clough, P. T. (2003), 'Affect and Control: Rethinking the Body Beyond Sex and Gender', *Feminist Theory*, 4:3, pp. 359–364.

Cohen, N. (2007), *What's Left? How Liberals Lost Their Way*, London: Harper Perennial.

Collard, A. (1989), 'Investigating "Social Memory" in a Greek Context', in Tonkin, E., McDonald, M. and Chapman, M. (eds), *History and Ethnicity*, London: Routledge, pp. 89–103.

Commission for Racial Equality (2001), *Anti-Islamic reactions in the EU after the terrorist acts against the USA: United Kingdom second country report*, London: CRE.

Commission on British Muslims and Islamophobia (2004), *Islamophobia: Issues challenges and action*, London: Trentham Books.

Copsey, N. (2004), *Contemporary British Fascism: The British National Party and the Quest for Legitimacy*, London: Palgrave.

Coulter, A. (2007), 'Have you hugged an Islamo-fascist today?', (posted 24 Oct.), http://www.anncoulter.com/cgi–local/article.cgi?article=218

Cowan, J. (1990), *Dance and the Body Politic in Northern Greece*, Princeton: Princeton University Press.

Crampton, J. W. (2002), 'Thinking Philosophically in Cartography: Toward a Critical Politics of Mapping', *Cartographic Perspectives*, 42, pp. 12–31.

Curzon, G. N. (1967), *Russia in Central Asia in 1889 and the Anglo-Russian Question*, London: Frank Kass.

Daily Mail, The (2006), 'The real intelligence failure of Forest Gate,' (9 Jun.).

Dalrymple, W. (2008), 'A triumph of style over knowledge', (27 Jan.), *Sunday Times*.

Danielson, V. (1987), 'The "Qur'an" and the "Qasidah": Aspects of the popularity of the repertory sung by Umm Kulthum', *Asian Music*, 19:1, pp. 26–45.

Davies, B. (1999), *From Voluntaryism To Welfare State: A History Of The Youth Service In England*, Leicester: Youth Work Press.

Davies, M. (2002), *Asking the law question: The dissolution of legal theory*, Sydney: Lawbook Co.

De Lange, S. L. (2008), *From Pariah to Power: Explanations for the Government Participation of Radical Right-Wing Populist Parties in West European Parliamentary Democracies*, Unpublished PhD Thesis, Antwerp: Universiteit Antwerpen.

De Leeuw, M. and van Wichelen, S. (2005), '"Please, Go Wake Up" Submission, Ayaan Hirsi Ali and the "War on Terror" in the Netherlands', *Feminist Media Studies*, 5:3, pp. 325–340.

Delafosse, M. (1912), *Haut-Sénégal-Niger (Soudan Français)*, vol. III: *Les Civilisations*, Paris: Émile Larose.

Delanty, G. and O'Mahony, P. (2002), *Nationalism and Social Theory*, London: Sage.

Deleuze, G. (2006), *Foucault*, London: Continuum.

Deleuze, G. and Guattari, F. (2004), *A Thousand Plateaus*, London: Continuum.

Delvoye, F. (1994), 'Indo-Persian literature on art-music: Some historical and technical aspects', in Delvoye, F. (ed.), *Confluence of Cultures*, New Delhi: Manohar, pp. 93–130.

Delwit, P. and De Waele, J. M. (1998), *L'extrême droite en Flandre et en Belgique*, Bruxelles: Complexe.

Department for Communities and Local Government (2008), *Preventing Violent Extremism: Next Steps for Communities*.

Derrida, J. (1976), *Of Grammatology*, trans. from French by Gayatri Chakravorty Spivak, London: John Hopkins University Press.

Derrida, J. (1990), Force of Law: The 'mystical foundation of authority', *Cardozo Law Review*, 11:5–6, pp. 919–1045.

Desmet, Y. (2002), 'Over kut-Marokkaantjes, hondendrollenen Jean-Marie Le Pen', (24 Feb.), *De Morgen*.

Devji, F. (2007), 'Apologetic Modernity', *Modern Intellectual History*, 4:1, pp. 61–76.

Diken, B. and Laustsen, C.B. (2002), 'Zones of Indistinction: Security, Terror, and Bare Life', *Space and Culture*, 5:3, pp. 290–307.

Dillon, M. and Reid, J. (2001), 'Global Liberal Governance: Biopolitics, Security and War', *Millenium: Journal of International Studies*, 30:1, pp. 41–66.

Dilthey, W. (1976), *Selected Writings*, Cambridge: Cambridge University Press.

Dinet, E. and Sliman Ben Ibrahim, E.H. (1918), *The Life of Mohammed, The Prophet of Allah*, Paris: Paris Book Club.

Dinnet, E. and Sliman Ben Ibrahim, E.H. (n.d. [1922]), *L'Orient Vu de L'Occident*: Essai critique, Paris: Piazza-Geuthner.

Dinnet, E. and Sliman Ben Ibrahim, E.H. [Hadji Nacir Ed Dine, E. Dinet and el Hadj Sliman Ben Ibrahim Baâmer] (1930), *Le Pélerinage a la Maison Sacrée d'Allah*, Paris: Hachette Livre.

Dinet, E. and Sliman Ben Ibrahim, E.H. (1937), *La Vie de Mohammed, Prophète d'Allah*, G.P. Maisonneuve, pp. 61–76.

Djait, H. (1976), 'Dimensions de L'Orientalisme Islamisant', in Moniot, J. (ed.), *Le Mal de Voir. Ethnologie et Orientalisme*, Cahiers Jussieu 2, Paris: Collection 10/18, pp. 258–266.

Djait, H. (1978), *L'Europe et L'Islam*, Paris: Seuil.

Djait, H. (1985), *Europe and Islam*, Heinegg, P. (trans.), Berkeley: University of California Press.

Doornaert, M. (2004), 'Kritiek hebben op de islam mag', (15 Sept.), *De Standaard*.

Dostoyevsky, F. (2002), 'Dnevnik Pisatelya za 1877 (Writer's Diary for 1877)', *Russkaja Ideya (Russian Idea)*, Moscow: Iris Press, pp. 154–162.

Dougary, G. (2006), 'The voice of experience', (9 Sept.), *The Times*.

Dussel, E. (2000), 'Europe, Modernity and Eurocentrism', *Nepantla: Views from South*, 1:3, pp. 465–478.

Dworkin, R. (1986), *Law's Empire*, London: Fontana.

Eagleton, T. (2007), *Ideology: An Introduction*, Oxford: Blackwell.

Ebrey, P. (1996), 'Surnames and Han Chinese Identity', in Brown, M. J. (ed.), *Negotiating Ethnicities in China and Taiwan*, Berkeley: University of California Institute for East Asian Studies, pp. 19–36.

Eddy, C. (1931), *Greece and the Greek Refugees*, London: Allen & Unwin.

Elia, N. (2006), 'Islamophobia and the "Privileging" of Arab American Women', *NWSA Journal*, 18:3, pp. 155–161.

Elias, N. (2000), *The Civilizing Process*, Oxford: Blackwell.

Elman, B. A. (2000), *A Cultural History of Civil Examinations in Late Imperial China*, Berkeley: University of California Press.

EUMC (2002), *EUMC Report on Islamophobia after September 11*, Vienna: EUMC.

Fabian, J. (1983), *Time and The Other*, New York: Columbia University Press.

Falk, R. (2005), 'The Global Setting: US Foreign Policy and the Future of the Middle East', in Danchev, A. and MacMillan, J. (eds), *The Iraq War and Democratic Politics*, London: Routledge, pp. 20–34.

al Faruqi, L. I. (1985), 'Music, musicians and Muslim law', *Asian Music*, 17:1, pp. 3–36.

Fattah, M. A. and Butterfield, J. (2006), 'Muslim Cultural Entrepreneurs and the Democracy Debate', *Critique: Critical Middle Eastern Studies*, 15:1, pp. 49–78.

Fazl, A. (1902), *Akbarnama, vol. ii*, Beveridge, H. (trans.), Calcutta: Baptist Mission Press.

Fei, X. (1989), 'Configuration of Plurality and Unity of the Chinese Nation', in Fei, X., Chen, L., Jia J. and Gu, B. (eds), *Zhonghua Minzu Duoyuan Yiti Geju (Configuration of Plurality and Unity of Chinese Nation)*, Beijing: Central Institute for Ethnic Minorities Press, pp. 1–36.

Fekete, L. (2004), 'Anti-Muslim racism and the European Security state', *Race & Class*, 46:1, pp. 3–29.

Fekete, L. (2009), *A Suitable Enemy: Racism, Migration and Islamophobia in Europe*, London: Pluto Press.

Field, C. D. (2007), 'Islamophobia in Contemporary Britain: The Evidence of the Opinion Polls, 1988–2006', *Islam and Christian-Muslim Relations*, 18:4, pp. 447–477.

Fitzpatrick, P. (1992), *The Mythology of Modern Law*, London: Routledge.

Foucault, M. (1991), 'Governmentality' in Burcell, G., Gordon, C. and Miller, P. (eds), *The Foucault Effect: Studies in Governmentality*, Chicago: Chicago University Press, pp. 111–119.

Foucault, M. (1992 [1984]), *The History of Sexuality, 2: The Use of Pleasure*, London: Penguin Books.

Foucault, M. (2000 [1984]), 'Polemics, Politics and Problematizations', in Rabinow, P. (ed.), *Essential Works of Foucault, vol. 1: Ethics*, London: Penguin Books, pp. 111–119.

Fourest, C. and Venner, F. (2003), 'Islamophobie?' *ProChoix*, 26/27, pp. 13–16.

Frank, K. (2006), Agency, *Anthropological Theory*, 6:3, pp. 281–302.

Fredrickson, G. (2002), *Racism: A Short History*, Princeton: Princeton University Press.

Friedman, M. (2005), *The Neoconservative Revolution: Jewish Intellectuals and the Shaping of Public Policy*, Cambridge: Cambridge University Press.

Frum, D. and Perle, R. (2003), *An End to Evil: How to win the War on Terror*, New York: Random House.

Fuchs, B. (2001), *Mimesis and Empire: The New World, Islam and European Identities*, Cambridge: Cambridge University Press.

Gaffney, Jr., F. J. (2006), 'Islamofascist "coup" in Turkey', (14 Mar.), *Jewish World Review*, www.jewishworldreview.com/cols/gaffney031406.asp

Gallant, T. W. (1997), 'Greek Exceptionalism and Contemporary Historiography: New Pitfalls and Old Debates', *Journal of Modern Greek Studies*, 15:2, pp. 209–216.

Gandhi, L. (1998), *Postcolonial Theory: A Critical Introduction*, Edinburgh: Edinburgh University Press.

Gandy, M. (2006), 'Zones of indistinction: Bio-political contestations in the urban arena', *Cultural Geographies*, 13:4, pp. 497–516.

Gardesse, C. (n.d.), 'Islamophobie: Essai de définition', *Hermés: (Histoire en réseu des méditerranées)*, http://www.hermes.jussieu.fr/repjeunes.php?id=2

Garland, J. and Rowe, M. (2001), *Racism and Anti-Racism in Football*, Basingstoke: Palgrave.

Gatagova, L. (2006), Mezhdu strakhom i nenavistju: islamofobiya v Rossii (Between fear and hatred: Islamophobia in Russia), *Rodina*, 6, http://www.istrodina.com/rodina_articul.php3?id=1911&n=99

Gates, H. (1996), *China's Motor: A Thousand Years of Petty Capitalism*, Ithaca, New York: Cornell University Press.

Geaves, R. (2005), 'Negotiating British Citizenship and Muslim Identity', in Abbas, T. (ed.), *Muslim Britain: Communities Under Pressure*, London: Zed Books, pp. 66–77.

BIBLIOGRAPHY

Geisser, V. (2003), *La Nouvelle Islamophobie*, Paris: La Découverte.

Gilroy, P. (1987), *There Ain't No Black in the Union Jack*, London: Hutchinson.

Gilroy, P. (2002), *There Ain't No Black in the Union Jack*, London: Routledge Classics.

Gilroy, P. (2004), *Between Camps: Nations, Cultures and the Allure of Race*, London: Routledge.

Gladney, D. C. (1999), 'Making Muslims in China: Education, Islamicization and Representation' in Postiglione, G. A. (ed.), *China's National Minority Education: Culture, Schooling, and Development*, London: Falmer Press, pp. 55–94.

Gladney, D. C. (2004), *Dislocating China: Reflections on Muslims, Minorities and Other Subaltern Subjects*, Chicago: University of Chicago Press.

Goddard, V. (ed.) (2000), *Gender, Agency and Change: Anthropological perspectives*, New York: Routledge.

Goel, S. R. (n.d.), *Hindu Society Under Siege, New Delhi: Voice of India*, http://voiceofdharma.org/books/hsus [Last accessed on 5 Jul. 2009].

Goldberg, D.T. (2006), 'Racial Europeanization', *Ethnic and Racial Studies*, 29:2, pp. 331–364.

Göle, N. (1996), *The Forbidden Modern: Civilization and Veiling*, Ann Arbor: University of Michigan Press.

Goodhart, D. (2004), 'Too Diverse?', (Feb.), *Prospect*.

Gordon, L. (2006), *Disciplinary Decadence: Living Thought in Trying Times*, Boulder: Paradigm Publishers.

Gottschalk, P. (2007), 'A Categorical Difference: Communal Identity in British Epistemologies', in Hinnells, J.R. and King, R. (eds), *Religion and Violence in South Asia: Theory and Practice*, London: Routledge, pp. 195–210.

Gottschalk, P. and Greenberg, G. (2008), *Islamophobia: Making Muslims the Enemy*, New York: Rowman & Littlefield Publishers.

Gourgouris, S. (1992), 'Nationalism and Oneirocentrism: Of Modern Hellenes in Europe', *Diaspora*, 2, pp. 43–71.

Gourgouris, S. (1996), *Dream Nation: Enlightenment, Colonization and the Institution of Modern Greece*, Stanford: Stanford University Press.

Gove, M. (2006), *Celsius 7/7*, Weidenfeld & Nicolson.

Greek Helsinki Monitor, (2003) 'Easter Stories of Church-State Interweaving', (24 Apr.).

Gresh, A. (2004), 'A Propos de l'Islamphobie', *Oumma*, http://oumma.com/A-propos-de-l-islamophobie

Griffiths, A. (2002), 'Legal Pluralism' in Banakar, R. and Travers, M. (eds), *An Introduction to Law and Social Theory*, Oxford: Hart Publishing, pp. 289–311.

Griffiths, J. (1986), 'What is Legal Pluralism?', *Journal Of Legal Pluralism and Unofficial Law*, 24, pp. 1–56.

Grossberg, L. (1993), 'The formation of Cultural Studies: An American in Birmingham', in Blundell, V., Shepherd, J. and Taylor, I. (eds) *Relocating Cultural Studies: Developments in Theory and Research*, London: Routledge, pp. 21–66.

BIBLIOGRAPHY

Guardian Leader (2008), 'In praise of... Martin Amis', (1 Feb.), *The Guardian*.

Guardian Letters (2007), 'Ian McEwan: Martin Amis is not a racist', (21 Nov.), *The Guardian*.

Gunn, T.J. (2005), 'Fearful Symbols: The Islamic Headscarf and the European Court of Human Rights', paper submitted to the seminar on *The Islamic head scarf Controversy and the Future of Freedom of Religion or Belief*, (28–30 Jul.), Strasbourg, France.

Gupta, C. (2001), *Sexuality, Obscenity, Community: Women, Muslims, and the Hindu Public in Colonial India*, Delhi: Permanent Black.

Hacking, I. (1990), 'Two Kinds of "New Historicism" for Philosophers', *New Literary History*, 21:2, pp. 343–364.

Hacking, I. (2002), 'Inaugural Lecture', *Economy and Society*, 31:1, pp. 1–14.

Hacking, I. (2007), 'Kinds of People: Moving Targets', *Proceedings of the British Academy*, 151, pp. 285–318.

Hage, G. (2000), *White Nation: Fantasies of White supremacy in a multicultural society*, London: Routledge.

Hagopian, E. C. (ed.) (2004), *Civil Rights in Peril: The Targeting of Arabs and Muslims*, London: Pluto Press.

Hall, S. (1992), 'The West and the Rest: Discourse and Power', in Hall, S. and Gieben, B. (eds.), *Formations of Modernity*, Cambridge: Polity Press, pp. 275–331.

Hall, S. (1997), 'The Spectacle of the "Other"', in Hall, S. (ed.) Representation: Cultural Representations and Signifying Practices, Milton Keynes: Open University, pp. 223–279.

Hall, S. (2000), 'Conclusion to the Multi–cultural Question', in Hesse, B. (ed.) *Unsettled Multiculturalisms: Diasporas, Entanglements, Transruptions*, London: Zed Books, pp. 209–241.

Hall, S. (2006), 'Black Diaspora Artists in Britain: Three "Moments" in Post-War History', *History Workshop Journal*, 61, pp. 1–24.

Hall, S. et al. (1978), *Policing the Crisis: Mugging, the state and law and order*, London: Macmillan.

Halliday, F. (1999), '"Islamophobia" Reconsidered', *Ethnic and Racial Studies*, 22:5, pp. 892–902.

Halper, S. and Clarke, J. (2004), *America Alone: The Neoconservatives and The Global Order*, Cambridge: Cambridge University Press.

Hansen, R. (2006), 'The Danish cartoon controversy: A defence of literal freedom', *International Migration*, 44:5, pp. 7–16.

Hansen, T. B. (1996), 'Recuperating Masculinity: Hindu Nationalism, Violence and the Exorcism of the Muslim "Other"', *Critique of Anthropology*, 16:2, pp. 137–172.

Hansen, T. B. (1999), *The Saffron Wave: Democracy and Hindu Nationalism in Modern India*, Princeton: Princeton University Press.

Hardt, M. and Negri, A. (2000), *Empire*, Cambridge: Harvard University Press.

Hari, J. (2008), 'Ken Livingstone: The Interview', http://www.johannhari.com/2008/04/13/ken-livingstone-the-interview

Haritaworn, J. (2008), 'Loyal repetitions of the nation: Gay Assimilation and the "War on Terror"', (May), *Dark Matter*, Issue 3, http://www.darkmatter101.org/site/2008/05/02/loyal-repetitions-of-the-nation-gay-assimilation-and-the-war-on-terror/

Haritaworn, J., Tamsila, T. and Erdem, E. (2008), 'Gay Imperialism: The Role of Gender and Sexuality Discourses in the "War on Terror"' in Miyake, E. and Kuntsman, A. (eds), *Out of Place: Queerness and Raciality*, York: Raw Nerve Books, pp. 71–95.

Harrell, S. (1995), 'Introduction: Civilizing Projects and the Reaction to Them', in Harrell, S. (ed.) *Cultural Encounters on China's Ethnic Frontiers*, Seattle: University of Washington Press, pp. 3–36.

Hart, H.L.A. (1994), *The Concept of Law*, 2nd edn., Oxford: Clarendon Press.

Hart, W. D. (2000), *Edward Said and the Religious Effects of Culture*, Cambridge: Cambridge University Press.

Hasan, Q. (1663), *Sarud al-Bahr*, Salar Jung Museum Library, Hyderabad, Mus.

Hassan, S.D. (2002), 'Arabs, Race and the post September 11 National Security State', *Middle East Report*, 224, pp. 16–21.

Hawkes, T. (1992), *Meaning by Shakespeare*, London: Routledge.

Hedetoft, U. (1993), 'National Identity and the Mentalities of War in Three EC Countries', *Journal of Peace and Research*, 30, pp. 281–300.

Hellenic Republic, Embassy of Greece, 'Islam does not Identify itself with Terrorism, Greek PM Says', Washington DC, http://www.greekembassy.org/embassy/Content/en/ArticlePrint.aspx?... [Last accessed on 31 Jan. 2009].

Herring, J. (2009), *Family Law*, 4th edition, Pearson, Longman.

Herzfeld, M. (1985), *The Poetics of Manhood: Contest and Identity in a Cretan Mountain Village*, Princeton: Princeton University Press.

Herzfeld, M. (2000), *Anthropology: Theoreitcal Practice in Culture and Society*, Oxford: Blackwell.

Herzfeld, M. (2002a), 'The Absent Presence: Discourses of Crypto-Colonialism', *South Atlantic Quarterly*, 101:4, pp. 899–926.

Herzfeld, M. (2002b), 'Ethnographic Phenomenology of the Greek Spirit' in Revel, J. and Levi, G. (eds), *Political Uses of the Past: The Recent Mediterranean Experience*, London: Frank Cass, pp. 13–26.

Herzfeld, M. (2005), *Cultural Intimacy*, New York: Routledge.

Hess, A. (2007), 'Horowitz's "Islamofascism Awareness Week"', (5 Oct.), http://www.counterpunch.org/hess10052007.html

Hesse, B. (1997), 'White Governmentality: Urbanism, Nationalism, Racism', in Westwood, S. and Williams, J. (eds), *Imagining Cities: Scripts, Signs, Memory*, London: Routledge, pp. 85–102.

Hesse, B. (2003), 'New Directions in African Diasporic Thought', (Spring), *The Diaspora*, pp. 6–7.

Hesse, B., (2004), 'Discourse on Institutional Racism, the genealogy of a concept', in Law, I, Philips, D, and Turney, L, *Institutional Racism in Higher Education*, London: Trentham Books, pp. 131–148.

Hesse, B. (2004), 'Im/plausible Deniability: Racism's conceptual double bind', *Social Identities*, 10:1, pp. 9–29.

Hesse, B. (2007), 'Racialized Modernity: An analytics of white mythologies', *Ethnic and Racial Studies*, 30:4, pp. 643–663.

Hesse, B. and Sayyid, S. (2006), 'Narrating the Postcolonial Political and the Immigrant Imaginary' in Ali, N., Kalra, V.S. and Sayyid, S. (eds), *A Postcolonial People: South Asians in Britain*, London: C. Hurst & Co., pp. 13–31.

Hesse, B. and Sayyid, S. (forthcoming), *Paradoxes of Racism*, London: Pluto Press.

Hindess, B. (2004), 'Liberalism—What's in a name?', in Larner, W. and Walters, W. (eds), *Governing International Spaces*, London: Routledge, pp. 23–39.

Hirschkind, C. and Mahmood, S. (2002), 'Feminism, the Taliban, and Politics of Counter-Insurgency', *Anthropological Quarterly*, 75:2, pp. 339–354.

Hitchens, C. (2007), 'Defending the term Islamofascism', (22 Oct.), *Slate*, http://www.slate.com/id/2176389

HM Government (2009), *United Kingdom's Strategy for Countering International Terrorism*, (Mar.).

Ho, E. (2004), 'Empire Through Diasporic Eyes: A view from the Other Boat', in Tirman, J. (ed.), *The Maze of Fear: Security and Migration After 9/11*, New York: The New Press, pp. 17–44.

Hodgson, M.G.S. (1974), *The Venture of Islam, vol. 3: The Gunpowder Empires and Modern Times*, Chicago: University of Chicago Press.

Holden, D. (1972), *Greece Without Columns: The Making of the Modern Greeks*, London: Faber & Faber.

Home Office (2000), *A choice by right: The report of the working group on forced marriage*, London: Home Office Communications Directorate, http://www.fco.gov.uk/Files/KFile/AChoiceByRightJune2000.pdf

Home Office Task Force (2005), *Working Together To Prevent Extremism*, London, Home Office, Cohesion and Faith Unit.

Hughes, A. W. (2007), *Situating Islam: The Past and Future of an Academic Discipline*, London: Equinox.

Hume, M. (2003), 'Whatever happened to RIP?', (2 Jun.), *Spiked*, http://www.spikedonline.com/Articles/00000006DDD5.htm [Last accessed on 10 Sept. 2004].

Huntington, S. (1993), 'The Clash of Civilizations?', *Foreign Affairs*, 72:3, pp. 22–49.

Huntington, S. (1996), *The Clash of Civilizations and the Remaking of World Order*, New York: Simon & Schuster.

Huntington, S. (2004), *Who Are We? The Challenges to America's National Identity*, New York: Simon & Schuster.

Husband, C. (2003), 'Doing Good by Stealth, Whilst Flirting With Racism: Some contradictory dynamics of British multiculturalism', Public Lecture, Perth: Office of Multicultural Interests and University of Western Australia, http://www.omi. wa.gov.au/Publications/Seminar/doing%20good%20by%20stealth.pdf

Hutchinson, J. (2005), *Nations as Zones of Conflict*, London: Sage.

Independent, The (2008), 'Petty fraudster was informant in botched Forest Gate raid', (4 May).

Independent, The (2007) 'Thinking allowed; Martin Amis', (5 Dec.).

INSET (2007), *The search for common ground*, London: GLA.

Islam, I. (2006), 'The rise of Anti-Americanism in the Muslim world: A Sceptic's Guide', in O'Connor, B. and Griffiths, M. (eds), *Rise of Anti-Americanism*, London: Routledge, pp. 68–90.

Islamic Human Rights Commission (IHRC) (2002), *The hidden victims of September 11: The backlash against Muslims in the UK*, Islamic Human Rights Commission.

Islamic Human Rights Commission (IHRC) (2005), 'Enormous upsurge in anti-Muslim backlash', Islamic Human Rights Commission press release, (22 Jul.).

Ismail, Q. (1991), 'A Bit of This and a Bit of That: Rushdie's Newness', *Social Text*, 29, pp. 117–124.

Ismail, Q. (2002), 'Something like a response to 11 September', *Inter-Asia Cultural Studies*, 3:1, pp. 149–155.

Ismail, Q. (2008), '(Not) At Home in (Hindu) India', *Cultural Critique*, 68, pp. 210–247.

Jackson, R. (2006), 'Religion, Politics and Terrorism: A Critical Analysis of Narratives of "Islamic Terrorism"', University of Manchester Centre for International Politics Working Paper Series, no. 21, Oct. 2006.

Jacobs, D. (1998), *Nieuwkomers in de Politiek: Het parlementair debat omtrent kiesrecht voor vreemdelingen in Nederland en België (1977–1997)*, Gent: Academia Press.

Jacobs, D. and Swyngedouw, M. (2002), 'The extreme-right and enfranchisement of immigrants: Main issues in the public 'debate' on integration in Belgium', *Journal of International Migration and Integration*, 3:3–4, pp. 329–344.

Jairazbhoy, N. (2001), 'Musical perspectives on music and September 11: A roundtable on music, community, politics, and violence', (12 Oct.), Department of Ethnomusicology, UCLA. Reproduced in ECHO 3:2, http://www.humnet.ucla.edu/echo/volume3–issue2/sept11–roundtable/jairazbhoy.html

Jamal, G. (2004), *Osvobojdenije Islama (Liberation of Islam)*, Moskva: Ummah.

Jarvie, G. (1991), *Sport, Racism and Ethnicity*, Falmer: London.

Jay, M. (1985), '[review of:] The Legitimacy of the Modern Age by Hans Blumenberg', *History and Theory*, 24:2, pp. 183–196.

Jayawardena, K. and De Alwis, M. (eds) (1998), *Embodied Violence: Communalising Women's Sexuality in South Asia*, London: Zed.

Jenkins, G. H. (2009), *Between Fact and Fantasy: Turkey's Ergenekon Investigation*, Central Asia Caucasus Institute and Silk Road Studies Programme.

Jones, K. W. (1981), 'Religious Identity and the Indian Census', in Barrier, N. G. (ed.), *The Census in British India: New Perspectives*, New Delhi: Manohar Publications, pp. 73–101.

Joppke, C. (2009a), *Veil: Mirror of Identity*, Cambridge: Polity Press.

Joppke, C. (2009b), 'Limits of integration policy: Britain and her Muslims', *Journal of Ethnic and Migration Studies*, 35:3, pp. 453–472.

Just, R. (1989), 'The Triumph of the Ethnos' in Tonkin, E., Chapman, M. and McDonald, M. (eds) *History and Ethnicity*, London: Routledge and Kegan Paul, pp. 71–88.

Kadish, R. (2001), 'My Zionism is Bigger than Your Zionism: Israeli Lesbians, Gay Men, Gay Rights and National Identity', PhD Dissertation, Berkeley: University of California.

Kant, I. (1960), *Observations on the Beautiful and the Sublime*, (trans.) Goldthwait, J., Berkeley: University of California Press.

Kapur, R. (2005), *Erotic Justice, Law and the New Politics of Postcolonialism*, London: Glass House Press.

Karakasidou, A. (1997), *Fields of Wheat, Hills of Blood: Passages to Nationhood in Greek Macedonia 1870–1990*, Chicago: University of Chicago Press.

Kavakci, M. (2004), 'Headscarf Heresy', (May), *Foreign Policy*, 142, http://www.foreignpolicy.com/articles/2004/05/01/headscarf_heresy

Kelman, M. (1987), *A Guide to Critical Legal Studies, Cambridge:* Harvard University Press.

Khalid, A. (2001), 'Nationalizing the revolution in Central Asia: The transformation of Jadidism, 1917–1920', in Suny, R.G. and Martin, T. (eds), *A State of Nations: Empire and Nation-Making in the Age of Lenin and Stalin*, Oxford: Oxford University Press, pp. 145–162.

Khan, K. (1977), *Muntakhab al-Lubab*, in Syed, A.J. (ed.), *Aurangzeb in Muntakhab-al-lubab*, Bombay: Somaiya.

Khan, M. G. (2006), 'Towards a National Strategy for Muslim Youth Work', Youth and Policy, 92, pp. 7–18.

Khan, M. G. (2007), 'My First Death Committee', (30 Mar.), *The Muslim News*.

Khan, S. (2006), 'Muslim!', in Ali, N., Kalra, V.S. and Sayyid, S. (eds), *A Postcolonial People: South Asians in Britain*, London: C. Hurst & Co. pp. 182–187.

King, A. (2000), 'Football fandom and post-national identity in the New Europe', *British Journal of Sociology*, 51:3, pp. 419–442.

Kipnis, A. (2006), '*Suzhi*: A Keyword Approach', *China Quarterly*, 186, pp. 295–313.

Kirriemuir, J. (2007), 'Snapshots of Second Life use in UK HE and FE', *Eduserv Foundation*, http://en.wikipedia.org/wiki/Eduserv_Foundation [Last accessed on 4 Aug. 2008].

Kitromilides, P. (1989), '"Imagined communities" and the Origins of the National Question in the Balkans', *European History Quarterly*, 19:2, pp. 149–192.

Kitromilides, P. (1992), *Mikrasiatiki Katastrophi ke Elliniki Koinonia*, Athens.

Klyuchevsky, V. (1937), *Kurs Russkoi Istorii (A course in Russian history), vol. 5*, Moscow: Nauka.

Kouriannidis, Y. (2006), 'Karachasan Candidacy: Playing with Fire', (10 May), http://www.e-grammes.gr/print.php?id+2086 [Last accessed on 31 Jan. 2009].

Krishnaswami (n.d.), *Islam and Pseudo-Secularists*, Delhi: Shradha Prakashan.

Kristol, W. and Kagan, R. (1996), 'Toward a Neo-Reaganite Foreign Policy', *Foreign Affairs*, 75:4, pp. 18–32.

Kristol, W. and Kagan, R. (1998), 'Bombing Iraq is not Enough', (30 Jan.), *New York Times*.

Krugman, P. (2003), 'Channels of influence', (25 Mar.), *New York Times*.

Krymin, A. and Engelgardt, G. (2003), 'Islamophobia', *Otechestvennye Zapiski*, 5, http://www.strana-oz.ru/?numid=14&article=652

Kundnani, A. (2007a), *The End of Tolerance: Racism in 21ˢᵗ Century Britain*, London: Pluto Press.

Kundnani, A. (2007b), 'Integrationism: The politics of anti-Muslim racism', *Race & Class*, 48:4, pp. 24–44.

Kundnani, A. (2008), 'Islamism and the roots of liberal rage', *Race & Class*, 50:2, pp. 40–68.

Kuntsman, A. (2008a), 'Written in Blood: Contested Borders and the Politics of Passing in Israel/Palestine and in Cyberspace', *Feminist Media Studies*, 8:3, pp. 267–283.

Kuntsman, A. (2008b), 'The Soldier and the Terrorist: Sexy Nationalism, Queer Violence', *Sexualities*, 11:1–2, pp. 142–170.

Kureishi, H. (1986), *My Beautiful Laundrette*, London: Faber & Faber.

Kureishi, H. (1990), *The Buddha of Suburbia*, London: Faber & Faber.

Kureishi, H. (1992), *Outskirts and Other Plays*, London: Faber & Faber.

Kureishi, H. (1995), *The Black Album*, London: Faber & Faber.

Kureishi, H. (1997), *My Son the Fanatic*, London: Faber & Faber.

Laclau, E. and Mouffe, C. (2001), *Hegemony and Socialist Strategy*, London: Verso.

Lawrence, J. (2007), *Integrating Islam: A New Chapter in 'Church-State' Relations (Transatlantic Task Force on Immigration and Integration)*, http://www.migrationpolicy.org/pubs/LaurenceIslamicDialogue100407.pdf

Lazaridis, G. and Wickens, E. (1999), '"Us" and the "Others": Ethnic Minorities in Greece', *Annals of Tourism Research*, 26:3, pp. 632–655.

Lazzarato, M. (2006), 'The Concepts of Life and the Living in the Societies of Control', in Fugslang, M. and Sørensen, B.M. (eds) *Deleuze and the Social*, Edinburgh: Edinburgh University Press, pp. 171–190.

Lefort, C. (1986), *The Political Forms of Modern Society: Bureaucracy, Democracy, Totalitarianism*, (ed. and trans.) Thompson, J. B., Cambridge: Polity Press.

Lewis, M. E. (1999), *Writing and Authority in Early China*, Albany: State University of New York Press.

Leyens, J. et al. (1994), *Stereotypes and Social Cognition*, London: Sage.

Leyers, J. (2007), '"Ik ben een Christen: En Karel De Gucht ook" interview met Jan Leyers door Walter Pauli', (27 Oct.), *De Morgen*.

Lipman, J. N. (1997), *Familiar Strangers: A History of Muslims in Northwest China*, Seattle and London: University of Washington Press.

Loomba, A. (1998), *Colonialism/Postcolonialism*, London: Routledge.

Loomba, A. (1999), "'Delicious Traffick": Alterity and Exchange on Early Modern Stages', *Shakespeare Survey*, 52, pp. 201–214.

Loomba, A. (2000), "'Delicious Traffick": Racial and religious difference on early modern stages', in Alexander, C.M.S. and Wells, S. (eds), *Shakespeare and Race*, Cambridge: Cambridge University Press, pp. 203–221.

Loomba, A. (2002), *Shakespeare, Race and Colonialism*, Oxford: Oxford University Press.

Loomba, A. (2003), 'Remembering Said', *Comparative Studies of South Asia, Africa and the Middle East*, 23:1–2, pp. 12–14.

Loomba, A. (2005), *Colonialism/Postcolonialism*, 2nd edn., London: Routledge.

Lopez, F. B. (2009), *Islamofobia y Antisemitismo: La construcción discursiva de las Amenazas Islaámica y Judía*, PhD Thesis, Universidad Autónoma de Madrid.

Ludden, D. (ed.) (1996), *Making India Hindu: Religion, Community, and the Politics of Democracy in India*, New Delhi: Oxford University Press.

Lynch, T. J. (2008), 'Kristol Balls: Neoconservative Visions of Islam and the Middle East', *International Politics*, 45, pp. 182–211.

Lyon, S. (2005), 'In the Shadow of September 11: Multiculturalism and Identity Politics', in Abbas, T (ed.), *Muslim Britain: Communities Under Pressure*, London: Zed Books, pp. 78–91.

MacMaster, N. (2008), 'Islamophobia in France and the "Algerian Problem"', in Qureshi, E. and Sells, M. (eds), *The New Crusades: Constructing the Enemy Within*, New York: Columbia University Press, pp. 288–313.

Mahmood, S. (2006a), 'Secularism, Hermeneutics and Empire: The Politics of Islamic Reformation', *Public Culture*, 18:2, pp. 323–347.

Mahmood, S. (2006b), *Politics of Piety, The Islamic Revival and the Feminist Subject*, Princeton: Princeton University Press.

Mahmood, S. and Hirschkind, C. (2002), 'Feminism, the Taliban, and the politics of counter-insurgency', *Anthropological Quarterly*, 75:2, pp. 339–354.

Maldonado-Torres, N. (2007), 'On the Coloniality of Being: Contributions to the Development of a Concept', *Cultural Studies*, 21:2–3, pp. 240–270.

Malik, A. (2006), 'Sites—Sights of Memory and Mourning', Said Adrus' Lost Pavillion, http://www.darkmatter101.org/site/2007/07/11/sites-sights-of-memory-and-mourning-said-adrus-lost-pavilion-2006/

Malik, K. (2005), 'Are Muslims hated?', *30 Minutes*, broadcast on (8 Jan.), Channel 4, transcript available online, www.kenanmalik.com/tv/c4_islamophobia.html [Last accessed on 13 Sept. 2007].

Malik, K. (2009), *From Fatwa to Jihad: The Rushdie Affair and its Legacy*, London: Atlantic Books.

Mamdani, M. (2002), 'Good Muslim, Bad Muslim: A Political Perspective on Culture and Terrorism', *American Anthropologist*, 104:3, pp. 766–775.

Mamdani, M. (2004), *Good Muslim, Bad Muslim: America, the Cold War and the Roots of Terror*, New York: Pantheon.

Manucci, N. (1907), *Storia do Mogor; or Mogul India, 1653–1708*, Irvine, W.J., (trans.) London: John Murray, vol. ii, p. 8.

Marable, M. and Aidi, H.D. (2009), *Black Routes to Islam*, New York: Palgrave Macmillan.

Marcos, S. (2006), *Taken from the Lips: Gender and Eros in Mesoamerican Religions*, Leiden: Brill.

Marcus, S. L, (2007), *Music in Egypt: Experiencing music, expressing culture*, Oxford: Oxford University Press.

Martin, T. (2001), *Affirmative Action Empire: Nations and Nationalism in the Soviet Union, 1923–1939*, Ithaca: Cornell University Press.

Massad, J. (2007), *Desiring Arabs*, Chicago: University of Chicago Press.

Matar, N. (1998), *Islam in Britain 1558–1685*, Cambridge: Cambridge University Press.

Matar, N. (1999), *Turks, Moors & Englishmen in the Age of Discovery*, New York: Columbia University Press.

Maussen, M. (2006), 'Anti-Muslim sentiments and mobilization in the Netherlands: Discourse, policies and violence', in Cesari, J. (ed.), *Securitisation and Religious Divides in Europe: Muslims in Europe After 9/11: Why the term Islamophobia is more a predicament than an explanation*, Brussels: European Commission, pp. 100–142, http://www.libertysecurity.org/IMG/pdf_Challenge_Project_report.pdf

Mayer, E. (1999), *Islam and Human Rights*, New York: Westview Press.

Mazower, M. (1998), *Dark Continent: Europe's Twentieth Century*, London: Allen Lane.

McCargo, D. (2008), *Tearing Apart the Land: Islam and Legitimacy in Southern Thailand*, Ithaca: Cornell University Press.

McCarney, J. (2003), 'Hegel's Racism? A response to Bernasconi', *Radical Philosophy*, 119, pp. 32–35.

McEwan, I. (2007), 'Martin Amis is not a racist', (21 Nov.), *The Guardian*.

Meer, N. (2006), 'Get off your knees!' Print media public intellectuals and Muslims in Britain', *Journalism Studies*, 7:1, pp. 35–59.

Meer, N. (2007), 'Less equal than others', *Index on Censorship*, 36:2, pp. 114–118.

Meer, N. (2008), 'The politics of voluntary and involuntary identities: Are Muslims in Britain an ethnic, racial or religious minority?', *Patterns of Prejudice*, 41:5, pp. 61–81.

Meer, N. and Modood, T. (2009), 'Refutations of racism in the Muslim question', *Patterns of Prejudice*, 43:3–4, pp. 332–351.

Meer, N. and Noorani, T. (2008), 'A sociological comparison of anti-Semitism and anti-Muslim sentiment in Britain', *The Sociological Review*, 56:2, pp. 195–219.

Meeropol, R. (ed.) (2005), *America's Disappeared: Secret Imprisonment, Detainees, and the 'War on Terror'*, London: Seven Stories Press.

Menski, W. F. (2006), *Comparative Law in a Global Context: The legal systems of Asia and Africa*, 2nd edn., Cambridge: Cambridge University Press.

Michot, Y. (1997), 'Muslims in Belgium', *Muslim Politics Report: Council on Foreign Relations*, 15.

Mignolo, W. (2007), 'Delinking: The rhetoric of modernity, the logic of coloniality and the grammar of decoloniality', *Cultural Studies*, 21:2–3, pp. 449–514.

Mignolo, W. (2002), 'The Enduring Enchantment: (or the Epistemic Privilege of Modernity and Where to Go from Here)', *The South Atlantic Quarterly*, 101:4, pp. 927–954.

Mignolo, W. (2006), 'Islamophobia/Hispanophobia': The (Re)Configuration of the Racial/Imperial Colonial Matrix', *Human Architecture: Journal of the Sociology of Self-Knowledge*, 5:1, pp. 13–26.

Mignolo, W. and Tlostanova, M. (2006), 'Theorizing from the Borders: Shifting to Geo- and Body-Politics of Knowledge', *European Journal of Social Theory*, 9:1, pp. 205–221.

Miles, R. (1982), *Racism and Migrant Labour*, London: Kegan Paul.

Miles, R. (1984), 'The riots of 1958: Notes on the ideological construction of "race relations" as a political issue in Britain', *Immigrants & Minorities*, 3:3, pp. 252–275.

Miles, R. (1986), 'Labour Migration, Capital Accumulation in Western Europe Since 1945', *Capital and Class*, 28:1, pp. 49–86.

Miles, R. (1988), 'Racism, Marxism and British Politics', *Economy and Society*, 17:3, pp. 428–460.

Miles, R. (1989), *Racism*, London: Routledge.

Miles, R. (1993), *Racism After 'Race Relations'*, London: Routledge.

Miles, R. and Brown, M. (2003), *Racism*, London: Routledge.

Miller, P. and Rose, N. (2008), *Governing the Present*, Cambridge: Polity.

Mishra, P. (2007), 'A paranoid, abhorrent obsession: Talented writers nibbling on clichés is a depressing spectacle, but a public conversation about Islam should not be avoided', (8 Dec.), *The Guardian*.

Misra, A. (2004), *Identity and Religion: Foundations of anti-Islamism in India*, New Delhi: Sage.

Mobasher, N. (2005), 'The Production of the Muslim Race', *Hot Coals*, http://hot-coals.org/?p=30

Modood, T. (1996), 'If Races Do Not Exist Then What Does? Racial Categorisation and Ethnic Realities', in Barot, R. (ed.) *The Racism Problematic: Contemporary Sociological Debates on Race and Ethnicity*, New York: Edwin Mellen Press, pp. 89–105.

Modood, T. (1997), '"Difference", Cultural Racism and Anti-Racism', in Werbner, P. and Modood, T. (eds) *Debating Cultural Hybridity: Multi–Cultural Identities and the Politics of Anti-Racism*, London: Zed Books, pp. 154–172.

Modood, T. (2005), *Multicultural Politics: Racism, Ethnicity and Muslims in Britain*, Edinburgh: Edinburgh University Press.

Modood, T. (2006), 'Obstacles to Multicultural Integration', *International Migration*, 44:5, pp. 51–62.

Modood, T. (2008a), 'Is multiculturalism dead?', *Public Policy Research*, pp. 84–88.

Modood, T. (2008b), 'Multicultural Citizenship and the anti-Sharia storm', http://www.opendemocracy.net/article/faith_ideas/europe_islam/anti_sharia_storm.

Mohanty, C. (1991), 'Under Western Eyes: Feminist scholarship and colonial discourse' in Mohanty, C.T., Russo, A. and Torres, L. (eds), *Third World Women and the Politics of Feminism*, Indianapolis: Indiana University Press, pp. 61–88.

Mojab, S. (2006), 'In the Quagmire's of Ethnicity: A Marxist critique of liberal "exit" strategies', *Journal of Ethnicities*, 5:3, pp. 341–361.

Moore, S. F. (1978), *Law as process: An anthropological approach*, London: Routledge & Kegan Paul.

Moors, A. (2009), 'The Dutch and the face-veil: A politics of discomfort', *Social Anthropology*, 17:4, pp. 393–408.

Morgan, K. (1991), 'Women and the Knife: Cosmetic Surgery and the Colonization of Women's Bodies', *Hypatia*, 6:3, pp. 25–53.

Morlino, R. (2004), '"Our Enemies Among US!": The Portrayal of Arab and Muslim Americans in Post-9/11 American Media', in Hagopian, E.C. (ed.), *Civil Rights in Peril: The Targeting of Arabs and Muslims*, London: Pluto Press, pp. 71–103.

Morris, C. (2007), 'The absurd world of Martin Amis', (25 Nov.), *The Observer*.

Murphy, R. (2004), 'Turning Chinese Peasants into Modern Citizens: "Population Quality", Demographic Transition, and Primary Schools', *China Quarterly*, 177, pp. 1–20.

Murray, D. (2006), 'What are we to do about Islam?', speech to the Pim Fortuyn Memorial Conference on Europe and Islam, (Feb.), *The Hague*.

Murray, N. (2004), 'Profiled: Arabs, Muslims and the Post-9/11 Hunt for the 'Enemy Within', in Hagopian, E.C. (ed.), *Civil Rights in Peril: The Targeting of Arabs and Muslims*, London: Pluto Press, pp. 27–68.

Naqshbandi, M. (2006), *Problems and Practical Solutions to Tackle Extremism; and Muslim Youth and Community Issues*, Shrivenham Papers 1, Defence Academy Of The United Kingdom.

Nasser, N. (2005), 'Expressions of Muslim Identity in Architecture and Urbanism in Birmingham, UK', *Islam and Christian-Muslim Relations*, 16:1, pp. 61–78.

National Bureau of Statistics and State Ethnic Affairs Commission (2003), *Tabulation on Nationalities of 2000 Population Census of China*, Beijing: The Ethnic Publishing House.

Nawaz, A. (2004), '"Islam for me was more punk than punk": Aki Nawa interviewed', *Open Democracy*, http://www.opendemocracy.net/globalization-world/article_2138.jsp

Negri, A. (2003), *Reflections on Empire*, Cambridge: Polity.

Norrie, A. (2005), *Law and the Beautiful Soul*, London: Glasshouse Press.

Northrop, D. (2004), *Veiled Empire: Gender and Power in Stalinist Central Asia*, Ithaca: Cornell University Press.

Okin, S. M. (1999), 'Is Multiculturalism Bad for Women?', *Boston Review*, 22, http://www.bostonreview.net/BR22.5/okin.html

Open Democracy (2008), http://www.opendemocracy.net/

[Örnek, Özden], [excerpts from Diary], *Nokta: Weekly Political News Magazine*, 1:22 (29 May–4 Apr. 2007).

Otterbeck, J. and Bevelander, P. (2006), [*Islamofobi*] *Islamophobia: English Summary*, Stockholm: Living History Forum.

Ouseley, H. (2001), *Community Pride Not Prejudice—Making Diversity Work For Bradford*, Bradford: Bradford Vision.

Ownby, D. (2008), *Falun Gong and the Future of China*, Oxford: Oxford University Press.

Ozanne, W. I. (2006), 'Review of Confronting Islamophobia in educational practice', in van Driel, B. (ed.), 2004 *Comparative Education*, 42:2, pp. 283–297.

Padamsee, A., (2005), *Representations of Indian Muslims in British Colonial Discourse*, Basingstoke: Palgrave-Macmillan.

Parekh, B. (2006), 'Europe, liberalism and the "Muslim question"' in Modood, T., Triandafyllidou, A. and Zapata-Barrero, R. (eds), *Multiculturalism, Muslims and Citizenship: A European Approach*, London: Routledge, pp. 179–203.

Parekh, B. (2008), *A New Politics of Identity: Political Principles for an Interdependent World*, Basingstoke: Palgrave MacMillan.

Pasto, J. (1998), '"Islam's Strange Secret Sharer": Orientalism, Judaism, and the Jewish Question', *Comparative Studies in Society and History*, 40:3, pp. 437–474.

Peramos Homepage, The (1998), http://members.aol.com/peramos [Last accessed on 12 Dec. 2005].

Petzen, J. (2005), 'Wer liegt oben? Türkische und deutsche Maskulinitäten in der schwulen Szene' in Ifade (ed.), *Insider-Outsider: Bilder, ethnisierte Räume und Partizipation im Migrationsprozess*.

Pew Global Attitudes Project (2008), 'The Great Divide: How Westerners and Muslims View Each Other', http://pewglobal.org/reports/display.php?PageID=833 [Last accessed 9 Mar. 2009].

Phillips, A. and Dustin, M. (2004), 'UK initiatives on forced marriage: Regulation, dialogue and exit', *Political Studies*, 52:3, pp. 531–551.

Phillips, M. (2006), *Londonistan: How Britain Is Creating A Terror State Within*, London: Gibson Square.

Phillipse, H. (2004), 'Stop the tribalisation of the Netherlands', (19 May), *NRC Handelsblad*.

Pierce, G. (2008), 'Was it like this for the Irish?', (10 Apr.), *London Review of Books*.

Pierce, G. (2009), 'Make sure you say that you were treated properly', (14 May), *London Review of Books*.

Pipes, D. (2002a), 'Who is the enemy?', (Jan.), *Commentary*, vol. 13, no. 1, pp. 21–28.

Pipes, D. (2002b), 'Jihad and the Professors', (Nov.), *Commentary*, vol. 114, no. 4, pp. 17–22.

Pipes, D. (2005a), 'Good News Could End in Mideast', (8 Mar.), *New York Sun*.

Pipes, D. (2005b), 'Methods Matter Less Than Goals', (22 Mar.), *New York Sun*.

Pipes, D. (2006), 'How to end terrorism with moderate Islam', (5 Dec.), *New York Sun*.

Podhoretz, N. (2002), 'How to Win World War IV', (Feb.), *Commentary*, vol. 113, no. 2, pp. 19–30.

Podhoretz, N. (2004), 'World War IV: How it Started, What it Means and Why We Have to Win', (Sept.), *Commentary*, vol. 118, no. 2, pp. 17–55.

Poillon, F. (1997), *Les deux vies d'Étienne Dinet, peintre en Islam: L'Algérie et l'heritage colonial*, Paris: Balland.

Polanyi, K. (1944), *The Great Transformation*, Boston: Beacon Press.

Pollis, A. (1992), 'Greek National Identity: Religious Minorities, Rights, and European Norms', *Journal of Modern Greek Studies*, 10:2, pp. 171–196.

Pollitt, K. (2006), 'Wrong War, Wrong Word', (11 Sept.), *The Nation*.

Poole, E. (2002), *Reporting Islam*, London: I B Tauris.

Poynting, S. and Mason, V. (2007), 'The resistible rise of Islamophobia: Anti-Muslim racism in the UK and Australia before 11 September 2001', *Journal of Sociology*, 43:1, pp. 61–86.

Prakash, G. (1995), 'Orientalism Now', *History and Theory*, 34:3, pp. 199–212.

Pravoslavie i islam (Orthodox Christianity and Islam), http://www.pravoslavie-islam. ru/

Prins, B. (2002), 'The Nerve to Break Taboos: New Realism in the Dutch Discourse on Multiculturalism', *Journal of International Migration and Integration*, 3:3–4, pp. 363–379.

Prins, B. (2004 [2000]), *Voorbij de onschuld. Het debat over integratie in Nederland*, Amsterdam: Van Gennep.

Pryce-Jones, D. (2004), 'Islamization of Europe', *Commentary*, (Dec.), vol. 118, no. 5, pp. 29–33.

Puar, J. (2005), 'Queer Times, Queer Assemblages', *Social Text*, 23:3–4, pp. 84–85.

Puar, J. (2007), *Terrorist Assemblages: Homonationalism in Queer Times*, Durham: Duke University Press.

Purkayastha, B. (2009a), 'Conclusion: Human Rights, Religions, Gender' in Narayan, A. and Purkayastha, B. (eds), *Living Our Religions, Hindu and Muslim South Asian American Women Narrate Their Experiences*, Kumarian Press, pp. 285–295.

Purkayastha, B. (2009b), 'Transgressing the Sacred-Secular, Public-Private Debate' in Narayan, A. and Purkayastha, B. (eds), *Living Our Religions, Hindu and Muslim South Asian American Women Narrate Their Experiences*, Kumarian Press, pp. 23–46.

Purwar, N. and Rughuram, P. (2003), *South Asian Women in the diaspora*, Oxford: Berg, pp. 160–164.

Quayson, A. (2005), 'Translations and transnationals: Pre- and Postcolonial', in *Postcolonial Approaches to the European Middle Ages*, Jahanara, A. and Williams, D. (eds), Cambridge: Cambridge University Press, pp. 253–268.

Quijano, A. (2000), 'Coloniality of Power, Eurocentrism, and Latin America', *Nepantla*, 1:3, pp. 533–580.

Ramadan, T. (2002), 'Europeanization of Islam or Islamization of Europe?', in Hunter, S. (ed.), *Islam, Europe's Second Religion: The New Social, Cultural and Political landscape*, Westport: Praeger, pp. 207–218.

Ramamurthy, A. (2006), 'The Politics of Britain's Asian Youth Movements', *Race & Class*, 48:2, pp. 38–60.

Rana, J. (2007), 'The Story of Islamophobia', *Souls: A Critical Journal of Black Politics, Culture, and Society*, 9:2, pp. 148–162.

Ranasinha, R. (2002), *Hanif Kureishi*, Devon: Northcote House Publishers.

Rath, J. (1991), *Minorisering: De sociale constructie van minderheden*, Amsterdam: Sua.

Rattansi, A. (2005), 'The Uses of Racialisation: The Time-spaces and Subject-objects of the Raced Body', in Murji, K. and Solomos, J. (eds), *Racialization: Studies in Theory and Practice*, Oxford: Oxford University Press, pp. 271–301.

Rattansi, A. (2007), *Racism: A Very Short Introduction*, Oxford: Oxford University Press.

Razack, S. (2008), *Casting Out: The Eviction of Muslims from Western Law & Politics*, Toronto: Toronto University Press.

Reisigl, M. and Wodak, R. (2001), *Discourse and Discrimination: Rhetorics of Racism and Anti-Semitism*, London: Routledge.

Report of the All Party Parliamentary Inquiry into Anti-Semitism (2006), London: HMSO.

Richardson, J. E. (2004), *(Mis)representing Islam: The racism and rhetoric of British broadsheet newspapers*, Amsterdam: John Benjamin.

Richardson, J.E. (2005), *New Approaches to Islamophobia*, Leicester: Markfield.

Richardson, J.E. (2006), 'On delineating "reasonable" and "unreasonable" criticisms of Muslims', *Fifth Estate Online—International Journal of Radical Mass Media Criticism*, http://www.fifth-estateonline.co.uk/criticsm/ondelineatingreasonable and-unreasonable.html

Robson, G. (2004), *'No One Likes Us, We Don't Care': The Myth and Reality of Millwall Fandom*, Oxford: Berg.

Roded, R. (2002), 'Modern Gendered Illustrations of the Life of the Prophet of Allah—Etiénne Dinet and Sliman Ben Ibrahim', *Arabica*, 49:3, pp. 325–359.

Rorlich, A. (2004), 'The challenge of Belonging: The Muslims of the late imperial Russia and the contested Terrain of Identity and Gender', in Ro'I, Y. (ed.) *Democracy and pluralism in Muslim Eurasia*, London: Frank Cass, pp. 39–52.

BIBLIOGRAPHY

Rose, N. (1999), *Powers of Freedom*, Cambridge: Cambridge University Press.

Rotthier, R. and Filip Rogiers, P. (2001), 'Hoe de democraten het Vlaams Blok misbruikten', (29 Sept.), *De Morgen*.

Roudometof, V. (1999), "Nationalism, Globalization, Eastern Orthodoxy: 'Unthinking' the 'Clash of Civilizations' in Eastern Europe", *European Journal of Social Theory*, 2:2, pp. 233–247.

Runnymede Trust (1994), *A Very Light Sleeper: The persistence and dangers of anti-Semitism*.

Runnymede Trust (1997a), *Islamophobia: A challenge for us all*, Report of the Runnymede Trust Commission on British Muslims and Islamophobia, London.

Runnymede Trust (1997b), *Islamophobia: Its Features and Dangers*, London: The Runnymede Trust.

Rushdie, S. (1983), *Shame*, London: Jonathan Cape.

Rydgren J. (2003), 'Meso-level Reasons for Racism and Xenophobia: Some Converging and Diverging Effects of Radical Right Populism in France and Sweden', *European Journal of Social Theory*, 6:1, pp. 45–68.

Rydgren, J. (2004), *The Populist Challenge: Political Protest and Ethno-Nationalist Mobilization in France*, Oxford: Berghahn Books.

Rymaszewski, M.; Au, W. J.; Wallace, M.; Winters, C.; Ondrejka, C. and Batstone-Cunningham, B. (2007), *Second Life: The Official Guide*, New Jersey: John Wiley and Sons.

Sahni, K. (1997), *Crucifying the Orient*, Bangkok: White Orchid Press.

Said, E. (1978), *Orientalism*, London: Penguin.

Said, E. (1984), 'Permission to Narrate', *Journal of Palestine Studies*, 13:3, pp. 27–48.

Said, E. (1985a), 'Orientalism Reconsidered', *Cultural Critique*, 1, pp. 89–107.

Said, E. (1985b), 'Orientalism Reconsidered', *Race & Class*, 27:2, pp. 1–15.

Said, E. (1985c), 'Orientalism Reconsidered', in Barker, F. et al. (eds), *Europe and Its Others*, Colchester: University of Essex, pp. 14–27.

Said, E. (1994), 'Travelling Theory Reconsidered', in Polhemus, R. M. and Henkle, R. B. (eds), *Critical Reconstructions: The Relationship of Fiction and Life*, Stanford: Stanford University Press, pp. 251–265.

Said, E. (1995), *Orientalism: Western Conceptions of the Orient*, London: Penguin Books.

Said, E. (1997), *Covering Islam: How the Media and the Experts determine how we see the Rest of the World*, London: Vintage.

Said, E. (1998), 'In Conversation with Neeladri Bhattacharya, Suvir Kaul, and Ania Loomba', [New Delhi, 1997], *Interventions*, 1:1, pp. 81–96.

Said, E. (2003 [1978]), *Orientalism*, London: Penguin.

Salaita, S. G. (2006), 'Beyond Orientalism and Islamophobia: 9/11, Anti-Arab Racism, and the Mythos of National Pride', *CR: The New Centennial Review*, 6:2, pp. 245–266.

Samad, Y. and Eade, J. (2002), *Community perceptions of forced marriage*, London: Foreign and Commonwealth Office.

Sanctorum, J. (2008), *De Islam in Europa: Dialoog of clash?*, Leuven: Van Halewyck.

Sandler, B. (1986), 'The Campus Climate Revisited: Chilly for Women Faculty, Administrators, and Graduate Students', Washington, D.C.: Association of American Colleges.

Sardar, Z. (2002), 'The excluded minority: British Muslim identity after 11 September', in Griffith, P. and Leonard, M. (eds), *Reclaiming Britishness*, London: Foreign Policy Centre, pp. 51–55.

Sarkar, T., (2002), 'Semiotics of Terror: Muslim Children and Women in Hindu Rashtra', (13 Jul.), *Economic and Political Weekly*, vol. 28.

Sayyid, S. (1997), *A Fundamental Fear: Eurocentrism and the Emergence of Islamism*, London: Zed Books.

Sayyid, S. (2000), 'Beyond Westphalia: Nations and Diasporas—The Case of the Muslim Umma', in Hesse, B. (ed.), *Un/settled Multiculturalisms: Diasporas, Entanglements, Transruptions*, London: Zed Books, pp. 33–50.

Sayyid, S. (2003), *A Fundamental Fear: Eurocentrism and the emergence of Islamism*, 2nd edn., London: Zed Books.

Sayyid, S. (2004), 'Slippery People: The Immigrant Imaginary and the Grammar of Colour', in Law, I., Phillips, D. and Turney, L. (eds.), *Institutional Racism in Higher Education*, London: Trentham Books, pp. 149–160.

Sayyid, S. (2006a), 'Islam and Knowledge', *Theory, Culture & Society*, 23:2–3, pp. 177–179.

Sayyid, S. (2006b), 'BrAsians: Postcolonial People, Ironic Citizens', in Ali, N., Kalra, V.S. and Sayyid, S. (eds), *A Postcolonial People: South Asians in Britain*, London: C. Hurst & Co., pp. 1–10.

Sayyid, S. (2008), 'Racism and Islamophobia', *Dark Matter*, http://www.darkmatter101.org/site/2008/03/26/racism-and-islamophobia/

Sayyid, S. and Tyrer, D. (2002), 'Ancestor worship and the irony of the 'Islamic' Republic of Pakistan', *Contemporary South Asia*, 11:1, pp. 57–75.

Scheffer, P. (2000a), 'The multicultural drama', (29 Jan.), *NRC Handelsblad*.

Scheffer, P. (2000b), 'Het Multiculturele Drama', (29 Jan.), *NRC-Handelsblad*.

Scheffer, P. (2004), 'The discomfort in Islam', (17 Sept.), *Trouw*.

Scheffer, P. (2007), *Het Land van Aankomst*, Amsterdam: De Bezige Bij.

Schirokauer, C. (1981), 'Introduction', in I. Miyazaki *China's Examination Hell: The Civil Service Examinations of Imperial China*, (trans.) C. Schirokauer, New Haven: Yale University Press, pp. 7–10.

Schmitt, C. (2007), *The Concept of the Political*, London: The University of Chicago Press.

Schwartz, S. (2002), 'Democracy and Islam After September 11', (13 Dec.), *Weekly Standard*.

BIBLIOGRAPHY

Schwartz, S. (2004), 'Is Cat Stevens a Terrorist', (22 Sept.), *Weekly Standard.*

Schwartz, S. (2005), 'The 'Islamophobes' That Aren't', (28 Apr.), *FrontPage Magazine*, www.frontpagemag.com/Articles/Read.aspx?GUID=448A41BB-FCAA-4A8F-A288-538DD09269EA

Schwartz, S. (2006a), 'What Is "Islamofascism"?', (17 Aug.), *Weekly Standard,*

Schwartz, S. (2006b), 'Radical Roadshow', (31 Jan.), *Weekly Standard.*

Scott, J. C. (1998), *Seeing Like a State*, New Haven: Yale University Press.

Scott, J. W. (2007), *The Politics of the Veil*, Princeton: Princeton University Press.

Scruton. R. (2006), 'Islamofascism: Beware of a Religion Without Irony', (20 Aug.), *Wall Street Journal.*

Seddon, M. S. (2004), *British Muslims Between Assimilation and Segregation: Historical, Social and Legal Realities*, Markfield: The Islamic Foundation.

Select Committee on Religious Offences in England and Wales, vol. II: *Oral Evidence* (Session 2002–2003), London: Parliamentary Papers—House of Lords.

Seremetakis, N. (1996), 'In Search for Barbarians: Borders in Pain', *American Anthropologist*, 98:3, pp. 489–491.

Shachar, A. (2001), *Multicultural Jurisdictions, Cultural Differences and Women's Rights*, Cambridge: Cambridge University Press.

Shah, P. (2005), *Legal Pluralism in Conflict: Coping with Cultural Diversity in Law*, London: Glass House Press.

Shaheen, J.G. (2001), *Reel Bad Arabs: How Hollywood Vilifies a People*, Northampton, MA: Interlink.

Shaikh, N. (2007), *The Present as History: Critical Perspectives on Global Power*, New York: Columbia University Press.

Shaw, M. (2000), *Theory of the Global State: Globality as an Unfinished Revolution*, Cambridge: Cambridge University Press.

Sheridan, L. (2006), 'Islamophobia pre and post September 11th 2001', *Journal of Interpersonal Violence*, 21:3, pp. 317–336.

Sheth, F. A. (2009), *Towards a Political Philosophy of Race*, Albany: State University of New York Press.

Silverstein, P. A. (2008), 'The context of anti-Semitism and Islamophobia in France', *Patterns of Prejudice*, 42:1, pp. 1–26.

Singhal, A. (2005), Public Speech during VHP Dharma Sansad, (13–14 Dec.), Hardwar, India.

Singhal, A. (n.d.), *Secularwadiyon dwara hindu samaj par uttpan chaturdik hamla* [Total attack on Hindu society due to Secularists], New Delhi: VHP.

Sirisakdamkoeng, P. (2009), 'Perspectives of Thailand's Southernmost Muslim People in Virtual Communities', Five Years of the Southern Fire Conference, Deep South Watch, Hat Yai.

Sivanandan, A. (2006), 'Race, terror and civil society', *Race & Class*, 47:3, pp. 1–8.

Sivanandan, A. et al. (2007), 'Race, Liberty and the War on Terror', *Race & Class*, 48:4, pp. 45–96.

Skopetea, E. (1999), *Fallmerayer*, Athens: Themelio.

Slokum, J. (2005), 'Kto I kogda byli inorodtsami? (Who and when were the born others?)', in Vert, P. Kabytov, P. and Miller, A. (eds), *Rossiiskaja Imperija v Zarubezhnoi Instoriografii*, Moscow: Novoye Izdatelstvo, pp. 502–531.

Smith, A. D. (1986), *The Ethnic Origins of Nations*, Oxford: Blackwell.

Smith, M. L. (1973), *Ionian Vision: Greece in Asia Minor 1919–1922*, New York: St Martin's Press.

Sokolov, A. (2002), 'Polozheniye Chechentsev (The Conditions of Chechenians)', *Natsionalism, Ksenofobia i Neterpimost v Sovremennoy Rossii (Nationalism, Xenophobia and Intolerance in Modern Russia)*, Moscow: Moscow Helsinki Group, pp. 351–394.

Solomos, J. (1991), 'Political language and racial discourse', *European Journal of Intercultural Studies*, 2:1, pp. 21–34.

Songben, Z. and Matsumoto, M. (2003), *A Study of Ethnic Policies of China: Nationalism from the End of Qing Dynasty to 1945*, Zhonghui, Z. (trans.), Beijing: The Ethnic Publishing House.

Spalek, B. and Imtoual, A. (2007), 'Muslim Communties and Counter-Terror Responses: 'Hard' Approaches to Community Engagement in the UK and Australia', *Journal of Muslim Minority Affairs*, 27: 2, pp. 185–202.

Special Issue of Nea Michaniona Press (1993), *70 Years Since the Foundation of Michaniona, 1923–1993*.

Spivak, G. (1988), 'Can the subaltern speak?' in Nelson, N. and Grossberg, L. (eds) *Marxism and the Interpretation of Culture*, Chicago: Illinois University Press , pp. 271–313.

Spohn, W. (2005), 'National Identities and Collective Memory in an Enlarged Europe', in Eder, K. and Spohn, W. (eds), Collective Memory and European Identity, Aldershot: Ashgate, pp. 1–16.

Spritzer, D. A. (2009), 'Fear and loathing in Europe: Islamophobia and the challenge of integration', *JTA News*, http://jta.org/news/article/2009/02/05/1002796/fear-and-loathing-in-europe-islamophobia-and-the-challenge-of-integration (Last accessed 9 Mar. 2009).

St Louis, B. (2002), 'Post-race/post politics? Activist-intellectualism and the reification of race', *Ethnic and Racial Studies*, 25:4, pp. 652–675.

Steans, J. (2008), 'Telling Stories about Women and Gender in the War on Terror', *Global Society*, 22:1, pp. 85–202.

Stewart, C. (1991), *Demons and the Devil*, Princeton: Princeton University Press.

Sunder, M. (2005), 'Enlightened Constitutionalism', *Connecticut Law Review*, vol. 37.

Sutton, D. (1998), *Memories Cast in Stone: The Relevance of the Past in Everyday Life*, Oxford, New York: Berg.

Swarup, R. (n.d.), *Understanding Islam through Hadis: Religious Faith or Fanaticism?*, New York: Exposition Press, http://bharatvani.org/books/uith [Last accessed on 3 Jul. 2009].

Syal, M. (1992), *Bhaji on the Beach*, (dir.), Gurindher Chada.

Syal, M. (2000), *Life Isn't All Ha Ha Hee Hee*, London: Transworld.

Tayob, A. I. (2007), 'Religion in Modern Islamic Thought and Practice', in Fitzgerald, T. (ed.), *Religion and the Secular: Historical and Colonial Formations*, Equinox Publishing, pp. 177–192.

Ternisien, X., (2004), 'En France, le terme "Islamophobie" suscite un débat', (15 Feb.), *Le Monde*.

Terranova, T. (2007), 'Futurepublic: On Information Warfare, Bio-racism and Hegemony as Noopolitics, *Theory, Culture and Society*, 24:3, pp. 125–145.

Thoburn, N. (2007), 'Patterns of Production: Cultural Studies after Hegemony', *Theory, Culture & Society*, 24:3, pp. 79–94.

Thomson, I. (2005), *Heidegger and Ontotheology: Technology and the politics of education*, Cambridge: Cambidge University Press.

Tibi, B. (2007), 'The Totalitarianism of Jihadist Islam and its Challenge to Europe and Islam', *Totalitarian Movements and Political Religions*, 8:1, pp. 35–54.

Tlostanova, M. (2003), *A Janus-Faced Empire: Notes on the Russian Empire in Modernity Written from the Border*, Moscow: Blok.

Tlostanova, M. (2005), 'Seduced by Modernity: Why Turkey can be/become Europe and Russia can not?' in Mendes, C. (ed.), *Islam, Latinite, Transmodernite*, 11ᵉᵐᵉ Colloque International Ancara—Istanbul, (12–16 Avril), Rio de Janeiro: Academie de la Latinite, pp. 305–335.

Tlostanova, M. (2006a), 'Imperial discourse and post-utopian peripheries: suspended epistemologies in Soviet non-European (ex) colonies', *Desarollo e Interculturalidad, Imaginario y Diferencia: La Nacion en el Mundo Andino, 14ᵗʰ Conferencia Internacional de Academia de la Latinidad*, Textos de referencia, Rio de Janeiro: Academie de la Latinite, pp. 296–331.

Tlostanova, M. (2006b), 'Why Cut the Feet in Order to Fit the Western Shoes? Caucasus and Central Asia and the Modern Colonial Gender System' Central Asian Gender Net', www.genderstudies.info [Last accessed on 27 Sept. 2006].

Tlostanova, M. (2008), 'The Janus-faced empire distorting orientalist discourses: Gender, race, and religion in the Russian/(post)Soviet constructions of the Orient', Worlds and Knowledges Otherwise, a Web Dossier, http://www.jhfc.duke.edu/wko/dossiers/1.3/documents/TlostanovaWKO2.2_000.pdf

Todorova, M. (1997), *Imagining the Balkans*, New York: Oxford University Press.

Tonkin, E. (1992), *Narrating Our Pasts: The Social Construction of Oral History*, Cambridge: Cambridge University Press.

Townsend, J. (1992), 'Chinese Nationalism', *The Australian Journal of Chinese Affairs*, 27, pp. 97–130.

Toynbee, P. (2001), 'Last Chance to Speak Out', (5 Oct.), *The Guardian*.

Toynbee, P., (2005), 'My right to offend a fool', (10 Jun.), *The Guardian*.

Turner, B. S. (1994), *Orientalism, Postmodernism and Globalism*, London: Routledge.

Tyrer, D. (forthcoming), '"Fact" as MacGuffin: Islamophobia, "Race" and Muslim Identities', *Ethnic and Racial Studies*.

Tzanelli, R. (2002), 'Haunted by the "Enemy" Within: Brigandage, Vlachian/Albanian Greekness, Turkish "Contamination," and Narratives of Greek Nationhood in the Dilessi/Marathon Affair (1870)', *The Journal of Modern Greek Studies*, 20:1, pp. 47–74.

Tzanelli, R. (2004), 'Giving Gifts (and then Taking Them Back): Identity, Reciprocity and Symbolic Power in the Context of Athens 2004', *The Journal of Cultural Research*, 8:4, pp. 425–446.

Tzanelli, R. (2006), 'Not My Flag! Citizenship and Nationhood in the Margins of Europe (Greece, October 2000/2003)', *Ethnic & Racial Studies*, 29:1, pp. 27–49.

Tzanelli, R. (2007), 'The Politics of "Forgetting" as Poetics of Belonging: Between Greek Self-Narration and Reappraisal (Michaniona 2000/3)', *Nations and Nationalism*, 13:4, pp. 675–694.

Tzanelli, R. (2008a), *Nation-Building and Identity in Europe*, Basingstoke: Macmillan.

Tzanelli, R. (2008b) 'The Nation has Two Voices', *European Journal of Cultural Studies*, 11:4, pp. 489–508.

Tzanelli, R. (2009), *The 'Greece' of Britain and the 'Britain' of Greece Performance, Stereotypes, Expectations and Intermediaries in 'Neohellenic' and Victorian Narratives (1864–1881)*, Saarbrücken: Verlag Dr Müller, part I.

Ulf, H. (1993) 'National Identity and the Mentalities of War in Three EC Countries', *Journal of Peace Research*, 30, pp. 281–300.

Urry, J. (1990), *The Tourist Gaze*, London and New Delhi: Sage.

van Amerongen, A. (2008), *Brussel: Eurabia*, Amsterdam: Atlas.

van den Broek, B. (2000), 'Het kaartenhuis van de multiculturele samenleving', (22 Jul.), *De Morgen*.

Vertovec, S. (2002), 'Islamophobia and Muslim Recognition in Britain', in Haddad, Y. Y. (ed.), *Muslims in the West: From Sojourners to Citizens*, Oxford: Oxford University Press, pp. 19–35.

Waggoner, M. (2005), 'Irony, Embodiment and the "Critical Attitude": Engaging Saba Mahmood's Critique of Secular Morality', *Culture and Religion*, 6:2, pp. 237–261.

Weitz, E. D. (2002), 'Racial Politics without the Concept of Race: Re-evaluating Soviet Ethnic and National Purges', *Slavic Review*, 61:1, pp. 1–29.

Weldon, F. (1989), *Sacred Cows*, London: Chatto & Windus.

Weller, P. (2009), *A Mirror for Our Times: The Rushdie Affair and the Future of Multiculturalism*, London: Continuum.

Wendell, S. (1990), 'Oppression and victimization; choice and responsibility', *Hypatia*, 5:3, pp. 120–141.

Werbner, P. (2005), 'Islamophobia: Incitement to religious hatred—legislating for a new fear?', *Anthropology Today*, 21:1, pp. 5–9.

Wetherell, M. and Potter, J. (1992), *Mapping the Language of Racism: Discourse and the Legitimation of Exploitation*, New York: Columbia University Press.

Wilby, P. (2007), 'On the press: Why we should all debate racism', (22 Oct.), *The Guardian*.

Wilfred, S. (2005), 'National Identities and Collective Memory in an Enlarged Europe', in Eder, K. and Spohn, W. (eds), *Collective Memory and European Identity*, Aldershot: Ashgate, pp. 1–14.

Williams, J., Dunning, E. and Murphy, P. (1992 [1984]), *Hooligans Abroad: The Control of English Fans in Continental Europe*, London: Routledge.

Williams, M. C. (2005), 'What is the National Interest: The neoconservative Challenge in IR Theory', *European Journal of International Relations*, 11:3, pp. 307–337.

Wilson, A. (2006), *Dreams, questions, struggles: South Asian women in Britain*, London: Pluto Press.

Winter, T. (2003), 'Muslim Loyalty and Belonging: Some Reflections on the Psychosocial Background', in Seddon, M.S., Hussain, D. and Malik, N. (eds.), *British Muslims: Loyalty and Belonging*, Leicester: The Islamic Foundation and the Citizen Organising Foundation, pp. 3–22.

Wolf, N. (1991), *The Beauty myth: How images of beauty are used against women*, New York: Doubleday.

Wolfe, P. (2002), 'Can the Muslim Speak?', *History and Theory*, 41, pp. 376–380.

Xiao, J. (1995), 'An Historical Investigation of the Course of Chinese Ethnic Minorities Identifying with Confucianism', *Kongzi Yanjiu (Studies of Confucius)*, 2, pp. 96–102.

Ye'or, B. (2005), *Eurabia: The Euro-Arab Axis*, Madison: Fairleigh Dickinson University Press.

Yeğenoğlu, M. (1998), *Colonial Fantasies: Towards a Feminist Reading of Orientalism*, Cambridge: Cambridge University Press.

Yi, L. (2005), 'Muslim Narratives of Schooling, Social Mobility and Cultural Difference: A Case Study in Multiethnic Northwest China', *Japanese Journal of Political Science*, 6:1, pp. 1–28.

Yi, L. (2006), 'Choosing between ethnic and Chinese citizenship: the educational trajectories of Tibetan minority children in northwestern China', in Fong, V. and Murphy, M. (eds), *Chinese Citizenship: views from the margins*, London and New York: Routledge, pp. 41–67.

Yi, L. (2007), 'Ethnicization through Schooling: The Mainstream Discursive Repertoire of Ethnic Minorities', *The China Quarterly*, 192, pp. 933–948.

Yi, L. (2008), *Cultural Exclusion in China: State Education, Social Mobility and Cultural Difference*, London: Routledge.

Yosef, R. (2002), 'Homoland: Interracial Sex and the Israeli–Palestinian Conflict in Israeli Cinema', *GLQ: A Journal of Lesbian and Gay Studies*, 8:4, pp. 553–580.

Youmans, W. (2004), 'The New Cold Warriors', in Hagopian, E.C. (ed.) *Civil Rights in Peril: The Targeting of Arabs and Muslims*, London: Pluto Press, pp. 105–130.

Yuval-Davis, Y. (1992), 'Fundamentalism, Multiculturalism and Women in Britain', in Donald, J. and Rattansi, A. (ed.), *Race, Culture and Difference*, London: Sage, pp. 278–291.

Zhongguo Lishi [History of China] (1995), vol. 4, Beijing: The People's Education Press.

Zizek, S. (1999), *The Ticklish Subject: The Absent Centre of Political Ontology*, London: Verso.

Zizek, S. (2000), *The Fragile Absolute or, Why is the Christian Legacy Worth Fighting for?*, London: Verso.

Zizek, S. (2002), *The Puppet and the Dwarf*, London: Verso.

Zwagerman, J. (2009), *Hitler in de Polder & Vrij van God*, Antwerp and Amsterdam: Uitgeverij De Arbeiderspers.

INDEX

Abdelhamid, Ahmed Hossam Hussein (Mido): racist chants directed at by Newcastle United FC fans, 255

Abdulhamid II, Caliph-Sultan, 19

Adrus, Said: 'The Labelled Story', 41–2

Afghanistan, 176; insurgency in, 232; invasion of (2001), 121, 130, 159; ruled by Taliban, 46, 161–2; War in, 113, 124

Albania: and Greek Islamophobia, 221–3, 227

Ali, Ayaan Hirsi: *Submission*, 160

al-Qaeda: threat of, 120, 161

Amis, Martin: anti-Muslim rhetoric of, 79–80, 83; defenders of, 81–2

Anglican Church: social mission of, 124; negotiation broker, 124

Anti-Judaism: definition of, 7–8

Anti-Semitism, 3, 76; definition of, 6, 8, 83; forms of, 71; movement from Jew hatred to, 77; Runnymede Trust Report on (1994), 7; relationship with racism, 9

Anti-Zionism: definition of, 7–8

Aslam, Nadeem: *Maps for Lost Lovers*, 259, 261–2, 264

Aurangzeb: alleged banning of music in Mughal Empire, 45, 49; connoisseur of North Indian art, 46; death of (1707), 46

Austin, John: intellectual focus of, 137

Austrian Freedom Party: opposition to Turkey as member of EU, 69

Bangladesh, 265; sense of identity, 42–3

Belgium, 235; Belang Party, 236; Flemish population of, 238; labour shortage after Second World War, 238; Muslim population of, 236, 240–1; Royal Agency for Migration Policy, 239; Vlaams Blok, 236, 238–40

Bentham, Jeremy: intellectual focus of, 137

Bosnia: Muslim population of, 10

Bouyeri, Muhammad: background of, 160; murderer of Theo van Gogh, 160

British Muslims for Secular Democracy: launch of (2008), 97

British National Party (BNP), 60; increased presence of, 53–4; use of language when referring to Islam and Muslims, 54, 70

Bush, George W., 226; and Global War on Terror, 19, 33, 35, 86; opposition to, 49; use of term 'Islamo-fascism', 130

Byzantine Empire, 226; Aghia Sofia, 230; and Orthodox Christianity, 172;

architecture of, 228; fall of, 218;
siege of Constantinople (1543), 219

Canada, 131
Catholicism, 208; influence of in
Europe, 123, 172, 246
China, 276; and Global War on Terror,
194; and Orientalism, 191;
Buddhism in, 190–1, 194; Communist Party of, 191–2; culture of, 186,
188, 192–3; ethnic minority
population of, 186–7, 190–2; Falun
Gong, 194; history of, 186, 188–9;
Islamophobia in, 194; language of,
186, 188; Manchurian Qing regime,
190; Ming Dynasty, 189; Muslim
population of, 3, 186, 189–92, 194;
rise in power of, 120; Song Dynasty,
189; Tang Dynasty, 189; Ugyur riots
(2009), 185, 194; Xinjiang Ugyur
Autonomous Region, 185; Yellow
River, 187; Yuan Dynasty, 189
Christianity, 166–7, 169; and
Crusades, 20; and Thailand, 231;
Greek Orthodoxy, 213, 226–7;
political uses of, 152; Protestantism,
169, 172, 208; Russian Orthodoxy,
165, 171–6, 178
Cold War, 129; end of, 117, 120, 159,
241; ideological battle of, 165,
168–9; legacy of, 237
Columbia: embassy in Second Life, 65
Commission for Racial Equality
(CRE), 57; second monitoring
report for EUMC, 56, 58, 61
Crusades, 117: activity in Palestine and
Syria, 21; and Christianity, 20;
occupation of territory, 21–2; origins
of, 20; perceived justification for, 20

Daily Mail: anti-Muslim language in
articles in, 96

de Menezes, Jean Charles; shooting of
(2005), 107

Egypt: Cairo, 143; Muslim population
of, 143
Erbakan, Necmettin: leader of Refah
Party, 200
Erdogan, Recep Tayyip: government of,
199; leader of AKP, 202; Prime
Minister of Turkey, 131, 202
European Convention on the Defence
of the Fundamental Human Rights:
and Greece, 227
European Monitoring Centre for
Racism and Xenophobia (EUMC),
59, 75; implementation of monitoring mechanism across member states,
(2001), 57; second CRE report for,
56, 58, 61
European Union (EU): and Turkey, 69;
borders of, 221; Maastricht Treaty
(1992), 239

First World War, 38, 217; end of, 109;
Muslim participation in, 39
Former Republic of Yugoslavia (FRY):
Muslim population of, 71
Former Yugolsav Republic of Macednia
(FYROM), 223
Forum Against Islamophobia and
Racism (FAIR), 59; structure of, 56
France, 171; Algerian community, 276;
and Greece, 215–17; Islamophobia
in, 32, 36, 242; language of, 36,
40–1; Le Monde, 126; Moroccan
community, 276
Front National: led by Le Pen,
Jean-Marie, 66; literature on
'Islamisation of France', 70

Geneva Convention: and Guantanamo
Bay inmates, 119

Germany, 171; gay and lesbian activists of, 111–12, 114; Islamophobia in, 62; Jewish population of, 10; Turkish community, 62, 276

Global War on Terror, 88–89, 97–99, 102, 104, 111, 185, 251; and Bush, George W., 19, 33, 86; and China, 194; and Greece, 224; and USA, 194; complicity of liberal gay politics in, 115; perception of war on Islam, 126–7

Gogh, Theo van: murdered by Muhammad Bouyeri, 51, 160; *Submission*, 160

Greece, 238; and Albania, 221–3, 227; and France, 215–17; and Global War on Terror, 224; and Orientalism, 228, 230; and Ottoman Empire, 218, 226; and Russian Empire, 215; and UK, 215–17; architecture of, 228; Athens Organising Committee (ATHOC), 225; Civil War of (1944–49), 217, 222; culture of, 213–14, 222, 228–30; Democratic Party, 225; ethnic minority population of, 222–3; Islamophobia in, 32, 213–16, 221; La. O.S. (*Laikos Orthodoxos Synagermos*), 225; Ministry of Foreign Affairs, 227; Ministry of Public Health, 221; modern history of, 215–16; Muslim population of, 222, 225, 227–8; Orthodox Church of, 213, 226–7; signed European Convention on the Defence of the Fundamental Human Rights, 227; territory of, 217

Guantanamo Bay prison, 119, 122

Gul, Abdullah: AKP Turkish presidential nominee (2007), 196, 203

Harman, Harriet: remarks regarding *niqab*, 126

Hegel, Georg Wilhelm Friedrich, 71

Hinduism, 252; Hindutva, 266–7, 269–70; relationship with nationalism, 266–7, 269–70

Horowitz, David: organiser of 'Islamo-fascism Awareness Week', 130

Huntington, Samuel: *The Clash of Civilizations*, 165, 169

India: Bajrang Dal, 267, 269; colonial history of, 32; film industry of, 265; Hindu population of, 268–69; Islamophobia in, 15, 265, 267–68, 270; Muslim population of, 3, 265, 268; Partition of (1947), 42, 252–3, 265 Sangh Parivar, 268; sense of identity, 43; traditional music of, 46

Iran: clerics of, 37; traditional music of, 46

Iraq: Abu Ghraib prison, 111, 194; insurgency in, 232; Invasion of (2003), 18, 121, 129, 132; War in, 49, 113, 124, 159

Islam, 23, 30, 131, 159, 174, 211, 244, 246; and Global War on Terror, 126–7; and Russian Federation, 165–6; European hostility toward, 39–40; fundamentalist, 46, 106; monolithic concept of, 73; perceived conflict with the West, 145; personal interpretations of, 73, 236, 242; *sharia*, 151–3; presence in politics, 196, 243; *ummah*, 251; viewed by Crusaders, 20

Islamic Human Rights Commission; claim of mass attacks on Muslims following 9/11, 55–6; critics of, 37; structure of, 56

Islamism, 1, 80, 125; and Turkey, 197–9; interpretation of *jihad*, 133;

perceived threat of, 120, 123, 133, 199, 202

Islamophobia, 24, 30–1, 59, 79, 85, 115, 123, 134, 165, 174, 205, 252, 272, 277–8; and China, 194; and France, 32, 36, 242; and Germany, 62; and Greece, 32, 213–16; and India, 15, 265, 267–8, 270; and McCarthy, Joseph, 200; and Russia, 15, 170; and Serbia, 32; and Sikhism, 254; and Turkey, 32, 36, 62, 195, 200, 204–5; and UK, 136; and USA, 15, 225, 275; and USSR, 170; application of 'governmentality' theory to, 120, 126; concept of, 15, 17, 75, 83, 96, 101–4, 110, 117, 213, 244, 274; football chants, 255–6; necessary factors for, 58; lack of social penetration, 62–3; origin of term, 38, 40, 72, 169–70, 271–2; perceptions of, 1–3, 7, 13; relationship with Orientalism, 2, 26, 104, 120; relationship with Muslim identity, 43, 95; relationship with racism, 12–13, 259, 273; Runnymede Trust Report on (1997), 7–9, 14, 23

Israel: attacks on Gaza strip, 18; conflict with Palestine, 11; gay community in, 112, 115; government of, 11; Law of Return, 113; neoconservative support for, 130; Occupied Territories, 112; opposition to, 8, 10; Soviet immigrants, 113

Israeli Defence Force (IDF): gay men serving in, 113

Jinnah, Mohammed Ali: criticisms of, 101; founder of Pakistan, 101

Kant, Immanuel: *Observations on the Feeling of the Beautiful and the Sublime* (1764), 167; view of Arabic peoples, 168

Kelly, Ruth: Preventing Violent Extremism (PVE) announcement (2007), 85

Kemal Atatürk, Mustafa: house of, 230; legacy of, 199, 203–5, 213; policies of, 195

Kureishi, Hanif, 264; *My Son the Fanatic*, 259–61; *My Beautiful Laundrette*, 261–2; *The Black Album*, 259–62; *The Buddha of Suburbia*, 262

Le Pen, Jean-Marie: leader of Front National (FN), 66

Livingstone, Ken: Yusuf al-Qaradawi controversy (2008), 101–2, 105

McCarthy, Joseph: allegorical use in Islamophobia study, 200; influence of, 130

Middlesbrough FC, 255

Mohammed, Binyam: torture of, 122

Mughal Empire: Muslim population of, 45; *padishah*, 252; persecution of Sikhs, 252–3

Muhammad, Prophet: hymns on life of, 47; offensive depictions of, 67; opposed by Makkan aristocracy, 16

Muslim, 247; community in Belgium, 236, 240–1; community in Bosnia, 10; community in China, 3, 186, 189–92, 194; community in Greece, 222, 225, 227–28; community in India, 3, 265, 268; community in Netherlands, 158–9, 163–4; community in Pakistan, 80, 260; community in Palestine, 21; community in Russian Empire, 171, 174; community in Russian

Federation, 3, 165, 177, 182–4; community in Thailand, 3, 232–3; community in Turkey, 195; community in UK, 17–18, 55, 142–4, 151, 155–6, 210, 259; community in USSR, 171, 178–79, 181; concept of female subjectivity, 136, 139–40, 145, 153–4; divorce proceedings, 153; views of sense of identity as, 27, 93–4, 97–98, 108, 122, 183, 195–6, 276

Muslim Council of Britain: focus of, 124; formation of (1997), 124

Muslim Youthwork Foundation: view of policy responses affecting young Muslims, 86; warnings issued by, 88

Netherlands: borders of, 238; Equal Treatment Commission (CGB), 158, 160; government of, 157–8, 161; Ministry of Education, 159; Ministry of the Interior, 159; Muslim population of, 158–59, 163–4; opposition to public wearing of *burqa*, 157–9, 161–4

Newcastle United FC, 255

North Atlantic Treaty Organization (NATO), 17; military forces of, 225

Organisation of the Islamic Conference (OIC): membership of, 3

Orientalism, 38, 115, 134, 237; and China, 191; and Greece, 228, 230; and USA, 275; concepts of, 167–8; critiques of, 26–8, 34, 39; culturalist accounts of, 241; development of, 7, 26, 208–9, 216; gender elements of, 111; influence of, 25; post-Enlightenment, 211; question of relationship with Islamophobia, 2, 26, 104, 120

Ottoman Empire, 171, 213, 220; and Greece, 218, 226; fall of, 195, 218–9; invasion of Europe, 20; power of, 172; siege of Constantinople (1543), 219; territory of, 218

Ozkok, Hilmi: head of Turkish military, 202

Pakistan, 265; and Jinnah, Mohammed Ali, 101; Muslim population of, 80, 260; sense of identity, 42–3

Palestine, 19; conflict with Israel, 11; Crusader activity in, 21; Muslim population of, 21

Phillips, Melanie: 'victim culture' assertion, 88

Qur'an, 156, 243; *aya*, 67; conspiracy theories regarding, 254; depiction in *Submission*, 160; education courses on, 196; first Revelation of, 38; recitation of, 47–8; schools of, 125

Racism, 37; Cultural, 29; Eurocentric concept of, 11–13, 29, 166, 274; relationship with anti-Semitism, 9; relationship with Islamophobia, 12–13, 259, 273

Rana, Junaid: *The Story of Islamophobia*, 37

Runnymede Trust: Commission on British Muslims and Islamophobia, 34, 52–4, 63–4, 72, 74; report on anti-Semitism (1994), 7; report on Islamophobia (1997), 7–9, 14, 23, 34–5, 52, 72, 170, 272–3

Rushdie, Salman, 37; fatwa issued against (1989), 31, 42–3, 124, 260; *Satanic Verses*, 124; *Shame*, 259–60

Russian Empire, 183; and Greece, 215; historical development of, 172, 180;

Inorodsty Act (1822), 175; Islamophobia in, 170, 172, 182; Jewish population of, 175; Muslim population of, 171, 174; Orthodox Church of, 171–6, 178; political isolation of, 171; Tatars, 176–7; territorial expansion goals of, 173

Russian Federation: and Islam, 165–6; Chechnya conflict, 181; ethnic population of, 166; Islamophobia in, 16, 170, 182; Muslim population of, 3, 165, 177, 182–4; Orthodox Christian population of, 165, 182–3

Sarkozy, Nicholas: President of France, 126; proposal for banning of *niqab*, 126

Second Life (SL): Ahl as-Sunnah wa Jamaat, 66; Avatarians, 67; Ithna Ashari Ahmaddiya, 66; presence of national embassies in, 65; racist activity in, 66; structure of, 65; virtual Makkah, 66

Second World War, 78; resultant labour shortage in Belgium after, 238

Serbia: Battle of Kosovo, 32; Islamophobia in, 32

Shinawatra, Thaksin: Prime Minister of Thailand, 232

Sikhism: and Islamophobia, 254; Diaspora in UK, 251, 253–4; persecution in Mughal Empire, 252–3; sense of identity as, 252–3

Sookhdeo, Rev. Dr. Patrick: criticisms of Runnymede Trust Report on Islamophobia, 35

Soviet Union (USSR), 176–7, 183; collapse of (1991), 165, 169; division of labour, 180; Islamophobia in, 170, 179, 181–2; migrants to Israel, 113; Muslim population of, 171, 178–9, 181; territory of, 180

Stone, Richard: chair of Uniting Britain Trust, 35

Straw, Jack: remarks on *niqab*, 97

Sweden: embassy in Second Life, 65

Sufism, 124; *sama'*, 46

Swiss People's Party: anti-Muslim campaign posters, 70

Syal, Meera: *Bhaji on the Beach*, 264; *Life Isn't All Ha Ha Hee Hee*, 264

Syria: Crusader activity in, 21

Taliban: rulers of Afghanistan, 46; use of music, 47, 49

Teziç, Erdogan: head of Council of Higher Education, 203

Thailand: Buddhism, 231, 233; anti-Muslim sentiment in, 234; Christian population of, 231; Department of Religion, 231; Islamic Council of, 232; Ministry of Culture, 231; National Office of Buddhism, 231; National Reconciliation Commission (NRC), 233; military of, 233; Muslim population of, 3, 232–3; *pondok*, 232; Supreme Sangha Council, 231; territory of, 232; Wat Phromprasit attack (2005), 231

Toynbee, Polly: 'In Defence of Islamophobia', 35, 94

Turk's Head: origin of, 208–9; presence in British culture, 207, 209, 211

Turkey, 174; accession to EU, 69; and Germany, 62, 276; and Islamism, 197–9; Council of State, 198; *Cumburiyet* attack (2006), 198; economic depression (2001), 202; foundation of Republic, 197; Grand National Assembly of, 132, 201; *Imam-Hatip* schools in, 200–1; Islamophobia in, 32, 36, 62, 195,

200, 204–5; Istanbul University, 200; Justice and Development Party (AKP), 196, 202–3; military coup in (1980), 199–200; military coup in (1998), 201; military coup in (2007), 196–7, 200; Muslim population of, 195; *Refah* Party (Islamic Welfare Party), 200, 203; Social Democratic Party, 201; Supreme Court of, 201

Uniting Britain Trust: chaired by Richard Stone, 35
United Kingdom (UK), 108, 171, 274; 7/7 attacks, 60, 74, 86, 124, 260; and Greece, 215–17; Asian community of, 142, 146, 156, 209, 251, 254, 256, 259, 262, 264, 276; Black Arts movement, 42; Community Cohesion and Preventing Violent Extremism, 86; detainees at Guantanamo Bay prison, 122; Forest Gate Raid (2006), 107; gay community of, 111, 113–15; government of, 85, 90, 106, 125; Department for Children, Schools and Families (DCSF), 88; football culture of, 256–7; Forced Marriage Protection Act (2007), 146; Foreign and Commonwealth Office (FCO), 146; government of, 217; Home Office, 86; House of Lords, 123, 149; Human Rights Act (1998), 149; Islamophobia in, 136; legal issue debates in, 142, 148; legal system of, 151–2; Marriage Act (1949), 145; Matrimonial Causes Act (1973), 145–6; Muslim population of, 17–18, 55, 142–4,

151, 155–6, 210, 259; navy of, 216, 260–2, 264, 274; post-World War II racist activity in, 78; *Pink Paper*, 113–14; Preventing Extremism Together task force (PET), 86, 90; rise of professional *nasheed* singers and groups in, 48; sense of identity in, 209–10; Shariah Councils of, 155; Sikh Diaspora in, 251, 253–4; Terrorism Act (2006), 86–7; Youth Offending Service, 87
United States of America (USA), 129; 9/11 attacks, 31, 35, 54, 56, 74–6, 98, 106, 112, 118, 120, 126–7, 129–30, 162, 168, 171, 181, 185, 241, 248, 260, 275; and Global War on Terror, 194; and Orientalism, 275; Civil Rights Movement of, 18; emigration to, 238; gay community of, 115; government of, 217; immigration agenda in, 275; Islamophobia in, 15, 225, 275; National Security Council, 100; USA PATRIOT Act (2001), 109

Vienna: Church Council, 208
Voorhamme, Robert: Antwerp aldermn of education, 237; controversial comments on immigration and integration, 237

Wilders, Geert, 163; resolution for prohibition of wearing of *burqa* (2005), 158–62
Williams, Dr. Rowan, 152; controversial comments made by, 151–4

Zionism: and Runnymede Trust Report on anti-Semitism (1994), 11; support for, 11